African American
Biographies, 3

Also by Walter L. Hawkins
and from McFarland

Black American Military Leaders: A Biographical Dictionary (2007; paperback 2009)

African American Biographies, 2: Profiles of 332 Current Men and Women (1994)

African American Generals and Flag Officers: Biographies of Over 120 Blacks in the United States Military (1993)

African American Biographies [1]: Profiles of 558 Current Men and Women (1992)

African American Biographies, 3

Profiles of 909 Current Men and Women

WALTER L. HAWKINS

McFarland & Company, Inc., Publishers
Jefferson, North Carolina, and London

Library of Congress Cataloguing-in-Publication Data

Hawkins, Walter L., 1949–
African American biographies, 3 : profiles of 909 current men and women / Walter L. Hawkins.
p. cm.

ISBN 978-0-7864-4131-0
softcover : 50# alkaline paper ∞

1. African Americans — Biography — Dictionaries.
2. United States — Biography — Dictionaries.
I. Title. II. Title: African American biographies, three.
E185.96.H383 2009 920'.009296073 — dc22 2009004520

British Library cataloguing data are available

Cover photograph: 2008 Presidential Candidate Barack Obama
©2009 Shutterstock

Manufactured in the United States of America

McFarland & Company, Inc., Publishers
Box 611, Jefferson, North Carolina 28640
www.mcfarlandpub.com

To my granddaughters,
Kailyn Mackenzie Hasan and
Hay-lei Gabrielle Hasan

Acknowledgments

First and foremost, I thank God.

This book could not have been written without the love and support of my wife, Carol Hooks Hawkins. Thank you, thank you, thank you for your constant strength and love. Also to my children Winter, Donta, Whitney and Faheem (son-in-law). To my grand-girls, Kailyn and Hay-Lei. Thanks to my mother, Helen Johnson Hawkins, my mother-in-law, Sylvia Hooks; my father-in-law, Ephriam Hooks; my brothers and sisters, Milton, Maurice, Daniel, Eugene, Carolyn, Ellen, and Deborah. To all of you: Thanks.

Special thanks to a few of the many family and friends whose love and support have always encouraged me and contributed to me being who I am: Samuel Johnson, Sarah Johnson Nelson, Richard L. Fain, William David Fain, Kristin K. Hawkins, Bennie Hawkins, Betty Hawkins, O'Neal Johnson, Lewis Mann, Brenda Jordan, Marlin Ellis, Charlotte Cook, Clarence Greene, Jo Ann Campbell Moore, Lillian Hooks, Alvin Hooks, Melvin Hooks, Sheryl Hooks Grayson, Mansfield Arnold, Betty Alexander, Waddell Duckett, Karen I. Duckett, Percy Butler, Barbara Paxton, Blake Walker, Altonia Walker, Will Jackson, Isaac Oliver, Charles Johnson, Russell Hodo, Cary Hodo, Albert Garrett, Linda Morris, Bensonetta Tipton-Lane, Larry Thomas, Larry Gilpin, Leroy Ware, James Hill, James O. Wyatt, Henry Dodson, Juanita Brady, Vickye Byron, Ronald Reese and Major General Joe Turner.

Table of Contents

Preface

This book is a collection of profiles on living African Americans who are leaders in their professions and personal endeavors, tracing their steps as they rise into roles that shine with innovation, success, and service.

What started out as a hobby has turned into a mission. For over 20 years, I have been gathering information on famous and not-so-famous African American history makers, logging their accomplishments, updating their existing biographies and writing to total strangers for information to share in these pages. Throughout my years as a U.S. Army Reserve command sergeant major, Atlanta police officer and detective, Fulton County, Georgia, police sergeant and a postal police captain, it has been a dream to provide biographical portraits as an offering of information and inspiration.

This book aims to dispel any notions that people, including black people, may have about a lack of black role models. This reference work demonstrates that success comes in every field for African Americans in the United States: technology, education, medicine, military, science, entertainment, media, sports and many more. Furthermore, this work follows several other compilations of African American biographies; the stories of successful and inspirational people are too numerous to be confined to the contents of one book in one slice of time. Other biographical sketches may be found in my books *African American Biographies [1]: Profiles of 558 Current Men and Women* (1992), *African American Generals and Flag Officers* (1993), *African American Biographies, 2: Profiles of 332 Current Men and Women* (1994), *Black American Military Leaders* (2007), and *American Black Military Leaders* (a pictorial history) (2007). These books are used in black studies programs colleges and universities across the United States, often providing information on individuals that cannot be found in any other source.

Through these books, I hope to create a literary "book binding," a network of leadership, a forum that will add perspective and direction to the achievements of excellence in all facets of life for the community at large. There is a deep and continuing need to expand people's awareness of everyday heroes who are often out of the public eye. I wanted role models we could see and touch. I believe it's important for us to know about these significant achievers and their achievements now, while they are taking place. Readers will find in these pages the stories of individuals who represent the best of this nation and serve as examples of what one can accomplish if given the opportunity.

The 909 profiles are arranged alphabetically with all individuals either born or having spent their childhood years in the United States. A few exceptions were made when foreign-born figures lived most of their adult lives in the United States. The standards used to measure contribution and accomplishment include membership in professional and community organizations; notable athletic achievements and records; career successes; national, state or local leadership; major honors, Olympic medals or selection to any hall of fame. Also profiled are those African Americans who were the first in a profession, field or position.

This book does not attempt to chronicle the full range of African American contributions in the United States. Rather, its intent is to identify those individuals who have served as role models, ensuring that their achievements are noted and recorded for the generations to follow.

The Biographies

James Abbington

MUSIC. James Abbington received a bachelor of arts degree in music from Morehouse College in Atlanta, Georgia. He earned his master of music and doctor of musical arts degrees in church music and organ from the University of Michigan at Ann Arbor, where he was a student of Marilyn Mason. He was minister of music and church organist of the Hartford Memorial Baptist Church in Detroit from 1983 to 1996. He was national director of music for the Progressive National Baptist Convention, Inc., from 1990 to 1994 and national music director for the NAACP from 1988 to 1992.

Abbington was an associate professor of music and chair of the Department of Visual and Performing Arts at Shaw University in Raleigh, North Carolina, from 1998 to 2003. He has served as a professor of music in the Department of Fine Arts at Morgan State University. He is currently an associate professor of music and worship at Candler School of Theology, Emory University, Atlanta, Georgia.

Sheila Abdus-Salaam

JUDICIAL. Sheila Abdus-Salaam received a bachelor of arts in economics from Barnard College in 1974 and earned a juris doctor degree from Columbia Law School in 1977. She was a staff attorney at Brooklyn Legal Services Corp. from 1977 to 1980. She served as an assistant attorney general for the New York State Department of Law from 1980 to 1988. In 1988, she was general counsel for the New York City Office of Labor Services. From 1991 to 1993, she was a judge on the New York City Civil Court. In 1993, she was elected a justice, New York County Supreme Court, and was still serving in 2008.

Lilia A. Abron

ENGINEERING. Lilia A. Abron received a bachelor of science degree in chemistry from LeMoyne College and a master of science in environmental engineering from Washington University. She is the first African American woman in the United States, and the third woman at the University of Iowa, to receive a doctorate in chemical engineering.

Abron became the founder and chief executive officer of PEER Consultants, an environmental consulting firm headquartered in Washington, D.C. The firm has grown to include branch offices in 10 major cities throughout the U.S. She has been active in a number of community organizations, including serving as president of the Washington, D.C., chapter of Jack and Jill of America, Inc. She serves numerous technical societies and professional organizations, is a mentor for several students each year, and is active on the lecture circuit. She is also a member of the University of Iowa College of Engineering Advisory Board.

Gregory A. Adams

JUDICIAL. Gregory A. Adams received a bachelor of science degree in criminal justice from Georgia State University in 1981 and earned his juris doctor degree from the University of Georgia School of Law in 1983. Adams was the chief judge of the Georgia DeKalb County Juvenile Court for ten years, where he presided over a staff of 103 employees with annual budget of nearly six million dollars. As a result of Judge Adams' work he was honored with a portrait that will hang in the DeKalb County Juvenile Court, making him the first African American jurist in DeKalb County to have a portrait displayed in a county building.

Adams made history when he was elected to the Georgia Superior Court of the Stone Mountain Judicial Circuit on July 20, 2004, by running unopposed for an open seat. He is currently a Superior Court judge in Stone Mountain Judicial Circuit at DeKalb County Courthouse in Decatur, Georgia.

Robert "Bobby" Adams

EDUCATION. Robert Adams grew up in South Central Los Angeles and graduated from Los Angeles High School. He attended Los Angeles City College and Philander Smith College. He received a bachelor of arts degree in psychology at Loyola Marymount University in Los Angeles. He earned a master of education degree from the University of Southern California and a Ph.D. in educational management from Pepperdine University.

Adams began his career at Santa Monica College in 1974, serving as a counselor in outreach and as an Equal Opportunity Program Specialist (EOPS). He served as Counseling Department chair from 1981 to 1986 and was dean of student life from 1986 to 1996 and associate vice president of student affairs from 1996 to 1998. In 1998, he was hired as vice president of student affairs at Santa Monica College. On May 22, 2007, the Peralta Community College District Board of Trustees unanimously approved the appointment of Adams as president of Merritt College. His appointment as Merritt College's president comes after 33 years of service at Santa Monica College.

Willie Adams

SPORTS. Willie Adams is a graduate of Cass Technical High School and attended Highland Park Community College and Wayne State University. Adams' career as one of the most prominent martial artists in America began in the late 1950s and early 1960s, when he earned his black belt in isshinryu karate under Masters Don Nagle, James Chapman and Doug Noxon. Adams also had the opportunity to study other martial arts, including shotokan under Master Ozaki, kung fu under Masters Lee and Wong, aikido under Master Yusuda, judo under Master John Osako, and the arts of quan tao and poke lon under Master Phil Reeders. He won the 1966 International Karate Championship's black belt kumite division. He also won several Illinois, Indiana, Michigan, Ohio and Pennsylvania state championships in the weapons and empty-hand kata, kumite and breaking divisions. He was a member of the United States International Karate Team in 1964. In the 1970s, as captain of the Detroit All-Stars Karate Team, he led his fighters to two years of undefeated success in tournaments throughout the East Coast and Midwest

Adams has owned and operated a number of successful businesses outside of the dojo, including a limousine service, the Worldwide Import-Export Company, Renaissance Security Investigation Company and Panther brand karate uniform company. Today, he owns one of the most successful karate schools in Michigan, and trains all of the major police departments in the area, including the Wayne County Sheriff's Department, the Detroit and the Southfield Police Departments, and several other law enforcement agencies. He is licensed by the state of Michigan as a private investigator and is active in the Southfield Police Department D.A.R.E. (Drug Abuse Resistance Education).

Ilesanmi Adesida

EDUCATION. Ilesanmi Adesida received a bachelor of science degree, a master of science degree and a Ph.D. in electrical engineering from the University of California at Berkeley. He was an IBM postdoctoral fellow at the National Research and Resource Facility for Submicron Structures. Adesida served in the mid–1980s as a visiting assistant professor in electrical engineering department at Abubakar Tafawa Balewa University in Bauchi, Nigeria. He joined the Illinois faculty in 1987 and currently holds appointments as a professor of electrical and computer engineering and materials science and engineering. He is a researcher at the Coordinated Science Laboratory and the Beckman Institute for Advanced Science and Technology.

His research interests include nanofabrication and nanotechnology, and high-speed semiconductor optoelectronic devices and circuits. He was the director of the Micro and Nanotechnology Laboratory and the Center for Nanoscale Science and Technology. Adesida is currently the Donald Biggar Willett professor of engineering at the University of Illinois at Urbana

Champaign. He was named interim dean in June 2005 and named the 13th dean of the College of Engineering at the University of Illinois since the inception of the College of Engineering in 1870.

John O. Agwunobi

PUBLIC HEALTH. John O. Agwunobi completed his pediatric residency at Howard University Hospital in Washington, D.C., rotating between Children's National Medical Center and the District of Columbia General Hospital, then one of the nation's busiest inner-city hospitals. In addition to his medical degree, Dr. Agwunobi bolds a master of business administration from Georgetown University in Washington, D.C., and a master of public health from the Johns Hopkins School of Public Health in Baltimore, Maryland. He is also a certified managed care executive.

Dr. Agwunobi is a seasoned public health professional with experience in health care delivery, managed care, and health policy. He served as Florida's secretary of health and state health officer from October 2001 to September 2005. He confronted many public health challenges during his tenure, including leading the state's public health and medical response to the unprecedented four major hurricanes that struck Florida in 2004. The day after being named secretary, he led the Florida Department of Health in its response to the nation's first-ever intentional anthrax attack. He subsequently guided the state's nationally recognized efforts to prepare for, prevent, respond to, and mitigate the effects of a bioterrorism attack.

He was confirmed by the U.S. Senate on December 17, 2005, as the assistant secretary of health, U.S. Department of Health and Human Services, and as an admiral in the U.S. Public Health Services Commissioned Corps. He oversees the U.S. Public Health Service and its Commissioned Corps for the secretary.

Claudia Alexander

SCIENCE. Claudia Alexander received a master of science degree in geophysics and space physics from the University of California at Los Angeles and earned her Ph.D. in space plasma physics at the University of Michigan. She is a research scientist at NASA's Jet Propulsion Laboratory in Pasadena, California. She was one of the project managers of NASA's *Galileo* mission to Jupiter, which ended September 21 with a plunge into the planet's atmosphere. She is also project scientist for the U.S. role in the European Space Agency's *Rosetta* mission to a comet. She is the recipient of an Emerald Honor for Women of Color in Research and Engineering. The award is given by Career Communications Group, Inc., publisher of *Black Engineer and Information Technology* magazine.

Renita D. Alexander

MILITARY. Renita D. Alexander received a bachelor of arts degree in communication from the University of Alabama in 1982 and a master's degree in public administration from Webster University. She also earned a master's degree in strategic studies from the United States Army War College at Carlisle, Pennsylvania. Her military education includes Squadron Officer School at Maxwell Air Force Base in Alabama; Air Command and Staff College; Armed Forces Staff College at Norfolk, Virginia; and Air War College. Alexander was commissioned through the Air Force Reserve Officer Training Corps (ROTC) in 1982. She has served in key leadership positions at the squadron, group, wing and unified command levels.

Her most recent assignments include: July 1995 to July 1998, joint petroleum officer at Headquarters Command in Stuttgart, Germany; July 1998 to September 2000, commander, 375th Supply Squadron, at Scott Air Force Base in Illinois; September 2000 to August 2002, deputy commander, 375th Logistics Group at Scott Air Force Base in Illinois; from June 2003, commander of Defense Energy Support Center (DESC) Americas West in San Pedro, California; and July 2005 to August 2006, deputy commander of the 374th Mission Support Group, Yokota Air Base in Japan. In August 2006, she was assigned as commander of the 28th Mission Support Group at Ellsworth Air Force Base in South Dakota. She is responsible for seven squadrons of approximately 1,600 members responsible for installation security, communications, personnel support, contracting, logistical readiness, civil engineering and base services for nearly 8,000 military and civilian personnel and their families.

Winser Alexander

ENGINEERING, EDUCATION. Winser Alexander received a bachelor's degree in electrical engineering from North Carolina A&T State University in 1964. He earned a degree in engineering in 1966 and a doctoral degree in electrical engineering in 1974 from the University of New Mexico.

Alexander has served as chairman of the Department of Electrical Engineering at North Carolina A&T State University. His areas of research specialty include digital signal processing, special purpose computer architecture and image processing. He joined the faculty of North Carolina State University in Raleigh,

North Carolina, 1982, serving as a professor of electrical and computer engineering. He has received the Presidential Award for Excellence in Science, Mathematics and Engineering Mentoring. Administered by the National Science Foundation, the prestigious award honors outstanding mentors and role models in the sciences. Alexander is one of 10 individual honorees who received the presidential award at the White House on September 10, 1998, in Washington, D.C. President William J. Clinton greeted the awardees in the Oval Office prior to the ceremony.

Anita L. Allen

EDUCATION. Anita L. Allen received a bachelor of arts degree from New College in 1974 and a master of arts degree from the University of Michigan in 1976. She earned a Ph.D. in philosophy from the University of Michigan in 1980 and a juris doctor from Harvard University School of Law in 1984.

She was a member of the faculty of Georgetown University Law Center as associate dean. She also was the first African American woman to teach philosophy at Carnegie-Mellon and the first African American woman on the University of Pittsburgh law faculty. She has been a visiting professor at Yale Law School, Villanova Law School, Princeton University, the University of Arizona, Hofstra University and Harvard Law School. She was the first Robert H. Levi professor of bioethics and public health at Johns Hopkins University. She has served as a commentator for MSNBC and appeared on *Good Morning America, 20/20, Nightline, 60 Minutes, Burden of Proof,* and *Talk of the Nation.* Allen is the Henry R. Silverman professor of law and professor of philosophy at the University of Pennsylvania Law School.

Cheryl L. Allen

JUDICIAL. Cheryl L. Allen is a native of Pittsburgh, Pennsylvania. She received a bachelor's degree from Penn State University and earned her juris doctor degree from the University of Pittsburgh School of Law. Allen was an elementary school teacher in the Pittsburgh Public Schools. After obtaining her law degree, she served as an attorney with a Neighborhood Legal Service, the Pennsylvania Human Relations Commission, and the Allegheny County Law Department. She was appointed as judge to the Pennsylvania Superior Court of Common Pleas in Allegheny County. She has since been elected and retained by the voters for over 17 years.

Danielle Allen

EDUCATION. Danielle Allen received a bachelor of arts in classics (with a political theory minor) summa cum laude from Princeton University in 1993 and won that university's Samuel D. Atkins Thesis Prize. She went on to earn a master of arts degree in 1994 and a Ph.D. in classics from King's College, Cambridge, in 1996, winning the Hare Prize in ancient Greek history for her dissertation. She immediately began work in political theory in Harvard University's government department, earning a master of arts degree in 1998 and a Ph.D. in 2001.

Allen joined the University of Chicago humanities faculty as an assistant professor in classical languages and literature in 1997, was appointed associate professor in 2000, and received the college's Llewellyn John and Harriet Manchester Quantrell Award for Excellence in Undergraduate Teaching in 2001. In 2003, she was named professor of classical languages and literatures, political science, and to the committee on social thought at the University of Chicago.

While serving as the MacArthur fellow and classics professor, at age 32 she was named dean of the Division of the Humanities beginning July 1, 2004. She is the first MacArthur fellow to become a dean at the University of Chicago. She was also named to the board of trustees of Amherst College and was named to the Pulitzer Prize board in 2006. Allen was appointed the UPS Foundation professor in the School of Social Science at the Institute for Advanced Study at Princeton University in July 2007.

David J. Allen

MILITARY. David J. Allen enlisted in the U.S. Marine Corps in September 1980 and attended recruit training at Marine Corps Recruit Depot Parris Island, South Carolina. He was transferred to Camp Lejeune, North Carolina, with 8th Engineer Battalion. He is a gradu-

ate of the Drill Instructor School at Marine Corps Recruit Depot in San Diego.

Allen was deployed in support of Operation Desert Storm and Operation Iraqi Freedom. He held numerous key leadership positions, including serving as a drill instructor for a weapons field training battalion; as the first sergeant for Headquarters and Service Company at Marine Corps Recruit Depot San Diego in 2001; as the first sergeant of Alpha Company, Infantry Training Battalion; and as first sergeant for the Light Armored Vehicle Company, School of Infantry, at Camp Pendleton, California. He is the sergeant major for the CLB-17, 1st Marine Logistics Group, at Camp Pendleton, California.

Ivye L. Allen

BUSINESS, EDUCATION. Ivye L. Allen received a bachelor's degree in economics from Howard University and a master of business administration in marketing and international business from New York University. She earned a Ph.D. in social policy from Columbia University. Allen has served as a consultant to nonprofit organizations and taught graduate public policy and urban affairs courses at Jackson State University and Hunter College. She was director of fellowship programs for the Rockefeller Brothers Fund in New York. She served as chief operating officer for MDC, Inc., in Chapel Hill, North Carolina, a nonprofit organization that works to advance equality issues and opportunities in the American South. She was named president of the Foundation for the Mid South on March 13, 2006. The foundation promotes racial, social, and economic equity in Arkansas, Louisiana, and Mississippi.

Maxine Allen

MINISTRY. Maxine Allen is a native of Arkansas and attended Little Rock public schools. She received a bachelor's degree in philosophy and religion from Philander Smith College in Little Rock, Arkansas, and earned a master of divinity degree from Interdenominational Theological Center's Gammon Seminary (UM), Atlanta, Georgia. Allen has served as a pastor, a teacher of religion and a mentor of young clergy, and has participated in mission trips to Haiti, Jamaica, the Democratic Republic of the Congo and Russia. She currently serves as the minister of missions and ethnic ministries for the Arkansas Conference of the United Methodist Church. She is the first African American woman to be an ordained elder in the United Methodist Church in Arkansas. The Reverend Allen was appointed to the Arkansas Judicial Discipline and Disability Commission in 2007 by Governor Mike Beebe.

Ronald Allen

MILITARY. Ronald Allen is a native of Benton, Mississippi, and a graduate of Benton High School. After graduation he enlisted in the United States Navy on March 13, 1978. He has completed the master training specialist course and Senior Enlisted Academy. He has served at Naval Station Guam in the Service Craft Department. His sea commands includes USS *Sierra*, USS *Shenandoah*, USS *Conyngham*, USS *South Carolina*, USS *Portland*, and USS *Kauffman*, where he served as command master chief. Allen's shore commands include shore intermediate maintenance activity, Little Creek, Virginia, and Navy Recruiting District, Montgomery, Alabama, where he served as recruiter and recruiter in-charge. Other shore commands were Fleet Training Center, Norfolk, as branch head of Main Propulsion Maintenance School, and Southeast Regional Maintenance Center as command master chief.

Roosevelt Allen

MILITARY, MEDICINE. Roosevelt Allen graduated magna cum laude with a bachelor of arts degree from

Lincoln University in Pennsylvania and a doctor of dental surgery from Howard University College of Dentistry in Washington, D.C. He also earned a master of science degree in national resource strategy, Industrial College of the Armed Forces, at Fort Lesley J. McNair in Washington, D.C. His military education includes the Air Command and Staff College, Air War College, and the Interagency Institute for Federal Healthcare Executives at George Washington University in Washington, D.C.

Colonel Allen received a direct commission in 1986. He has been a clinician, educator, commander and advocate for dentistry at various assignments throughout his military career. He served as chief of the East Coast Port Mortuary Forensic Dental Service while at Dover Air Force Base in Delaware. He deployed to Senegal, West Africa, in support of MEDFLAG, a humanitarian mission. He has led or participated in remains identification of fallen comrades in the terrorist bombings of the U.S. embassies in Kenya and Tanzania, the Arizona MV-22 Osprey crash, and the USS *Cole* terrorist bombing. He was chief of dental services while deployed to Turkey for Operation Provide Comfort and Saudi Arabia for Operation Southern Watch. Colonel (Dr.) Allen is commander of the 5th Medical Group and director of base medical services at Minot Air Force Base in North Dakota.

Deborah L. Alleyne

BUSINESS. Deborah I. Alleyne received a bachelor of arts degree in sociology from the University of Pennsylvania and earned a master of science degree in insurance management from Boston University. She holds professional designations for Chartered Property Casualty Underwriter (CPCU), Associate in Risk Management (ARM), Associate in Reinsurance (ARE), Associate in Management (AIM), and Associate in Research and Planning (ARP).

Alleyne began her insurance career with ACE predecessor organization Insurance Company of North America in 1977 in the underwriting program and subsequently spent several years at AIG and Home Insurance. She joined ACE USA in July 1994 as a home office underwriter for ARM in Philadelphia. She joined the Excess Workers Compensation unit in January 2003 and assumed the underwriting manager position within a year. She currently is senior vice president, Excess Workers Compensation for ACE Risk Management. ACE USA is based in Philadelphia.

Linda L. Ammons

EDUCATION. Linda L. Ammons received a bachelor of arts from Oakwood College. She also earned a master of arts and a juris doctor from Ohio State University. She has served as executive assistant to Ohio Governor Richard Celeste and as special assistant to the director of the Department of Administrative Services for the state of Ohio. As a member of the faculty of the National Judicial College, she instructs judges new to the bench in areas of her legal specialties, as well as experienced judges who desire additional legal education. She is an expert in federal and Ohio administrative procedure law. She has also held several positions in the field of journalism and communications. She joined the Cleveland-Marshall faculty in the fall of 1991 and served as a professor of law and associate dean. Ammons was selected to serve as the dean of Widener University School of Law. She is the first woman and the first African American to lead the school.

Arthur B. Anderson

ENGINEERING. Arthur B. Anderson received a bachelor of science degree in chemical engineering from the University of Florida in Gainesville. He began his career at Procter and Gamble, where he spent 20 years in research and development roles, including director of research and development for the feminine care, facial tissues, and personal care new products groups. He served for

nearly a decade at Kraft Foods in leadership roles, culminating as vice president of operations and research and development strategy. He served as senior vice president of advanced technology for PepsiCo. Anderson was appointed senior vice president for global research and development and quality in June 2005. He also serves as a member of Campbell's Corporate Leadership Team.

Benjamin Anderson

MILITARY. Benjamin Anderson received a bachelor of science degree in architecture from Tuskegee University in Alabama and a master of science degree in public administration from Troy State University in Alabama. He earned a second master's degree, in strategic studies, from the Air War College at Maxwell Air Force Base in Alabama. His military education includes Squadron Officer's School at Maxwell Air Force Base; Air Command and Staff College at Maxwell Air Force Base; Armed Forces Staff College, Joint Professional Military Education, Phase II, in Virginia; and the Air War College at Maxwell.

Anderson entered the U.S. Air Force on May 20, 1983. He has served in a variety of Air Force civil engineer positions at the base, major command, U.S. Air Force, and joint staff level. He served in the U.S. Army from 1979 to May 1983, was assigned to Fort Stewart, Georgia, and completed the basic parachutist course (airborne) at Fort Benning, Georgia. In 1982, he was approved for an inter-departmental service transfer to the U.S. Air Force. From August 1993 to August 1995 he was joint civil engineering staff officer at the American Embassy in Cairo, Egypt. From August 1995 to February 1998, he was commander of the 355th Civil Engineer Squadron, Davis-Monthan Air Force Base, Arizona. In March 1998, he was assigned as director of the Infrastructure Section at Headquarters Airsouth (NATO), Naples, Italy. From August 2002 to July 2004, he was commander of the 823rd Red Horse Squadron at Hurlburt Field in Florida. In July 2004, he became commander and professor of aerospace studies, Air Force ROTC Detachment 320, Tulane University, New Orleans, Louisiana.

Frank J. Anderson

LAW ENFORCEMENT. Frank J. Anderson grew up in Indianapolis and graduated from Shortridge High School. He began his career in law enforcement in 1956 in the United States Navy as a shore patrol officer and was honorably discharged in 1959. Anderson was a Marion County sheriff's deputy from 1961 to 1965.

He served 12 years in the U.S. Marshal's Service, first as a deputy marshal, and later as an inspector and security specialist. He helped found and later direct the U.S. Federal Witness Protection Program. He served as U.S. marshal for the Southern District of Indiana, the chief federal police official in more than half of Indiana, first from 1977 to 1981. From 1983 to 1994, he was district director of the Federal Protective Service for the U.S. General Service Administration. From 1994 to 2001, he once again served as U.S. marshal for the Southern District of Indiana. As marshal, he oversaw federal law enforcement for 62 Indiana counties with offices in Indianapolis, Evansville, Terre Haute and New Albany. In 2001, Anderson received the Martin J. Burke Award, given to the most outstanding marshal in the nation. In 2002, he was elected Marion County sheriff and became the first African American elected to the post in Marion County.

Linda Randle Anderson

JUDICIAL. Linda Randle Anderson is a native of Homes County, Mississippi, and was educated in the Holmes County Public Schools. She received an associate degree from Holmes Junior College. She earned a bachelor's degree and a master's degree in music education from Jackson State University. She received her juris doctor degree from Mississippi College School of Law.

Anderson was an elementary music teacher for Jackson Public Schools from 1977 to 1985. Upon completing law school, Anderson was a law clerk in the Mississippi Supreme Court from 1985 to 1987. From 1987 to 1999, she was an assistant district attorney in the Seventh Judicial Court District of Hinds County (1987 to 1999) and assistant attorney in the Office of the U.S. Attorney for the Southern District of Mississippi and the U.S. Department of Justice from 1999 to 2006. In 2006, she was appointed as

U.S. magistrate judge for the Southern District of Mississippi. Anderson is the first African American female U.S. magistrate judge in Mississippi.

Marcia Mahan Anderson

MILITARY. Marcia Mahan Anderson received a bachelor of arts degree in political science from Creighton University and a juris doctor degree from Rutgers University School of Law in Newark, New Jersey. She also earned a master of strategic studies degree from the United States Army War College. Her military education includes the Adjutant General Officer Basic and Advanced Courses, the United States Army Command and General Staff College, and the U.S. Army War College.

Her most recent staff and command assignments in the U.S. Army Reserves include commander, 6th Brigade (Professional Development), 95th Division (Institutional Training), Topeka, Kansas; assistant commander for operations, Headquarters, 95th Division (Institutional Training), Oklahoma City, Oklahoma; and commander, Training Support Division West, Regional Support Group, Arlington Heights, Illinois, beginning September 2007. She was promoted to brigadier general in September 2007. Anderson's civilian career includes serving as the clerk of court, U.S. Bankruptcy Court, Western District of Wisconsin, in Madison.

Reuben V. Anderson

JUDICIAL. Reuben V. Anderson received a bachelor of arts degree from the University of Mississippi and earned his juris doctor from the University of Mississippi Law School. Anderson served in private law practice in Mississippi; as a judge for the City of Jackson Municipal Court in Mississippi; as a Hinds County Court judge; as a judge for the Mississippi 7th Circuit Court District; as chair of law and government at the University of Mississippi; and as a member of the board of directors that govern the Jackson Medical Mall Foundation.

Shelly "Butch" Anthony

BUSINESS. Shelly "Butch" Anthony is a native of Tampa, Florida, where he helped his parents operate their family owned restaurant. He relocated to Atlanta and worked for a few years in the corporate sector. Anthony took his corporate knowledge and opened his first restaurant in 1977, Slide In BBQ, which achieved tremendous success. He sold it in 1980.

In 1983, Mr. Anthony and his wife Barbara founded This Is It! BBQ and Seafood. Heralded as local pioneers of southern and home-style cuisine, their corporate focus is to promote quality food and family pride. Anthony's This Is It! BBQ and Seafood restaurants are recognized for their exceptional hospitality and home-style, health conscious recipes. His restaurants are recognized as one of the Top 100 Restaurants throughout America and the World. Anthony is founder, president and chief executive officer of the restaurants, with Georgia locations in Lithonia, Fayetteville, Smyna, and two locations in Decatur.

Treena Livingston Arinzeh

ENGINEERING. Treena Livingston Arinzeh received a bachelor of science degree in mechanical engineering from Rutgers University in New Brunswick, New Jersey, in 1992 and a master of science in biomedical engineering from Johns Hopkins University in 1994. She earned a Ph.D. in bioengineering from the University of Pennsylvania in 1999.

Arinzeh served for several years as a project manager at a stem cell technology company, Osris Therapeutics, Inc., based in Baltimore, Md., where she developed stem cell based therapies for orthopedic applications. She is currently at the New Jersey Institute of Technology, Department of Biomedical Engineering, as an assistant professor. Her research focuses on tissue engineering and applied biomaterials, specializing in the design of biomaterials for

stem cell based tissue repair. She is also investigating optimum biomaterial surfaces to direct adult stem differentiation into neural cells for treating spinal cord injuries. She was honored at the White House when John H. Marburger III, science advisor to the president and director of the White House Office of Science and Technology Policy, presented her with the Presidential Early Career Award for Scientists and Engineers.

Anton Armstrong

MUSIC. Anton Armstrong received a bachelor's degree from St. Olaf College in 1978 and a master of music degree from the University of Illinois. He earned a doctor of musical arts degree from Michigan State University. Armstrong served for more than 20 years on the summer faculty of the American Boyschoir School in Princeton, New Jersey, and was conductor of the St. Cecilia Youth Chorale, a 75-voice treble chorus based in Grand Rapids, Michigan, from 1981 to 1990. He has guest conducted such noted ensembles as the Utah Symphony and Symphony Chorus, the Mormon Tabernacle Choir and the St. Paul Chamber Orchestra. He returned to St. Olaf in 1990 as the Harry R. and Thora H. Tosdal professor of music at St. Olaf College and conductor of the St. Olaf Choir. He is also on the faculty of Calvin College and conducted the Campus Choir, the Calvin College Alumni Choir and the Grand Rapid Symphony Chorus.

Since returning to St. Olaf in 1990, Armstrong has taken the St. Olaf Choir on tours throughout the United States and to Denmark, Norway, Australia, New Zealand and Central Europe (France, Germany, Switzerland, Austria, Slovakia and the Czech Republic). On May 5, 2005, he sang for President George W. Bush and guests at the White House to commemorate the National Day of Prayer. A month later he led the St. Olaf Choir on a three-week tour of Norway with the St. Olaf Band and the St. Olaf Orchestra to celebrate Norway's 100 years of independence from Sweden and 100 years of friendship between St. Olaf College and Norway. Armstrong has won the Robert Foster Cherry Award for Great Teaching, a $200,000 prize awarded by Baylor University in Waco, Texas, where he began teaching in 2007. The St. Olaf music department received $25, 000 as part of Armstrong's award.

Marvin S. Arrington, Sr.

JUDICIAL. Marvin S. Arrington, Sr., is a native of Atlanta, Georgia, and graduated from Henry McNeil Turner High School in 1959. He received a bachelor of arts degree from Clark Atlanta University. He attended Howard University School of Law and transferred to Emory University School of Law, where he earned his juris doctor degree in 1967. He received an honorary doctorate degree from Clark Atlanta University.

Judge Arrington has served in private law practice. In 1969, he was elected to the Atlanta Board of Alderman (now called City Council); in 1980, he was elected president of the Atlanta City Council and would serve in that capacity until he stepped down in 1997 to unsuccessfully run for mayor of Atlanta. He was appointed judge on the Fulton County Superior Court by Governor Roy Barnes in 2002, and was then elected to that position. Judge Arrington serves on the board of trustees of Clark Atlanta University and Emory University Law School.

Charles P. Austin, Sr.

LAW ENFORCEMENT, LOCAL GOVERNMENT. Charles P. Austin, Sr., received a bachelor's degree from South Carolina State University and a master's degree from Erskine Theological Seminary. He earned a doctorate in pastoral ministry from Graham Bible College and a doctor of divinity degree from Carolina Theological Bible Institute. He also holds a doctor of public service degree from South Carolina State University. He is a graduate of the John F. Kennedy School of Government for senior executives in state and local government at Harvard University.

He has served with the Greenville and Easley, South Carolina, police departments as a patrolman. He worked with the South Carolina State Law Enforcement Division as a narcotics investigator and as a protective services officer. In 1986, Austin was named chief of South Carolina State University's campus police department. He served with the Chatham County, Georgia, Police Department as deputy chief of police. He was hired as deputy chief in the Columbia Police Department in 1990, a position that he held until 2001, when he became the assistant city manager for public safety. In 2003, Austin was named city manager for Columbia, South Carolina. He is the first African American to serve as Columbia's city manager.

Robert Auten

ENGINEERING. Robert Auten received a bachelor of science degree in electrical engineering from Santa Clara University and a master of science degree with emphasis on digital signal processing and digital controls systems from Loyola Marymount University in Los Angeles.

At Northrop Grumman he was spacecraft bus segment manager on a deep-space craft, responsible for a work package that exceed $1 billion. He has served as design engineer and functional manager as well as deputy and program manager for some of the nation's most critical programs, providing technical direction, management and leadership to multi-disciplinary design and development teams. Auten led conceptual design and development efforts for the avionics, flight software and guidance, navigation and control for space exploration systems and worked on the company's proposal efforts. He is currently deputy manager of avionics and guidance, navigation and control at Northrop Grumman Space Technology sector, Redondo Beach, California.

Claudia S. Averette

EDUCATION. Claudia S. Averette received a bachelor's degree and earned her master's degree in health administration and public health and education from Arcadia University (formerly Beaver College). She has served as vice president of marketing and communications for United Bank of Philadelphia. She spent 24 years in the health care industry assessing and developing innovative approaches that would ensure access to health care for underprivileged and underinsured communities. She was director of community development and outreach for Albert Einstein Medical Center in Philadelphia.

Averette joined the School District of Philadelphia in 1998 and has held multiple roles with increasing levels of responsibility. She began her career with the district as a post-secondary readiness coordinator. In 200, she joined the Office of Learning and Technology Support as the assistant director and as deputy of school police. In 2003, she was administrative director to the chief of staff and was appointed chief of staff for the School District of Philadelphia. As chief of staff, she oversees the day to day operations of the 7th largest urban public school district in the country.

Curry Avery

HEALTH. Curry Avery received a bachelor of science degree in psychology from Howard University and a Ph.D. in clinical and school psychology from Hofstra University. She is enrolled in the master of divinity cooperative program of Hartford Seminary and Yale Divinity School. Avery is a licensed psychologist on staff at an inner city public high school in Connecticut. She maintains a private practice in New London, Connecticut, where she helps children and adults of various backgrounds to cope with daily life. She worked for the Department of Children and Family in two locked facilities: one for psychiatrically impaired youth and the other for adjudicated adolescents.

Gloria Addo Ayensu

HEALTH. Gloria Addo Ayensu received a master of public health in international health from Tulane School of Public Health in 1988 and earned her medical degree from Tulane University School of Medicine in 1994. She was a member of the Loma Linda University Preventive Medicine Faculty Group from 1996 to 1999. During that period, she was also a consultant for the San Bernardino County STD program and the Riverside County HIV Early Intervention Program.

She has a background in parapsychology. She joined the Fairfax County Health Department in November 1999 as assistant health director for the Mount Vernon District Office of the Fairfax County Health Department. She has served as deputy health director, providing medical direction for the agency's emergency preparedness and communicable diseases programs. On August 4, 2003, the Fairfax County Board of Supervisors appointed Dr. Ayensu as the director of the Fairfax County Department of Health.

Lloyd Ayers

PUBLIC SAFETY. Lloyd Ayers graduated from Murrell Dobbins High School in 1969 as a machinist's apprentice. He is a graduate and associate of the Carl Holmes Executive Development Institute at Dillard University in New Orleans, Louisiana. He earned a master's of human services degree from Lincoln University in May 2004 and completed additional course work at the National Fire Academy in Emmetsburg, Maryland.

Ayers served four years in the U.S. Coast Guard. He began his career with the Philadelphia Fire Department in 1974. He has served in every rank in the Philadelphia Fire Department, ranging from lieutenant to commissioner. He was deputy commissioner of operations and managed the activities of the Philadelphia Fire Academy, Fire Fighting Force of Division 1 and Division 2, the Aviation and Marine Units and the Safety Office. Prior to that, he was the deputy commissioner of technical services, responsible for the Fire Marshal's Office, Hazardous Materials Administration, the Fire Prevention Unit, Fire Code Unit, and other critical service functions. He was sworn in as the City of Philadelphia fire commissioner on December 1, 2004.

Jerry L. Bailey

MILITARY. Jerry L. Bailey enlisted in the U.S. Marine Corps in December 1981 from Salisbury, Maryland, and completed recruit training at Marine Corps Recruit Depot Parris Island, South Carolina, in July 1982. He reported to Motor Transport Schools Company, Marine Corps Base, Camp Lejeune, North Carolina, for training as a heavy vehicle operator. He is a graduate of the Airborne School at Fort Benning, Georgia.

Bailey was assigned in February 1983 to the 2nd Force Reconnaissance Company, Camp Lejeune, as a heavy vehicle operator. After several deployments, he was assigned to Motor Transport Schools Company as a heavy vehicle operator instructor. He was deployed in support of Operations Desert Shield and Desert Storm. In 1991, he was assigned to Headquarters and Support Battalion, Marine Corps Base, Camp Pendleton, as the commanding general's driver. The following year, he was transferred to Headquarters and Service Company, I Marine Expeditionary Force, as the commanding general's driver, deployed to Operation Restore Hope in Somalia. His next assignment was as a Marine recruiter with the 1st Marine Corps District in Garden City, New York. In July 1997, he was assigned to Truck Company, Headquarters Battalion, 2nd Marine Division, Camp Lejeune, as a section leader for 4th Platoon. In May 1999, he was transferred to Headquarters Battalion, Camp Fuji, Japan, for duty as the company gunnery sergeant. He returned to Camp Lejeune in July 2000 as the Marine Corps Base roadmaster. After his promotion to first sergeant in April 2001, he was assigned to Company B, H&S Battalion, at Marine Corps Base, Camp Lejeune. In 2003 he was reassigned to Company A within the same battalion. He was promoted to sergeant major in April 2005 and transferred to Headquarters and Headquarters Squadron at Marine Corps Air Station, Iwakuni, Japan.

John H. Bailey

MILITARY. John H. Bailey is a graduate of Doty High School in McKinney, Texas. He received a bachelor's degree in aeronautics from Embry Riddle Aeronautical University and a master's degree in education administration and supervision from Alcorn State University. He enlisted in the U.S. Army in 1959. After basic training he completed Basic Airborne School with the 82nd Airborne. In 1962, he transferred to the 8th Infantry Division in Bad Kreuznach, Germany. Three years later he was transferred to the 101st Airborne Division, where he was promoted to staff sergeant and selected for Advanced Airborne School and Officer Candidate School. He was then commissioned a second lieutenant in the U.S. Army. Bailey served in Vietnam as a paratrooper with the 101st Airborne Division. He went on to become a fixed wing aviator, accumulating 1265 combat hours with the First Aviation Brigade. Among his 17 awards and honors are the Soldiers Medal for heroism and the Vietnam Cross of Gallantry for bravery.

After leaving active duty he returned to Texas and joined the Texas National Guard. He also began a distinguished career in military science education. In 1984 he joined Clear Creek Independent School District in southeast Houston as director of military science. He now oversees a junior ROTC program that includes 926 cadets and 14 instructors at four high schools and seven intermediate campuses.

In 1991, Bailey became the first African American to attain the rank of brigadier general in the Texas State Guard, an honor bestowed by Governor Ann Richards. In 1994, Governor George W. Bush promoted Bailey to major general and appointed him commanding general of the Texas State Guard. He served in that capacity until his retirement from the guard in 1997.

Ronald L. Bailey

MILITARY. Ronald L. Bailey is a native of St. Augustine, Florida, and graduated from Austin Peay State University in Clarksville, Tennessee. He received a master's degree from the National War College in Washington, D.C., in 1998. He received his second master's from the Army Command and General Staff College in 1993. He graduated from the Amphibious Warfare School at Quantico, Virginia, in 1984.

Brigadier General Bailey has held a wide variety of military assignments, including as series commander, Battalion S-3, and commanding officer at the Marine Corps Recruit Depot Parris Island, South Carolina. In June 1998, he was assigned to Headquarters Marine Corps, Manpower Management office, as the ground lieutenant colonel's monitor; in June 2000, he was assigned as deputy, Joint Contact Team Program, and plans officer, Headquarters U.S. European Command, Stuttgart, Germany. From 2002 to 2004, Colonel Bailey commanded the 2nd Marine Regiment; from 2004 to 2005, he was assigned as the CMC national fellow at the Council on Foreign Relations. In July 2005, he became director, Expeditionary Warfare School. He is the deputy commander at the National Military Command Center.

Anthony E. Baker, Sr.

MILITARY. Anthony E. Baker, Sr., is a native of Baltimore, Maryland. He received a bachelor of science in criminal justice from LaSalle University in 1983 and a master of science in human resource management in 1995. He earned a master of arts degree in organizational communication from Bowie State University. His military education includes graduating from the Command and Staff College and the Army War College Senior Service College Fellowship Program at Carnegie Mellon University in Pittsburgh, Pennsylvania.

Baker was commissioned through the Maryland Officer Candidate School program in 1983 and has served in a variety of positions with the Maryland Army National Guard and the National Guard Bureau. He has participated in several key assignments, including serving as acting division chief, Fulltime Support Division, Army National Guard; chief, Policy and Program Branch , Staff Management Office, Army National Guard; human resources realignment officer, Army National Guard; and operations and training and mobilization officer, Office of the Secretary of Defense. Colonel Baker assumed duties as chief of family programs, National Guard Bureau, Joint Staff, on July 5, 2004.

Arlene Holt Baker

BUSINESS. Arlene Holt Baker has over 30 years of experience as a union and grassroots organizer. From the late 1970s to the mid 1990s she worked as a union organizer and later international union area director in California for the American Federation of State County and Municipal Employees. In 1995 she went to work for the AFL–CIO, a national federation of labor organizations, as executive assistant to the executive vice president, and later served as assistant to the president. From September 2004 until January 2006, Baker was president of Voices for Working Families, a nonpartisan voter education and mobilization organization. She returned to the AFL–CIO in January 2006 and as assistant to the president; she oversees the AFL–CIO's Gulf Coast recovery efforts. She was named executive vice president of the AFL–CIO, becoming the first African American to serve as one of the top three executive officers for the 10-million member federation.

Dawn Rivers Baker

BUSINESS. Dawn Rivers Baker is a native of Philadelphia and a graduate of Foxcroft School in Middleburg, Virginia. She has attended Princeton University and Columbia University. Ms. Baker has served in legal administration for the Atlantic Recording Corporation and for a premier Manhattan-based law firm. She currently serves as the president and chief executive officer of Wahmpreneur Publishing, Inc., and the editor and publisher of the *MicroEnterprise Journal*. She is also the founder and board chairman of the Microbusiness Research Institute, a non-profit, non-partisan research organization whose mission is to collect and publicize data on microbusinesses in the United States and their impact on the U.S. economy.

Delbert W. Baker

EDUCATION. Delbert W. Baker is a native of Oakland, California. He served as special assistant to the president and director of diversity at Loma Linda University, a health science institution in Loma Linda, California. During his tenure, he was also a professor and taught in four of the six schools on campus. Baker was appointed the 10th president of Oakwood College. He has a rich background of professional experience which includes work as a pastor in Ohio and Virginia.

Nannette A. Baker

JUDICIAL. Nannette A. Baker received a bachelor of science degree from the University of Tennessee Knoxville and earned her juris doctor degree from St. Louis University School of Law. She was a consumer reporter for KSDK-TV in St. Louis, Missouri. She served as chair of the St. Louis Board of Election Commissioners. She worked in private law practice and as a law clerk for Judge Odell Horton, U.S. District Court for the Western District of Tennessee. She served as a circuit court judge in the City of St. Louis from 1999 to 2004. In 2004, she was appointed a judge on the Missouri Court of Appeals for the Eastern District.

Richard S. Baker

MEDICINE. Richard S. Baker received a bachelor's degree in physics from Stanford University. He was awarded his medical doctor degree from Harvard Medical School with concurrent doctoral training in health sciences technology from the Massachusetts Institute of Technology. Upon completion of medical school, Dr. Baker was awarded a fellowship at the Joslin Diabetes Center, Harvard Medical School. He then went on to complete an internship in general surgery at the University of Minnesota. Then Dr. Baker was awarded a National Institute of Health Fellowship in Biostatistics and Epidemiology at the University of Minnesota. He completed his ophthalmology residency training at the Charles R. Drew University of Medicine and Science.

Dr. Baker currently holds dual faculty appointments as an associate professor of ophthalmology at Charles R. Drew University and the Jules Stein Eye Institute at the University of California at Los Angeles School of Medicine. Dr. Baker is associate vice president for research; director of the National Institutes of Health sponsored Biomedical Research Center at Charles R. Drew University; director of the Drew Center for Health Services Research; director of the Urban Telemedicine Center of Excellence; and acting director of the Drew Urban Community Health Institute. He is the principal investigator of multiple studies and a published author in the field of ophthalmology, telemedicine, epidemiology and health services research. He has served on numerous expert panels for the National Institutes of Health and the agency for Research for Quality and Health. He has over 200 scientific publications, book chapters, and presentations.

Thurbert E. Baker

STATE GOVERNMENT. Thurbert E. Baker is a native of Rocky Mount, North Carolina. He received a bachelor of arts degree from the University of North Carolina at Chapel Hill in 1975. At UNC he was a member of the fencing team and the 1975 Atlantic Coast Conference (ACC) individual saber champion. In 2002, the ACC recognized Baker as one of the top fencers in conference history, naming him to its fiftieth anniversary fencing team. He earned his juris

doctor degree from the Emory University School of Law in 1979.

Baker's legal career began in private law practice. He served as an attorney with the U.S. Environmental Protection Agency and managed his own law firm. In 1988, he won the first of five elections to represent part of DeKalb County in the Georgia House of Representatives. In 1991, after just one term in the General Assembly, he was chosen by Governor Zell Miller to serve as his assistant administration House floor leader. In 1993, Governor Miller elevated him to the position of House floor leader.

He was appointed Georgia's fifty-second attorney general by Miller on June 1, 1997, following the resignation of Attorney General Michael Bowers. Baker became the first African American to serve as Georgia's attorney general. On November 3, 1998, he was elected to serve a four year term as attorney general, and he was re-elected by the voters of Georgia in 2002 and 2006.

Vicki Ballou-Watts

JUDICIAL. Vicki Ballou-Watts was born in Montgomery, Alabama. She received a bachelor of arts degree cum laude from Howard University in 1980 and earned her juris doctor degree from the University of North Carolina School of Law in 1983. She was admitted to the Maryland bar in 1984. Ballou-Watts served in private law practice from 1984 to 1999. From 1999 to 2000, she was an associate judge for the District Court of Maryland for Baltimore. Since May 29, 2002, she has served as an associate judge on the Baltimore County Circuit Court, 3rd Judicial Circuit.

Ed Banks

LAW ENFORCEMENT. Ed Banks received a bachelor of science degree in physical education and history from North Carolina A&T State University. Banks was among the first group of African American men hired in the Department of Correction to work at the McLeansville Prison in Guilford County, North Carolina, in 1961. He began his 35 years of service in the North Carolina prison system as a sergeant of the guard. He served as athletic director and coach at Goldsboro Correctional Center. He was coordinator of the Committed Youthful Offender program, the statewide Jaycee program and the Central Classification Board. He was superintendent of Greene Correctional Center from 1973 to 1975, then moved to Goldsboro Correctional Center in Goldsboro, North Carolina, where he was superintendent for 20 years.

Jacqueline Bardwell

MEDICINE, EDUCATION. Jacqueline Bardwell is a native of Chicago, Illinois. She received her medical doctor degree from the University of Illinois College of Medicine and completed her training in family medicine in 1987 at the Rush-Christ Hospital family practice residency program. Dr. Bardwell is a certified instructor in advanced life support obstetrics. She has served as co-coordinator for undergraduate medical education at Christ Medical Center, as medical director for Anchor Life Weight Management and as medical director for University of Illinois HMO (health management organization). She joined the faculty of the family medicine residency program at Christ Hospital in 1992 after working for five years at the Anchor HMO in Chicago. Dr. Bardwell is currently the medical director of family medicine obstetrics and director of Anchor Life Weight Management at the University of Illinois Christ Medicine Center.

Lisa Barker

ENGINEERING. Lisa Barker is a graduate of the University of California at Los Angeles and the University of Southern California. She joined Ball Aerospace in 2000 and has worked on NASA's Mars exploration rovers and the Deep Impact program, as well as commercial space programs. She also works with the company's intern program, and outside of Ball, serves

Denver neighborhood boards and non-profits. She currently serves as the principal engineer for the Ball Aerospace and Technologies Corp. She is the integrated product lead for star tracker assembly electronics redesign at Ball Aerospace.

Valerie Barnes

MILITARY. Valerie Barnes resides in Washington, D.C. Currently she is an Active Guard/Reserve (AGR) since 1998. Chief Master Sergeant Barnes joined the U.S. Air Force Reserve Advisory Council in October 2005 upon assignment as superintendent, policy integration, at the Headquarters United States Air Force at the Pentagon. During her tenure in the personnel career field, she served on active duty for twelve years, was a traditional reservist, an individual mobilization augmentee and an Air National Guardsmen.

Joyce Anne Barr

FEDERAL GOVERNMENT. Joyce Anne Barr is a native of Tacoma, Washington. She received a bachelor of arts in business administration magna cum laude from Pacific Lutheran University and a master of public administration from Harvard University. She also received a master of science in national resource strategy from the Industrial College of the Armed Forces. She has also received both Swedish and Russian language training.

Barr joined the Department of State in September 1979. She has served in assignments abroad in Stockholm, Sweden, in 1980; Budapest, Hungary, in 1982; Nairobi, Kenya, in 1985; Khartoum, Sudan, in 1989; and Ashgabat, Turkmenistan, in 1998. Her most recent assignment was as counselor for management affairs in Kuala Lumpur, Malaysia. She has served as a post management officer in the Bureau of East Asia and Pacific Affairs, where she provided managerial support and guidance for several United States embassies to include extensive logistical planning and multi-lateral negotiations to obtain property on behalf of the government. She has served as a senior watch officer in the State Department's crisis center. Other assignments include recruitment officer in the Bureau of Personnel; human rights officer for the Middle East and South Asia in the former Bureau of Human Rights and Humanitarian Affairs; and while assigned to the Bureau of International Organizations, desk officer for the United States Industrial Development Organization and the World Tourism Organization. Barr was nominated as U.S. ambassador to Namibia by President George W. Bush and was confirmed by the U.S. Senate. She began her appointment on October 4, 2004.

Jacquelyn Harris Barrett

LAW ENFORCEMENT. Jacquelyn Harris Barrett is a native of Charlotte, North Carolina, and a graduate of Harding High School. Her class was the first to enter high school under an order to desegregate in Charlotte public school system. She received a bachelor of arts degree in sociology, concentrating in criminology, from Beaver College in Glenside, Pennsylvania, in 1972. She earned a master's degree in criminology from Atlanta University in Atlanta, Georgia, in 1973. In 2001, she received an honorary doctorate of laws degree from Arcadia College in Pennsylvania.

Barrett has been an adult basic education teacher with the Atlanta Board of Education. She worked as a criminal justice planner for the cities of East Point, College Park and Hapeville, Georgia. In 1976, she accepted a curriculum specialist position with the Georgia Peace Officer Standards and Training Council. She was appointed chief administrative officer for Georgia's first elected African American sheriff, Richard B. Lankford, in Fulton County. She was appointed the first director of the new Fulton County Law Enforcement Academy by the Board of County Commissioners. On November 3, 1992, Barrett was elected to the office of sheriff, Fulton County, in Atlanta, Georgia. She is the first African American Woman in the history of the United States to win election as a sheriff.

Douglas L. Barry

PUBLIC SAFETY. Douglas L. Barry was born and raised in the South Bay, attending Narbonne High School, Los Angeles Harbor College, and California State University at Long Beach. He joined the Los Angeles Fire Department as a firefighter on February 16, 1975, and was quickly promoted to apparatus operator in 1979 and engineer in 1980. He was promoted

to captain I in 1986 and captain II in 1989. In 1993, he assumed command of Los Angeles Fire Department's Battalion 13, covering five fire stations in South Los Angeles. As head of Battalion 13, he maintained strong relationships with community block clubs and churches, as well as the Los Angeles Police Department and the Los Angeles County Fire Department.

In 1995, Barry took command of the Los Angeles Fire Department's operations office, and in 1997, he assumed command of the department's Battalion 11. In 2000, he took command of Battalion 6 in the Harbor area, overseeing operations at nine fire stations responsible for fire protection at the Port of Los Angeles, three major refineries and a host of heavy commercial occupancies.

In 2004, Barry was appointed assistant chief of Los Angeles Fire Department Division 2, covering all of South Los Angeles, including the Los Angeles International Airport and the Port of Los Angeles. He most recently served as assistant fire marshal, managing the day-to-day operations of the Fire Prevention Bureau. Barry was appointed acting fire chief and assumed command of the Los Angeles Fire Department on January 1, 2007.

John R. Batisle

LAW ENFORCEMENT. John R. Batisle received a bachelor's degree in law enforcement administration from City University in Washington State and is currently working on his master's degree in organization and human resource management. He began his career with the Washington State Patrol in March 1976. He was promoted through the ranks from sergeant to deputy chief and served in numerous positions of increasing responsibility, including field operations, District 1, Tacoma; research and development; and Human Resources Division. He retired from the Washington State Patrol in April 2002 with over 26 years of service. He also was the assistant chief of the Tacoma Police Department and the deputy chief of the Port of Seattle Police Department. Governor Christine Gregoire appointed Batisle the 21st chief of the Washington State Patrol on February 14, 2005. He is the first African American in this position.

Donald L. Battle

MILITARY. Donald L. Battle is a native of Greenville, North Carolina. Upon graduation from high school, he entered One Station Unit Training (OSUT) as an armor crewman at Fort Knox, Kentucky. He received an associate degree in general studies from Central Texas College and a bachelor's degree from Thomas Edison State College in administration of justice. He is currently pursuing a master's degree in human relations from the University of Oklahoma. His military education includes all courses in the noncommissioned officer education system, M1A1 tank master gunner course, and first sergeant course. He is a graduate of the U.S. Army Sergeants Major Academy (Class 22).

Battle has served in numerous positions in armor and cavalry units, including drill sergeant and senior drill sergeant, tank platoon sergeant, tank platoon leader and company executive officer, company and battalion master gunner, first sergeant, inspector general noncommissioned officer in charge, operations sergeant major and (currently) command sergeant major. He was with the 3rd Armored Division during Operations Desert Shield and Desert Storm as a tank commander. He deployed to Bosnia as Task Force 4-67 armor master gunner from May 1996 to September 1996. He deployed to Camp Able Sentry, Macedonia, in 1999 as Team Alpha providing force protection. In May 2003, he deployed to Operation Iraqi Freedom as Task Force 1-35 operation sergeant major. From March 2004 to March 2005, he deployed with the 1st BDE Combat Team, 1st Cavalry Division, in support of Operation Iraqi Freedom II.

Eliot F. Battle, Jr.

MEDICINE. Eliot F. Battle, Jr., received his dermatology residency and medical doctor degree from Howard University and a three year laser surgery fellowship from Harvard Medical School. Dr. Battle is co-founder and director of laser surgery for Washington, D.C.'s Cultura Cosmetic Medical Spa, a groundbreaking medical practice merging dermatology, laser surgery, plastic surgery, and spa therapy. He combines physician directed skin care, non-ablative cosmetic laser therapy and minimally invasive plastic surgery. Dr. Battle's laser research at Harvard helped to pioneer the new generation of non-invasive "color blind" cosmetic lasers. He is known as the leading authority on cosmetic laser therapy for darker skin types.

Michael A. Battle

EDUCATION, MINISTRY. Michael A. Battle is a native of St. Louis, Missouri. He received a bachelor of arts degree from Trinity College. He earned a master of divinity degree from Duke University and a doctor of

ministry from Howard University. He received certifications from the Institute of Educational Management at Harvard University, the Executive Leadership Institute of Hampton University, and American Association of State College and Universities Millennium Leadership.

Battle served from 1976 to 1996 as dean of the University Chapel at Hampton University, pastor of the Hampton University Memorial Church and executive secretary and treasurer of the Hampton University Minister's Conference. From 1996 to 1998, he was associate vice president of student affairs at Virginia State University, where under his leadership, the institution's successful planning and assessment was widely acknowledged. In 1998, he was hired as vice president of student affairs at Chicago State University. He is the seventh president of the Interdenominational Theological Center in Atlanta, Georgia.

Stanley F. Battle

EDUCATION. Stanley F. Battle received a bachelor of science degree in sociology from Springfield College and a master of social work in casework from the University of Connecticut. He earned both his master of public health in maternal and child health and his Ph.D. in social work welfare policy from the University of Pittsburgh. He was president of Coppin State University in Baltimore, Maryland, for four years. He was the fourth person in the institution's 107 year history to hold the position. On July 1, 2007, he assumed the role of chancellor at North Carolina Agricultural and Technical State University. He is the eleventh chancellor and president to serve at the helm of the land grant university since its inception in 1891.

Anthony W. Batts

LAW ENFORCEMENT. Anthony W. Batts' education includes a bachelor of science in law enforcement administration, a master's degree in business management, and a doctorate in public administration. He is a graduate of several executive programs: Harvard University's executive development course; the FBI national executive development course; the FBI National Executive Institute, police executive training course; the University of Southern California's Delinquency Control Institute; the FBI National Academy Leadership; Long Beach Law Enforcement Command College; and International Association of Chiefs of Police SWAT Commander School.

Batts was an Explorer Scout with the Los Angeles Police Department, a police cadet with the Santa Monica Police Department, and a reserve officer with the Hawthorne Police Department. He was hired by the Long Beach Police Department as a community relations assistant in 1982 before being accepted into the police academy as a recruit officer that year. In October 2002, he was named chief of police for the Long Beach, California, Police Department.

Frank E. Batts

MILITARY. Frank E. Batts received a bachelor of science degree in electrical engineering in 1977 and a master of science degree in electrical engineering in 1981, both from North Carolina A&T State University in Greensboro. He also holds a master of science degree in strategic studies from the United States War College in 2004.

Batts was commissioned through the Army ROTC program at North Carolina A&T State University on December 17, 1976. He served in both the West Virginia and Tennessee Army National Guards before joining the Virginia Guard in 1985. He has served in command positions from battery through brigade level. Prior to his current assignment, he was the commander of the 54th Field Artillery Brigade. In one of his most recent assignments he was mobile liaison team chief in Kabul, Afghanistan, as part of OPERATION ENDURING FREEDOM from May 2004 through April 2005. Batts is the deputy commander, Joint Force Headquarters, Virginia, Virginia National Guard. He is responsible for the headquarters element of the Joint Force Headquarters.

Randolph Baxter

JUDICIAL. Randolph Baxter is a native of Columbia, Tennessee. He received a bachelor's degree from Tuskegee University and earned a juris doctor degree from the University of Akron School of Law. Baxter is a former captain in the U.S. Army who was awarded the Bronze Star for Valor in the Republic of Vietnam. He was appointed as judge to the U.S. Bankruptcy Court for the Northern District of Ohio, a 14-year term, in 1985. He is currently serving his second 14-year appointment as chief judge of the U.S. Bankruptcy Court for the Northern District of Ohio. His district covers all bankruptcy courts in the northern half of Ohio, including those in Cleveland, Toledo, Akron, Canton, and Youngstown. He is principally assigned to handle cases in metropolitan Cleveland but has also been assigned as visiting judge in New York, Michigan, Tennessee, and Florida. Baxter is active in his community and plays trumpet with the Cleveland Clinic Orchestra and his church's orchestra.

Sheila R. Baxter

MILITARY. Sheila R. Baxter received a bachelor of science degree in physical education from Virginia State College in 1977 and earned a master of arts degree in health service administration from Webster University. Her military education includes the U.S. Army medical department officer basic and advanced courses; U.S. Army Command and General Staff College; and the United States Army War College. She entered the U.S. Army with an ROTC commission as a second lieutenant on July 11, 1978. Key leadership assignments include: from December 1983 to January 1986, commander, B Company, 3d Battalion, Academy of Health Sciences, Fort Sam Houston, Texas; September 1993 to May 1995, chief, Logistics Division, U.S. Army Medical Department Activity at Fort Huachuca, Arizona; May 1995, commander of the 226th Medical Battalion (Logistics, Forward), V Corps in Germany; and June 1998, executive officer to the director of logistics, Office of the Surgeon General, Falls Church, Virginia. She was promoted to colonel on May 1, 2000.

In May 2000, Colonel Baxter was assigned as commander of the U.S. Army Medical Materiel Center, Europe, Germany; from April 2002 to June 2003, she was chief of staff at the U.S. Army Medical Research and Materiel Command, at Fort Detrick, Maryland; from June 2003 to June 2005, she was assistant surgeon general for force sustainment and deputy chief of staff for force sustainment/chief, U.S. Army Medical Service Corps, U.S. Army Medical Command at Fort Sam Houston, Texas. She was promoted to brigadier general on August 1, 2003. Since June 2005, Baxter has been the commanding general of Western Regional Medical Command/Lead Agent, Tricare Region 11, U.S. Army Medical Service Corps at Tacoma, Washington.

A.D. Baylor

LAW ENFORCEMENT. A. D. Baylor serves as the chief of police of Montgomery, Alabama. Montgomery is the capital city of Alabama, and its police department employs 510 sworn police officers and 200 civilians. It is responsible for 202,000 citizens in the city of Montgomery as well as nearly 150,000 others within the metro Montgomery area on a daily basis.

Karen Baynes

JUDICIAL. Karen Baynes received a bachelor's degree from Wake Forest University in 1989 and earned her juris doctor degree from the University of California at Berkeley in 1992. She served from 1995 to 2002 with the Fulton County Georgia, juvenile court system, most recently as an associate judge. She also led the Court Appointed Special Advocates program that trains volunteers who advocate for the best interests of abused and neglected children in the courts.

James A. Bell

BUSINESS. James A. Bell is a native of Los Angeles, California. He received a bachelor's degree in accounting from California State University at Los Angeles. He began his career with Rockwell in 1972 and held positions of increasing responsibility, including corporate senior internal auditor, manager of accounting and manager of general and cost accounting.

He has served over thirty-five years with the Boeing Company in management positions, including vice president of contracts and pricing for Boeing Space and Communications; vice president at the operating group level in 1996; and as the director of business management of the space station electric power system at the Boeing Rocketdyne unit. On November 24, 2003, he was named chief financial officer of the Boeing Company and was formally elected to the position by the Boeing board of directors in January 2004. From March through June 2005, in addition to his chief financial officer duties, Bell was Boeing president and chief executive officer on an interim basis.

Robert Mack Bell

JUDICIAL. Robert Mack Bell is a native of Rocky Mount, North Carolina, and was raised in Baltimore, Maryland. He received a bachelor of arts degree from Morgan State College in 1966 and earned a juris doctor degree from Harvard University Law School in 1969. Bell worked in private law practice from 1969 to 1974; from 1975 to 1980, he was a judge for Maryland District Court District One in Baltimore City. From 1980 to 1984 he as associate judge, Baltimore City Circuit Court, for the Eighth Judicial Circuit; he served as judge for the Court of Special Appeals, Sixth Appellate Circuit, in Annapolis, Maryland, from 1984 to 1991. He was an associate judge on the Maryland Court of Appeals in Baltimore, Maryland, from 1991 to 1996. Since 1996, Bell has served as the chief judge, Court of Appeals, 6th Appellate Circuit, in Baltimore.

Verdelle Bellamy

HEALTH. Verdelle Bellamy is a native of Birmingham, Alabama. She received a diploma degree from Grady Memorial Hospital's School of Nursing and a bachelor's degree from Tuskegee Institute and became a registered nurse in 1958. She earned a master's of nursing from Emory University's Nell Hodgan Woodruff School of Nursing in Atlanta, Georgia, in 1963. She is one of first African Americans to graduate from Emory University.

Bellamy joined the U.S. Veterans Affairs Medical System after graduating from Emory University. She designed and implemented policies and procedures for the Atlanta Veterans Administration Center that ultimately become models for veterans affair centers throughout the nation. She retired from the Veterans Affairs Medical System as an associated chief of geriatrics in the long-term care facility. She was the Veteran Affairs Medical Center's first African American administrator. She retired in 1998. Bellamy was the first African American elected to the executive committee of the Nurses Association of Georgia in 1971, and the first African American to receive a gubernatorial appointment to the Georgia Board of Nursing, from Governor Jimmy Carter in 1974.

Ray L. Belton

EDUCATION. Ray L. Belton received an associate degree from Southern University at Shreveport and a bachelor of science degree from Southern University A&M College in Baton Rouge. He earned a master of arts degree from the University of Nebraska and a Ph.D. from the University of Texas at Austin. Belton was executive vice chancellor, vice chancellor of student affairs, chairman of the Health and Human Services Department, coordinator of the mental health/mental retardation associate degree program, and faculty senate president at Southern University at Shreveport. He was named

chancellor and professor health and human services at Southern University.

Regina Marcia Benjamin

MEDICINE. Regina Marcia Benjamin received a bachelor of science degree in chemistry from Xavier University in New Orleans, Louisiana. She was a student intern-trainee for the Central Intelligence Agency. She earned a medical doctor degree from the University of Alabama in Birmingham in 1984, serving her internship and residency in family practice at the Medical Center of Central Georgia at Macon. She earned a master of business administration degree in 1991.

From 1990 to 1995, Dr. Benjamin was a medical director at several nursing homes, and in 1993 she went on a medical mission to Honduras. In 1995 she was named a "Person of the Week" on ABC *World News Tonight* with Peter Jennings. She practices as a country doctor in rural Alabama. As founder and chief executive officer of the Bayou La Batre Rural Health Clinic, Dr. Benjamin is making a difference to the underserved poor in a small fishing village on the Gulf Coast of Alabama. She is the first African American woman to become president of the state medical society of Alabama.

James K. Bennett

MEDICINE. James K. Bennett is a native of Georgia. He received a bachelor's degree (summa cum laude) from Clark College in Atlanta in 1976 and received his medical doctor degree from Duke University in 1979. Dr. Bennett attended Emory University, where he completed an internship in surgery and a residency in urology.

Dr. Bennett is an activist in the treatment and education of prostate cancer. He was the first Georgia urologist to perform cryosurgical abalation of the prostate. He also created an educational film featuring Dr. Louis Sullivan titled *Prostate Cancer in Black Men*, which has been used nationwide by the American Cancer Society. Dr. Bennett's video credits include *The Next River to Cross*, narrated by Les Brown, and *Prostate Cancer* narrated by Sidney Poitier. Dr. Bennett is clinically affiliated with Emory University and Morehouse School of Medicine and is co-director of the Department of Urology at Shepherd Center. He is the author of many medical articles on urologic topics and often conducts symposia in the medical field. He is the founder of Midtown Urology and Surgical Center in Atlanta, Georgia.

Karen Bennett-Haron

JUDICIAL. Karen Bennett-Haron is a native of Las Vegas, Nevada. She received a bachelor's degree in political science from Hampton University and earned her juris doctor from Thurgood Marshall School of Law. She began as a law clerk for the Honorable Thomas Foley. She later served as an assistant federal public defender. She has also served in private law practice and as general counsel to the Las Vegas Housing Authority. She was appointed to the Las Vegas Justice Court bench in May 2002 and became the first African American female appointed to the state's justice system at any level.

Marilyn Benoit

MEDICINE. Marilyn Benoit received a master's degree in health service management and policy and earned her medical doctor degree from Georgetown University in Washington, D.C. Dr. Benoit has served on the faculties of Howard University and George Washington University. She is a clinical associated professor of psychiatry at Georgetown University Medical Center, from where she received the Vicennial Silver Medal of Honor for 20 years of distinguished service. Dr. Benoit is a past president (2001–2003) of the American Academy of Child and Adolescent Psychiatry. She initiated a collaborative relationship with the Child Welfare League of America to establish a national coalition of

major stakeholders in the foster care system in order to improve mental health services to children in the system.

Lisa D. Benton

MEDICINE. Lisa D. Benton received her doctor of medicine degree from Jefferson Medical College, completed a general surgery residency at the University of Medicine and Dentistry of New Jersey Rutgers Robert Wood Johnson Medical School, and completed plastic surgery training at the University of California in San Francisco. Dr. Benton serves as a board certified attending general surgeon at Stanford University Hospital and Clinics with private practice offices in Palo Alto and Alameda, California. She is a bioterrorism, environmental and occupational health public health medical officer for the state of California, and as medical director of Project New Start Oakland, a laser tattoo removal program. She is also an advisory commissioner and vice-chair for the Alameda County Public Health Department and president of the East Bay Metropolitan Unit of the American Cancer Society.

Irene Berger

JUDICIAL. Irene Berger received a bachelor's degree in mathematics from West Virginia University in 1976 and earned her juris doctor from West Virginia University College of Law in 1979. She is a judge for the 13th Judicial Circuit in Kanawha County, West Virginia. She was named 2006 Outstanding Alumna of West Virginia University. In 2004, Governor Bob Wise presented her with the Distinguished West Virginia Award.

Daniel O. Bernstine

EDUCATION. Daniel O. Bernstine received a bachelor's degree in political science from the University of California at Berkeley. He earned a juris doctor from Northwestern School of Law in Chicago and an LL.M. from the University of Wisconsin Law School. He began his legal career at the U.S. Department of Labor. He served as interim dean and professor of law at Howard University School of Law in Washington, D.C., and general counsel for Howard University and Howard University Hospital. He served for seven years as dean and professor of law at the University of Wisconsin Law School and was president of Portland State University in Oregon from 1997 to 2007.

Rosie Phillips Bingham

EDUCATION. Rosie Phillips Bingham is a native of Memphis, Tennessee. She received a bachelor's degree in sociology and education from Elmhurst College in Elmhurst, Illinois. She earned a master of arts degree in counseling and guidance and a Ph.D. in counseling psychology from the Ohio State University. She started her career in higher education in 1972 at the Ohio State University and moved to the University of Florida in 1978. She was the associate director of the counseling center at the University of Florida prior to being hired as director for the Center for Student Development at the University of Memphis in 1985. She held this position until 1993, when she became the assistant vice president for student affairs and student development. After a national search, Bingham was selected as vice president for student affairs in 2003 and has articulated a division mission of "Students Learning through Engagement and Involvement."

Adolpho A. Birch, Jr.

JUDICIAL. Adolpho A. Birch, Jr., received a bachelor of arts degree and his juris doctor degree from Howard University. He was awarded the doctor of civil law honoris causa by the University of the South. Birch worked in private law practice. He moved to Davidson County, Tennessee, where he was assistant public defender from 1964 to 1966; assistant district attorney general from 1966 to 1969; judge of the Court of General Sessions from 1967 to 1978; judge of the Criminal Court, 1978

to 1987; and associate judge, Tennessee Court of Criminal Appeals, 1987 to 1993.

Judge Birch was appointed to the Tennessee State Supreme Court by Governor Ned McWherter in December 1993. He was confirmed as a Supreme Court justice by a statewide election in 1994 and retained by a statewide election in 1998. He was chief justice from May 16, 1996, until July 7, 1997, becoming the first African-American to serve as the chief justice of the Tennessee Supreme Court. He is currently on the faculty of the Nashville School of Law. He has served as adjunct professor in legal medicine at Meharry Medical College, a lecturer in law at Fisk and Tennessee State University and as a distinguished jurist in residence at the University of Memphis, Cecil C. Humphreys School of Law.

Andre Birotte, Jr.

LOCAL GOVERNMENT. Andre Birotte received a bachelor's degree from Tufts University and a juris doctor degree from Pepperdine University. He has taught legal writing and advocacy at the University of Southern California Law School. Birotte has served as a deputy public defender in Los Angeles, where he represented indigent clients charged with felony and misdemeanor offenses in several phases of criminal proceedings. He served with the United States Attorney's Office, where he investigated and prosecuted numerous violent crime, fraud and narcotics trafficking cases. He next worked in private law practice in Los Angeles. He joined the Office of the Inspector General in 2001. In 2003, he was appointed inspector general of the Los Angeles Police Department by the Los Angeles Board of Police Commissioners. Birotte has a staff of approximately 32 employees, including lawyers and professional auditors, to ensure compliance with Los Angeles Police Department policies and mandates for the Federal Consent Decree.

Clyde Bishop

JUDICIAL. Clyde Bishop is a native of Delaware. He received his bachelor of arts in sociology from Delaware State College in 1964 and a master of arts in sociology from Delaware University in 1972. He earned a Ph.D. from the University of Delaware in public policy analysis in 1976. He is fluent in Italian, Spanish and Portuguese. Bishop has served in the U.S. Department of State as a consular and economic officer in Palermo, Italy. His previous Foreign Service postings include Hong Kong, Bambay, Rio de Janeiro, and Korea. He was principal officer in Naples, Italy. He was the consul general at the U.S. Embassy in Santo Domingo, Dominican Republic. He was nominated by President George W. Bush in 2006 and confirmed as U.S. ambassador to the Republic of the Marshall Islands on September 28, 2006, by the U.S. Senate. Ambassador Bishop assumed his duties on December 5, 2006.

Sanford Dixon Bishop, Jr.

FEDERAL GOVERNMENT. Sanford Dixon Bishop, Jr., is a native of Mobile, Alabama, and attended public schools there. He received a bachelor of arts degree from Morehouse College in Atlanta, Georgia, in 1968 and a juris doctor degree from Emory University School of Law in Atlanta in 1971. He served in private law practice; served in the United States Army from 1969 to 1971; was elected a member of the Georgia State House of Representatives (1977–1991); and was elected to the Georgia State Senate (1991–1993). Bishop was elected a Democrat to the 103rd and to the seven succeeding Congresses (January 3, 1993, to present).

Angela Glover Blackwell

PUBLIC POLICY. Angela Glover Blackwell received a bachelor's degree from Howard University and a law degree from the University of California at Berkeley. She was a partner with Public Advocates, a nationally known public interest law firm representing the underrepresented. In 1987, she founded the Urban Strategies Council in Oakland, California, and received national recognition for pioneering a community building approach to social change through in-depth understand-

ing of local conditions, community-driven systems reform, and an insistence on accountability.

Blackwell founded PolicyLink after serving as senior vice president for the Rockefeller Foundation for three and a half years. She directed the foundation's domestic and cultural divisions and developed the Next Generation Leadership and Building Democracy programs, centered on issues of inclusion, race, and policy. Since its inception in January of 1999, PolicyLink has partnered with a cross-section of stakeholders to ensure that questions of equity received the highest priority in addressing major policy issues. Blackwell is the co-author of *Searching for the Uncommon Common Ground.* She is chief executive officer of PolicyLink.

J. Kenneth Blackwell

STATE GOVERNMENT. J. Kenneth Blackwell received bachelor of science and master of education degrees from Xavier University in Ohio. He was a scholar-in-residence at the Urban Morgan Institute for Human Rights at the University of Cincinnati College of Law. He has also served on the boards of directors of Physicians for Human Rights, the International Republican Institute and the Congressional Human Rights Foundation. He was a member of the advisory panel of the Federal Elections Commission; a member of the board of directors of the John M. Ashbrook Center for Public Affairs at Ashland University; vice president of the National Association of Secretaries of State; and member of the board of directors of the Campaign Finance Institute in Washington, D.C. He has been mayor of Cincinnati, undersecretary at the U.S. Department of Housing and Urban Development, U.S. ambassador to the United Nations Human Rights Commission, and treasurer of the state of Ohio. Blackwell was elected the 51st secretary of state of Ohio.

Angela Small Blalock

MUSIC. Angela Small Blalock is a graduate of Savannah State College and Ohio State University. She was a former associate artist with the Opera Columbus Company, Columbus Light Opera, and the Columbus Ensemble Singers. Additionally, she was the recipient of a travel scholarship from Ohio State University School of Music for study abroad in Graz, Austria, with the American Institute of Music Studies. She is on the music faculty of South Carolina State University, Orangeburg, and an assistant professor on the music faculty of Savannah State University in Georgia.

Blalock has performed benefit concerts for the Orangeburg Arts Council and made her South Carolina Philharmonic Orchestra debut the 1997–1998 season in its performance of Carl Orff's "Carmina Burana." She recently reprised this role in the 2003–2004 season opening performance of the South Carolina Philharmonic, Nicholas Smith, conductor. She has also appeared as a solo artist with the Augusta Symphony Orchestra and the University of South Carolina Symphony Orchestra with maestro Donald Portnoy. She was soloist with the South Carolina Philharmonic Orchestra in its performance of Haydn's *Creation*, and the Savannah Symphony Chamber Orchestra's performance of Handel's *Messiah.* Other solo appearances include performances of the requiems of Mozart, Brahms, Faure, and Rutter, the Bach *Magnificat,* Rutter *Magnificat*, and Mendelssohn's *Elijah* and *Hymn of Praise.* She was the soprano soloist for the South Carolina Philharmonic's 2003-2004 closing season performance of Gershwin's *Porgy and Bess.* She appeared as a guest artist in the Trinity Cathedral Performing Arts series in January 2006, in its Mozart Festival, commemorating the 250th anniversary of the composer's birth, and as the soprano soloist in the performance of the *Mozart Requiem* with the South Carolina Philharmonic Orchestra in January 2006.

Stephanie T. Bolden

LOCAL GOVERNMENT. Stephanie T. Bolden is a native of Wilmington, North Carolina, and a graduate of Howard High School. She received a bachelor's degree from Delaware State College (now University) in

1969 and earned a master's degree in urban education from Boston College. Bolden has served as a school teacher and community activist. In 1992 she was elected to the Wilmington City Council. She is the second African American female elected to the Wilmington City Council. She was re-elected in 1996, 2000 and 2004.

Edward L. Bolton, Jr.

MILITARY. Edward L. Bolton, Jr., received a bachelor of science degree in electrical engineering from the University of New Mexico in Albuquerque in 1983 and a master of science degree in systems management from the University of Southern California Los Angeles. He has also earned a master of science degree in national security strategy from the National War College at Fort Lesley J. McNair in Washington, D.C. His military education includes the Squadron Officer School at Maxwell Air Force Base, Alabama; the program manager course, Defense Systems Management College, Fort Belvoir, Virginia; Air Command and Staff College, Maxwell Air Force Base (distinguished graduate); the executive program manager course, Defense Systems Management College at Fort Belvoir in 2003; and senior executive fellow at Harvard University in Cambridge, Massachusetts, in 2006.

Bolton began his Air Force career as an enlisted cost and management analyst. In 1980, he was selected for the Airmen Education and Commissioning Program and was commissioned as a second lieutenant in 1983 after receiving his degree. His staff experience includes serving as systems requirements manager at Headquarters Air Force Systems Command and chief of the Spacelift Vehicles Requirements Branch at Headquarters Air Force Space Command. For two years he was director for defense policy at the National Security Council in the executive office of the president.

He was commander of the 30th Range Squadron and 30th Operations Group at Vandenberg Air Force Base in California; materiel wing director, Satellite and Launch Control Systems Program Office at the Space and Missile Systems Center, Los Angeles Air Force Base; and materiel wing director for the Space and Missile Systems Center's Space Launch and Range Systems Program Office. In August 2006, he was selected to serve as deputy director for system engineering, National Reconnaissance Office, in Chantilly, Virginia. Bolton was promoted to brigadier general on June 22, 2007.

Barry Lamar Bonds

SPORTS. Barry Lamar Bonds is a native of Riverside, California. He attended Junipero Serra High School in San Mateo, California. Ha batted .467 his senior year and was honored as a prep all–American. He is the son of former Major League All-Star Bobby Bonds, the godson of Hall of Famer Willie Mays, and a distant cousin of Hall of Famer Reggie Jackson. He attended Arizona State University, where he played baseball three years, hitting .347 with 45 home runs and 175 RBIs. He was named All-Pac 10 all three years. In 1985 he hit 23 home runs with 66 RBIs and a .368 batting average. He was a *Sporting News* All-American selection that year. He received a bachelor's degree in criminology from Arizona State University.

Bonds was drafted by the Pittsburgh Pirates in the first round (sixth overall) of the 1985 Major League Baseball draft. He played with the minor league Prince William Pirates and Hawaii Islanders before making his major league debut on May 30, 1986. In 1986, he finished 6th in Rookie of the Year voting, hitting 16 home runs and stealing 36 bases. He hit 25 home runs in his second season, along with 32 stolen bases and 59 RBIs. He won his first MVP award in 1990, hitting .301 with 33 home runs and 114 RBIs. In 1991 he led the Pirates to the National League East division title. In 1993, he left the Pirates to sign with the San Francisco Giants. On August 4, 2007, Bonds hit a 382 foot home run against Clay Hensley of the San Diego Padres for home run number 755, tying Hank Aaron's all-time record. He holds the all-time Major League home run record, after hitting his 756th home run in a game against the Washington Nationals on August 7, 2007, surpassing Hank Aaron. He currently has a total of 761 career home runs. He also is the all-time career leader in both walks (2,550) and intentional walks (684). He holds numerous single-season records, among them the single-season Major League record for home runs (73), set in 2001. He has won a record seven Most Valuable Player awards.

Fred Bonner

JUDICIAL. Fred Bonner received a bachelor of arts degree in sociology from Wiley College in 1968 and earned his juris doctor from the University of Washington School of Law in 1974. He passed bar exams in Washington and Minnesota. Bonner has served as a law clerk, City of Seattle Corporation Counsel; as a legal intern for King County Prosecutor's Office; law clerk, National Labor Relations Board; investigator, Depart-

ment of Licenses and Consumer Affairs; attorney for the National Labor Relations Board; commissioner, Municipal Court of Seattle; and magistrate on the Municipal Court of Seattle. Since 1989 he has served as a judge on the Seattle Municipal Court. Judge Bonner was the presiding judge on the Seattle Municipal Court from 2003 to 2006.

Charles L. Booker

MILITARY. Charles L. Booker entered the U.S. Marine Corps in January 1983. Upon graduation from Parris Island in April 1983, he received orders to his basic military occupational specialty school in Little Creek, Virginia. He completed Marine Security Guard School in May 1987. Booker has held key positions at U.S. embassies in Cairo, Egypt, and in Abu Dhabi, United Arab Emirates. While assigned to the attachment at Abu Dhabi he served as assistant detachment commander. In November 1989, he received orders back to the Fleet Marine Force and was assigned to Marine Air Control Squadron 1, Camp Pendleton, California. He assumed the billet of embarkation chief for the squadron. In August 1990, he embarked his squadron to Saudi Arabia in support of Operations Desert Shield and Desert Storm; his unit remained until November 1990. He was assigned to the American embassies at Kiev, Ukraine, and Pretoria, South Africa. In April 1999, he was promoted to first sergeant, and in May 1999, assigned to the 7th Engineer Support Battalion at Camp Pendleton, California, as the first sergeant for Alpha Company. He was first sergeant of Fox Company, Pretoria, South Africa. While in that billet, he covered 16 countries within East Africa and three detachments to Brazil.

In August 2003, he was promoted to sergeant major. In October 2003, he was assigned to Marine Corps Air Station Miramar, California, as the squadron sergeant major for Marine Medium Helicopter Squadron 161. In February 2004, his squadron was deployed in support of Operation Iraqi Freedom. In November 2004 he transferred to Marine Heavy Helicopter Squadron 465, were he was the sergeant major. He currently is the sergeant major for Marine Light Attach Training Squadron 303.

Cory A. Booker

PUBLIC SERVICE. Cory A. Booker was born in Washington, D.C., and grew up in Harrington Park in Bergen County, New Jersey. He graduated from Northern Valley Regional High School at Old Tappan and received a bachelor of arts in political science in 1991 and a master of arts degree in sociology in 1992 from Stanford University. He attended Oxford as a Rhodes scholar and received an honors degree in modern history in 1994. In 1997, he earned his law doctor degree from Yale University.

Booker has spent his entire professional life in Newark, New Jersey. His career includes serving as an attorney, as a program coordinator of the Newark Youth Project, and in 1998 he was elected Newark's Central Ward councilman. During his four years of service, he earned a reputation for his innovative ideas and bold actions, from increasing security in public housing to building new playgrounds. He ran for mayor of Newark in 2002, narrowly losing to the incumbent. He was elected mayor of the City of Newark 2006, becoming the 36th person to hold that post.

Voresa E. Booker

MILITARY. Voresa E. Booker is a native of Jackson, Tennessee. She received a bachelor of science degree in business administration from Lane College and a master's degree in systems management from the Naval Postgraduate School in Monterey, California. She completed Manpower School. Booker first enlisted in the U.S. Navy in February 1983, and following Recruit Training and Personnelman "A" school, she was assigned to the Personnel Support Detachment at Naval Station Roosevelt Roads, Puerto Rico. During her first enlistment, she was selected for Officer Candidate School in Newport, Rhode Island, and was commissioned in March 1985.

In May 1991, she served the Navy Recruiting District

Seattle as the Officer Programs Department head; she served on the staff of the commander, U.S. Fleet Forces Command, as a manpower analyst; and completed her second department head tour as officer in charge, Personnel Support Detachment at Naval Air Station in Oceana, Virginia. She assumed command of the Military Entrance Processing Station in Tampa, Florida, before transferring in August 2002 to the staff of the commander, Special Operations Command, where she was the chief of Navy and Marine Corps personnel and Navy element commander. In April 2005, she reported for duty as the executive officer of Navy Recruiting District Nashville and assumed command in July 2006.

Eric M. Bost

FEDERAL GOVERNMENT. Eric M. Bost is a native of Concord, North Carolina. He received a bachelor of arts degree in psychology from the University of North Carolina at Chapel Hill and a master of arts degree in special education from the University of South Florida.

He served as commissioner and chief executive officer of the Texas Department of Human Services for four years. In 2001, he was appointed as the under secretary for food, nutrition, and consumer services at the United States Department of Agriculture, responsible for the administration of the fifteen USDA nutrition assistance programs with a combined budget of over $58 billion, including the Food Stamp Program, the Special Supplemental Nutrition Program for Women, Infants and Children, the National School Lunch and School Breakfast Programs, and the Commodity Distribution Program.

He was nominated by President George W. Bush as U.S. ambassador to the Republic of South Africa in 2006. He was confirmed by the U.S. Senate on June 29, 2006, and was sworn in on July 20, 2006.

Terry Bowie

FEDERAL GOVERNMENT. Terry Bowie received a bachelor of science in accounting, finance and economics. He earned a master of public finance from American University in Washington, D.C. Bowie served with the U.S. Department of Housing and Urban Development for 12 years in various financial management positions. From 1995 to 2000, he was deputy chief financial officer of the U.S. Mint. From 2000 to 2005, was the director of financial management operations for the U.S. Department of Education. In May 2005, he assumed the position of deputy chief financial officer for the National Aeronautics and Space Administration (NASA).

Charles E. Box

STATE GOVERNMENT. Charles E. Box is a native of Rockford, Illinois. He received a bachelor of arts degree in history from Dartmouth College in 1973 and earned his juris doctor degree from the University of Michigan Law School in 1976. Box was an attorney in Rockford from 1976 to 1981. He served as the Rockford City administrator from 1987 to 1988 and as mayor from 1989 to 2001. On January 10, 2006, he was appointed chair of the Illinois Commerce Commission by Illinois Governor Rod Blagojevich. He is the first African American to head the agency.

Gwendolyn Elizabeth Boyd

ENGINEERING. Gwendolyn Elizabeth Boyd is a native of Montgomery, Alabama, where she attended public schools. She received a bachelor of science degree in mathematics with a double minor in physics and music, summa cum laude, from Alabama State University. She was awarded a fellowship to pursue graduate work at Yale University. She was the first African American female to earn a master of science degree in mechanical engineering from Yale University. Boyd is an engineer and the assistant for development programs at the Johns Hopkins University Applied Physics Laboratory. She serves on the Advisory Council of the College of Engineering, Architecture and Physical Science for Tuskegee University. She is affiliated with Society of Women Engineers and the Metropolitan Area Network of Minority Women in Science. She has also served as the national president of Delta Sigma Theta Sorority, Inc.

Gwendolyn V. Boyd

LAW ENFORCEMENT. Gwendolyn V. Boyd holds associate and bachelor's degrees in criminal justice; she earned a master's degree in public administration and a Ph.D. in adult education and human resource development from Florida International University. She is a graduate of the Southern Police Institute and the John F. Kennedy School of Government at Harvard.

Boyd began her law enforcement career in 1974 with the City of Miami Police Department as a public service aide in a police apprenticeship program. She worked various assignments as a street officer and as an investigator on several major undercover operations before becoming the first African American female officer assigned to the police academy. She advanced through the ranks, becoming the first African American female sergeant, lieutenant, captain, and major. In her 13-year tenure as a police major, she commanded such areas as personnel resource management, community relations, criminal investigations, and two of the three police substations. She is an adjunct professor at Florida International University.

After almost 25 years of distinguished service with the Miami Police Department, on November 25, 1997, Boyd was sworn in as police chief of the Prichard, Alabama, Police Department. In May 1999, she was appointed chief of police of the Miramar, Florida, Police Department and became the first African American to hold that position in Broward County. In April 2000, she was named vice president of administrative services by Florida International University, becoming the first alumni to serve on the executive council. In January 2002, she was selected as chief of police of the North Miami Police Department, becoming the first African American in that position.

Wilson G. Bradshaw

EDUCATION. Wilson G. Bradshaw received a bachelor of arts degree in psychology in 1971 and a master of arts degree in experimental psychology in 1973, both from Florida Atlantic University in Boca Raton. He earned a Ph.D. in psychobiology from the University of Pittsburgh in Pennsylvania in 1980. He has held numerous faculty appointments and administrative positions, including assistant professor of pharmacology at Florida A&M University/VA Medical Center in Miami from 1981 to 1983; associate professor of psychology at Florida Atlantic University in Boca Raton from 1984 to 1990; and professor of psychology at Georgia Southern University in Statesboro, Georgia, from 1990 to 1995. In 2001, he began as professor of psychology at Metropolitan State University in St. Paul, Minnesota. From 1988 to 1990 he was dean of graduate studies at Florida Atlanta University; from 1995 to 2000, he was provost and vice president for academic affairs at Bloomsburg University of Pennsylvania. Since 2000, Bradshaw has served as president of Metropolitan State University in St. Paul–Minneapolis, Minnesota.

Nelvia Brady

EDUCATION. Nelvia Brady was raised in public housing on Chicago's West Side. She received a bachelor's degree in sociology from the University of Illinois and a master's degree in guidance and counseling at the University of Wisconsin. She earned a doctorate degree in pupil personnel administration at Michigan State University.

Brady joined the Chicago Public Schools system in 1981 to help implement the city's desegregation plan. Seven years later, she was appointed chancellor of the largest community college district in Illinois, with more than 120,000 students spread over eight colleges. She was the first African American and the only female to have served as the chancellor of the City Colleges of Chicago. She was also the first African American and female to serve as lead counselor of the Minneapolis Public Schools. In 2003, she became the first director of ethnic diversity at Trinity Christian College, where she also teaches in the business department. She was the vice president and executive search consultant at Carrington and Carrington, Ltd., placing African Americans, Hispanics, women, and other minorities in senior management and high-level positions at Fortune 500 companies.

Rosalind Brewer

BUSINESS. Rosalind Brewer received a bachelor of science degree in chemistry from Spelman College in

Atlanta, Georgia. She has also completed the Advanced Management Program at the Wharton School of Business. Brewer serves as president and corporate officer of Kimberly-Clark Corporation. She currently leads the Global Nonwovens sector, which includes research and development, engineering, and manufacturing. The sector operates 27 nonwoven base machines in the U.S., Great Britain and South Korea.

Shirley Bridges

ENGINEERING, BUSINESS. Shirley Bridges received a bachelor's degree in mathematics from Clark Atlanta University and earned a master's degree in project management from George Washington University. Bridges has more than 30 years of project management and information technology experience. She worked in a variety of positions with Bridgehaus, Inc., and Norfolk Southern Railroad. She joined Delta's Information Technology department in 1990 as senior project manager. During her time with Delta and Delta Technology, she has served as director of finance systems, and director of engineering research projects systems and large systems engineering. She served as vice president of airline operation systems and now as the chief information officer for Delta Air Lines, Inc., and serves as president and chief executive officer for Delta Technology in Atlanta, Georgia.

Timothy K. Bridges

MILITARY. Timothy K. Bridges received a bachelor of science degree in civil engineering from Virginia Military Institute in Lexington, Virginia, and a master's degree in business management and supervision from Central Michigan University. His military education includes Squadron Officer School at Maxwell Air Force Base in Alabama, Air Command and Staff College, and Air War College at Maxwell. Bridges was commissioned in 1979 as a distinguished graduate of the Air Force Reserve Officer Training Corps program at Virginia Military Institute. He served in various roles at the base level, including design, planning, contract management, operations and Red Horse, and twice served as a base civil engineer and squadron commander. He has had a tour as an Air Force ROTC professor, and he worked at the major command and Air Force levels in the readiness environmental and resources arenas.

His last assignments in the Air Force were as chief, Programs Division, Directorate of the Civil Engineer, Headquarters Pacific Air Force at Hickam Air Force Base in Hawaii, and as deputy command civil engineer and later as command civil engineer, Directorate of Installations and Mission Support, Headquarters Air Force Materiel Command at Wright-Patterson Air Force Base in Ohio. He retired from active duty in the rank of colonel in July 2006 and entered the senior executive service. Since July 2006, he has been director of installations and mission support at Headquarters at Air Force Materiel Command, Wright-Patterson Air Force Base in Ohio.

Anthony Brinkley

MILITARY. Anthony Brinkley received an associate degree in information management a degree in personnel administration from the Community College of the Air Force. He is a graduate of the United States Air Force Senior Non-Commissioned Officer Academy at Maxwell Air Force Base and the Chiefs Leadership Course, Maxwell Air Force Base, Gunter Annex, in Alabama. Brinkley is a native of Roanoke Rapids, North Carolina. He entered the Air Force on January 12, 1984. He began his career as an administrative specialist and later retrained into the first sergeant career field. He has led several deployments in support of operations Desert Fox and Southern Watch in Saudi Arabia, as well as conducting fact finding activities in Kyrgyzstan to enhance quality of life for deployed troops. He serves as the command

chief master sergeant for the 8th Fighter Wing, Kunsan Air Base in the Republic of Korea. In this position he represents the 3,000 Airmen of the Wolf Pack and serves as the principal adviser to the commander on all enlisted issues.

Dale Bronner

MINISTRY. Dale Bronner is a native of Atlanta, Georgia, and received a bachelor's degree from Morehouse College. He earned his doctor of ministry degree from the Christian Life School of Theology. Bronner began ministry in his local public high school as president and founder of the Praise the Lord Club. He is the founder and senior pastor of Word of Faith Family Worship Cathedral, an interdenominational ministry founded in 1991, thriving with more than 10,000 members. He is the author of the books *Get a Grip, Guard Your Gates, A Check Up from the Neck Up* and most recently, *Treasure Your Silent Years.*

Carolyn B. Brooks

EDUCATION, SCIENCE. Carolyn B. Brooks received her bachelor of science and master of science degrees in biology from Tuskegee University. She earned a Ph.D. in microbiology from the Ohio State University. Brooks has served as a principal investigator in nutrition programs at Kentucky State University. At the University of Maryland Eastern Shore, she was the principal investigator on several research programs in microbiology and biotechnology and has taught undergraduate and graduate courses in these areas. Her research endeavors have included work in Togo, Nigeria, Senegal, Cameroon, and Egypt. She was a recipient of the Faculty Award for Excellence in Science and Technology from the White House. She is as the dean of the School of Agricultural and Natural Sciences and the 1890 research director at the University of Maryland Eastern Shore, and serves as chair of the Association of 1890 Research Directors.

Peggy Brooks-Bertram

EDUCATION. Peggy Brooks-Bertram is a native of Baltimore, Maryland, and moved to Buffalo, New York, in 1986 after a career in public health. She received a bachelor of arts degree in political science from Goucher College in Baltimore, Maryland. She earned a master's degree and a doctorate degree from the Johns Hopkins University School of Hygiene and Public Health. She received a second doctorate in American studies from the University of Buffalo, the State University at New York.

Brooks-Bertram has written children's books, produced radio and television programs, and researched in the areas of education, public health, and African American history. She has also developed a faith-based hospice center, worked as an advocate of the parents of public school children, and founded, among other things, an independent consultant firm, Jehudi Educational Services, of which she is the chief executive officer. She is an adjunct assistant professor and director of undergraduate studies in the Department of African American Studies at the University of Buffalo, New York.

Anita Brown

EDUCATION, MINISTRY. Anita Brown is a native of New York City and grew up in Albany, Georgia. She received her early education in the Dougherty County School System, graduating with honors from Monroe. She received a bachelor of science degree from Albany State University in 1969 and a master of education from American University in Washington, D.C., in 1973. In June 2000, she received a Ph.D. in curriculum and instruction from the University of Sarasota, Florida.

Brown has taught in Alabama; Washington, D.C.; Lee County, Georgia; and Dougherty County, Georgia; she is a retired assistant principal of Dougherty Middle School in Albany, Georgia. Since 1997, she has served as the senior pastor of Harvest Temple of the Kingdom of God in Hawkinsville, Georgia.

Charles Q. Brown, Jr.

MILITARY. Charles Q. Brown, Jr., received a bachelor of science in civil engineering from Texas Tech University, in Lubbock, Texas, and master of aeronautical science from Embry-Riddle Aeronautical University in Daytona Beach, Florida. His military education includes the United States Air Force Fighter Weapons School, Nellis Air Force Base, Nevada; Squadron Officer School at Maxwell Air Force Base, Alabama; Distinguished Graduate Air Command and Staff College at Maxwell; Air War College at Maxwelle; and National Defense Fellow, Institute for Defense Analyses, Alexandria, Virginia.

Brown was a distinguished graduate of the Air Force Reserve Officer Training Corps (ROTC) at Texas Tech University and received a commission in the U.S. Air Force in 1984. He has held various squadron and wing level positions during operational assignments, including instructing in the F-16 Division, U.S. Air Force Weapons School. His staff tours include aide-de-camp to the chief of staff of the Air Force and Air Operations Officer, United States Central Command. Colonel Brown commanded the 78th Fighter Squadron at Shaw Air Force Base in South Carolina. He was a national defense fellow at the Institute for Defense Analyses, Alexandria, Virginia, and deputy chief, Program Integration Division, Directorate of Programs, Headquarters, United States Air Force in Washington, D.C. Prior to his current assignment, he was the commandant for the U.S. Air Force Weapons School, 57th Wing, at Nellis Air Force Base in Nevada. Colonel Brown is the commander of the 8th Fighter Wing at Kunsan Air Base, Republic of Korea. He commands more than 2,700 personnel, four groups and 15 squadrons, including two F-15 fighter squadrons.

Cherry Houston Brown

HEALTH, LOCAL GOVERNMENT. Cherry Houston Brown is a native of Aiken County, South Carolina. She attended Aiken and Barnwell County schools and graduated from Williston Elko High. She earned a bachelor's degree in social welfare and a master's degree in rehabilitation counseling from South Carolina State University.

Brown serves as the director of behavioral health services at John de la Howe School and has more than 23 years of experience working with behavior disordered children. She served from 1990 to 1998 as the District 1 representative on the McCormick County Council, South Carolina, where she helped lead improvements for the nursing home, water installation and a number of other community-based projects. In 2007, Brown was named to represent McCormick County on the Piedmont Technical College Area Commission in South Carolina. Members of the governing board are recommended by their respective county councils and appointed by the governor for four-year terms.

Frederick L. Brown

JUDICIAL. Frederick L. Brown received a bachelor's degree from Harvard College in 1954 and earned his juris doctor degree from Harvard Law School in 1967. He served as regional counsel for the United States Department of Housing and Urban Development. He has also taught at Boston University Law School and Northeastern Law School and has published a number of articles in scholarly legal journals. In 1976, he was appointed to the Massachusetts Appeals Court, becoming the first African American to serve on the Appeals Court in Massachusetts.

Jim Brown

SPORTS. Jim Brown is a native of St. Simons, Georgia. He was abandoned by his father about two weeks after his birth, and his mother left when he was 2 to take a job as a maid on Long Island, New York. His great-grandmother raised him, and they shared a house with his grandmother. At the age of 8, his mother sent for him; it was the first time he seen his mother in six years. He attended mostly white Manhasset High School, where he earned 13 letters playing football, basketball, baseball, lacrosse and running track. As a senior, he averaged 14.9 yards a carry in football and 38 points a game in basketball. He is a graduate of Syracuse University in New York, where he played football, basketball, lacrosse and ran track.

In his sophomore year he was Syracuse's

second leading scorer in basketball, averaging 15 points, and the football team's second leading rusher. As a junior, he rushed for 666 yards (5.2 per carry), averaged 11.3 points in basketball and was named a second-team All-American in lacrosse. In his senior year, Brown was first-team All-American in both football and lacrosse (43 goals in 10 games to tie for the national scoring championship). In football he averaged 6.2 yards in running for 986 yards, third most in the country despite Syracuse playing only eight games, and scored 14 touchdowns. He was the Cleveland Browns' first-round draft choice at number 6 overall, and was the league's Rookie of the Year in 1957, leading all running backs with 942 yards. The next year, the fullback was named most valuable player after leading the league in rushing with 1,527 yards and touchdowns with 18. In 1963, he became the first back to run for more than a mile with his 1,863-yard total. He caught passes, returned kickoffs, and even threw three touchdown passes. His 12,312 rushing yards and 15,459 combined net yards put him in a class by himself for his time.

Brown was a unanimous first-team All-NFL pick eight times. He was recognized as the NFL's most valuable player by many media organizations. In all, he earned league MVP honors four times (1957, 1958, 1963, and 1965). In the summer of 1966, while working on the movie *The Dirty Dozen* in London during the off season, he stunned the sports world with his announcement that he was retiring. He never missed a game in nine years. His number 32 was retired by the Browns and he was inducted into the Pro Football Hall of Fame in 1971.

Brown has appeared in 32 movies; among the best were *The Dirty Dozen, Ice Station Zebra, Rio Conchos, 100 Rifles, El Condor, Slaughter, Black Gunn, Three the Hard Way, The Running Man, I'm Gonna Git You Sucka, Mars Attacks, Oliver Stone* and *Any Given Sunday*. He also appeared in guest spots on TV shows such as *CHiPs* in 1977 and *Knight Running Man* in 1987. He is active with his Amer-I-Can Program, which teaches self-help principles to ex-convicts and gang members. Brown is an executive advisor with the Cleveland Browns Organization, helping to build relationships with Browns players and to further enhance the NFL's wide range of sponsored programs through the Browns' player programs department.

Joe Brown

JUDICIAL. Joe Brown was born in Washington, D.C., grew up in South Central Los Angeles and later moved to the Crenshaw area, where he graduated from Dorsey High School. He received a bachelor's degree in political science and earned his juris doctor from the University of California at Los Angeles. Brown worked with the Equal Employment Opportunity Commission . He was selected to serve as a prosecutor for the City of Memphis, Tennessee, the first African American in that position. He was later named director of the City of Memphis Public Defender's Office. In 1978, he entered private law practice. He was elected to serve as judge of Division 9 of the Tennessee State Criminal Courts for Shelby County. He was a judge of the Shelby Criminal Courts in Memphis, Tennessee, from 1990 to 2000. In 2008 he was in his eleventh season of his TV show *Judge Joe Brown*, a daily half-hour syndicated reality court.

Kevin M. Brown

MILITARY. Kevin M. Brown joined the United States Navy on February 16, 1982. Upon completion of recruit training at Recruit Training Center San Diego, California, he attended Quartermaster "A" School at Service School Command, Naval Training Center, Orlando, Florida. His key assignments include serving onboard USS *Hue City*. As chief petty officer he deployed to the Mediterranean and Adriatic Seas. His next duty station was at Broaden Opportunity for Officer Selection and Training in Newport, Rhode Island, from August 1995 to September 1998. He was assigned to the USS *Theodore Roosevelt* in Norfolk, Virginia, from October 1998 to July 2002. While aboard he was advanced to senior chief petty officer. He took follow-on orders to Commander Amphibious Group Two in Norfolk, Virginia, from August 2002 to May 2004. During this tour, he was advanced to master chief petty officer and was selected for the command master chief program. After completing training at the Senior Enlisted Academy in Newport, Rhode Island, Brown transferred to the HSL-51 Warlords at the U.S. Naval Air Facility, Atsugi, Japan, as the command master chief.

Linda E. Brown

JUDICIAL. Linda E. Brown received her juris doctor from Indiana University Law School, Indianapolis, Indiana. She began her career in 1992 in private law practice with her sister. While in private practice, she worked part-time as a public defender with the Marion County Public Defender Agency. From 1992 to 1996, she served as judge pro-tempore for Judge John Hesseldenz of Center Township of Marion County Small Court. After the death of Judge Hesseldenz in 1996, she continued as a commissioner for his succes-

sor until the summer of 2000. Also, during this time she sat as judge pro-tempore in the Initial Hearing Court and Marion Superior Courts, Criminal Divisions 14, 15, and 19. She became a master commissioner for the Marion Superior Courts in 2000 and was elected Marion County Superior Court judge in November of 2000. She currently serves as the presiding judge in Marion County Superior Court, Criminal Division 10.

Manson K. Brown

MILITARY. Manson K. Brown is a native of Washington, D.C. He graduated from the U.S. Coast Guard Academy in 1978 with a bachelor of science degree in civil engineering. He earned a master of science degree in civil engineering from the University of Illinois at Champaign Urbana and a master of science degree in national resources strategy from the Industrial College of the Armed Forces. He is a registered professional civil engineer. He assumed command of Maintenance and Logistics Command Pacific in June 2006.

Brown's previous commands include commander, Coast Guard Sector, Honolulu, and commander, Coast Guard Group, Charleston. From 1999 to 2002, he was the military assistant to the U.S. secretary of transportation, including duty as the acting deputy chief of staff for six months after the terrorist attack of September 11, 2001. In May 2003, he became the chief of officer personnel management at the Coast Guard Personnel Command. From April to July 2004, he was temporarily assigned as the senior advisor for transportation to the Coalition Provisional Authority in Baghdad, Iraq. Working in a combat zone, he oversaw restoration of Iraq's major transportation systems, including two major ports. He is the first recipient of the Coast Guard's Captain John G. Witherspoon Award for Inspirational Leadership.

Mark Brown

MILITARY. Mark Brown received a bachelor of science degree in accounting from Tuskegee University in Alabama in 1986 and a master of public administration degree from Troy State University in 1992. He earned a master's degree in strategic studies at Air Command and Staff College in 2001 and a master's degree in national security strategy from the National Defense University, National War College, at Fort McNair, Washington, D.C. He is a graduate of the Air Command and Staff College and Air University at Maxwell Air Force Base, Alabama.

Brown was commissioned into the U.S. Air Force through the Reserve Officer Training Corps program at Tuskegee University. He has served in comptroller, command, and staff positions at all levels of the Department of Defense. He has commanded two squadrons, deployed in support of Operation Provide Comfort, and served as the assistant executive officer for the 17th Air Force chief of staff. His was commander and regional accounting and finance officer, 32nd Accounting and Finance Squadron, at Incirlik Air Base in Turkey. In March 2002, he served as assistant executive officer to the Air Force chief of staff at Headquarters United States Air Force, Pentagon, Washington, D.C. From October 2003 to July 2004, he was congressional liaison, Headquarters U.S. Air Force. He is deputy director of budget and appropriations affairs in the Office of the Secretary of Defense, Office of the Comptroller, Pentagon, in Washington, D.C. As the senior military assistant to the under secretary of defense comptroller, he assists and provides military advice to the comptroller on oversight of Department of Defense financial management activities, including a budget of over $600 billion.

Thomas E. Brown

LAW ENFORCEMENT. Thomas E. Brown was educated in the Atlanta public school system. He received two associate degrees from DeKalb Community College and a bachelor of science degree in public administration from Brenau College in 1990. Brown joined the Atlanta Fire Bureau

in September 1972. During more than 12 years of service in Atlanta, he advanced through the ranks of fire fighter-paramedic, fire captain and chief of rescue services to deputy fire chief.

In June 1985, he was chosen by the DeKalb County chief executive officer to serve as the fifth fire chief of DeKalb County. At that time, he was the youngest fire chief in the United States of departments protecting populations of over 100,000. He was selected as public safety director of DeKalb County on January 8, 1990. As director, he was responsible for the administration of police, fire and emergency medical services, the 911 communication center, and animal control. Brown won a special election in March of 2001 with 83 percent of the votes cast, becoming the 48th sheriff of Dekalb County. He was elected to his second term in 2004, running unopposed.

Tulanda D. Brown

ENGINEERING. Tulanda D. Brown received a bachelor's degree in nuclear engineering from the University of Cincinnati. She joined Martin Marietta's Portsmouth Gaseous Diffusion Plant in 1990, serving as nuclear criticality safety representative for all fissile waste products. Two years later Brown joined Fluor, where she performed safety assessments for several on-site projects at Fernald. From 1995 until 2002, she worked for the Department of Energy's (DOE) Ohio Field Office as the lead safety engineer and was responsible for all nuclear safety issues at five DOE sites in Ohio and New York. That work included developing a DOE technical certification program for 100 engineers and scientists in the Ohio field office. She is one of the nation's experts in the cleanup of radioactive environments and is safety and health manager with Fluor Fernald, Inc.

Rodney Bryan

MILITARY. Rodney Bryan is a native of Cambridge, Maryland. He received a bachelor of science degree in art education and was commissioned in the United States Air Force in 1975 as a graduate of the University of Maryland, Eastern Shore, through the Reserve Officer Training Corps. He earned a master's degree in management and human relations from Webster College at Altus Air Force Base in Oklahoma. His military education includes Squadron Officer School, Air Command and Staff College, and Air War College. Bryan entered the United States Air Force as a transportation officer and has held various positions in base transportation, aerial port and mobile aerial port units, as well as plans and programs. In June 1990, he joined the 459th Airlift Wing as an air reserve technician at Andrews Air Force Base in Maryland, where he was the chief of logistics plans. He transferred to the 932nd Airlift Wing, at Scott Air Force Base, Illinois, in April 1993, to be chief of wing plans. Since October 2001, he has served as commander, 446th Mission Support Group, at McChord Air Force Base in Washington.

Vanessa Lynne Bryant

JUDICIAL. Vanessa Lynn Bryant is a native of Queens, New York. She received a bachelor of arts degree from Howard University in 1975 and earned her juris doctor from the University of Connecticut School of Law in 1978. Bryant began her career in private law practice (1978 to 1981); as counsel for Aetna Life and Casualty Company from 1981 to 1989; as counsel to Shawmut Bank, 1989 to 1990; as vice president and general counsel for the Connecticut Housing Finance Authority, 1990 to 1992; and as a Superior Court judge in Connecticut from 1998 to 2007. Bryant was nominated by George W. Bush on January 9, 2007, to serve as U.S. District Court judge in the District of Connecticut. She was confirmed on March 28, 2007, and received her commission and appointment on April 2, 2007.

Walter G. Bumphus

EDUCATION. Walter G. Bumphus received bachelor's and master's degrees from Murray State University and a doctoral degree from the University of Texas at Austin. Bumphus began his career as director of minority affairs and residence halls at Murray State University in western Kentucky. He also has served with colleges in Arkansas and Virginia. He consults with universities on issues of instructional and administrative technologies, designing model student development programs and instructional training to attract and

retain high-risk students. Bumphus was vice president and dean of student of Howard Community College in Columbia, Maryland, from 1987 to 1991, and served as president of Brookhaven College in Dallas County, Texas, from 1991 to 1997. He is president of the High Education Division of Voyager Expanded Learning in Dallas.

Roy A. Burrell

ENGINEERING. Roy A. Burrell received a bachelor of science degree in mathematics and pure and applied sciences from the University of Louisiana at Monroe (formerly Northeast Louisiana University). He served 22 years as a plant and network planning engineer at Bell South Telecommunications Company in Bossier City. In 1994, he was elected to the Shreveport City Council and in 2003 he was elected to the Louisiana House of Representatives for District 2.

Karyn L. Butler

MEDICINE. Karyn L. Butler received her medical degree from Morehouse School of Medicine and completed her surgical training at Howard University College of Medicine. She held fellowships at Bayley-Seton Hospital, Staten Island, New York, and University of Maryland–New Jersey Medical School, Newark, New Jersey. She was a National Institutes of Health trauma research fellow at the University of Colorado Health Sciences Center, Denver.

Dr. Butler is a trauma surgeon and associate professor of surgery in the Division of Trauma and Critical Care at the University of Cincinnati Medical Center. She conducts research at the Cardiovascular Research Center on myocardial ischemia-reperfusion injury (the loss or reduction in blood flow to part of the muscular tissue of the heart and resulting injury). Dr. Butler serves on the publications committee of the Society of University Surgeons and is a member of the executive committee of the Society of Black Academic Surgeons.

Percy Dean Butler

BUSINESS. Percy Dean Butler was born in Prichard, Alabama, and was raised in Prichard and Gulfport, Mississippi. He graduated from Thirty-Third Avenue High School, Gulfport, and attended college at Los Angeles City College and the University of California at Los Angeles before enlisting in the Army in May 1964.

Butler's twenty year Army career was spent specializing in human resources and management, staff operations and planning, and analysis. During his military tenure, he earned a bachelor of science degree in business administration awarded by American Technological University and pursued his postgraduate work in master of science business administration with Boston University's European Campus. He consistently progressed in rank to become a chief warrant officer four, W-4, serving in various posts in the United States, Republic of West Germany, and two combat tours to the Republic of Vietnam. He received numerous awards and decorations.

After retiring from the military, Butler launched a financial consulting and insurance business in the Greater Atlanta area, specializing in advising clients on asset protection through family financial and estate planning. The education of children and retirement funding has been fundamental aspect of his business and he has received government approval as a certified federal employee benefits counselor. He is the president and founder of the Advantage Capital Group, Inc., in Atlanta.

Butler has been active throughout the continental United States, serving as a presidential appointee on the Veterans Administration Advisory Committee on National Cemeteries and Memorial, for which he was elected as vice chairman and chairman for more than four years. He has served as assistant vice president for Veterans Affairs, is a lifetime member of the United States Army Warrant Officers Association, and is a member of Veterans of Foreign Wars and the American Legion. Butler is a member of Christians for Change Baptist Church, where he is on the trustee board. He has been active in the NAACP, the former Atlanta Exchange and numerous business and civic organizations. He is the founder of the Business Forum of Atlanta. He is a master Mason, 32nd degree, and Shriner. He participates in mentoring programs in the educational system, public speaking engagements and by providing financial seminars.

Veronica Butler

MEDICINE. Veronica Butler received her medical doctor degree from Howard University College of Medicine in Washington, D.C., and her master's in public health from the University of Michigan. Dr. Butler is co-author of a breakthrough research study on the benefits to health and quality of life of Vedic architecture, published in the *Journal of Social Behavior and Personality*. She is a board-certified family practitioner, director of women's programs for the Institute of Natural Medicine and Prevention, and director of the Family Practice Center in Ottumwa, Iowa.

Michael B. Calvin

JUDICIAL. Michael B. Calvin received a bachelor of arts degree from Monmouth College in Illinois and earned his juris doctor from St. Louis University. He served in private law practice from 1976 to 1978. He was elected magistrate judge of the City of St. Louis in 1978. In 1979, he became an associate circuit judge in the 22nd Circuit in St. Louis. He was appointed circuit judge in 1988. Judge Calvin was retained in 1990, 1996 and 2002. His term expires December 31, 2008.

Cloves Campbell, Jr.

PUBLISHING, STATE GOVERNMENT. Cloves Campbell, Jr., is a native of Phoenix, Arizona, and attended East Phoenix High School and Pitzer College in Claremont, California. Campbell has spent his entire career with the *Arizona Informant* newspaper, a family owned and operated publication in its 37th year. He has served on the Governor's African American Advisory Board. He was elected to serve as the State Representative for District 16, Arizona House of Representatives.

Michael "Mike" Carey

SPORTS. Michael Carey received a bachelor's degree in biology from Santa Clara University in Santa Clara, California, in 1971. He played football for four years until an ankle injury sidelined him. He maintained his ties to Santa Clara University by serving on the Board of Regents from 1992 to 1996 and then as a member of the Board of Trustees, where he chaired the Student Affairs Committee. Carey began his officiating career in 1972 with the Pop Warner football games in the San Diego, California, area. In 1985, he joined the Western Athletic Conference. Carey was hired by the National Football League in 1990 as a side judge before being promoted to referee for the start of the 1995 NFL season. He was only the second African American official to become a referee after Johnny Grier in 1988. He served as an alternate referee for Super Bowl XXXVI (36) in 2002.

Of all the active referees in the NFL, he has ejected the most players. On the field, he wears the uniform number 94. On October 3, 2005, he and his brother, Don Carey, a back judge, became the first brothers to officiate an NFL game together when they were assigned to the game between the Carolina Panthers and Green Bay Packers. Carey was the referee during the January 7, 2006, NFC wild card playoff game between the Washington Redskins and Tampa Bay Buccaneers. During his 18th year as an official, he was selected to serve as the referee for NFL's Super Bowl XLII (42) on February 3, 2008, in Glendale, Arizona. Carey became the first African American in the 41-year history of the NFL to lead the Super Bowl's officiating crew, serving as the referee.

Pamela Carmouche

MILITARY. Pamela Carmouche is a native of Midland, Texas. She received an associate in science degree in general studies from Central Texas College and a bachelor's degree in human resources management from Troy State University. She also earned a master's degree in human resources development from Webster State University. Her military education includes all the noncommissioned officer courses; postal operations course; Nuclear Biological Chemical course; alcohol and drug course; basic instructor training course; Drill Sergeant School; equal opportunity advisor course; first sergeant course; and the U.S. Army Sergeants Major Academy.

Carmouche enlisted into the United States Army Reserve through the delayed entry program in June 1986

as an administrative specialist. She attended basic combat training and advanced individual training at Fort Jackson, South Carolina. After 11 months on reserve status, she enlisted in the regular Army on December 1, 1987.

Carmouche has held numerous leadership assignments, including serving as the equal opportunity sergeant major for the U.S. Army Training and Doctrine Command; administrative supervisor, Joint Command Southcent, Larissa, Greece; first sergeant, Alpha Battery and Echo Battery, 1st Battalion, 19th Field Artillery, Fort Sill, Oklahoma; postal noncommissioned officer in charge, Camp Coiner, Korea; administrative sergeant, White Sands Missile Range, New Mexico; drill sergeant at Fort Jackson, South Carolina; and senior postal clerk, 147th AG Company, Heidelberg, Germany. She currently is the command sergeant major for the U.S. Garrison in Kaiserslautern, Germany, the largest U.S. community outside of the continental United States.

Benjamin S. Carson, Sr.

MEDICINE. Benjamin S. Carson, Sr., is a native of Detroit, Michigan. He received a bachelor's degree from Yale University and his doctor of medicine degree from the University of Michigan School of Medicine in 1977. He served surgical and neurosurgical residencies and fellowships at Hopkins, and also trained at Sir Charles Cairdner Hospital in Western Australia. He has been awarded 22 honorary doctorate degrees. Dr. Carson serves as director of pediatric neurosurgery at the Johns Hopkins Children's Center, a position he held since 1984 at age 33, the youngest physician to head a major division at Johns Hopkins. He holds appointments in the departments of neurosurgery, oncology, plastic surgery, and pediatrics at the Hopkins School of Medicine.

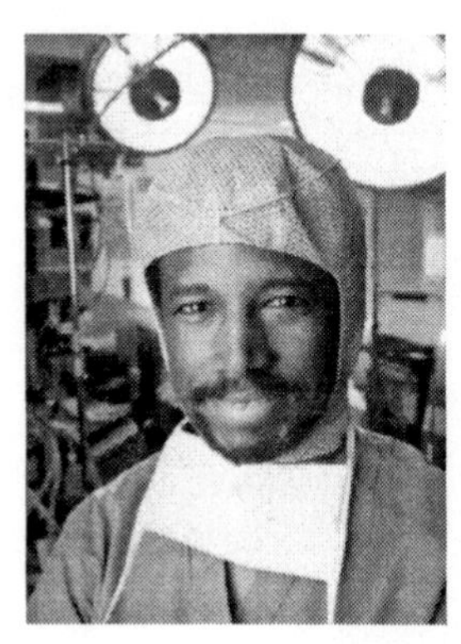

Dr. Carson pioneered the first intrauterine surgical procedure to relieve pressure on the brain of a hydrocephalic fetal twin in 1986. He performed the first successful separation of conjoined twins joined at the head in 1987. Dr. Carson was the primary neurosurgeon among the 70-member medical team that successfully separated seven-month-old German craniopagus twin boys. The 22-hour procedure is believed to be the first time hypothermia (the lowering of body temperature) was coupled with circulatory bypass and deliberate cardiac arrest to spare brain tissue for such a procedure. The boys returned to Germany after seven months at Johns Hopkins.

In 1997, he led a team of doctors in South Africa in the first completely successful separation of vertical craniopagus twins from Zambia. The procedure required 28 hours of surgery. The boys, who were 11 months old at the time, show no signs of impairment. In recent years, Dr. Carson has developed, with Hopkins's plastic surgery division, a craniofacial program in which children with congenital deformities undergo combined neurosurgical and plastic surgical reconstruction. He is part of a group studying the problems of achondroplastic children and has particular interest in cervicomedullary compression and its treatment.

Joseph C. Carter

MILITARY, LAW ENFORCEMENT. Joseph C. Carter received a bachelor of arts degree in organizational management from Lesley University in Cambridge, Massachusetts, in 1988 and a master of arts degree in criminal justice administration from Atlanta University in Atlanta, Georgia. He also received a master of science degree in strategic studies from the U.S. Army War College at Carlisle, Pennsylvania, in 2002, and was a graduate of the U.S. Army Command and General Staff College in 1992. He is also a graduate of the 140th Session of the FBI National Academy; a 1986 graduate of Police Executive Research Forum's Senior Management Institute for Police; and a 1991 graduate of the American Bar Association National Judicial College's administrative law judge course.

Carter began his military career on July 17, 1979, as a second lieutenant with the Massachusetts Army National Guard in Braintree, Massachusetts. Since that time he has held numerous staff and command assignments. His most recent include from January 2005 to September 2007 as assistant adjutant general at Joint Force Headquarters, Massachusetts National Guard, in Milford, Massachusetts; and from September 21, 2007, as adjutant general at Joint Force Headquarters. Major General Carter is the first African American to serve as the adjutant general for the Massachusetts National

Guard. He was promoted to brigadier general in March 2006 and to major general in September 2007.

Carter began his law enforcement career in 1978 with the Boston Police Department and served as superintendent from 1985 to 1998. From 1998 to 2003, he was chief of police of Oak Bluffs, Massachusetts, and from 2003 to 2007 as chief of police, Massachusetts Bay Transportation Authority. He also served as the president of the International Association of Chiefs of Police from 2006 to 2007.

Warrick L. Carter

EDUCATION. Warrick L. Carter was born in Charlottesville, Virginia, and graduated from Burley High School. He received a bachelor of science degree from Tennessee State University in 1964 and completed advanced percussion study at Blair Academy of Music. He earned a master of music degree from Michigan State University in 1966 and then a Ph.D. in music education from Michigan State University.

He served in 1966, 1967, and 1971 as an assistant professor in the Department of Music at the University of Maryland and at Michigan State University. He was a member of the Lansing (Michigan) Symphony Orchestra in 1965 and from 1968 to 1970. In 1971 he was hired as a professor at Governors State University in Park Forest South, Illinois. He remained at that institution for 14 years, during which time he held several titles, including coordinator of music (1971–1976) and coordinator of fine and performing arts (1976–1984). As division chairman, Carter oversaw the administration of four departments: music, theater, visual arts, and photography. In 1984, he assumed the position of dean of Berklee College of Music in Boston, serving as dean of faculty and then as provost and vice president of academic affairs. In 1996, he joined Disney's education, training and performance programs as director of entertainment arts, the corporation's arts advocacy arm. In 2000, he was named president of Columbia College in Chicago. He is a past president of the International Association of Jazz Educators.

Wilmer Amina Carter

STATE GOVERNMENT. Wilmer Amina Carter graduated from San Bernardino High School and attended San Bernardino Valley College. She earned both her bachelor's degree and master's degree from California State University at San Bernardino. Carter served as a staff member to Congressman George Brown for 26 years; during that time, she was District Director. She served on the Rialto Unified School District Board for sixteen years. Carter was elected to the California State Assembly in 2006, for the 62nd Assembly District.

Gwen Chandler

EDUCATION. Gwen Chandler received a bachelor of science degree from Alabama State University and a master of science in library science from Catholic University of America. She also earned a master of science from the University of North Florida and a Ph.D. in education from Nova University. Chandler has served as a librarian with the Jacksonville Public Library System and worked at the National Security Agency in Ft. Meade, Maryland. She served from 1995 to 2003 as a member of the Jacksonville City Council. She currently is employed by Florida Community College at Jacksonville as department chair of the Downtown Campus Library and is a professor of education technology.

Karen Chandler

EDUCATION, MUSIC. Karen Chandler is a native of Nashville, Tennessee. She received a bachelor's degree in music education from Hampton University in Virginia. She earned a master's degree in music education from Columbia University in New York and a Ph.D. in arts and humanities from New York University. Her first job was at Saint Paul's College in Virginia, where she was pre-

sented with a project that would inspire her to become involved in arts management. This request included all aspects of the show, consisting of fundraising and marketing, along with the multiple tasks involved with assembling a concert series.

She relocated to Washington, D.C., where she worked as an assistant professor of arts management at American University. In 1999 she began teaching at the College of Charleston and directing the school's prestigious Avery Research Center for African American History and Culture. Chandler, alongside Jack McCray, a longtime Charleston journalist and jazz expert, established the Charleston Jazz Initiative in 2003. The ongoing research project documents the American jazz tradition in Charleston and the South Carolina Low County, and its widespread movement throughout the United States and Europe in the late 19th century. Chandler also took the time to look into the lives and backgrounds of the jfk Center volunteers in Washington, D.C.

Farrell J. Chiles

LOCAL GOVERNMENT. Farrell J. Chiles earned a bachelor of science degree in political science from the State University of New York. He is a graduate of the Greater Los Angeles Federal Executive Board's leadership associates program; he has completed the organizational leadership for executive program and the personnel management for executives course. He began his federal government career in 1992 with the United States Army Reserve's 300th Military Police Command, Inkster, Michigan, as a military personnel specialist. In 1993, he accepted a management analyst position with the West Los Angeles Veterans Administration Hospital. In 1996, he became chief of the Special Actions Branch at the 63rd Regional Readiness Command until he was promoted to his current position. He is a Vietnam veteran and a chief warrant officer in the United States Army Reserve with over 33 years of service to his country.

He was elected president of the Los Angeles/Long Beach Area Chapter of Blacks in Government in January 2000. As president, he increased the chapter's membership significantly. In January 2001, he joined Blacks in Government's National Board of Directors representing Region 9. He was elected chairman of the board in January 2002 and re-elected as chairman in 2003 and 2004.

Mark S. Clanton

MEDICAL. Mark S. Clanton received a bachelor's degree from Howard University and a medical doctor degree from Tulane University Medical School. He completed his pediatric training at Baylor Pediatric Residency Program in Houston, Texas, and earned a master's in public health from Harvard School of Public Health. Dr. Clanton was appointed deputy director, Office of the Director, of the National Cancer Institute, and he leads the National Cancer Institute's initiatives in cancer care delivery systems. His principal efforts are focused on applying systems thinking to increase the impact that National Cancer Institute has on the quality of cancer care, cost and reimbursement of cancer care, and the reduction of cancer health disparities. Dr. Clanton was appointed to the World Health Organization's Cancer Technical Group, charged with writing the first Global Cancer Control Plan.

Constance R. Clark

EDUCATION. Constance R. Clark holds a Ph.D. in education and has served in public education as a teacher, principal, assistant superintendent, deputy superintendent for the District of Columbia Public Schools, and director for the College Board Upward Bound Program. At the higher education level she was an adjunct professor at George Washington University, Educational Leadership Department, C.W. Post, Long Island University School of Education and New Rochelle College. Clark currently is the superintendent of Westbury Public Schools in Nassau County, New York. She also serves as the president of the Nassau County Council of School Superintendents and has been appointed to the National Superintendent's Roundtable.

H. Westley Clark

HEALTH. H. Westley Clark received a bachelor of arts in chemistry from Wayne State University in Detroit, Michigan. He earned a medical degree and a master's in public health from the University of Michigan

in Ann Arbor, where he completed a psychiatric residency at University Hospital, Neuropsychiatric Institute. He obtained his juris doctor degree from Harvard University Law School and completed a two-year substance abuse fellowship at the Department of Veteran Affairs Medical Center in San Francisco. Dr. Clark is a licensed to practice medicine in California, Maryland, Massachusetts and Michigan. He is also a member of the Washington, D.C., Bar Association.

He is the former chief of the Associated Substance Abuse Programs at the Department of Veterans Affairs Medical Center in San Francisco and associate clinical professor of psychiatry, Department of Psychiatry, at the University of California in San Francisco. Dr. Clark has served as a senior program consultant to the Robert Wood Johnson Substance Abuse Policy Program, as well as a co-investigator on various National Institute on Drug Abuse–funded research grants in conjunction with the University of California at San Francisco. He was appointed director of the Center for Substance Abuse Treatment under the Substance Abuse and Mental Health Services Administration, U.S. Department of Health and Human Services, and leads the agency's national effort to provide effective and accessible treatment to all Americans with addictive disorders.

Richard M. Clark

MILITARY. Richard M. Clark was born in Frankfurt, Germany, and grew up in Oakland, California, and Richmond, Virginia. He received a bachelor of science in management from the United States Air Force Academy in 1986 and a master of arts in human resource development from Webster University in St. Louis, Missouri. He earned a master of strategic studies from the Naval Command and Staff College at the Naval War College in Rhode Island, a master of airpower studies from the School of Advanced Air and Space Studies at Maxwell Air Force Base in Alabama, and a master of national security studies from the National War College at Fort McNair in Washington, D.C. He is a graduate of the United States Air Force Weapons School, B-1 Division, Ellsworth Air Force Base in San Diego and the Air War College at Maxwell Air Force Base in Alabama.

Clark has held numerous key leadership assignments, including serving from August 2000 to August 2001 as a fellow, President's Commission on White House Fellowships in Washington, D.C. In August 2001 he was assigned as assistant director of operations for the 77th Bomb Squadron at Ellsworth Air Force Base in San Diego. In May 2002 he became commander, 34th Bomb Squadron at Ellsworth Air Force Base; in June 2005, he was assigned as the vice wing commander of the 12th Flying Training Wing at Randolph Air Force Base in Texas. Colonel Clark now serves as the commander of the 12th Flying Training Wing. He has over 4,000 flight hours.

Vincent E. Clark

MILITARY. Vincent E. Clark received a bachelor's degree in economics and business from the University of Tennessee in Knoxville in 1985. He has earned a dual master's in aeronautical science (aviation aerospace operations and management) with distinction from Embry-Riddle Aeronautical University. He is level III certified in acquisition logistics and level II certified in program management in the Department of Defense. He is a graduate of the avionics courses at the Naval Technical Training Center in Millington, Tennessee.

He enlisted in the delayed entry program in June 1987. He reported to Marine Corps Recruit Depot Parris Island, South Carolina, in February 1988 and was a lay leader and Platoon 1038 honor graduate. He completed the aircraft maintenance officers' course in Pensacola, Florida, and Amphibious Warfare School at Quantico, Virginia. He was selected for, then attended, resident professional military education at the Australian Command and Staff College in January 2003.

Lieutenant Colonel Clark's key leadership assignments include an assignment to Marine Aviation Logistics Squadron 16 (Forward), Marine Aircraft Group 16 (Forward) at Marine Corps Air Station Tustin, and then as the assistant aircraft maintenance officer during the initial deployment into Somalia, Africa (Operation Restore Hope). In August 2000, he reported to navairsyscom program offices, where he served as a deputy assistant program manager for the logistic and operational test liaison officer. He currently serves as the commanding officer of Marine Aviation Logistics Squadron 39.

Stephen Clarke

ENGINEERING. Stephen Clarke grew up in Jamaica and later moved to Miami, Florida. He received technical training at McFatter Technical School and the National Cable Television Institute. He completed the Great Nondic Nettest Network training course in 2001, fiber optics technician course in 2002, and the advance technician course in 2003. He received the mechanical drafting certificate in 1992, the AutoCAD drafting certificate in 1992 and the forward and reverse certification training in 1998.

Clarke's career began as a lead technician with tci of South Florida in Miami, Florida, where he performed aerial and underground coaxial splicing and troubleshooting of hfc systems. He also responded to system outages and performed routine quality control on install and service calls. From 1998 to 2005, he served as project manager for Cougar Communication Services in Wheat Ridge, Colorado. He preformed system bi-directional sweep, certification and node optimization of the High Fiber Count systems and provided end of line testing and reports of system performances to the technical operation manager. He also performed fiber optic splicing, restoration, bi-directional testing, troubleshooting and provided reports of splice loss budget in a customized fiber network analysis document. He provided a system preventive maintenance program to ensure that the system integrity was maintained after delivery, and maintained a personnel and inventory control to ensure that delivery date was met.

Since 2005, Clarke has served as operations manager for Broadband Solutions Inc., in Fayetteville, Georgia. He is responsible for all the company's operations, including system sweep, certification, node optimization, ingress mitigation and end of line testing. He provides as-built print to system for correction and performs new built splicing, balancing and activating and power supply maintenance and upgrade.

Roy L. Clay, Sr.

BUSINESS, LOCAL GOVERNMENT. Roy L. Clay, Sr., was the first African-American to serve on the City Council for the City of Palo Alto (1973 to 1979) and to serve as the city's vice mayor from 1976 to 1977. Clay was a key figure in the development of Hewlett-Packard's (HP) computer division. In the early 1970s, at the beginning of Silicon Valley, Kleiner Perkins Caufield and Byers selected him as the computer consultant for prospective investments in start up companies such as Tandem Computers, Compaq and Intel Corporation.

He led the team that engineered HP's first foray into the computer market with the development of the 2116A computer in 1966. Not only was he the first director of the HP research and development software and hardware group, he was a founding member of the HP computer division. He served as interim general manager. He is the chief executive officer of rod-1 Electronics, the inventor of the automated dielectric withstand (hipot) tester, and world leader in development of electrical safety testing equipment.

William Lacy Clay, Jr.

FEDERAL GOVERNMENT. William Lacy Clay, Jr., is a native of St. Louis, Missouri, and a graduate of Springbrook High School in Silver Spring, Maryland, in 1974. He received a bachelor of arts degree from the University of Maryland in College Park in 1983. Clay's career of public service began in 1983, when he was elected a member of the Missouri State House of Representatives (1983 to 1991). In 1991, he was elected to the Missouri State Senate (1991 to 2001). He was elected as a Democrat to the 107th and to the three succeeding Congresses (January 3, 2001, to present).

Norma Clayton

ENGINEERING. Norma Clayton is a native of Orange, New Jersey. She received a bachelor of science degree in industrial administration with a concentration in industrial engineering and finance from the New Jersey Institute of

Technology in 1981. Clayton has held positions in manufacturing, procurement, project management and plant operations at Lockheed Martin, General Electric, RCA and General Motors. She joined the Boeing Company in 1995 as director of the machining center in St. Louis, Missouri. She is now vice president of lean manufacturing and quality at the Boeing Military Aircraft and Missile Systems Group. She is the first African American and the first woman to be a senior manufacturing executive at Boeing Aircraft and Missile Systems Group.

Emanuel Cleaver II

FEDERAL GOVERNMENT. Emanuel Cleaver II is a native of Waxahachie, Texas, and a graduate of Booker T. Washington High School in Wichita Falls, Texas. He received a bachelor of science degree from Prairie View A&M University in Prairie View, Texas, in 1972, and earned a master of divinity from St. Paul School of Theology in Kansas City, Missouri, in 1974. Cleaver has served as a pastor, radio show host, and member of the Kansas City, Missouri, City Council from 1979 to 1991. He was elected mayor of Kansas City, Missouri, from 1991 to 1999. Cleaver was elected as a Democrat to the 109th Congress and to the succeeding Congress (January 3, 2005, to present).

Linda Clement-Holmes

ENGINEERING. Linda Clement-Holmes received a bachelor of science degree in industrial management and computer science from Purdue University. She served over twenty years at Procter and Gamble, where her assignments included many leadership roles across a multitude of technology areas. She worked to standardize the company's workstation environment, develop an artificial intelligence system that provides stain removal advice, and create the long-term strategy and vision for the company's e-mail system. She took on the responsibility for managing the support and shared infrastructure engineering organization for Procter and Gamble. She now serves as manager, information and decision solution, of infrastructure services and governance in the global business service organization at Procter and Gamble.

Sonya Summerour Clemmons

SCIENCE. Sonya Summerour Clemmons is a native of Gainesville, Georgia. She is a graduate of the dual-degree program between Georgia Tech and the Atlanta University Center; she received a bachelor of science degree in physics from Spelman College and a bachelor of science degree in mechanical engineering from Georgia Tech in 1994. She earned a master of business administration, a master of science in bioengineering in 1996 and a Ph.D. in bioengineering from the University of California, San Diego, in 1999, becoming the university's first African American woman to receive a Ph.D. in bioengineering. Clemmons has worked in the San Diego biotechnology industry as a scientist and principal engineer for a number of years. She serves as director of business development with MediVas, a company that is creating bio-absorbable polymers for use in drug, gene and biologic delivery, and is the founder of a biotechnology consulting company, SSC Enterprises.

U.W. Clemon

JUDICIAL. U.W. Clemon is a native of Fairfield, Alabama. He received a bachelor of arts degree from Miles College in 1965 and earned a juris doctor degree from Columbia Law School. Clemon worked in private law practice from 1969 to 1980. In 1974, he became one of the first two African Americans elected to the Alabama State Senate since Reconstruction, serving from 1975 to 1980. He was nominated by President Jimmy Carter on January 10, 1980, to be a federal judge to a new seat created by legislation. He was confirmed by the U.S. Senate on June 26, 1980, and he received his commission on June 30, 1980, as a judge to

the U.S. District Court for Northern District of Alabama. He served as that court's chief judge from 1999 to 2006.

Tanya Clemons

BUSINESS. Tanya Clemons received a bachelor of arts degree in psychology from the University of New Orleans and earned a Ph.D. in organizational psychology from Louisiana State University. Clemons has served as a senior executive with extensive experience in leadership and organization change at Microsoft and IBM. She served as corporate vice president for people and organization capability at Microsoft, where she was responsible for leadership development, talent management, employee learning and training, organization development and enterprise-wide change initiative. She held leadership roles at IBM, Georgia-Pacific and Anheuser-Busch. She was appointed vice president and chief talent officer at Pfizer. She reports to the senior vice president for worldwide talent development and human resources. She is a member of the human resources leadership team and Pfizer senior management team.

Arlene W. Clinkscale

EDUCATION. Arlene W. Clinkscale received a bachelor of science from Hampton Institute in Hampton, Virginia, and a master's degree and professional diploma from Teachers College, Columbia University. She was awarded an honorary doctorate from St. Thomas Aquinas College in Sparkhill, where she served on the Board of Trustees.

Clinkscale's professional career began in 1950 as an elementary teacher in Virginia. She moved to Rockland County, New York, in 1960. She taught in Pearl River and Spring Valley for six years before assuming a series of senior administrative positions in the East Ramapo and Nyack Central School districts, rising to the rank of District Superintendent in Nyack in 1981. After six years in that position, she left for Englewood Public Schools, serving as principal, assistant superintendent and acting superintendent. She also served as an educational consultant for minority affairs in Roslyn, Long Island, New York. She was the first African American woman in New York to lead a school district, and in April 2004 was appointed by the Rockland County Legislature to the College's Board of Trustees.

James Enos Clyburn

FEDERAL GOVERNMENT. James Enos Clyburn is a native of Sumter, South Carolina, and a graduate of Mather Academy in Camden, South Carolina, in 1957. He received a bachelor of science degree from South Carolina State University in Orangeburg in 1961. Clyburn has served as a teacher, an employment counselor with the South Carolina state employment security commission, director of the Charleston County, South Carolina, neighborhood youth corps and new careers projects, executive director of South Carolina state commission for farm workers, and a member of the staff of South Carolina Governor John C. West. He was appointed to the South Carolina Human Affairs Commission from 1974 to 1992. Clyburn was elected as a Democrat to the 103rd and to the seven succeeding Congresses (January 3, 1993, to present).

Tom Colbert

JUDICIAL. Tom Colbert is a native of Oklahoma City and a graduate of Sapulpa High School. He earned an associate degree from Eastern Oklahoma State College in 1970 and a bachelor of science degree from Kentucky State University in 1973. While at Kentucky State he was named an All-American in track and field. He earned a master of education degree from Eastern Kentucky University in 1976 and his juris doctor from the University of Oklahoma in 1982.

Colbert taught in the public schools in Chicago. He was an assistant dean at Marquette University Law School from 1982 to 1984 and an assistant district attorney in Oklahoma County from 1984 to 1986, before working in private law practice from 1985 to 2000. He also served as an attorney for the Oklahoma Department of Human Services from 1988 to 1989 and in 1999.

In March of 2000, he became the first African American appointed to the Oklahoma Court of Civil Appeals. He served as chief judge of the Court of Appeals in 2004. On October 7, 2004, Governor Brad Henry appointed Justice Colbert to the Supreme Court of Oklahoma. He is the first African American to serve on the Supreme Court of Oklahoma.

Lora Cole

LAW ENFORCEMENT. Lora Cole is a native of Mound Bayou, Mississippi. She is a graduate of Delta State University with a bachelor of arts in criminal justice and a bachelor of science in guidance and counseling. Cole has served as board and advisory board member for several community organizations and has held adjunct instructor positions at Jackson State University and Hinds Community College. She began her career with the Mississippi Department of Corrections as a correctional officer and correctional counselor at the Mississippi State Penitentiary in Parchman.

Over the next 28 years she served in progressively higher supervisory positions, including classification case manager supervisor; Mississippi State Penitentiary Unit 29 programs coordinator; Mississippi State Penitentiary Unit 30 correctional superintendent of security; deputy warden for programs and classification at the Central Mississippi Correctional Facility in Pearl, Mississippi; and correctional warden, associate superintendent for central satellite facilities and programs at Central Mississippi Correctional Facilities. She was named interim deputy commissioner and then deputy commissioner of the Division of Community Corrections for the Mississippi Department of Corrections.

Thomas Cole

EDUCATION. Thomas Cole is a native of Texas. He received a bachelor of arts degree with honors from Wiley College in Marshall, Texas, and earned a Ph.D. in organic chemistry from the University of Chicago. He received honorary doctorate degrees from West Virginia State College, the University of Charleston, Allegheny College, and Wiley College.

Cole has served as president of Wiley College. He became Clark Atlanta University's first president in 1989 following the consolidation of Clark College and Atlanta University in 1988. He served simultaneously as president of Clark College and Atlanta University for a year prior to consolidation. He served as president of Clark Atlanta University from 1989 to 2002. Cole was chancellor of the West Virginia Board of Regents, president of West Virginia State College, and president and chief executive officer of Great Schools Atlanta. He was appointed interim chancellor of the University of Massachusetts at Amherst in September 2007.

Y. Laketa Cole

LOCAL GOVERNMENT. Y. Laketa Cole is a native of Cincinnati, Ohio, and a graduate of the Cincinnati Public Schools system. She received a bachelor of arts in political science from Wittenberg University in 1995. Cole, at the age of twenty-nine on April 23, 2003, became the first African American woman appointed to serve on the Cincinnati City Council. In November that year, she was elected to her council seat. In 2005 she was re-elected to the council with a 3rd place finish out of 31 candidates and was elected president pro-tem for the second time by her colleagues.

Marsha Coleman-Adebayo

FEDERAL GOVERNMENT. Marsha Coleman-Adebayo received a bachelor of arts degree in foreign affairs and economics from Barnard College and earned a Ph.D. from the Massachusetts Institute of Technology. She joined the Environmental Protection Agency (EPA) as an African affairs specialist in 1990. While serving in the Gore-Mbeki Commission, she reported that toxic waste generated by an American company was poisoning African workers and their families. She won a landmark discrimination case in federal court against the EPA in August 2000, and $600,000 in damages for emotional strain caused by discrimination. Having seen what could happen to those who expose unfair practices at work, she went to Congress seeking whistleblower safeguards for federal workers. In 2002, the Notification and Federal Employee Anti-discrimination and Retaliation (No fear) Act became law. She proudly stood in the Oval Office and watched President George W. Bush sign the act, the first civil rights law of the 21st century. Coleman-Adebayo has remained at the EPA and is currently a senior advisor in the Office of Pollution Prevention and Toxics.

Beverly Coleman-Miller

MEDICINE, PUBLIC HEALTH. Beverly Coleman-Miller received a bachelor of science degree in nursing from the University of Pennsylvania in Philadelphia. She earned her medical doctor degree from Temple University School of Medicine and completed her residency in internal medicine at Thomas Jefferson University Hospital, Philadelphia, Pennsylvania. Dr. Coleman-Miller began her professional career as a medical and surgical nurse for 15 years, with a concentration in community and mental health issues, before entering medical school. She served as special assistant for medical affairs to the District of Columbia commissioner of public health and spent many years providing direct medical care to high-risk, low-income patients in federally funded clinics.

She has served as an advisor to the secretary of health and human services and a consultant to the World Health Organization. Dr. Coleman-Miller is a nationally renowned authority on domestic violence and the impact of community social and environmental issues on public health. The president of bcm Group, Inc., she is also a visiting scholar at the Harvard School of Public Health.

Allen J. Coles

EDUCATION. Allen J. Coles is a native of New York. He received his bachelor's and master's degrees from Hofstra University. He earned a doctorate degree in administration, curriculum and instruction from the University of Nebraska at Lincoln and is a Danforth Fellow. He has served as a high school teacher, college instructor, building principal and as an area superintendent. He was a region superintendent for the Clark County School District in Las Vegas, Nevada. Coles was named superintendent of Richland School District One in Columbia, South Carolina.

Wanda Collier-Wilson

LOCAL GOVERNMENT. Wanda Collier-Wilson joined the Jackson (Mississippi) Convention and Visitors Bureau in 1983 and has served as executive director since mid–1998. She is the first African American woman to hold the executive director position in the City of Jackson, and the first person from within the bureau to be promoted to the top spot. Her duties include fiscal responsibility and overall management of the bureau and a staff of 15, as well as maintaining a quarter-million dollar grant program designed to assist non-profit tourism entities in the city with marketing projects. The focus of the Jackson Convention and Visitors Bureau is developing programs and projects designed to further tourism and position the city as a premier convention and tourist destination.

Alfred Collins, Sr.

MILITARY. Alfred Collins, Sr., is a native of Warner Robins, Georgia. He enlisted in the United States Navy in 1972 and advanced through the rank of operations specialist chief petty officer. He attended the University of South Alabama, National University and the University of California in San Diego. He earned a master's degree in national resource strategy from National Defense University Industrial College of the Armed Forces.

Collins was commissioned an officer in the U.S. Navy in August 1983 through the limited officer program. He has held numerous management assignments. In October 1992, he was assigned to the Bureau of Naval Personnel in Washington, D.C., as branch head for enlisted bonus programs in the Compensation and Policy Coordination Division. On July 7, 1995, he took command of the USS *Gladiator* in Lisbon, Portugal, followed by command of the USS *Ardent* in the Persian Gulf; in 1998, he was assigned as the executive assistant to the commander, Naval Surface Forces, United States Pacific Fleet. He took command of USS *Fitzgerald* in April 1999 and next served at the Pentagon in Washington, D.C., assigned to the operations directorate on the Joint Staff as chief, Network Operations Division. Next Captain Collins was assigned as the commander of Destroyer Squadron One.

Elroy Combs, Jr.

MILITARY. Elroy Combs, Jr., was born in Gibsland, Louisiana. He received an associate of applied science and technology from the Community College of the Air Force and a bachelor of science degree in marketing and sales from Grambling State University at Grambling, Louisiana. He also earned a master of arts degree in industrial and organizational psychology at Louisiana Tech University, Ruston, Louisiana. He is a graduate of the Senior Noncommissioned Officer Academy.

Combs enlisted in the United States Air Force Reserve on June 30, 1988, and attended basic training at Lackland Air Force Base in Texas. After graduation from jet engine mechanic apprentice school at Chanute Air Force Base, in Illinois, he reported to the 917th Wing, where he worked as an aircraft maintenance technician on both the A-10 and B-52 until January 1996. He then took a position as assistant section supervisor on the A-10. In November 1997, he became a career assistance advisor for two years, and in March 1999, he became the assistant flight chief, 917th Propulsion Flight. In January 2002, he moved to the position of accessory flight chief, and in April 2005, he was selected to serve as the 917th Wing's command chief master sergeant. He advises the commander on matters influencing the health, morale, welfare and effective utilization of more than 1,500 reserve enlisted members within the wing and serves as the commander's representative to numerous committees, councils, boards and military and civilian functions.

Sean Combs

ENTERTAINMENT. Sean Combs was born in New York, New York, to Melvin and Janice Combs. His father was murdered when he was two years old. His mother moved him to Mount Vernon, New York. He attended Howard University in Washington, D.C. While at Howard, Combs took an internship at Uptown Entertainment in New York. He was named director of artists and repertoire (A&R) for Uptown at age 19. Shortly thereafter, in 1991, he engineered the careers of Uptown artists Jodeci and Mary J. Blige, producing their music and influencing their image.

In 1993, he left Uptown and later that year emerged with his own company, Bad Boy Entertainment. In 1997, Combs released his first solo CD and in 1999, he released his second CD. As of October 2006, his nickname and recording name is Diddy. Previously, he had been known as Puff Daddy and later as P. Diddy. His businesses include Bad Boy Records and the clothing lines Sean John and Sean by Sean Combs. His job titles include recording executive, back up singer, performer, producer, clothing designer, and Broadway actor. He is the third richest hip-hop entertainer (after Jay-Z and 50 Cent as of 2007), having a net worth estimate of $346 million.

Barbara A. Cooper

MILITARY. Barbara A. Cooper is a native of Philadelphia, Pennsylvania. She enlisted in the United States Navy on March 28, 1988. She completed U.S. Navy recruit training and Hospital Corps" "A" School. She also completed Preventive Medicine Technician" "C" School in Oakland, California.

Cooper was assigned to the National Medical Center, Bethesda, Maryland, from August 1988 to April 1990. She served at the United States Naval Hospital in Guam and completed a successful tour in 1992. She reported to Naval Hospital in Philadelphia, Pennsylvania, from December 1992 to October 1995. She received orders to Navy Environmental and Preventive Medicine Unit Seven in Sigonella, Italy, before being assigned to the Navy Environmental Health Center in Norfolk, Virginia, in November 1998. In September 2001, Chief Cooper reported for duty onboard the USS *Harry S. Truman* (CVN-75), where she was the as the ship's senior preventive medicine technician and divisional leading chief petty officer for the Medical Department. She detached from the USS *Harry S. Truman* in June 2005 and reported to the Navy Environmental and Preventive Medicine Unit Six, Pearl Harbor, in Hawaii, where she is serving as the senior enlisted leader.

Lisa A. Cooper

EDUCATION. Lisa A. Cooper received a bachelor of arts degree from Emory University in 1984 and a med-

ical doctor degree from the University of North Carolina at Chapel Hill in 1988. She earned a master of public health degree from Johns Hopkins University Bloomberg School of Public Health in 1993. Dr. Cooper serves as a professor of medicine in the Epidemiology and Health Policy and Management Department at Johns Hopkins Bloomberg School of Public Health. She has authored several articles and book chapters, including a chapter on patient-physician communication published in the Institute of Medicine's 2003 Report" "Unequal Treatment."

Willie W. Cooper II

MILITARY. Willie W. Cooper II received a bachelor of business administration from Mercer University in Macon, Georgia, and a master of national resource strategy at the Industrial College of the Armed Forces, Fort McNair, Washington, D.C. His military education includes: aircraft munitions and maintenance officer course at Chanute Air Force Base in Illinois; the Air Command and Staff College; Squadron Officer School; and advanced logistics officers course at Lackland Air Force Base. Cooper has spent his career in the tactical air, military airlift, air combat and air mobility commands. A career logistics officer, his past assignments include maintaining such diverse weapon systems as the F4-D/E and F-16 fighters; HH-3 and HH-60 Pave Hawk helicopters; and the HC-130 tankers, C-5 Galaxy, C-17 Globemaster III, and C-130H2 aircraft.

Colonel Cooper served as maintenance supervisor for the 304th Expeditionary Rescue Squadron at Incirlik Air Base in Turkey; as commander of the 920th Consolidated Maintenance Squadron, Patrick Air Force Base, Florida; as the commander of the 512th Logistics Group at Dover Air Force Base; and from October 2002 to August 2007, as commander of the 512th Maintenance Group at Dover Air Force Base. In August 2007, he was assigned as commander of the 440th Maintenance Group at Pope Air Force Base in North Carolina.

Claudette A. Copeland

MINISTRY. Claudette A. Copeland is a native of Buffalo, New York. She received a bachelor of arts degree in psychology from the University of Connecticut and a master of divinity in pastoral care and counseling from the Interdenominational Theological Center in Atlanta, Georgia. She earned her doctorate of ministry degree from United Theological Seminary in Dayton, Ohio.

Copeland has been a licensed evangelist since age 8 in the Church of God in Christ, and, ordained in 1979, she has served in West Africa, East Africa and Haiti. In 1980, she was commissioned into the United States Air Force chaplaincy. She and her husband were the first African American clergy couple in the history of the U.S. military. Copeland is the founder of c.o.p.e. Professional Services, a consulting agency for personal effectiveness training in the public sector. She has also served as pastor and co-founder of the New Creation Christian Fellowship of San Antonio, Texas, for over 22 years.

Elaine Johnson Copeland

EDUCATION. Elaine Johnson Copeland received a bachelor of science degree from Livingston College and a master of arts degree from Winthrop University. She earned a master of business administration from the University of Illinois and a Ph.D. in counseling from Oregon State University. She was an associate professor of educational psychology, former associate dean of the Graduate College and associate vice chancellor for academic affairs at the University of Illinois at Urbana-Champaign.

Copeland was selected to serve as the president of Clinton Junior College, founded in 1894 by the Reverend Nero Crockett, presiding elder of the Yorkville District of South Carolina Conference of the African Methodist Episcopal Zion Church, and the Reverend W.M. Robinson, pastor of the Clinton Chapel A.M.E. Zion Church. The college was named after Bishop Isom Caleb Clinton, the presiding bishop of South Carolina at the time.

Edward E. Cornwell III

MEDICINE. Edward E. Cornwell III is a native of Washington, D.C. He attended Sidwell Friends School and then received his undergraduate education at

Brown University in Providence, Rhode Island, graduating with a degree in biology in 1978. He then attended Howard University College of Medicine and graduated with honors and as class president in 1982. He received his surgical training (internship and residency) at the Los Angeles County and University of Southern California Medical Center (1982–1987) and his trauma and critical care fellowship at the Maryland Institute for Emergency Medical Services Systems in Baltimore, Maryland (1987–1989). He has been certified and re-certified in both general surgery and surgical critical care by the American Board of Surgery.

Dr. Cornwell received clinical appointments at the Howard University College of Medicine (1989–1993), the University of Southern California (1993–1997), and Johns Hopkins School of Medicine (1998–present). He is presently professor of surgery and chief of adult trauma at the Johns Hopkins Hospital. He has served as president of the Society of Black Academic Surgeons.

RoseMary Covington

LOCAL GOVERNMENT. RoseMary Covington has 29 years of experience in the transportation industry, both in the private and public sectors. She has most recently worked with Parsons Brinckerhoff and as Washington, D.C.'s, mass transit administrator. She has also served on high level task forces for the Federal Transit Administration and American Public Transportation Association. Covington serves as the assistant general manager of planning and transit system development for the Sacramento Regional Transit. She is responsible for transit and service planning throughout the district and ensuring consistency of planning.

Kirk D. Crawley

MILITARY. Kirk D. Crawley enlisted in the Navy in June 1979 and completed initial training at Recruit Training Command, Great Lakes, Illinois, in September 1979. He was advanced to seaman apprentice upon completion of recruit training and then reported to Quartermaster" "A" School at Naval Training Center, Orlando, Florida, in November 1979. He graduated from Basic Enlisted Submarine School, Groton, Connecticut, in December 1979. He completed the United States Navy Senior Enlisted Academy.

Crawley reported to his first submarine, the USS *Baton Rouge*, in January 1980. During this three and one-half year tour, he served in the Quartermaster Division and completed two Indian Ocean deployments and one Mediterranean Sea deployment. He transferred to Pre-Commissioning Unit Buffalo in June 1983. During his tour he served as the Quartermaster Division leading petty officer and qualified assistant navigator. In June 1984 he was transferred to USS *Atlanta* to fill a priority billet shortage in the Quartermaster Division. In October 2001 he was assigned to USS *Miami* as the chief of the boat until August 2004. During this tour he was selected for the Command Master Chief Program. He transferred in August 2004 to the Submarine Learning Facility in Norfolk, Virginia, serving as the command master chief. In September 2006, he assumed duties as command master chief of Navy Recruiting District Houston, Texas.

Romeo Crennel

SPORTS. Romeo Crennel is a native of Lynchburg, Virginia. He was a high school standout at Fort Knox, Kentucky, High and Central High in Amherst, Virginia. He received his bachelor's degree in physical education and a master's degree from Western Kentucky University. Crennel was a graduate assistant at Western Kentucky.

He was defensive line coach at Western Kentucky (1971–1974); defensive assistant coach at Texas Tech University (1975–1977); defensive ends coach at the University of Mississippi (1978–1979); defense line coach at Georgia Tech University (1980–1981); with the New York Giants as a special teams and defensive line coach (1981–1992); with the New England Patriots as a defensive line coach (1993–1996); de-

fensive line coach for the New York Jets (1997–1999); Cleveland Browns defensive coordinator (2000–2001); and New England Patriots defensive coordinator and defensive line coach (2001 to 2004).

Crennel was named head coach of the Cleveland Browns on February 8, 2005, the 11th full-time coach in franchise history. He brought a 3–4 defensive scheme to Cleveland. He was widely recognized as one of the top assistant coaches in the NFL. He crafted the defense for the New England Patriots and helped the team win three Super Bowls (2001, 2003, and 2004).

John Creuzot

JUDICIAL. John Creuzot is a native of New Orleans, Louisiana, and Houston, Texas. He received a bachelor of arts degree in philosophy from the University of North Texas in 1978 and earned his juris doctor degree from Southern Methodist University Law School in 1982. Creuzot served in a district attorney's office as a chief felony prosecutor until 1989. From 1989 to 1991, he worked in private law practice. In 1991, the George W. Bush, governor of Texas, appointed him a Texas state district judge in the Frank Crowley Courts in Fort Worth. He was elected to the position in 1992 and re-elected in 1996, 2000 and 2004. Judge Creuzot is the recipient of the 2002 President's Citation.

Timothy A. Crisp

MILITARY. Timothy A. Crisp is a native of Tulsa, Oklahoma, and joined the Marine Corps on November 8, 1983. He reported to Recruit Training at Marine Recruit Depot San Diego, California. He graduated in January 1984. He attended Basic Warehouse School, for supply training, at Barstow, California. He has completed Drill Instructor School.

Crisp has served as a drill instructor and noncommissioned officer in-charge of the rifle and pistol rangers at Camp Schwab and Camp Hansen. In 2001, he was re-assigned to H&S Company as acting first sergeant, subsequently being promoted to the rank of first sergeant in November 2002. In January 2003, he was assigned to General Support Company and deployed to Kuwait and Iraq in support of Operation Iraqi Freedom. In January of 2004 he was assigned as the first sergeant for H&S Company. In November 2005 he was transferred to Communications Company, Combat Logistic Regiment. He was assigned to Combat Logistic Regiment as the sergeant major in March 2006 and later selected to the rank of sergeant major in February 2007. Sergeant Major Crisp currently serves as the senior enlisted advisor of Marine Wing Support Squadron 171.

Denise L. Cross

JUDICIAL. Denise L. Cross received a bachelor of arts degree from Wilberforce University and earned her juris doctor degree from the University of Akron School of Law in 1978. She has served in private law practice; as an assistant public defender in Erie County, Pennsylvania; as the domestic relations supervising attorney at the Legal Aid Society of Dayton; and as assistant prosecuting attorney in the Montgomery County (Ohio) prosecutor's office. She was the legal director and chief magistrate of Montgomery County Juvenile Court. Judge Cross serves as the administrative judge of Montgomery County.

Jesse R. Cross

MILITARY. Jesse R. Cross received a bachelor of business administration in commerce marketing and merchandising degree from West Texas A&M University and a master of science in logistics management from Florida Institute of Technology. He earned a master of science in strategic studies from the Air War College at Maxwell Air Force Base in Alabama and the U.S. Army Command and General Staff College. He has completed the U.S. Army Logistics Management College at Fort Lee, Virginia.

Cross has held numerous command and leadership positions, including as commander, 125th Forward Support Battalion, 1st Armored Division, Fort Riley, Kansas; Senior Forward Support Battalion observer and controller, Combat Maneuver Training Center Operations Group, 7th Army Training Command, later Support Operations Officer, 3rd Corps Support Command, United States Army Europe and Seventh Army in Germany; chief of the Plans Division, J-4, United States Central Command, MacDill Air Force Base in Florida; and commander of the Defense Supply Center Philadelphia, Pennsylvania. Cross was selected to serve as the commanding general of the U.S. Army Quartermaster Center and School/Deputy Commanding General of Fort Lee, Virginia, in September 2007.

Delores Crowell

BUSINESS. Delores Crowell received a bachelor of science degree in sociology from State University College of New York at Buffalo. She is also a graduate of Leadership Georgia, Leadership DeKalb and the Regional Leadership Institute. Crowell was manager of the Office of Diversity for AT&T, which included the development and implementation of diversity and human resources programs supporting over 34,000 employees. She has served as district manager for regulatory and external affairs at BellSouth (now AT&T) since 2001. She manages corporate and regulatory affairs in the city of Atlanta and in DeKalb, Henry and Rockdale counties in Georgia.

Derrick D. Crowley

MILITARY. Derrick D. Crowley is a native of Jackson, Mississippi. He received an associate degree in applied health science from the Community College of the Air Force and a bachelor of science degree in occupational education from Wayland Baptist University. He earned a master of arts in organizational management from the University of Phoenix. He is a graduate of the Senior Noncommissioned Officer Academy at Maxwell Gunter Air Force Base in Alabama.

Crowley entered the Air Force in September 1982. He has held many positions both in and out of the medical arena, but his primary specialty is in the aerospace medical service career field. He has served in various tactical, operational and strategic level positions throughout the wing, medical community and the air staff, including a strategic-level position as the Air Force Medical Service enlisted force manager, and as chief of enlisted force development, Office of the Air Force Surgeon General, at Bolling Air Force Base in Washington, D.C. Crowley is the command chief master sergeant for the 79th Medical Wing at Andrews Air Force Base in Maryland. He is the principal advisor to the wing commander on all enlisted matters.

Mildred C. Crump

LOCAL GOVERNMENT, EDUCATION. Mildred C. Crump is a native of Detroit, Michigan, where she attended and graduated from the local public schools. She received a bachelor's degree from Wayne State University and was the recipient of the David D. McKenzie Honor Society Award. Ms. Crump was the first African American Braille teacher in the history the City of Detroit, and after moving to New Jersey in 1965, she became the first African American Braille teacher in that state. She was sworn in on July 1, 1994, as the first African American councilwoman in the 336 year history of Newark. On July 1, 2006, she was again sworn in as councilwoman at large. She created history once again when she was elected as the first female president of the Newark Municipal Council.

Elijah Eugene Cummings

FEDERAL GOVERNMENT. Elijah Eugene Cummings is a native of Baltimore, Maryland, and a graduate of Baltimore City High School in 1969. He received a bachelor of science degree from Howard University in Washington, D.C., in 1973 and earned his juris doctor

from University of Maryland School of Law in Baltimore in 1976. Cummings served in private law practice, as the chief judge for Maryland Moot Court Board, and as an elected member of the Maryland State House of Delegates (1983 to 1996), serving as speaker pro tempore in 1995–1996. He was elected as a Democrat to the 104th Congress by special election to fill the vacancy caused by the resignation of Rep. Kweisi Mfume, then was re-elected to the six succeeding Congresses (April 16, 1996, to present).

Simone Cummings

MEDICINE. Simone Cummings received a bachelor's degree in business administration from Washington University, a master's degree in health administration from Washington University School of Medicine, and a doctorate in health policy and administration from the University of North Carolina at Chapel Hill. Prior to receiving her doctorate, Dr. Cummings worked for several hospitals, including Barnes-Jewish Hospital, Children's Hospital, and St. Louis Regional Hospital in St. Louis, Missouri, as well as Columbia Hospital for Women in Washington, D.C. She has experience teaching a variety of courses, including payment and reimbursement, health care finance, health care accounting, and managerial accounting. Her research efforts are focused on improving access to care for vulnerable and minority populations.

Roosevelt Currie

JUDICIAL. Roosevelt Currie received a bachelor of arts degree summa cum laude from Washington State University and earned his juris doctor from the University of Missouri. His legal career includes serving in private practice in Tacoma, Washington, and as a special deputy prosecutor for the Cowlitz County Prosecuting Attorney's Office. He has provided pro tem services for the Pierce County No. One District Court. From 1991 to 1998, he was an assistant attorney general with the State Attorney General's Office representing a variety of state agency clients; from 1999 to 2002, he was an administrative law judge in the Seattle and Olympia Office of Administrative Hearings. Judge Currie was appointed chief administrative law judge of the Washington State Office of Administrative Hearings by Governor Christine Gregoire in April 2006.

H. James Dallas

BUSINESS. H. James Dallas received a bachelor of science degree in accounting from the University of South Carolina in Aiken, South Carolina, and earned a master of business administration from Emory University. He served as vice president and chief information officer at Georgia Pacific. During his 22-year career at Georgia Pacific, he held a series of progressively responsible information technology positions at the business, group and corporate level. In April 2006, Dallas was named senior vice president and chief information officer at Medtronic. He has responsibility for leading the information technology organization and developing and implementing information technology strategies on a global basis. He is also a member of Medtronic's executive committee and operating committee.

Angelita Blackshear Dalton

JUDICIAL. Angelita Blackshear Dalton is a native of Nashville, Tennessee, and a graduate of White Creek High School. She received a bachelor's degree from Lane College in 1993 and earned her juris doctor from the University of Toledo. Dalton served as an assistant prosecutor for the Davidson District Attorney General. In 2006, she was elected a judge to the General Sessions Court Division III of Metropolitan Nashville and Davidson County, Tennessee.

Bobby Dandridge

MILITARY. Bobby Dandridge was born at Bethesda's National Naval Medical Center and raised as a military dependent. He received an associate degree in applied science, personnel administration, from the Community College of the Air Force and a bachelor of science degree in social psychology from Park University in Parkville, Missouri. His military education includes all the noncommissioned officers education system courses; aerospace management certificate, Community College of the Air Force; U.S. Air Force First Sergeant Symposium at Yokota Air Base in Japan; Army Material Command Warfare Center deployed

first sergeant course at Fort Dix, New Jersey; and U.S. Senior Leadership Course.

His past assignments include installations in the Strategic Air Command, Military Airlift Command, U.S. Air Forces in Europe, Air Mobility Command, Pacific Air Forces and the U.S. Transportation Command. He has deployed to Central America, South Korea, Kingdom of Saudi Arabia and three president-approved flood relief missions. He has served in every leadership role from squad leader to command chief. Before assuming his current position, he served as combatant command first sergeant, U.S. Transportation Command, at Scott Air Force Base in Illinois. He serves as the command chief master sergeant of the 501st Combat Support Wing, Royal Air Force, Alconbury, United Kingdom.

Gilda R. Daniels

FEDERAL GOVERNMENT. Gilda R. Daniels is a native of Louisiana. She earned a bachelor's degree from Grambling State University and a juris doctor from New York University School of Law. She was a law clerk for the Honorable Joseph W. Hatchett, former chief judge, United States Eleventh Circuit Court of Appeals, and served as staff attorney with the Southern Center for Human Rights representing death row inmates and bringing prison condition cases in Alabama and Georgia. In 1995, she moved to Washington, D.C., to work for the Department of Justice as a staff attorney in the Civil Rights Division's Voting Section. Daniels left the Department of Justice in 1998 to work for the Lawyers' Committee for Civil Rights Under Law as a voting rights project staff attorney. In 2000, she returned to the department as a deputy chief in the Voting Section.

Carr L. Darden

JUDICIAL. Carr L. Darden is a native of Nashville, Tennessee, but has lived in Indiana most of his life. He received a bachelor of science degree from Indiana University School of Business in 1966 and earned his juris doctor degree from Indiana University School of Law in Indianapolis in 1970. He is a graduate of the Judicial College of Indiana in 1998 and in 2004, the Indiana Graduate Program for Judges. Darden was honorably discharged from the United States Air Force in 1959. He has served as the chief deputy state public defender in Indiana. He was a Marion County Municipal Court judge and a judge on the Marion County Superior Court in Indiana. Judge Darden was named to the Indiana Court of Appeals by Governor Evan Bayh in October 1994 and was retained by election in 1998.

Julie Dash

FILM. Julie Dash is a native of New York City. She received a bachelor of arts in film production from City College New York and a master of fine arts degree in film and television production at University of California at Los Angeles. She was also a fellow at the American Film Institute's Center for Advanced Film Studies. Dash remains one of Hollywood's most talented directors, writers and producers. Her directorial debut with *Daughters of the Dust* in January 1992 opened to critical acclaim and is viewed as a classic among cinema buffs. She became the first African American woman to have a full-length general theatrical release in the United States. In December 2004, the Library of Congress placed *Daughters of the Dust* in the National Film Registry; it joins 400 American films preserved as a national treasures.

She also directed the CBS network television movie *The Rosa Parks Story*, winner of NAACP Image Award, the Family Television Award, and the New York Christopher Award. Actress Angela Bassett received an Emmy nomination for her performance as Rosa Parks. In October 2005, Dash received the outstanding Achievement Award for Women in Film in Atlanta, Georgia.

Merryl David

MILITARY. Merryl David is a native of Bronx, New York. In her military career she has served as a naval

aviator, operating combat helicopters and airplanes in the Middle East and South America. Major David left the Navy to become first woman to fly the Air Force Elite U-2 spy plane. She is one of only five women and three African Americans to be accepted into the Air Force's elite First Squadron, where U-2 pilots get their training. Solo flights can exceed 70,000 feet and last nine hours, and U-2s, with their large wingspan, are one of the toughest crafts to land.

Amanda Davis

TELEVISION. Amanda Davis received a bachelor's degree magna cum laude from Clark College in Atlanta, Georgia. Her career began in Charlotte, North Carolina, with the former NBC affiliate WRET-TV. During her four years there, she became the main anchor and hosted a weekly magazine show. From Charlotte, she joined the Satellite News Channel (SNC) in Washington, D.C. She joined Fox 5-TV in Atlanta in 1986 from WSB-TV, where she was an anchor and reporter. At Fox 5 she serves as co-anchor for the top-rated 6 P.M. and 10 P.M. newscasts. Her true labor of love is her work to find permanent homes for Georgia's foster children. She began the project in 1997 with a series of stories called *A Place to Call Home*. The Freddie Mac Foundation then approached the station with the idea of presenting weekly profiles of children available for adoption, and *Wednesday's Child* was launched in November 2000. In its first year, 32 children were placed in homes. She also launched the successful *Good Day Atlanta* in 1992, before taking over the main anchor chair at Fox 5 in 1997.

Angela Yvonne Davis

EDUCATION, ACTIVISM. Angela Yvonne Davis is a native of Birmingham, Alabama, where she attended Parker High School. By her junior year, at age 14, she applied for and was accepted to a program of the American Friends Service Committee that placed black students from the South in integrated schools in the north. She chose to attend high school at Elizabeth Irwin High School in Greenwich Village, New York City. Upon graduation from high school, she was awarded a full scholarship to Brandeis University in Waltham, Massachusetts, one of three black students in her freshman class. She was accepted for the Hamilton College Junior Year in France program, moved to Paris and lived with a French family. She next attended the University of Frankfurt for graduate work in philosophy, graduating with a bachelor's degree magna cum laude in 1965. She earned a master's degree from the University of California in San Diego, and then returned to Germany for her Ph.D. in philosophy from the Humboldt University of Berlin.

Davis's career began in 1969 as an assistant acting professor in the Philosophy Department at the University of California Los Angeles. At that time she was a radical feminist and activist, a member of the Communist Party USA and associated with the Black Panther Party. Governor Ronald Reagan urged the Board of Regents of the University of California to fire her from her job in 1970 because of her membership in the Communist Party. She was later rehired after community uproar over the decision.

On August 11, 1970, the FBI issued a warrant for Angela Davis's arrest. She was accused of having bought the guns for the "Soledad Brothers" shootout in the Marin County Center and was charged with murder, kidnapping and conspiracy. On October 13, 1970, she was arrested by the FBI in New York. Her arrest evoked a world-wide political campaign for her defense. In 1972, after she spent sixteen months in prison, her trial finally started on February 27. Acting as her own co-counsel, she was judged by an all-white jury. On June 4, she was acquitted of all charges. She is currently professor of history of consciousness and presidential chair at the University of California, Santa Cruz. She is a founder of the anti-prison grassroots organization Critical Resistance.

Artur Davis

FEDERAL GOVERNMENT. Artur Davis is a native of Montgomery, Alabama, and a graduate of Jefferson Davis High School in Montgomery. He received a bachelor of arts degree from Harvard University in Cambridge, Massachusetts, in 1990 and earned his juris doctor degree from Harvard in 1993. He has served in private law practice; as a law clerk

for Judge Myron Thompson, Middle District of Alabama; and as an assistant United States attorney, Middle District of Alabama from 1994 to 1998. Davis was elected as a Democrat to the 108th and to the two succeeding Congresses (January 3, 2003, to present).

Danny K. Davis

FEDERAL GOVERNMENT. Danny K. Davis is a native of Parkdale, Arkansas, and a graduate of Savage High School. He received a bachelor of arts degree from Arkansas AM&N College in 1961 and a master of science degree from Chicago State University in Chicago, Illinois, in 1968. He also earned a Ph.D. from Union Institute in Cincinnati, Ohio, in 1977.

Davis was a clerk with the United States Postal Service in Chicago from 1961 to 1965; teacher with the Chicago Public Schools system from 1962 to 1968; executive director of the Greater Lawndale Conservation Commission in 1969; director of training at the Martin L. King Neighborhood Health Center from 1969 to 1971; executive director of Westside Health Center from 1975 to 1981; alderman on the Chicago City Council, 1979 to 1990; elected commissioner on the board of Cook County, Illinois, 1990 to 1996; college professor; and unsuccessful candidate for the U.S. House of Representatives in 1984 and 1986. Davis was elected as a Democrat to the 105th and to the five succeeding Congresses (January 3, 1997, to present).

Don D. Davis

MILITARY. Don D. Davis received a bachelor of science degree from Central State University in Edmond, Oklahoma, and a master of business administration from Central State University in Oklahoma. His military education includes: Squadron Officer School at Maxwell Air Force Base in Alabama; comptroller staff officer course at Sheppard Air Force Base in Texas; Professional Military Comptroller School at Maxwell Air Force Base; Air Command and Staff College at Maxwell Air Force Base; and the Air War College at Maxwell Air Force Base in Alabama.

Davis was commissioned a second lieutenant after completing Air Force Officer Training School in 1979. During his career, he has held a variety of financial management positions at wing, major command, and air staff levels. His most recent assignments include: from July 1997 to June 2000, commander, 37th Comptroller Squadron at Lackland Air Force Base in Texas; in July 2000, chief, Budget Division, Comptroller Directorate, Headquarters Air Mobility Command at Scott Air Force Base in Illinois; and in July 2002, chief, Financial Analysis, Comptroller Directorate, at the Headquarters Air Force Materiel Command, Wright-Patterson Air Force Base in Ohio.

In July 2005, Colonel Davis was assigned as comptroller at the Headquarters Air Mobility Command at Scott Air Force Base in Illinois. He oversees more than 640 financial managers providing vital services supporting Air Mobility Command units worldwide, including 12 major bases.

Erroll B. Davis, Jr.

BUSINESS, EDUCATION. Erroll B. Davis, Jr., is a native of Pittsburgh, Pennsylvania. He received a bachelor of science in electrical engineering from Carnegie Mellon University in 1965 and a master of business administration in finance from the University of Chicago in 1967. He served from 1978 to 1990 in senior management with Wisconsin Power and Light Company, starting as vice president of finance and ending as chief executive officer and president. His career also includes finance positions at Xerox Corporation and Ford Motor Company. He was president and chief executive officer of WPL Holdings from 1990 to 1998. He joined Alliant Energy in 1998 as president and chief executive officer. Davis retired from his dual roles as president and CEO in July 2005, and retained the chairman's post until his move to the University System of Georgia. Davis was named chancellor of the University System of Georgia, responsible for the state's 35 public colleges and universities. The University System has 253,500 students, 35,000 faculty and staff, and an annual budget of $3 billion.

Kenneth Davis, Jr.

MEDICINE. Kenneth Davis, Jr., received his medical degree from St. Louis University School of Medicine and completed his surgical training at Harlem Hospital in New York. Dr. Davis is a professor of surgery and clinical anesthesia, vice-chairman of the department of surgery, and assistant dean for diversity and cultural affairs at the University of Cincinnati College of Medi-

cine. He is a member of the Office of Diversity and Community Affairs and of the executive committee of the Society of Black Academic Surgeons.

Lynda Van Davis

JUDICIAL. Lynda Van Davis received her juris doctor degree from Indiana State Law School in 1996 and went to work as a law clerk for Judge Arthur Hunter, Jr. She was elected and sworn in as a judge in Orleans Parish Criminal District Court in New Orleans, Louisiana, in 2003. Davis is the youngest District Court judge in Louisiana. She takes time to explain to defendants all of their rights in a way they can understand, and if defendants are under the age of 18 and have dropped out of school, she almost always orders them to return to school.

Michael J. Davis

JUDICIAL. Michael J. Davis received a bachelor's degree from Macalester College in 1969 and earned his juris doctor from the University of Minnesota Law School in 1972. He also received an honorary doctor of laws degree in 2001 from Macalester College. He has served as a criminal defense lawyer at the Neighborhood Justice Center in St. Paul, Legal Rights Center in Minneapolis, and later as an assistant public defender in Hennepin County.

In 1983, he was appointed to the Fourth Judicial Municipal Court of Minnesota, and in 1984, elevated by appointment to the District Court bench, where he served before being appointed to the federal bench. Davis was appointed by President Bill Clinton as a federal judge and took the oath of office on March 30, 1994. He is the twenty-eighth federal judge selected in Minnesota history and the first African American.

Robert N. Davis

JUDICIAL. Robert N. Davis received a bachelor's degree from the University of Hartford in 1975 and earned his juris doctor degree from Georgetown University Law Center in 1978. He is a commander in the United States Naval Reserves. He was a full tenured professor of law at Stetson University College of Law, and has held teaching positions at the University of Mississippi School of Law, the University of South Florida, Georgetown University Law Center, the University of Memphis, and Washington and Lee University. President George W. Bush appointed Davis as judge to the United States Court of Appeals for Veterans Claims. Judge Davis's appointment is for a 15-year term.

Brian S. Dawson

MILITARY. Brian S. Dawson is a native of Columbia, Maryland. He received a bachelor of science degree in nursing from American University in Washington, D.C., in 1983, after which he received his commission in the United States Navy. He earned a master's degree in nursing management with a perioperative focus, graduating with honors, from Old Dominion University in Norfolk, Virginia. Dawson served in various leadership roles and operational assignments, including charge nurse, gyn surgical service at the Oakland Naval Hospital; department head, main operating room, Naval Hospital Cherry Point; and deployment aboard the USS *Guadalcanal* as a perioperative nurse while assigned to Fleet Surgical Team Two out of Little Creek, Virginia, in support of Operation Desert Storm. He served as the clinical coordinator of perioperative services, Naval Medical Center Portsmouth, where he coordinated the activities of a 12-room

surgical suite and a 4-room satellite ambulatory surgery center. He also was department head, surgical Technologist Training Program, Naval School of Health Sciences in Bethesda, Maryland; head of perioperative services, U.S. Naval Hospital, in Okinawa, Japan; and disaster preparedness officer for the command and coordinator of medical disaster response for Marine Corps bases in Japan.

Captain Dawson served in a variety of nursing and executive management roles as the assistant director for the Military and Family Health Directorate at National Naval Medical Center, Bethesda. His areas of responsibilities included the Mother Infant Care Center, nicu, primary care, ob/gyn and pediatrics clinics, and the behavioral health service. He served as assistant director, communications and customer care, and assisted in the establishment of the Executive Health Primary Care Clinic. He is the executive officer of the naval hospital at Camp Lejeune, North Carolina.

Silvester Dawson

LAW ENFORCEMENT. Silvester Dawson has been a member of the Florida Highway Patrol since March 1983. He was promoted through the ranks from sergeant to major, serving as the chief of the Florida Highway Patrol Training Academy from December 2001 to August 2006 and as the inspections administrator. Chief Dawson requested the opportunity to serve as and was assigned as chief investigator for the Florida Highway Patrol in September 2006.

Garry C. Dean

MILITARY. Garry C. Dean received a bachelor of science degree in computer science from the United States Air Force Academy in Colorado Springs, Colorado, in 1972. He completed undergraduate pilot training at Reese Air Force Base in 1979; was a distinguished graduate for fighter lead-in training at Holloman Air Force Base in New Mexico; and completed F-15 upgrade training in December 1983, the Air Command and Staff College in 1992, the Air War College in 1998, and the Joint Task Force commanders course in 2006.

Dean was commissioned into the U.S. Air Force in May 1978 as a second lieutenant. He was assigned to the 12th Tactical Fighter Squadron as an F-15 fighter pilot at Kadena Air Base, Japan. In 1987 he joined the Georgia Air National Guard as an F-15 flight instructor and mission commander. He transferred to the Oregon Air National Guard's 142nd Fighter Wing in 1990, where he served as an F-15 mission commander, flight examiner, instructor pilot, functional check pilot, chief of safety, maintenance staff officer, 142nd Aircraft Generation Squadron commander, 123rd Fighter Squadron commander, and vice commander, 142nd Fighter Wing. He took full command of the 142nd Fighter Wing in January 2001. In November 2003, he accepted a position as the state director of operations in the Oregon Joint Force Headquarters — Air Component in Salem, Oregon. After two and a half years, he is now serving as the assistant adjutant general for Air, Joint Force Headquarters in Salem, Oregon. Dean was promoted to brigadier general on May 31, 2006.

Mark E. Dean

ENGINEERING. Mark E. Dean is a native of Jefferson City, Tennessee. He received a bachelor of science in electrical engineering from the University of Tennessee in 1979 and a master of science in electrical engineering from Florida Atlantic University in 1982. He earned a Ph.D. in electrical engineering from Stanford University in 1992. He has papers published in the *ieee Computer Society Press*, *MIT Press*, and *IBM Research Journal*.

Dean joined IBM in 1980 and was named an IBM fellow in 1995, one of only 50 active fellows of IBM's 200,000 employees. He was the first African American to be honored with an IBM fellowship. He has held several engineering positions in the area of computer system hardware architecture and design at IBM in Boca Raton, Florida. In 1997, he was named to be both director of the Austin Research Laboratory and director of Advanced Technology Development for the IBM Enterprise Server Group.

He has held various positions in several different cities and IBM divisions, including vice president for hardware and systems architecture in IBM's Systems and Technology Group in Tucson, Arizona. Dean was a vice president in IBM's Storage Technology Group, focused on the company's storage systems strategy and technology roadmap. He served as vice president fro

Systems Research at IBM's Watson Research Center in Yorktown Heights, New York, where he was responsible for the research and application of systems technologies spanning circuits to operating environments.

Dean is currently an IBM fellow and vice president of IBM's Almaden Research Center in San Jose. He oversees more than 400 scientists and engineers doing exploratory and applied research in various hardware, software and services areas, including nanotechnology, materials science, storage systems, data management, web technologies, workplace practices and user interfaces. Dean holds three of the original nine patents on the computer that all PCs are based upon. He has more than 40 patents or patents pending.

Terri Dean

BUSINESS. Terri Dean received a bachelor of arts degree from Chatham College in Pittsburgh, Pennsylvania. In her career with Verizon Communications she has served in numerous positions of increasing responsibility, gaining experience in a variety of disciplines, including finance, marketing, sales, and operations. She was appointed senior vice president of global communications for Verizon Business, the unit formed by the merger of Verizon and MCI. She is responsible for advancing the Verizon Business vision and mission worldwide by communication to internal and external audiences about the company's strategic direction, progress toward key goals, products and services, advocacy positions and more. Dean is responsible for executive communications, industry analyst relations, and community investment for Verizon Business.

Cassandra Deck-Brown

LAW ENFORCEMENT. Cassandra Deck-Brown is a native of Franklin County, North Carolina. She holds a master's degree in public administration from North Carolina State University. She joined the Raleigh (North Carolina) Police Department shortly after graduating from college. In 2003 she became the first woman to command one of Raleigh's six police districts. She made history a second time when she became the first woman promoted to the rank of major. She has served over 20 years with the Raleigh Police Department, now in charge of the department's administrative services division, which provides training, administrative support and technical services to the department's 750 officers.

Willie A. Deese

BUSINESS. Willie A. Deese received a bachelor of arts degree in business administration from North Carolina A&T State University in 1977 and earned his masters of business administration from Western New England College in 1983. He served from 1977 to 1979 as a buyer for Digital Equipment Corporation and from 1980 to 1981 as a senior buyer. From 1981 to 1992, he was in management with the Digital Equipment Corporation; from 1992 to 1995, he served as director for purchasing at SmithKline Beecham Clinical Laboratory Sector. In 1995, he was named vice president and director for purchasing at SmithKline Beecham Pharmaceuticals. In 1996 he became vice president for purchasing at Kaiser Permanente; he returned to SmithKline Beecham Pharmaceuticals in 1997 to serve as senior vice president and director of purchasing, worldwide supply operations. He was then senior vice president for global procurement and logistics at Glaxo SmithKline (2001–2004) and senior vice president for global procurement at Merck and Company (2004–2005). In 2005, Deese was named president of Merck Manufacturing Division.

Ronald V. Dellums

LOCAL GOVERNMENT. Ronald V. Dellums is a native of Oakland, California. He grew up on Wood Street in West Oakland and received an associate degree from Oakland Tech, Merritt College. He received a bachelor of arts degree from San Francisco State College and a master of social work degree from the University of California at Berkeley.

Dellums served two years active duty in the United States Marine Corps. He was a psychiatric social worker for the California Department of Mental Hygiene. He then directed various programs in Bayview–Hunters Point before becoming director of the Hunters Point Youth Opportunity Center. Subsequently, he was director of employment programs for the San Francisco poverty program and then senior consultant on manpower programs for Social Dynamics, a leading Bay Area consulting firm.

In 1967, he was elected to the Berkeley City Council and in 1970 to the U.S. House of Representatives. He represented Oakland, Berkeley, and surrounding areas, in the Congress for 28 years, rising to become chair of the House D.C. Committee and then chair of the House Armed Services Committee. He was elected mayor of the City of Oakland, California, and was still serving in that position in 2008.

Clinton E. Deveaux

JUDICIAL. Clinton E. Deveaux was appointed to the Atlanta Municipal Court on January 20, 1981, by Mayor Maynard Jackson and elected to the court in 1985 and each Atlanta election since. From May 1994 to January 2003, his calendar contained domestic and family violence cases exclusively. In August 2004, Judge Deveaux was appointed presiding judge of the Atlanta Community Court Division. He has also served on the visiting faculty of the Family Institute of New Jersey and is a trustee of the National Judicial College.

Robert A. Dews

MILITARY. Robert A. Dews was born in Washington, D.C., and raised in Capitol Heights, Maryland. He received a bachelor of science degree in electronics engineering from Southern University A&M in Baton Rouge, Louisiana, in 1988, and a master's degree in business administration from New Hampshire College in 1992. He received his commission as an aviation maintenance duty officer after completing Aviation Officers Candidate School in Pensacola, Florida, in May 1989. His military education includes the U.S. Army Command and General Staff College at Fort Leavenworth, Kansas, and the Joint Forces Staff College in Norfolk, Virginia.

Dews has served as a maintenance control officer and was deployed aboard the USS *Dwight D. Eisenhower* in support of Operation Desert Storm and later aboard the USS *George Washington*. In March 1994, he reported to the Naval Strike Aircraft Test Squadron at Naval Air Station Patuxent River, Maryland, and served as the assistant aircraft maintenance officer and as the squadron's executive officer, garnering the" "Officer of the Year" award for 1996.

In 1997, he laterally transferred to the human resources officer community and was assigned as the enlisted programs officer at Navy Recruiting District Houston, Texas, from November 1997 to May 2000. He was the commanding officer of the Oklahoma City Military Entrance Processing Station from November 2001 through March 2004. In April 2004, he transferred to the Office of the Deputy Assistant Secretary of the Navy (Installations and Environment) and served as the lead analyst for mobilization and recruiting in support of the 2005 base realignment and closure.

Masicia Sonya Lee Diggs

MILITARY. Masicia Sonya Lee Diggs received an associate degree in applied science in law enforcement from Central Texas College and a bachelor of science cum laude in social psychology from Park University. Her military education includes the first sergeant's course (commandant's list); the U.S. Army Sergeants Major Academy (class 55); the command sergeants major course; the equal opportunity leader's course; Army force management course; unit prevention leader course; retention course; and cadre training course.

Diggs enlisted into the U.S. Army in August 1985 and received basic combat training at Fort McClellan, Alabama, and advanced individual training at Fort Benjamin Harrison, Indiana. Her first assignment was with Headquarters, 3rd Armored Division Support Command, in Frankfurt, Germany. Other assignments include the New Haven Recruiting Battalion, New Haven, Connecticut; Headquarters, 6th Infantry Division (Light), Fort Wainwright, Alaska; National Imagery and Mapping Agency with duty at Defense Mapping School, Fort Belvoir, Virginia; Headquarters, 8th Personnel Command, in Seoul, Korea; Headquarters, U.S. Army Materiel Command, Alexandria, Virginia; 369th Adjutant General Battalion and Headquarters, Training

Support Battalion, Soldier Support Institute, at Fort Jackson, South Carolina. Diggs has served as the command sergeant major for Combine Arms Center's Special Troops Battalion at Fort Leavenworth, Kansas, since May 15, 2006.

Walter L. Dixon

ENGINEERING. Walter L. Dixon is a native of Baltimore, Maryland, where he received an associate in arts degree in electronic technology from the Community College of Baltimore (Baltimore, Maryland). He received a bachelor of science in political science and community law in 1974, and a master of science in planning and administration from Antioch College, in Yellow Springs, Ohio, in 1978. His education also includes: bachelor of science in math from Towson University in Towson, Maryland, in 1985; bachelor of science in electronic engineering technology from Capitol College in Laurel, Maryland, in 1988; bachelor of science in electronic engineering from Capitol College in 1993; and a master of science in engineering from George Washington University in Washington, D.C., in 1999. He earned a Ph.D. in computer information systems from Nova Southeastern University in Fort Lauderdale, Florida.

His professional career began in 1978 and moved steadily upward, and in 1989 he entered government service at the Patuxent River Naval Air Station at Lexington Park, Maryland. Beginning as a project engineer for cruise missiles and unmanned aerial vehicles, he moved up to deputy director of advanced technology. He started with the Office of Naval Research in 1998 as a deputy program officer in aviation technology, went on to division head of information technology operations and chief engineer, and in 2005 he was selected to serve as a management information systems enterprise architect and chief engineer in the Office of Naval Research in Arlington, Virginia.

Carol A.M. Dockery

MILITARY. Carol A.M. Dockery received an associate degree in applied science in human resource management and personnel administration, Community College of the Air Force, and a bachelor of science degree in business administration and management studies, University of Maryland. Her military education includes all the noncommissioned officer courses and the U.S. Air Force Senior Noncommissioned Officer Academy at Gunter Air Force Base, Alabama; the U.S. Air Force senior leadership course, Center for Creative Leadership, La Jolla, California; Gettysburg Leadership Experience, Gettysburg College, Pennsylvania; and Keystone United States Joint Forces Command in Suffolk, Virginia.

Dockery entered the Air Force in 1983 after graduating from Beaufort High School. She held a variety of personnel positions, including opportunities within personnel flights, as personnel company team chief for an expeditionary air base group, Major Command (majcom) director of personnel staffs, majcom inspector general, the Air Force Personnel Center and HQ Air Force. Her assignments include bases in Florida, Japan, Illinois, San Antonio, Germany, Washington, D.C., Spain and a deployment to Bosnia.

Dockery is the principle advisor to the Warner Robins Air Logistics Center and 78th Air Base Wing commanders on matters concerning the effective utilization, training, education, development and combat readiness of over 3,000 enlisted Airmen, providing essential support to more than 28,000 personnel assigned to the center's 39 hosted units, including a major command headquarters, an air control wing, air mobility group and a large combat communications group on an 8,722-acre installation.

Larry Donaldson

MILITARY. Larry Donaldson received a bachelor's degree in business administration from Sullivan University in Louisiana. He is a graduate of the U.S. Army Sergeants Major Academy at Fort Bliss, Texas. He entered the U.S. Army in July 1984 as a petroleum supply specialist at Fort Leonard Wood, Missouri. His leadership assignments include serving as a drill sergeant at Fort Knox, Kentucky; platoon sergeant with the 123rd Maintenance Support Battalion in Dexheim, Germany; operations sergeant at the 561st Corps Support Battalion at Fort Campbell, Kentucky; first sergeant for the 102nd Quartermaster Company; and command sergeant major of the 260th Quartermaster Battalion at Hunter Army Airfield, Fort Stewart, Georgia. He was assigned as the command sergeant major of 505th Quartermaster Battalion at Okinawa, Japan, in July 2006.

Anne Doris

BUSINESS. Anne Doris received a bachelor of arts degree from City College of New York and a master of business administration from Long Island University, New York. She joined the cable television industry in

1988 and has held several marketing and programming management positions with leading companies such as Comcast Cable, Telecommunications International (Liberty Media International), United Artists Cable and ATC (Time-Warner Cable). She also led her own consulting practice in marketing operations, content acquisition and negotiation for U.S. and international cable and satellite companies.

She has served as vice president of marketing and programming for CableVision S.A., the leading pay television provider in Argentina; as vice president for marketing strategy and communication for Velocom, Inc.; and as vice president of operations for Cox Sports Television, a regional sports network serving approximately 930,000 customers throughout Louisiana and the Southeast. Doris, a twenty-year veteran of the cable television and communications industry, serves as vice president for Cox Communications with over 300,000 service subscribers in 13 communities throughout Southern Arizona.

Cheryl Dorsey

MEDICINE. Cheryl Dorsey grew up in Baltimore, Maryland. She received a bachelor of arts degree in history and science from Harvard-Radcliffe College. She earned her medical doctor degree from the Harvard Medical School and a master of public policy degree from the John F. Kennedy School of Government. Dr. Dorsey was a White House fellow in 1997, serving for a year as a special assistant to the U.S. secretary of labor, advising the Clinton administration on health care and other issues. She has served as president of Echoing Green since May 2002. Dr. Dorsey received an Echoing Green fellowship to study medicine at Harvard University. She became the first Echoing Green fellow to head the social venture fund, which has awarded more than $20 million in startup capital since 1987.

Myrtle Dorsey

EDUCATION. Myrtle Dorsey received her Ph.D. from the University of Texas in the community college leadership program. She began her career in higher education as reading specialist at both Bowie State University and the University of Maryland. In 1981, she moved to Howard Community College in Columbia, Maryland, where she held progressively responsible positions, including director of special services and associate dean of students. In 1991, she moved to Baltimore City Community College, an urban campus in Baltimore, Maryland. There she was vice president of student affairs, responsible for all aspects of student services and overseeing institutional advancement areas including a foundation, alumni affairs and grants.

Dorsey joined Georgia Perimeter College as vice president of student affairs and institutional advancement in 1996. This campus was one of a multi-campus system and had 16,000 credit and 22,000 non-credit students. In 2000, she joined the Cincinnati Technical and Community College, where she served as executive vice president. She had full responsibility for the college operation functions with the president focused on external partnerships. In 2002, Dorsey was appointed chancellor of the Baton Rouge Community College. As a leader in a new institution, she has been involved in both the tremendous growth of the student population and in the building of facilities at the college. Baton Rouge Community College is now the third largest in the state of Louisiana. She was a finalist for the president position of North Harris College.

Thomas W. Dortch

BUSINESS. Thomas W. Dortch is a native of Toccoa, Georgia, and a graduate of Whitman Street High School in 1968. He received a bachelor of arts degree in sociology from Fort Valley State University in 1972. He attended Georgia State University in Atlanta as a Ford fellow in urban administration and earned a

master of arts degree in criminal justice administration from Clark Atlanta University.

Dortch has served as a community development consultant for the Georgia Department of Human Resources and as associate director for the Democratic party of Georgia. From November 1978 to September 1987 he served as administrative aide to U.S. Senator Sam Nunn in Atlanta. In November 1990, he was appointed state director for Senator Nunn. In 1994, he became chief executive officer of the consulting firm twd, Inc., and Atlanta Transportation Systems, a Fulton County paratransit company. He has served as chairman of 100 Black Men of Atlanta and became the chairman of 100 Black Men of America's national board. He also founded the National Black College Alumni Hall of Fame Foundation.

Laura G. Douglas

JUDICIAL. Laura G. Douglas received a bachelor of arts degree from Hobart and William Smith College in 1979 and earned her juris doctor degree from the University of Pittsburgh School of Law in 1982. She has served in private law practice; as a law assistant with the New York State Unified Court System; as an associate law assistant to acting justice with New York State Unified Court System; and as principal law clerk, New York State Unified Court System. In 1991 she was elected judge to the New York City Civil Court in Bronx County; in 1998 she was appointed acting justice on the Supreme Court in Bronx County. In 2000 she was elected a Supreme Court justice, Bronx County.

Michael Douglas

JUDICIAL. Michael Douglas is a native of Los Angeles. He received a bachelor's degree from California State College in Long Beach in 1971 and earned his juris doctor from the University of California Hastings College of Law in 1974. Douglas came to Las Vegas in 1982 from Philadelphia, Pennsylvania, where he had served in private law practice. After two years at Nevada Legal Services, he was hired by the Clark County District Attorney's Office and served in the Civil Division until 1996. In January 1996, he was appointed judge to the Nevada Eighth Judicial District Court in Clark County and was retained in the election later that year. He was elected chief District Court judge in October 2003. He served on the Eighth Judicial District Court until in March 2004, becoming the first African American justice in Nevada's history.

George W. Draper III

JUDICIAL. George W. Draper III is a native of St. Louis, Missouri. He received a bachelor of arts degree in psychology from Morehouse College in Atlanta, Georgia, and earned his juris doctor from Howard University School of Law in Washington, D.C. He was a law clerk for Judge Shellie Bowers, District of Columbia Superior Court, from 1981 to 1982. From 1984 to 1994, he served in the Office of Circuit Attorney, City of St. Louis, Missouri, as first assistant from 1993 to 1994. He was appointed associate circuit judge in July 1994 and circuit judge in June 1998, both in the 21st Judicial Circuit. Draper was appointed as a judge of the Missouri Court of Appeals, Eastern District, in May 2000, and elected in November 2002 for a 12 year term expiring December 31, 2014.

Donald G. Drummer

MILITARY. Donald G. Drummer is a native of San Antonio, Texas. He received a bachelor of business administration degree from the University of Texas at Austin in 1979 and received a commission into the United States Army as a transportation corps officer. He earned a master of business administration degree from Kansas State University and master of science degree in strategic studies from the U.S. Army War College. He is a graduate of the Army War College, Army Command and Staff College, the Armed Forces Staff College, Combined Arms Services Staff School, transportation officer basic and advance courses, motor officer course, personnel management staff officer course, Airborne School, the Army Force management course, and the garrison commander course.

Drummer served from July 1993 to June 1996 with the 1st Cavalry Division at Fort Hood, Texas. He commanded the 10th Transportation Battalion at Fort Eustis, Virginia, from July 1996 to July 1998. In July 1998, he reported to the Pentagon to serve on the Department of the Army Staff as the watercraft and rail systems integrator in the office of the deputy chief of staff for operations. From July 2000 to July 2002, he was G3 operations, 19th Theater Support Command in Taegu, Korea. He served as director of logistics, U.S. Army Forces Command in Atlanta, Georgia. In this capacity, he also was director of the U.S. Army Forces Command Logistics Operations Center in support of Operations Noble Eagle, Enduring Freedom and Iraqi Freedom. He served as the commander of the 22nd Area Support Group in Vicenza, Italy. On August 16, 2005, he took the helm as chief of staff, U.S. Army Transportation Center and Fort Eustis.

Gregory C. Dudley

ENGINEERING. Gregory C. Dudley received a bachelor's degree in mechanical engineering from Virginia Polytechnic Institute and State University. He joined the Northrop Grumman Newport News Sector in 1997 and works in the reactor-plant planning yard for aircraft carriers, supporting the United States Naval Nuclear Propulsion Program through analysis of mechanical components and fluid systems. He is a senior engineer at the Northrop Grumman's Newport News Sector.

Charlene M. Dukes

EDUCATION. Charlene M. Dukes received a bachelor's degree from Indiana University of Pennsylvania. She earned a master's degree and a doctorate in administrative and policy studies with an emphasis in higher education from the University of Pittsburgh. Dukes has served as dean of students at the Community College of Allegheny County, Allegheny Campus. She also served as an adjunct faculty member for the Community College of Allegheny County, Prince George's Community College and the community college leadership doctoral program at Morgan State University. Dukes was appointed the eighth president and first female president of Prince George's Community College in Largo, Maryland.

Kerron R. Duncan

ENGINEERING. Kerron R. Duncan received a bachelor of science degree in electrical engineering from Morgan State University and a master of science degree in electrical engineering from Morgan State University in 2003. He has served with Northrop Grumman as a power systems integrated process team lead for a phased array radar system developed for unmanned aerial vehicle applications. He is currently serving as a power systems architect for several next-generation military radar programs with emphasis on helping to develop new designs that are on the cutting edge of transmit and receive modules and radar technology at Northrop Grumman.

Tony Dungy

SPORTS. Tony Dungy is a native of Jackson, Michigan. He attended Parkside High School, where he played guard position on the basketball team and quarterback on the football team. He was recruited by the University of Minnesota and started as the football team's quarterback. He received Minnesota's Most Valuable Player award twice. He has a career 576 pass attempts, 274 completions, 25 touchdown passes, and 3,577 yards passing. He finished fourth in career total offense in the Big Ten Conference. His professional football career began when he was signed as a free agent by the Pittsburgh Steelers of the National Football League as a defensive back. He played as a reserve special team player for the Steelers in 1977 and the Super Bowl champions during the 1978 season, leading the team in interceptions. In 1979, he was traded to the San Francisco 49ers, and then finished his career a year later in the training camp of the New York Giants.

Dungy began his coaching career in 1980 as a defensive backs coach with the University of Minnesota. He served from 1981 to 1988, first as a defensive backs coach and later as the defensive coordinator for the Pittsburgh Steelers. From 1989 to 1991, he was defensive backs coach with the Kansas City Chiefs. From 1996 to 2001, he was the head coach for the Tampa Bay Buccaneers. Under Coach Dungy, the Buccaneers went to the playoffs four times and won their division in 1999 only to lose to the St. Louis Rams in the NFC championship

game. He was named head coach of the Indianapolis Colts on January 22, 2002. He has directed the Colts to a 60–20 regular record, five playoff appearances, four AFC South titles, two afc championship game appearances and to a 29–17 victory over Chicago in Super Bowl XLI (41). The Colts earned their fourth World Championship in 2006, the first title game appearance by the franchise in 36 years. In 2007, Dungy began his 12th season as an NFL head coach. He became the first Colts head coach to earn five consecutive double-digit victory seasons. Indianapolis also became the only NFL team to open consecutive seasons with 9–0 records.

Leslie B. Dunner

MUSIC. Leslie B. Dunner is a native of New York. He holds advanced degrees in music from the University of Cincinnati's College Conservatory of Music, Queens College in New York City, and the University of Rochester's Eastman School of Music. From 1994 through 2001, Dunner was an assistant conductor to Kurt Masur and the New York Philharmonic, accompanying them in this capacity on their 1995 10-city European tour. From 1987 to 1994, he was music director of the Detroit Symphony Civic and Dearborn Symphony Orchestras, music advisor for the Harlem Festival Orchestra and a cover conductor for Erich Leinsdorf at the Chicago Symphony Orchestra. In addition, he was principal conductor of the renowned Dance Theatre of Harlem, leading performances throughout North and South America, the United Kingdom, Austria's Salzburg Festival, Denmark's Tivoli Festival, the former Soviet Union and on the troupe's historic 1992 debut tour of South Africa, during which they performed in the presence of Nelson Mandela. From 1996 to 1999, Dunner was music director of Canada's Symphony Nova Scotia; subsequently, he served five seasons as music director of the Annapolis Symphony Orchestra, where he reinvigorated that institution and brought it national recognition for its artistic achievements, wide-ranging programming, composer-in-residence forum and innovative educational experiences.

Early in 1999, Dunner ended an 11-season association with the Detroit Symphony Orchestra, having held the posts of resident, associate and assistant conductor. Dunner is the principal conductor of the Joffrey Ballet of Chicago, but also has performed with the Evansville and Prince George's Philharmonic Orchestras, San Jose's Symphony Silicon Valley and Chicago Sinfonietta, and other engagements. Dunner returned to the Baltimore Symphony Orchestra for a gala concert celebrating the Reginald F. Lewis Museum of Maryland African American History and Culture.

Jermaine Dupri

ENTERTAINMENT. Jermaine Dupri was born Jermaine Dupri Mauldin in Asheville, North Carolina, and moved to the Atlanta Georgia, area, where he grew up in the College Park community just south of the city. He took his mother's maiden name as a teenager. Dupri's music career began before he was ten years old. His father had coordinated a Diana Ross show in 1982. Dupri managed to get on stage dance along with Ross. He began performing around the country, appearing with Herbie Hancock and Cameo before he opened the New York Fresh Festival, with Run D.M.C., Whodini, and Grandmaster Flash. Dupri's production career began in 1987, when at the age of 14 he produced and secured a record contract for the Silk Tymes Leather. Dupri is founder, president, and chief executive officer of his own label, So So Def Records and Productions in Atlanta.

He has pursued a recording career of his own, which has resulted in hits such as" "Money Ain't a Thing" (1998, with Jay-Z)," "Welcome to Atlanta" (2001, with Ludacris) and" "Get Your Number" (2005, with Mariah Carey), and" "Gotta Getcha" featuring John Austin. So So Def, a label specializing in Southern hip hop, rhythm and blues, and bass music, was originally distributed through Sony Entertainment/Columbia Records. In 2003, Dupri was appointed president of Arista Black Music and moved So So Def and it artists there. In 2004, he was appointed executive vice president of Urban Music at Virgin Records and moved So So Def over to Virgin. Meanwhile, Dupri expanded his business ventures, buying into Chicago-based Distillery 3 vodka. He also opened a boutique restaurant, Café Dupri. In 2004–2005, he worked with R&B singers Usher and Mariah Carey on their releases. He also worked with his girlfriend singer Janet Jackson on her new album, *Twenty Years Old.*

Cheryl E. Easley

NURSING, EDUCATION. Cheryl E. Easley received a bachelor's degree in nursing from Columbia Union College in Takoma, Maryland. She earned her master's in nursing and Ph.D. in nursing both from the New York University. Easley's professional career includes serving in administrative and teaching positions at Sag-

inaw Valley State University, Rush-Presbyterian–St. Luke's Medical Center and Rush University, the University of Illinois at Chicago, the University of Michigan, Andrews University, and Herbert H. Lehman College of the City University of New York. She is a specialist in public health and human rights, health care for the underserved, and issues related to aging in Alaska. Easley was appointed to the position of dean and professor, College of Health and Social Welfare, at the University of Alaska in Anchorage on August 1, 2003.

William Eddins

MUSIC. William Eddins is a native of New York. He started playing piano at age 5 after his parents purchased a piano at a garage sale. He studied with David Effron at the Eastman School of Music in Rochester, New York, and completed his degree in piano performance in 1983 at age 18, one of the youngest graduates in the institution's history. He subsequently studied conducting with Daniel Lewis at the University of Southern California. In 1987, he was a founding member of the New World Symphony Orchestra in Miami, Florida.

Eddins has served as associate conductor of the Minnesota Orchestra, resident conductor of the Chicago Symphony Orchestra, and assistant to Daniel Barenboim at the Berlin State Opera. He spent 10 seasons as the assistant conductor of the Chicago Symphony and became its first resident conductor. He has worked with orchestras throughout the United States and Europe and has been the principal guest conductor for the National Symphony of Ireland.

The Edmonton Symphony invited candidates to guest conduct programs in 2004. Eddins performed in May and October. Following his latter appearance, members of the orchestra requested that the board end its search for a conductor and offer him the job. After negotiating with Eddins in December, the board unanimously approved his appointment. Eddins has been contracted as music director of the Edmonton Symphony Orchestra through the symphony's 2007-2008 season.

Robert Edmunds

MILITARY. Robert Edmunds graduated from Northgate Junior-Senior High School in Pittsburgh, Pennsylvania, in 1985. He attended Penn State University. He enlisted in the United States Navy in April 1989 and attended recruit training at Great Lakes, Illinois. In January 1994 he reported to the supreme allied commander, Atlantic representative in Europe, at nato Headquarters in Brussels, Belgium, as registry yeoman, facsimile operator, and documents control and leading petty officer. In April 1995, he served as shift chief at U.S. Command Post, Office of the U.S. National Military Representative Supreme Headquarters, Allied Powers Europe, in Shape, Belgium. His duty consisted of numerous missions such as Operation Deny Flight, Provide Promise, Provide Comfort, Sharp Guard, and Joint Endeavor. After this tour, he reported in February 1997 as administrative assistant and commanding officer's yeoman to Navy Recruiting District, Raleigh, North Carolina.

From May 1999 to August 1999, he participated in Joint Task Force Noble Anvil in Naples, Italy, as administrative assistant to the intelligent directorate. He then reported onboard the USS *Dubuque*, home ported in San Diego, California, where he was ship's secretary. Following his tour, Chief Edmunds reported to the Naval Reserve Officers Training Corps Unit at Virginia Tech in May 2004, where he is the administrative officer.

Anthony L. Edwards

MILITARY. Anthony L. Edwards is a native of Sanford, North Carolina. He received an associate degree from Minnesota State University. He enlisted in the United States Army as an infantryman on August 1, 1980, and attended infantry one station unit training at Fort Benning, Georgia. His military education includes all the noncommissioned officer courses, Airborne School, Air Assault School, the first sergeants course, and the U.S. Army Sergeants Major Academy.

Edwards's assignments include 1-87 Infantry Regiment; 82nd Airborne Division, Berlin Brigade; 1st Cavalry Regiment; 1-508th Airborne Battalion; 1st Armored Division; and the 101st Airborne Division (Air Assault). Edwards' duty and leadership positions include team leader, squad leader, team chief, section sergeant, pla-

toon sergeant, dill sergeant, rifle company first sergeant, headquarters and headquarters company first sergeant, battalion operations sergeant major, coscom operations sergeant major, and battalion command sergeant major. He currently serves as the command sergeant major of the 205th Infantry Brigade.

Herm Edwards

SPORTS. Herm Edwards is a native of Fort Monmouth, New Jersey, and was raised in Seaside, California. He received a bachelor's degree in criminal justice from San Diego State. He entered the NFL as a rookie free agent with Philadelphia in 1977 and went on to start 135 consecutive regular season contests at cornerback, producing a franchise-record 38 combined interceptions in regular and postseason action. Edwards began his pro coaching career as a participant in the NFL's minority coaching fellowship program with Kansas City in 1989 and is the first graduate of the program to go on to become the head coach of the franchise for which he served his fellowship. He rejoined the Chiefs after spending six seasons with Kansas City as a scout (1990–1991), defensive backs coach (1992–1994) and pro personnel scout (1995).

He joined Tony Dungy's staff in Tampa Bay as assistant head coach and defensive backs coach, spending five seasons (1996–2000) in that capacity. He then enjoyed a five-year stint as the head coach of the New York Jets (2001–2005). He led the Jets to 41 wins, the third-highest victory total in that franchise's history. Edwards was hired as the 10th head coach in Chiefs franchise history on January 9, 2006. He entered his sixth year as an NFL head coach and his 27th season in the league as either a player, a scout, or a coach. He also played in Super Bowl XV (15). He concluded his career with the L.A. Rams and Atlanta in 1986.

Ira Edwards, Jr.

LAW ENFORCEMENT. Ira Edwards, Jr., is a native of Dublin, Georgia, and graduated from Dublin High School in 1979. He received a bachelor of arts degree in sociology with a focus in criminal studies from the University of Georgia and a master of public administration degree with honors from Columbus State University. He is a 2002 graduate of the National Sheriff's Institute, where he was nominated as class president. He completed 280 hours of coursework to graduate from the Command College in December 2003. He is a graduate of the 2003 Georgia International Law Enforcement Exchange Program.

Edwards began his law enforcement career in 1985 with the Clarke County Sheriff's Office. After serving four years there, he transferred to the Athens–Clarke County Police Department, where he served 11 years until his election as sheriff of Clarke County in July of 2000. Sheriff Edwards is the first African American sheriff in the history of Athens–Clarke County. He is also the first African American to win a countywide election there. He is an ordained elder at Timothy Baptist Church.

Jules D. Edwards III

JUDICIAL. Jules D. Edwards III is a native of Louisiana. He received a bachelor of arts degree in sociology from Loyola University in New Orleans in 1981 and earned his juris doctor from Loyola University Law School in 1984. Edwards served in the U.S. Marine Corps Reserve. After law school he spent several years in private practice. He also served as an assistant district attorney and as an indigent defender in New Orleans. In 1993, he was appointed a judge in the 15th Judicial Circuit of Louisiana. He now serves as the chief judge of Louisiana's 15th Judicial District, covering the parishes of Lafayette, Acadia and Vermilion.

Teresa Dawn Edwards

EDUCATION, ENGINEERING. Teresa Dawn Edwards is a native of Nashville, Tennessee. She received a bachelor of arts degree in mathematics magna cum laude from Spelman College in 1976 and a master of science in operations research from Georgia Institute of Technology in 1979. She also earned a Ph.D. in industrial

and systems engineering from Georgia Institute of Technology in 1990.

Edwards's professional career includes serving as an associate professor at Spelman College and at Bennett College. Her research interests include nonlinear optimization, communication networks, and environmental science. She has investigated balancing loads on synchronous optical network (SONET) rings with a GTE colleague, and she worked with NASA and other atmospheric scientists on the 1997 Indonesia forest fires and presented her findings at an international meeting in Singapore in April 1998. She also supervises students on undergraduate research projects, with resulting competition awards and publications.

Edwards's professional activities have included organizing and hosting MATHFest93, a conference for undergraduates in mathematics; hosting the 1997 Master Association of American Systems Engineering section meeting and a Project Kaleidoscope Faculty 21 meeting; reviewing Environmental Protection Agency, National Science Foundation, and NASA proposals; and serving as the mathematics professor of 50 eighth grade minority students for the Summer Enrichment Program at the University of Massachusetts in Amherst.

Lisa Eghuonu-Davis

MEDICINE. Lisa Eghuonu-Davis received a bachelor of science degree from Massachusetts Institute of Technology (MIT) and a master of public health in epidemiology. She earned a master of business administration in health care management from Wharton and her medical doctor degree from Johns Hopkins School of Medicine. She completed her pediatric residency and Robert Wood Johnson Foundation clinical scholar fellowship at the University of Pennsylvania. Dr. Eghuonu-Davis is currently serving as a Pfizer sponsored scholar-in-residence at Spelman College to enhance women's health and reduce disparities in health care and to increase leadership opportunities for African American women in health and science. She previously served as vice president, United States Medical, in the U.S. Pharmaceuticals Division of Pfizer Global Pharmaceuticals.

Donna Elam

BUSINESS. Donna Elam received a bachelor of science degree from City University of New York. She earned a master of arts degree and an Ed.D. in the fields of special education and education policy from New York University. Elam has served as associate director for the Southeastern Equity Center, which serves eight southeastern states, and as director of New York University's Equity Assistance Center for New York, New Jersey, Puerto Rico and the Virgin Islands.

She has an outstanding record of work in diversity, disproportionality of minority students in special education referrals and placement, leadership, team building, standards-based instruction and parent education. She is the founder and chief executive officer of T.E.A.M. (Training, Evaluation, Assessment and Management) consulting, an organization based on her belief that all students are entitled to the quality of education necessary to maximize academic achievement.

Norman L. Elliott

MILITARY. Norman L. Elliott received a bachelor of science degree from the U.S. Air Force Academy and a medical degree from Yale University School of Medicine. He completed his internal medicine residency at Emory University Hospital System in 1982 and a fellowship in gastroenterology from the University of Alabama at Birmingham. He graduated from the School of Aerospace Medicine at Brooks Air Force Base in Texas in 1983, and received his flight surgeon wings.

Elliott entered the U.S. Air Force Academy in June 1966. After graduating in 1970, he entered undergraduate pilot training at Laughlin Air Force Base in Texas. He was awarded his pilot wings in August 1971. While on active duty, he flew as a pilot for the Rescue Service and for Weather Reconnais-

sance. After leaving active duty, he served as chief of Aerospace Medicine of the 117th Medical Squadron, Alabama Air National Guard, in Birmingham. In January 1990, he was assigned as commander of the 117th Medical Squadron with the Alabama Air National Guard in Montgomery. In March 2004, he was selected to serve as Air National Guard assistant to the surgeon general for Air Mobility Command at Scott Air Force Base in Illinois.

C. Jack Ellis

LOCAL GOVERNMENT. C. Jack Ellis is a native of Macon, Georgia, where he attended Ballard Hudson High School. He received a bachelor of arts degree from St. Leo College in Florida. Ellis served two years of combat duty in Vietnam as a paratrooper platoon sergeant with the 101st Airborne Division. He retired from the United States Army as a senior noncommissioned officer. He was awarded three Bronze Stars, the Army Commendation Medal for Valor and Heroism, and the Purple Heart for wounds received in combat. He is a former cable television executive and an executive with the United States Census Bureau. He is also the former host and producer of a local community affairs television program, *Community Forum.*

Ellis was elected the 40th mayor of the City of Macon, Georgia. He is currently serving his second term. Mayor Ellis was first sworn into office December 14, 1999, becoming the first African American mayor in the city's 176-year history. He was one of the speakers at the 2000 Democratic National Convention in Los Angeles, California.

Evelynn Ellis

EDUCATION. Evelynn Ellis is a native of Hale County, Alabama, and received a Bachelor of Arts degree from Concordia College. She earned a master's degree in music performance and a doctorate in higher education administration for Penn State.

Dr. Ellis has served at Penn State since 1985 in numerous positions, including in the office of student aid as the coordinator for recruitment and retention services; as an academic advisor and instructor at Penn State's College of Health and Human Services; as the director of multicultural programs and assistant to the associate dean for outreach; and at the cooperative extension at Penn State's College of Arts and Architecture. As senior director of the office of graduate educational equity program, she developed a strategic plan to attract students of color to Penn State's graduate programs.

Dr. Ellis was selected to serve as the director of equal opportunity and affirmative action at Dartmouth College. She assumed her new position on September 1, 2008.

Tellis B. Ellis III

MEDICINE. Tellis B. Ellis III is a native of Jackson, Mississippi, and a graduate of Jim Hill High School. He received a bachelor of science degree from Jackson State University in 1965. He was an outstanding football player for the university and was recruited by the National Football League to play professionally for the Green Bay Packers in Green Bay, Wisconsin. After sustaining a knee injury that ended his hopes for a career as a professional athlete, he decided to pursue a career in medicine. He earned his medical doctor degree from Meharry Medical College in Nashville, Tennessee, in 1970. He completed both his internship and residency in internal medicine at Meharry in 1974. Dr. Ellis then returned to Jackson, where he completed his cardiology fellowship at the University of Mississippi Medical Center in 1977. Dr. Ellis is board certified in internal medicine and cardiology.

Dr. Ellis is a founding partner of Jackson Cardiology Associates, where he practices with four other cardiologists. He is assistant clinical professor at the University of Mississippi Medical Center and an active staff physician at both St. Dominic–Jackson Memorial Hospital and Central Mississippi Medical Center in Jackson.

Cathy Ellison

LAW ENFORCEMENT. Cathy Ellison is a native of Dale, Texas, and later moved to Austin, Texas. She received a bachelor's degree in criminal justice from Southwest Texas University (now Texas State University). She is a graduate of the National Forum of Black Public Administrators, the Executive Leadership Institute, and the Law Enforcement Management Institute of Technology.

Ellison was commissioned as an Austin police officer

on February 23, 1979. Her assignments have included patrol officer; traffic enforcement, recruiting, and detective. She was promoted to sergeant, working in various divisions of the department, including child abuse, recruiting and northeast patrol. In 2003, she was appointed assistant chief. She was the City of Austin's first African American female to serve in that position. She has managed all nine patrol area commands of the city, in addition to providing leadership to Eastside Story program. Ellison was appointed chief of staff in April 2006, garnering another first. She supervised integrity crimes, internal affairs, administrative services, public information office and the inspections and accreditation units. On May 28, 2006, Ellison became the first African American woman to be named acting chief of police in the history of the Austin Police Department.

John H. England, Jr.

JUDICIAL. John H. England, Jr., is a native of Birmingham, Alabama, where he attended public school. He earned a bachelor of science degree in chemistry from Tuskegee University and earned his juris doctor from the University of Alabama Law School in Tuscaloosa, Alabama. England began his career in private law practice in Tuscaloosa. He was elected to the Tuscaloosa City Council and served as chairman of the finance and community development committee. After two terms on the city council, he was appointed by Governor Jim Folsom to the Sixth Judicial Circuit serving Tuscaloosa County in 1993. He was elected to the Sixth Judicial Circuit in 1994, where he served until 1999 when he was appointed to the Alabama Supreme Court from September 1999 until he returned to the Circuit Court of Tuscaloosa County in January 2001. Judge England was re-elected to the Circuit Court in 2002.

Paul Engola

ENGINEERING. Paul Engola is a native of New York, New York. He received a bachelor of science degree in aeronautics and astronautics from the Massachusetts Institute of Technology. He has also earned a master of science degree in aerospace engineering from Georgia Tech in 1994 and a master's of business administration from Stanford University's Graduate School of Business in Stanford, California.

His professional career began with the Boeing Satellite Systems in El Segundo, California, from 1994 to 1998 as a mechanical systems engineer, spacecraft manager and lead validation engineer. In 1998 he moved to Space Systems Loral in Palo Alto, California, as a systems engineer. He worked as a consultant to the Boston Consulting Group in Boston, Massachusetts, from 2000 to 2003, and joined Lockheed Martin as a business development director in 2003. Engola is the director of program management for Lockheed Space Systems in Denver, Colorado.

Charles H. Epps, Jr.

MEDICINE, EDUCATION. Charles H. Epps, Jr., is a native of Baltimore, Maryland, and graduated from Frederick Douglass High School. He received a bachelor of science in chemistry magna cum laude from Howard University and a medical doctor degree from Howard University in 1955. After medical school, he completed his internship and residency in orthopedic surgery at Howard University Hospital in Washington, D.C.

Dr. Epps served as a captain in the U.S. Army Medical Corps, and after his honorable discharge from the Army in 1962, he returned to Howard University as a member of the College of Medicine faculty and began a successful private practice. At age thirty-three, he was appointed chief of the division of orthopedic surgery at Howard. During his tenure as chief and professor, Dr. Epps trained more African American men and women in orthopedic surgery than anyone in the world. He has also served Howard in various other capacities, as dean of the College of Medicine, vice president for health affairs, the acting CEO of Howard Hospital and as special assistant to the president for health affairs. Howard University honored him with the Charles H. Epps, Jr., M.D., Endowed Chair in Orthopedics.

Charles T. Epps, Jr.

STATE GOVERNMENT. Charles T. Epps, Jr., received a bachelor's degree in history and elementary education from Bishop College in Dallas, Texas. He earned a master's degree in education administration and supervision from Seton Hall University and a doctorate in education from Rutgers University. In 2004, Epps

completed his residency at Oxford University in the United Kingdom.

Epps began his career in education in 1967, when he accepted a job as a seventh-grade teacher at Jersey City's Whitney M. Young School. He worked through the ranks of the Jersey City schools system as a teacher, supervisor, principal of adult evening programs, and director of funded programs. He was appointed as the district's associate superintendent for community and support services in 1998. Epps was named state district superintendent for the Jersey City Public Schools in September 2000. He was chairman of the Hudson County Community College Board of Trustees and a New Jersey State Representative for the 31st district, which consists of Bayonne and part of Jersey City.

Christopher B. Epps

LAW ENFORCEMENT. Christopher B. Epps is a native of Tchula, Mississippi. He received a bachelor of science degree in elementary education from Mississippi Valley State University and earned a master of arts in guidance and counseling from Liberty University in Lynchburg, Virginia.

Epps started his career with the Mississippi Department of Corrections in 1982 as a correctional officer at the Mississippi State Penitentiary. His experience with the Mississippi Department of Corrections includes chief of staff, deputy commissioner of institutions, deputy commissioner of community corrections, director of offender services, deputy superintendent, correction case management supervisor, director of treatment services, and corrections case manager. Additionally, he has served as disciplinary hearing officer, investigator and disciplinary hearing officer, and investigator and director of records for the agency.

He has held various leadership positions in the military since 1984. He is a commissioned officer in the Mississippi Army National Guard. Epps was appointed commissioner of the Mississippi Department of Corrections by Governor Ronnie Musgrove on August 30, 2002. He was reappointed to the post on January 13, 2004, by Governor Haley R. Barbour.

Clark Kent Ervin

FEDERAL GOVERNMENT. Clark Kent Ervin is a native of Houston, Texas. He received a bachelor of arts degree in government cum laude from Harvard University in 1980 and attended Oxford University from 1980 to 1982. He earned a master of arts degree in politics, philosophy and economics and a doctor of laws degree cum laude from Harvard University in 1985.

He worked in private law practice in Houston, Texas. Ervin was the associate director of policy for the Office of National Service at the White House from 1989 to 1991, assistant secretary of state of Texas from 1995 to 1999, and associate director of policy for the Office of National Service at the White House from 1999 until the spring of 2001. On August 3, 2001, he was sworn in as the inspector general of the Department of State. He was appointed the first inspector general of the U.S. Department of Homeland Security on December 26, 2003.

Warren Evans

LAW ENFORCEMENT. Warren Evans is a native of Detroit, Michigan. He has served as a police officer, correctional officer, supervisor, manager and administrator. He also has held executive positions in law enforcement, adult corrections, community corrections, juvenile detention, juvenile training schools and community based programs. Evans has held every rank within the Sheriff's Office of Wayne County, Michigan, starting as a deputy in 1970 and eventually serving as undersheriff from 1987 to 1991. In 1978, he became the department's youngest-ever lieutenant at age 28. He was also director for the two county jails in downtown Detroit.

Evans was recruited by Wayne County Executive Ed McNamara to create and run the Department of Community Justice. He was named chief of operations for the Wayne County Prosecutor's Office in 2001. He served for two years as chief of special operations at the Wayne County Prosecutor's Office. His areas of responsibility included the juvenile division, police shooting investigations, major drug prosecutions, drug house unit and auto theft. In January of 2003, Evans became sheriff of Wayne County. Since becoming sheriff, he has initiated several new crime reduction partnerships with city and suburban police chiefs.

Gloria D. Farrow

MILITARY. Gloria D. Farrow is a native of Marietta, Georgia. She received a bachelor of science degree in business management from Touro University International and is currently pursuing a master's degree in business administration from the same university. Her military education includes the first sergeants course, battle staff course, inspector general course, master fitness course, air assault course, instructor training

course, and the U.S. Army Sergeant Major Academy (Class 54).

Farrow entered the U.S. Army after high school in 1984. She completed basic combat training at Fort Dix, New Jersey. She has held every enlisted leadership position, including squad leader, section leader, platoon sergeant, first sergeant, operation noncommissioned officer, support operation noncommissioned officer in charge, petroleum operation supervisor, petroleum and water distribution supervisor, class III bulk supply manager, and assistant inspector general. She is the command sergeant major for the 505th Quartermaster Battalion.

Sergeant Major Farrow has deployed in support of Desert Shield and Desert Storm in Saudia Arabia; Operation Restore Hope, Mogadishu, Somalia; Task Force Bosnia-Herzegovina; Operation Enduring Freedom, Zamboanga, Philippines; and Operation Iraqi Freedom III, Taji, Iraq.

Gerald W. Felder

MILITARY, MINISTRY. Gerald W. Felder is a native of Birmingham, Alabama. He received a bachelor's degree from Lee College in Cleveland, Tennessee, and a master of divinity degree from the Church of God School of Theology in Cleveland, Tennessee. Felder enlisted in the U.S. Army in 1971 and completed boot camp at Fort Jackson, South Carolina. He was communications specialist while serving in the Army.

He was an alcohol and drug counselor for the Hiwassee Mental Health Center, overseeing four counties. He was commissioned into the U.S. Navy as a lieutenant junior grade in 1988 and served as the battalion chaplain for 1st Battalion, 8th Marines, and 2nd Light Armored Infantry Battalion at Camp Lejeune, North Carolina. During his time at Camp Lejeune, Chaplain Felder deployed to Desert Shield and Desert Storm. From 1991 to 1994, he served as one of six chaplains at Recruit Training Command and started the gospel service at Bluejacket Chapel. His command experience includes the USS *Gettysburg* (CG 64), the first United States ship to go to South Africa since apartheid. In addition, the USS *Gettysburg* rescued the victims from Achille Laurie. He was the senior protestant chaplain at the Mayport Chapel. Felder is serving as the Region Central chaplain, overseeing 7 districts covering 18 states. Presently, Commander Felder is also the command chaplain at Training Support Center, Great Lakes Naval Base.

Preston L. Felton

LAW ENFORCEMENT. Preston L. Felton has served with the New York State Police for over 22 years in a variety of assignments, including as a trooper, investigator and sergeant in Troop F, lieutenant within Internal Affairs, lieutenant in the Bureau of Criminal Investigation in Troop C, lieutenant in the Uniform Force in Troop K, captain in the Bureau of Criminal Investigation with the Executive Service Detail, and as a major-troop commander in Troop New York City. He was selected to serve as superintendent of the New York State Division of State Police. He is the first African American to be selected for this position.

Adrian M. Fenty

LOCAL GOVERNMENT. Adrian M. Fenty is a native of Washington, D.C., and grew up in the city's Mount Pleasant neighborhood. He received a bachelor of arts degree in economics and English from Oberlin College and earned a juris doctor from Howard University School of Law. Fenty served as a member of the Washington, D.C., Council from 2000 to 2006. He was elected mayor of the District of Columbia in November 2006, carrying every precinct in the city in both the primary and the general election. He assumed office on January 2, 2007.

Cedric Ferrell

BUSINESS. Cedric Ferrell received a bachelor of science degree in business from Purdue University's Krannert School of Business and a master of business administration degree from Southern Methodist

University's Cox School of Business. He was the senior vice president of business development and marketing for Towne AllPoints Communications, Inc., a Santa Ana based national direct marketing firm. He also held management positions around the country with Fortune 500 companies such as Masterfoods, PepsiCo, and Pillsbury.

He is an accomplished multi-unit franchisee for the Entrepreneur's Source, a leading business ownership consulting organization. He has served as an ambassador assisting other franchisees to grow and develop their businesses. He recently acquired the rights to another franchise concept, AIM Mail Centers, which provides multiple business services. The Entrepreneur's Source has more than 180 offices in the United States and Canada.

Gwen Keyes Fleming

LAW ENFORCEMENT. Gwen Keyes Fleming is a native of New Jersey. She received a bachelor of science degree in finance from Douglass College and earned her juris doctor from Emory University School of Law in 1993. Fleming has served as an assistant solicitor general in the DeKalb County (Georgia) Solicitor-General's Office, where she prosecuted domestic violence, drunk driving charges, and other misdemeanor cases. After being promoted to senior trial attorney, she was recruited to join the Fulton County District Attorney's Office as a senior assistant district attorney. In January 1999 she made history as the first African American, first female, and the youngest elected solicitor-general in DeKalb County. Fleming was elected district attorney and was sworn into office in December 2004. She made history as the first African American and the first female ever to serve the citizens of DeKalb County in this post.

Mark W. Flemon

MILITARY. Mark W. Flemon is a native of Baton Rouge, Louisiana, and at the age of two moved to Denver, Colorado, where he left high school early to enlist in the Navy on May 18, 1981. Upon completion of recruit training and Basic Electric and Electronics Training School in San Diego, California, he reported to Basic Enlisted Submarine School in Groton, Connecticut. Then he returned to San Diego for Sonar Technician "A" and "C" School. He is a graduate of the Navy Senior Enlisted Academy, Class 122 (Blue Group), and the command master chief course in Newport, Rhode Island. He and is currently pursuing a degree in human resource management.

Flemon's numerous leadership assignments include with the Naval Submarine Training Center Pacific Detachment, San Diego, California, where he was a department leading chief petty officer and contracting officer representative. He advanced to the rank of senior chief petty officer before transferring. His next assignment was Submarine Squadron One, Pearl Harbor, Hawaii, where he served as the squadron sonar assistant to the commodore and was briefly the acting command master chief. While at Submarine Squadron One, he was promoted to master chief petty officer and selected to the Chief of the Boat program. He was handpicked to be the chief of the boat on board the USS *Los Angeles* (SSN 688), which completed two successful Western Pacific deployments. He entered command master chief program. Flemon is assigned as command master chief, Navy Recruiting District San Diego, California.

Jeffrey Fletcher

MILITARY. Jeffrey Fletcher was born in Fort Bragg, North Carolina. He received a bachelor of science degree from Florida A&M University in Tallahassee, Florida, in 1988 and received a commission as a second lieutenant into the United States Army as an infantry officer. He also earned a master of science degree in administration from Central Michigan University in 2001. His military education includes the infantry officer basic course at Fort Benning, Georgia; the adjutant general officer advance course at Fort Benjamin Harrison, Indiana; and Command and General Staff College at Fort Leavenworth, Kansas.

Fletcher came to the U.S. Army Garrison Mannheim from the Senior Leader Development Office, where he was the human resource manager for the Army's Adjutant General, Finance, and Functional Area 43 colonels. His assignments include colonel's assignment manager, U.S. Army Human Resources Command; executive officer to the Army deputy G-1; executive officer, 55th Personnel Services Battalion; board recorder and later chief of the Department of the Army Secretariat for Senior Enlisted Selection Boards; adjutant general and finance team leader, Readiness Group Harrison; and commander, B Company, 30th Adjutant General Battalion. He serves as the commander, U.A. Garrison in Mannheim, Germany.

Eugene Flood, Jr.

BUSINESS. Eugene Flood, Jr., received a bachelor's degree in economics from Harvard University and earned a Ph.D. in economics from the Massachusetts Institute of Technology (MIT). Flood was a member of the faculty of Stanford University's Graduate School of Business, where he taught finance. He also lectured in a number of executive training programs, including those at the Sloan School of Management at the Massachusetts Institute of Technology, Nomura School of Advanced Management in Tokyo, Japan, the International Management Institute in Geneva, Switzerland, and the Graduate School of Business at Stanford University. In addition, he has worked as a consultant for a variety of private sector companies and government agencies.

Flood joined Morgan Stanley in 1987, serving as a portfolio manager in Morgan Stanley Asset Management. In January 2000, he was named president and chief executive officer of Smith Breeden Associates, a research and trading firm in the fixed-income market.

Elson S. Floyd

EDUCATION. Elson S. Floyd is a native of Henderson, North Carolina. He received a bachelor of arts degree in political science and speech, a master of education degree in adult education, and a doctor of philosophy degree in higher and adult education, all from the University of North Carolina at Chapel Hill.

Floyd began his career in 1978 at the University of North Carolina at Chapel Hill, where he held deanships in the Division of Student Affairs, the General College and the College of Arts and Sciences. From 1988 to 1990, he was assistant vice president for student services for the University of North Carolina system office, where he helped develop and articulate student affairs and academic affairs policy for the 16-campus university system. He spent two years as executive director of the Washington State Higher Education Coordinating Board, the agency responsible for statewide coordination, planning, oversight, policy analysis and student financial aid programs for Washington's post-secondary education system.

Floyd spent from 1995 to 1998 at the UNC Chapel Hill as chief administrative and operating officer and the senior official responsible for business and finance, human resources, auxiliary enterprises, student affairs, information technology, university advancement and development, and enrollment management. He served as president of Western Michigan University in Kalamazoo for more than four years. He was selected as the president of the four-campus University of Missouri system on November 11, 2002.

Ozena Floyd

HEALTH, MILITARY. Ozena Floyd received a bachelor's degree in nursing from California State University and earned a master's degree in public administration from San Francisco University. She received her nurse consulting certification from Kaplan College.

Floyd served over 22 years in the California Air National Guard and retired as a lieutenant colonel. During her military service, she earned several medals and commendations. In 1995, she was awarded the Air Force Commendation Medal of the overall success of the Operation Arch Angel during a statewide mass disaster training exercise in the state of Michigan. In November of 2003, she was named one of "24 Woman of Influence" by Fresno's KSEE-TV Channel 24, a program that recognizes women who have demonstrated unswerving dedication to the betterment of their families, their companies, and their communities at large.

Colonel Floyd has served with the California Department of Health for 20 years. She currently works with the California Department of Health Services, Licensing and Certification Division. She was recently appointed district administrator for the Fresno District Office and she was the first African American supervisor in that office.

Yvette Flunder

MINISTRY. Yvette Flunder is a native of San Francisco. She is a graduate of the ministry studies and master of arts program at the Pacific School of Religion in Berkeley, California. She received a doctor of ministry degree from San Francisco Theological Seminary in San Anselmo, California. Flunder is a third generation preacher with roots in the Church of God in Christ. She began performing and recording with Walter Hawkins and the Family and the Love Center Choir. She is also an ordained minister of the United Church of Christ.

In June 2003 Rev. Flunder was consecrated presiding bishop of Refuge Ministries/Fellowship 2000 a multi-denominational fellowship of more than 50 primarily African American Christian leaders and laity representing churches and faith-based organizations from all parts of the country and Africa. Rev. Flunder is the senior pastor of City of Refuge United Church of Christ. She founded the City of Refuge Community Church United Church of Christ in 1991 in order to unite a gospel ministry with a social ministry.

Joey A. Fondren

MILITARY. Joey A. Fondren was born in Chicago, Illinois. He joined the Navy in 1978 and completed recruit training in Great Lakes, Illinois. He served at sea on USS *Coral Sea* (CV 43) and the USS *Ogden* (LPD 5). Fondren has also served at Naval Air Station Moffett Field, Navy Recruiting District Los Angeles and Naval Mobile Construction Battalion Three. He returned to Navy Recruiting District Los Angeles as acting command master chief. He then reported to USS *Essex* (LHD 2) in San Diego, where he conducted the Navy's largest crew exchange and hull swap ever with USS *Belleau Wood* (LHA 3), forward deployed in Sasebo, Japan.

In May 2001, Fondren attended the Senior Enlisted Academy in Newport, Rhode Island. He returned to USS *Belleau Wood* as supply department leading chief petty officer. Selected into the command master chief program in February 2002, Fondren served as USS *Bunker Hill* (CG 52) command master chief. In September 2004, Master Chief Fondren reported to Navy Recruiting District Los Angeles to assume duties as command master chief.

Jenelle E. Foote

MEDICINE. Jenelle E. Foote is a native of Ohio. She received a bachelor's degree from Duquesne University in 1978 and earned a medical doctor degree from Temple University School of Medicine in 1984. She completed her internship and primary residency requirements in surgery at Albert Einstein Medical Center in Philadelphia. She completed her residency in urology at the University of Colorado Health Science Center in Denver. She also completed a fellowship in female urology, incontinence, and reconstructive surgery at Kaiser Permanente Medical Center in Los Angeles.

Dr. Foote gained recognition in a 2002 article in *Women in Medicine* magazine, as well as being named one of *Atlanta* magazine's "Best Docs" in 1999. Dr. Foote was also featured in the *Atlanta Tribune* article "Savy Doctor Battles Incontinence in Women," and in 2001, *Black Enterprise* named Dr. Foote as one of the "Top African American Doctors in the United States." Dr. Foote is a clinical assistant professor at Morehouse School of Medicine and Emory University. She is also a staff urologist at Shepherd Center. She has served as principal investigator for several urologic research studies and has published numerous articles and abstracts.

Aubrey Ford, Jr.

JUDICIAL. Aubrey Ford, Jr., is a native of Philadelphia, Pennsylvania. He received a bachelor's degree from Lincoln University in Lincoln, Pennsylvania, in 1970 and earned his juris doctor degree from Howard University School of Law in Washington, D.C. Ford joined the staff of the State Attorney General's Office as an assistant attorney general. After a year of service, he entered private law practice in Tuskegee, Alabama. On September 2, 1977, Alabama Governor George Wallace appointed him to serve as district judge for Macon County. In September 1999, Chief Justice Hooper appointed Judge Ford to serve on the Alabama Judicial

Study Commission; he also served as chair of the Board of Directors of the East Alabama Task Force for Battered Women, which provides services for victims of domestic violence in five eastern Alabama counties.

Niles Ford

PUBLIC SAFETY. Niles Ford received a bachelor's of public administration from Athens State University in Athens, Alabama, and a master's degree in management from Faulkner University in Montgomery, Alabama. He is currently pursuing a doctorate degree in organization and management from Capella University in Minneapolis. Ford's career began with the City of Bessemer, Alabama, as a public safety dispatcher, firefighter-paramedic, lieutenant fire inspector-investigator, and as a fire captain–medic. He served as deputy chief of logistics, support services, safety and member of the Fulton County, Georgia, Fire Department since 2003. In August 2007, Mayor Chris Beutler of Lincoln, Nebraska, appointed Ford the fire chief for the City of Lincoln, beginning October 1, 2007.

Steven Ford

MUSIC. Steven Ford is a native of Philadelphia. He was appointed head musician at the age of nine at his father's church. He completed his education in music composition and orchestration at Temple University in Philadelphia, Pennsylvania. Ford began his career as a studio musician, performing on numerous recording, television and radio commercials. His infatuation with recording and musical arranging soon became the driving force behind his maturity into a consummate musician, writer and producer.

His production skills have been a contributing factor for the success of over fifty album projects for such artists as Bishop TD Jakes, Richard Smallwood and Vision, Vickie Winans, Donnie McClurkin and the McClurkin Family, the Winans, Shirley Caesar, Maurette Brown-Clark, the Mighty Clouds of Joy, the Williams Brothers, John P. Kee, Bishop Carlton Pearson, Phyllis Hyman, Pieces of a Dream, the New York Voices, Bishop Merritt and the Straight Gate Mass Choir, the Dallas Ft. Worth Mass Choir, the Potter's House Mass Choir, and others. Ford has taught many symposiums and workshops on music ministry in the African American Church and the music industry.

Leana A. Fox

MILITARY. Leana A. Fox is a native of Saint Marys, Pennsylvania. She received a bachelor of science degree in nursing from Indian University of Pennsylvania in 1982 and a master of science degree in nursing administration and a certificate in nursing education from George Mason University, Fairfax, Virginia. She completed the Army Medical Department officer basic and advanced courses, the Command and General Staff College, and U.S. Army War College.

Fox began her military career in the U.S. Army Reserves as an enlisted soldier serving with units of the 99th Army Reserve Command. She received her commission through Reserve Officer Training Corps (ROTC) in 1980 and served as a platoon leader and personnel officer, Medical Clearing Company, Altoona, Pennsylvania. She began her active duty career as a medical surgical nurse. She participated in Reforger; as a senior clinical nurse, neonatal intensive care unit; as head nurse, OB/GYN clinic and evening night supervisor; chief, nurse education and staff development; chief nurse, 85th General Hospital, where she participated in the 1997 National Boy Scout Jamboree; head nurse, general medicine; as the commandant, Graduate School of Nursing, Uniformed Services University of the Health Sciences; and chief, nursing administration, 67th Combat Support Hospital, where she participated in Operation Iraqi Freedom as officer-in-charge. Colonel Fox currently serves as the deputy commander for nursing of the 18th Medical Command.

Betty Hager Francis

LOCAL GOVERNMENT. Betty Hager Francis is a native of Washington, D.C. She received a bachelor of

arts degree in political science from Howard University in 1967 and earned her juris doctor from Suffolk University Law School. Francis worked in the Capitol Hill office of Indiana Senator Birch Bayh and in the Ed Brooke U.S. Senate campaign. From 1980 to 1981, she worked as an attorney for Boston Legal Services, where she handled family and probate matters. She served with the Boston Housing Authority as an attorney.

In 1984, she was appointed commissioner of the Massachusetts Department of Public Works by Governor Michael Dukakis. She was appointed deputy chief counsel and chief administrative law judge with the Massachusetts Department of Public Works. In 1991, she was appointed director of Public Works in Washington, D.C. by Mayor Sharon Pratt Kelley. She was responsible for five thousand employees and an $800 million budget. In 1995, she was named director of the Prince George's County, Maryland, Department of Public Works and Transportation.

Tene Hamilton Franklin

SCIENCE. Tene Hamilton Franklin received a bachelor's degree in biology from the University of Virginia and earned a master's degree from Howard University in Washington, D.C. Franklin has served as a genetic counselor, providing information and guidance to families concerning genetic disorders, conditions, and the possibilities of such. She works with Tuskegee University's National Center for Bioethics and Health Care as a facilitator of a grant dealing with the Human Genome Project's ethical, legal, and social implications, especially concerning minorities. When the National Institute for the Humanities provided Tuskegee University the grant, she felt uniquely qualified and began her current work.

Greg Frazier

ENGINEERING. Greg Frazier attended the public schools of Baltimore, Maryland, and attended the prestigious Baltimore Polytechnic Institute, which trains high school students for careers in science and engineering. In 1985, he received a bachelor of science in aerospace engineering from the University of Maryland at College Park. He joined NASA in 1985 as an entry-level engineer and worked his way up to Interstellar Boundary Explorer (IBEX) mission manager. He works in aerospace engineering as the IBEX mission manager at NASA's Goddard Space Flight Center in Maryland. He is assisting Southwest Research Institute with evaluating the rocketry aspects of the mission, which includes the maneuvers that will occur when IBEX separates from the *Pegasus* launch vehicle.

Stephenie Frazier

BUSINESS. Stephenie Frazier is a native of Georgia. She received her bachelor's degree from Georgia Institute of Technology and earned her juris doctor degree from Howard University School of Law. Frazier has operated her own business and financial consulting firm in Washington, D.C., and opened the Atlanta office for a Mid-Atlantic asset-based lender, working to meet the needs of small to medium sized companies for more than 10 years. She is the founding chair of the Georgia Lenders Quality Circle, a trade association for lenders providing government-guaranteed loans to businesses. She is involved with the Atlanta Business League, serving as a member of the board of directors. She currently is vice president and relationship manager, Business Banking Group, for Wachovia Bank, N.A.

Everette J. Freeman

EDUCATION. Everette J. Freeman is a native of Washington, D.C. He received a bachelor of arts degree in sociology and economics from Antioch College in 1972 and a master of arts degree in labor and industrial relations from the University of Illinois in 1974. He earned an Ed.D. in education foundations from Rutgers University in 1983, and holds a certificate from the Institute for Educational Leadership at Harvard University and a certificate in economics from Fircroft College in Birmingham, England.

Freeman's rise through the academic ranks is evidenced by the caliber of programs he helped develop during his 14 years in higher education leadership and 19 years as a faculty member. He has held several cor-

porate positions and has specialized interest in organizational development, Equal Employment Opportunity Commission compliance and industrial relations.

Freeman was the executive assistant to the president at Tennessee State University, where he was also interim vice president for university relations and development. He served four years as senior vice president and provost at the University of Indianapolis. He was named the eighth president of Albany State University on September 7, 2005, by the Board of Regents of the University System of Georgia. He officially took office on October 10, 2005.

Myron Eugene Freeman

LAW ENFORCEMENT. Myron Eugene Freeman is a native of Atlanta, Georgia, and a graduate of Luther Judson Price High School in 1968. He received a bachelor of science degree in criminal justice and a master of public administration degree from Brenau College, Gainesville, Georgia. He is a graduate of the FBI National Academy in Quantico, Virginia.

Freeman served in the United States Army as a military policeman at Fort Dix, New Jersey, and was honorably discharged in 1971. He joined the Georgia State Patrol in 1972 and was assigned to the patrol post in Savannah, Georgia. He was assigned to the governor's mansion, becoming the first African American to work executive security. He was later promoted to corporal under Governor Jimmy Carter. While serving as security aide for Governor George D. Busbee, he was promoted to sergeant, lieutenant and captain. He was selected to serve as the supervisor and head of security for the Georgia governor and became the first African American to hold these positions. In 1983, he transferred to Georgia State Patrol Headquarters as administrative assistant in the personnel and training division. In 1989, he was named division director and promoted to the rank of major.

By 1993, he reached another first in Georgia history, when Governor Zell Miller appointed him the first African American deputy commissioner of the Office of Public Safety. Later, Governor Roy Barnes appointed him to the transition team for the newly created Office of Motor Vehicle Safety, where he would serve as the agency's accreditation and certification officer. He retired from the State Patrol at the rank of lieutenant colonel. On November 2, 2004, Freeman was elected sheriff of Fulton County, Georgia.

George T. French, Jr.

EDUCATION. George T. French, Jr., is a native of Louisville, Kentucky, and served at Miles College for nearly 10 years before being named its 14th president. He succeeded the late Albert J.H. Sloan II, who died in November 2005 after a long illness. French was interim president for the institution beginning December 14, 2005. Under his leadership, the college conducted the largest capital campaign fund drive in its history, raising $12 million. He was also the driving force behind construction projects totaling nearly $24 million in renovations and new buildings across campus.

Jeff Friday

FILM. Jeff Friday received a bachelor's degree cum laude in finance from Howard University and a master of business administration from New York University's Leonard Stern School of Business. Friday served as a product marketer, entertainment executive and entrepreneur. Before making his official entry into the film industry, he held marketing positions with Bristol Myers International, the Mingo Group, and Schieffelin and Somerset Company.

Friday entered the film business in 1996 when he became president of UniWorld Films, a division of UniWorld Group, Inc. His success there put him at the forefront of the independent black film movement and solidified his commitment to transforming the business of black cinema. Under his direction, the company founded the Acapulco Black Film Festival and assisted studios in marketing movies to the African American audience, including DreamWorks' film release *Amistad*. In 2001, he acquired UniWorld Films, re-

naming it Film Life, Inc., and assumed the position of CEO. The Acapulco Black Film Festival moved stateside in 2002 and became the American Black Film Festival (abff). He is also the creator and executive producer of the Black Movie Awards, a star-studded award ceremony celebrating black cinema. In October 2005, the Black Movie Awards made its national television debut on Turner Television Network.

Henry E. Frye

JUDICIAL. Henry E. Frye is a native of Ellerbe, North Carolina. He received a bachelor's degree from North Carolina A&T State University and earned his juris doctor degree from the University of North Carolina Chapel Hill School of Law, where he graduated with honors. Frye served two years in the United States Air Force and continued active duty in the Air Force Reserves, where he obtained the rank of captain. He founded Greensboro National Bank (now Mutual Community Savings Bank) and was its president from 1971 until 1981. In 1983, Frye was appointed to the North Carolina Supreme Court. This appointment made him the first African American to serve on the North Carolina Supreme Court. He successfully ran for eight-year terms on the Supreme Court in 1984 and 1992.

Kenneth Funderburg

MILITARY. Kenneth Funderburg received an associate in applied science degree in architectural science at Florida A&M University and an associate degree in applied science, intelligence and imagery analysis, at the Community College of the Air Force. His military education includes the material facilities management course, noncommissioned officer orientation course, target intelligence apprentice course, Noncommissioned Officer Leadership School, the U.S. Army survival instructor course, helicopter combat aircrew training, joint special operations intelligence course, Defense Intelligence College, Senior Noncommissioned Officer Academy, joint target course, Joint Targeting School, and U.S. Air Force senior leadership course.

Funderburg entered the U.S. Air Force in September 1978. Throughout his career, he has held positions in supply, early warning surveillance radar maintenance, intelligence, combat search and rescue, and special operations, at base, Major Command, and joint assignment levels. He specialized in kinetic and non-kinetic targeting, all source intelligence production, joint special operations at the air and ground component levels, joint operations planning, air operations at the air and ground component levels, and joint source intelligence production. He has deployed in support of Operations Just Cause, Desert Storm, Provide Promise, Restore/Uphold Democracy, and numerous classified and joint task force contingency operations. Before assuming his current position, he was the command chief master sergeant for the 480th Intelligence Wing. He serves as the command chief master sergeant, 55th Wing, Offutt Air Force Base in Nebraska. He is the principal enlisted advisor for more than 7,800 enlisted airmen assigned to the largest wing in the U.S. Air Force.

Brenda Gaines

BUSINESS. Brenda Gaines received a bachelor of arts degree from the University of Illinois at Urbana-Champaign and her master of public administration from Roosevelt University in Chicago, Illinois. Gaines has served as deputy chief of staff to Chicago's Mayor Harold Washington. She was responsible for the implementation of mayoral initiatives, development of policies and goals and co-management of the daily operations of the city's 42 operating departments. She also was commissioner of the Department of Housing for the City of Chicago and held a series of increasingly responsible positions at the regional level for the U.S. Department of Housing and Urban Development. She was named president and chief executive officer of Diners Club North America, a member of Citigroup.

Ronald Gaines

MILITARY. Ronald Gaines is a native of Manhattan, New York, and grew up in Wedgefield, South Carolina, where he graduated from Hillcrest High School in June 1980. He received a bachelor of science from Southern Illinois University. After attending Sumter Area Technical College in Sumter he joined the Navy as a fireman recruit in May 1983. He completed basic training in

Great Lakes, Illinois, and then went on to machinist, cryogenics and gas turbine system electrical schools. He also completed the senior enlisted propulsion course and the gas turbine marine inspector course.

Gaines's key leadership assignments include serving on board the USS *Caron* as main propulsion leading chief petty officer. After completion of his sea tour, he was transferred to Naval Training Center Great Lakes as an instructor and student advisor; there he was promoted to the rank of senior chief petty officer. He currently serves as the command master chief petty officer, U.S. Navy surface warfare specialist.

Willie E. Gary

BUSINESS. Willie E. Gary was born one of 11 children in Eastman, Georgia, and raised in migrant farming communities in Florida, Georgia and the Carolinas. He received a football athletic scholarship to college. He earned a bachelor's degree in business administration from Shaw University in Raleigh, North Carolina, where he was the co-captain of Shaw's football team during the 1969, 1970 and 1971 seasons. He earned his juris doctor from North Carolina Central University in Durham, North Carolina in 1974.

Gary serves in private law practice. His practice has grown into the a thriving national partnership consisting of 37 attorneys, a team of paralegals, and a professional staff of 120, including six nurses, two full-time investigators, an administrator, a certified public accountant, a public relations director, a general counsel, human resources director, and a full administrative staff. The firm operates out of three posh waterfront offices — two located on the St. Lucie River in historic downtown Stuart, Florida, and the third overseeing the Indian River Lagoon in Fort Pierce, Florida.

Gary is the chairman of the Black Family Channel, the nation's only African American owned and operated 24-hour cable channel devoted to wholesome "family values" programming aimed at urban viewers. In 1991, he donated $10.1 million to his alma mater, Shaw University. He has also donated hundreds of thousands of dollars to dozens of historically black colleges and universities throughout the United States. In 1994, he and his wife, Gloria, formed the Gary Foundation to carry out this formidable task. It provides scholarships, direction and other resources to youth so they can realize their dreams of achieving a higher education.

Leah Gaskin-Fitchue

MINISTRY. Leah Gaskin-Fitchue received a bachelor of arts degree in speech pathology from Rutgers University and a master of science degree in speech pathology from the University of Michigan. She earned a master of divinity degree from Princeton Theological Seminary and a Ph.D. in education administration, planning and social policy from Harvard University.

Gaskin-Fitchue is an ordained itinerant elder in the African Methodist Episcopal (A.M.E.) Church. She has served as an associate minister at Mother Bethel A.M.E. Church in Philadelphia, Pennsylvania, Jones Tabernacle A.M.E. Church in Philadelphia, and Mt. Zion A.M.E. Church in Trenton, New Jersey. She has served as the associate professor of urban ministry at Eastern Seminary, where she was the first full-time African American female faculty member in 1992. In 1995, she was appointed director of the doctor of ministry program in the Renewal of the Church for Mission.

Gaskin-Fitchue is the first African American woman to serve as director of a doctor of ministry program in the Association of Doctor of Ministry Educators. Also, in 1995 she became the first African American woman in the 70 year history of the seminary to receive tenure. In late 2003, Gaskin-Fitchue was named president of Payne Theological Seminary. She is the first woman to serve the seminary in that capacity in its 160 years.

Denise J. Gatling

BUSINESS. Denise J. Gatling received a bachelor's degree in business administration from North Carolina A&T State University and a master's in business administration from Meredith College in

North Carolina. Her career began with the former Glaxo Wellcome (now GlaxoSmithKline) in May 1986 as a marketing accountant. Throughout her career, she held various positions within finance, supporting numerous business units. In 1996, she transitioned to her current role as manager of supplier diversity. She is responsible for leading the company's supplier diversity initiative by implementing successful strategies and processes to ensure compliance and active participation.

Darrin P. Gayles

JUDICIAL. Darrin P. Gayles received a bachelor of arts degree from Howard University in 1990 and earned his juris doctor degree from George Washington University in 1993. Gayles' legal career includes serving as an assistant state attorney from 1993 to 1997; as an assistant district attorney from 1997 to 1999; and as an assistant United States attorney from 1999 to 2004. He was appointed a county court judge to the Miami-Dade Circuit in Florida.

Cedric George

MILITARY, ENGINEERING. Cedric George received a bachelor of science in electrical engineering from Norwich University in Vermont and a master of science in management from Troy State University in Alabama. He earned a master of military operational art and science (distinguished graduate) at Air Command and Staff College and a master of national resource strategy (distinguished graduate) at the Industrial College of Armed Forces. His military education includes Squadron Officer School, Maxwell Air Force Base in Alabama; Air War College at Maxwell; acquisition, all requisite courses; level III advanced program management certification; training senior acquisition course at Fort McNair in Washington, D.C.; training joint combat airspace command and control course; squadron and group commanders course; and the U.S. Army Airborne and Air Assault schools.

George has held numerous staff and command positions: from 2001 to 2003 as branch chief, Joint Strike Fighter, at the Pentagon in Washington, D.C.; in April 2003, deputy chief, Air Superiority Division, Pentagon; and in August 2003, commander, 49th Aircraft Maintenance Squadron, Holloman Air Force Base, New Mexico. In July 2006, he assumed his current assignment as commander, 35th Maintenance Group, 35th Fighter Wing, Misawa Air Base in Japan. He is responsible for approximately 1,300 aircraft and a budget of over $6 million.

Barbara Gilchrist

MILITARY. Barbara Gilchrist is a native of Blackstone, Virginia. She received a bachelor's degree (cum laude) in accounting from the University of North Carolina in Greensboro and a master's degree (summa cum laude) in business administration from Embry-Riddle Aeronautical University. She earned a master's degree in strategic studies at Air War College. Her military education includes: Squadron Officer School at Maxwell Air Force Base in Alabama; Marine Command and Staff College; Air Command and Staff College at Maxwell; Professional Military Comptroller School at Maxwell; and Air War College at Maxwell.

From July 1997 to July 2000 she was comptroller commander at Barksdale Air Force Base in Louisiana. From July 2000 to April 2002 she was chief of the Budget Operations Branch at Headquarters U.S. Air Force in Europe, at Ramstein Air Base in Germany. In April 2002, she became chief of the financial analysis division, Headquarters U.S. Air Force Europe. From June 2004 to May 2005 she was military assistant, assistant secretary of the Air Force (financial management) at the Pentagon. In May 2005, Colonel Gilchrist was assigned as comptroller at Headquarters Air Education and Training Command, Randolph Air Force Base, Texas. She has oversight of a budget of over $8 billion and pay services for over 100,000 personnel at 13 major bases.

Ida L. Gillis

LAW ENFORCEMENT. Ida L. Gillis is a native of Gary, Indiana. She graduated from Indiana State University, where she received a bachelor of science in 1974 and a master of science degree in 1977. She is a graduate of the U.S. Postal Inspector Academy and accounting at Roosevelt University, Chicago, Illinois, during 1981 through 1983. She passed the Uniform Certified Public Accountant (cpa) examination in 1985. She is licensed by the State of Pennsylvania Certified Public Accountancy Board. In 1988, she attended the Fuqua School of Busi-

ness executive program at Duke University. In August 1989, she completed training program for postal executives at the University of Virginia.

Gillis was appointed postal inspector in October 1978 and was assigned to the Chicago Division, recently renamed the Northern Illinois Division. While in Chicago, she worked a variety of investigations but was primarily assigned to external crimes and audit. In May 1985, she was promoted to program manager, Central Region, Chicago, Illinois. In January 1987, she was selected for the postal service career executive candidate list. Gillis was promoted to inspector in charge, Hartford Division, in November 1987. Effective April 1989, she was promoted to assistant regional chief inspector, Eastern Region. She became the first African American woman to serve in this position, with the oldest federal law enforcement organization.

In May 1993, Gillis was appointed inspector in charge of the Washington Division. On July 5, 1994, she was appointed to her current position, inspector in charge, Northern Illinois Division, in Chicago. In September 2001, she became deputy chief inspector for professional standards and resource development. She is the first African American woman to serve in this position with the U.S. Postal Inspection Service. She was also a member of the National Organization of Black Law Enforcement Executives (NOBLE). She received a one year sabbatical August 2000 to July 2001 to serve as the president and CEO of NOBLE. She has also served on numerous community and diversity groups and received numerous awards.

Andrew D. Gillum

LOCAL GOVERNMENT. Andrew D. Gillum is a native of Miami, Florida, and graduated from Gainesville High School in 1998. He received a bachelor's degree in political science from Florida A&M University and is a graduate of College Leadership Florida, Class IV. He was the first student member of the Florida A&M University's board of trustees and presidential search committee. At age 23, Gillum became the youngest person elected a commissioner to the Tallahassee City Commission in February 2003. At the time of the election, he was a student at Florida A&M University. In August 2004, he was re-elected by the citizens of Tallahassee to serve for a full four-year term.

Larry D. Gilpin

MILITARY. Larry D. Gilpin is a native of Thomson, Georgia. He is a 1979 graduate of the Career Academy School of Radio and TV Broadcasting, the Georgia Military College in 1997, and the Interdenominational Theological Center in 2006. His military education includes basic combat training, radio relay carrier attendant, senior leadership course, senior noncommissioned officer (NCO) course, unit supply course, Senior NCO Academy, intel analyst course, and the U.S. Army Sergeants Major Academy.

Gilpin entered the U.S. Army on March 16, 1966. During his 34 year career in the Army Reserves he has held numerous leadership positions, including with the 335th Signal Command in East Point, Georgia, as a radio relay chief, detachment sergeant, intel sergeant, chief supply sergeant, equal opportunity NCO, intel noncommissioned officer in charge, operations sergeant major, and chief log service supervisor. In December 1997, he was assigned as the command sergeant major of the 7th Battalion, 108th, 4th Brigade, Decatur, Georgia. Beginning December 2000, he was the command sergeant major of the 3rd Battalion 108th, 3rd Brigade at Fort Gordon, Georgia. He retired from the U.S. Army Reserves in January 2007.

Gilpin has served with the U.S. Postal Service as a human resources specialist in training. He manages a facility that provides training for more than 300 post offices in the Atlanta, Georgia, District. He is responsible for supervising the facilitators that train the post office sales and service associates, lead sales and services associates, driver instructors and the rural and city carriers.

Maria Goodloe-Johnson

EDUCATION. Maria Goodloe-Johnson holds a doctor of philosophy degree and is a graduate of the Broad Foundation's Urban Superintendent Academy, which provides intensive training for urban school district administrators. Goodloe-Johnson has spent two decades running schools, most recently as a superintendent, and before that as an assistant superintendent.

She has served as a cross country and girls' soccer coach; special education teacher in Colorado; administrative assistant, Hinkley High School, Aurora, Col-

orado; high school principal, Broomfield High School in Boulder, Colorado; and assistant superintendent, Corpus Christi (Texas) Independent School District. Goodloe-Johnson was named superintendent of Charleston County School District in South Carolina, overseeing 43,000 students at 80 schools over 1,000 square miles.

Della McGraw Goodwin

NURSING. Della McGraw Goodwin is a native of Claremore, Oklahoma, and moved to Little Rock, Arkansas, where she graduated from Paul Laurence Dunbar High School in 1950. She entered nursing training at Freedmen's Hospital at Howard University in Washington, D.C., and earned her diploma in nursing in 1955. She earned her bachelor of science degree in nursing in 1959 and a master's degree in nursing in 1962, both from Wayne State University in Detroit, Michigan.

Goodwin was a teacher in the nursing program of Providence Hospital from 1963 to 1964. In 1964, she was named director of nursing at Boulevard General Hospital. She became dean of the nursing program of Wayne County Community College in 1970. She retired as dean of the Wayne County Community College nursing program in 1986. She also served as president of the Comprehensive Health Planning Council of Southeastern Michigan.

Michelle Gourdine

PUBLIC HEALTH. Michelle Gourdine received her medical doctor degree from the Johns Hopkins School of Medicine in Baltimore, Maryland, and was a resident in the Department of Pediatrics there. Dr. Gourdine was selected to serve as the deputy director of the Maryland Department of Health and Mental Hygiene. She is the first African American health officer in Baltimore County and the second highest health officer in the state. In this position, she provides executive level management and leadership for all public health programs and county health departments throughout the state. As deputy secretary, Dr. Gourdine oversees seven administrations, along with the office of chief medical examiner, the anatomy board and 24 local health departments in Maryland.

Mirian Graddick-Weir

BUSINESS. Mirian Graddick-Weir received a bachelor of arts degree in psychology from Hampton University in 1976. She has earned a master of science degree and a Ph.D., both in industrial and organizational psychology and both from Penn State University. Graddick-Weir served for over twenty years with AT&T in human resources positions, as director, vice president, chief human resources officer and executive vice president. In 2006, she was named senior vice president of human resources at Merck and Company.

Wendell M. Graham

JUDICIAL. Wendell M. Graham received a bachelor of arts from Columbia University in 1978 and earned his juris doctor degree from the University of Miami in 1983. He was admitted to Florida bar in 1983. He has served as an assistant state attorney from 1983 to 1988; from 1989 to 1991, as a traffic magistrate judge; from 1990 to 1994, as a hearing officer for Dade County (Florida) Public Schools; and sole practitioner, criminal and administrative law, from 1988 to 1994. Since 1994, he served as a judge on the Dade County Court.

Terrance D. Grant-Malone

MINISTRY. Terrance D. Grant-Malone received a bachelor of arts degree in English from Huston-Tillotson College in Austin, Texas, and earned a master of arts from Aspen Christian College and Theological Seminary in Denver, Colorado. He completed studies at Lamar University and special seminars at the Seminario Evangelico in San Juan, Puerto Rico, and earned a Ph.D. in Christian education. Grant-Malone was baptized August 29, 1983, at the Sunlight Baptist Church in Beaumont, Texas. He accepted his call to the ministry at age fifteen. He was a licensed and ordained minister at Fellowship Baptist Church in Beaumont, Texas. Grant-Malone served as the former vice-president of the 1.5

million members of the National Baptist Youth and Young Adult Convention of America, Inc. He is the pastor of St. John Missionary Baptist Church in Houston, Texas.

Earl G. Graves, Jr.

PUBLISHING. Earl G. Graves, Jr., earned a bachelor of arts degree in economics from Yale University in 1984 and a master of business administration from Harvard University. He was a four-year starter and captain of the Yale basketball team. He became the school's all-time leading scorer and finished his college basketball career as the second leading scorer in Ivy League history. He was drafted in the third round by the National Basketball Association's Philadelphia 76ers in 1984 and enjoyed a brief professional basketball career with the Milwaukee Bucks and Cleveland Cavaliers.

Graves joined Black Enterprise in 1988 as senior vice president of advertising and marketing; in 1995, he was named the executive vice president and chief operating officer. In 1998, he was appointed president and CEO of Black Enterprise and Earl Graves Publishing, Inc., publisher of *Black Enterprise* magazine. He is responsible for the strategic positioning of the corporation and its overall profitability.

James E. Graves, Jr.

JUDICIAL. James E. Graves, Jr., is a graduate of Sumner Hill High School in Clinton, Mississippi, where he was valedictorian. He received a bachelor of arts degree in sociology from Millsaps College and his juris doctor degree from Syracuse University College of Law. He also earned a master of public administration degree from the Maxwell School of Citizenship and Public Affairs at Syracuse University, Syracuse, New York.

Graves has served in private law practice. As a special assistant attorney general, he was head of the Human Services Division of the Attorney General's Office of Mississippi. He was the director of the Division of Child Support Enforcement of the Mississippi Department of Human Services. In February 1991, he was appointed a Mississippi circuit judge. He gained the position in a special election in September 1991. He was re-elected without opposition in 1994 and 1998. Graves was appointed by the Mississippi governor to serve as a justice on the Mississippi Supreme Court on November 1, 2001. He was elected in November 2004 to a full term.

Bernadette Gray-Little

EDUCATION. Bernadette Gray-Little is a native of Washington, North Carolina. She received a bachelor's degree from Marywood College in Scranton, Pennsylvania, and a Ph.D. in clinical psychology from St. Louis University in 1970. She has earned fellowships from the National Research Council, the Fulbright program, the Ford Foundation and the National Institute of Mental Health. She is a fellow of the American Psychological Association and associate editor of the journal *American Psychologist.*

Gray-Little has served in numerous leadership positions at the University of North Carolina at Chapel Hill since joining the faculty in 1971. A professor of psychology, she was named executive associate provost in 2001, serving as the top advisor to the university's chief academic officer. She has also served as the director of the graduate program in clinical psychology (1983–1993), as chair of the department of psychology (1993–1998) and as a faculty affiliate at the Center for Creative Leadership (1998–2003). Gray-Little is currently the dean of the College of Arts and Sciences at UNC Chapel Hill.

Samuel A. Greaves

MILITARY. Samuel A. Greaves received a bachelor of science degree in electrical engineering from Cornell University, Ithaca, New York, in 1982 and a master of science in computer science from West Coast University, Los Angeles, California, in 1984. He has also received a master of strategic studies from the Air War College at Maxwell Air Force Base. His military education includes: Squadron Officer's School, Maxwell Air Force Base, Alabama (1986); level III acquisition professional development program certification in program management (1994); distinguished graduate, Air Command and Staff Course, Maxwell (1997); undergraduate space and missile training, staff course, Vandenberg Air Force Base in California (1997); Air War College (correspondence), with distinction "Excellent," Maxwell (1999); and program manager's course, Defense Systems Management College, Fort Belvoir, Virginia, in 2003.

Greaves was commissioned in 1982 through the Air

Force Reserve Officer Training Corps program after graduating from Cornell University. He has held a variety of assignments in operational, acquisition, and staff units. His assignments include positions at Headquarters Air Combat Command; the National Reconnaissance Office; within the Directorate of Operational Requirements and the Air Force Colonel Matters Office at Headquarters U.S. Air Force; and as material group director for the Air Force Satellite Control Network Program at Los Angeles Air Force Base. From June 2004 to August 2006, he was commander of the 45th Launch Group, 45th Space Wing, Cape Canaveral. Colonel Greaves has held the position of commander, Launch and Range Systems Wing, Los Angeles Air Force Base, California, since August 2006.

Bobbie Green

EDUCATION. Bobbie Green is a native of Las Cruces, New Mexico. She received a bachelor's degree in English from the University of Southern California and a master of business administration from City University in Seattle, Washington. She earned a Ph.D. from Seattle University. Green was selected to serve as the director of the master of business administration program in the New Mexico State University College of Business, Las Cruces, New Mexico.

Clifford Scott Green

JUDICIAL. Clifford Scott Green is a native of Philadelphia, Pennsylvania. He received a bachelor of science degree from Temple University in 1948 and earned his juris doctor from Temple University School of Law in 1951. He served in the United States Air Force from 1943 to 1946 (as sergeant). He was an instructor at William Penn Business Institute from 1951 to 1952. He worked in private practice in Philadelphia, Pennsylvania, from 1952 to 1964 and as a special deputy commonwealth attorney general, Pennsylvania, 1954 to 1955. He was a lecturer in law at Temple University from 1968 to 1971, then a judge on the County Court of Common Pleas in Philadelphia from 1964 to 1972.

Judge Green was nominated by President Richard M. Nixon on December 1, 1971, to serve as a federal judge to the U.S. District Court for the Eastern District of Pennsylvania. He was confirmed by the U.S. Senate on December 4, 1971, and received his commission on December 9, 1971. He assumed senior status on April 2, 1988.

Edgar L. Green

MILITARY. Edgar L. Green is a native of Pocomoke City, Maryland. He received a bachelor of science degree in education and a master's degree in management. He is a graduate of the Senior Enlisted Academy, Class 92 (Blue) in Newport, Rhode Island. Green enlisted in the Navy on May 11, 1981. He attended recruit training at Recruit Training Command, Great Lakes, Illinois, and Operations Specialist "A" School at Fleet Training Center, Dam Neck, Virginia Beach, Virginia. He has held numerous leadership positions, including serving on the USS *Harry S. Truman* (CVN 75) home ported in Norfolk, Virginia, as the operations department master chief. While onboard the *Truman*, he completed one Indian Ocean deployment and one Mediterranean deployment in support of Operations Enduring Freedom and Iraqi Freedom. He has also completed a tour of duty at Surfane Warfare Development Group, Little Creek, Virginia, as the staff command master chief. In November 2006 Green reported to the staff of commander second fleet as the leading chief of op plans. After being on board for a short period of time, he was selected by commander, Second Fleet, for the position of staff command master chief.

Henry W. Green, Jr.

JUDICIAL. Henry W. Green, Jr., is a native of Leavenworth, Kansas. He received a bachelor's degree with dual majors in history and political science from Kansas State University in 1972 and received his juris doctor from the University of Kansas Law School in 1975. Green was engaged in private practice of law from 1975 to 1993, and was a part-time instructor at the National College of Business in Shawnee Mission. From 1979 until his appointment to the court, he served as a member of the U.S. Panel of Bankruptcy Trustees for the District of Kansas. He currently is a judge on the Kansas Court of Appeals.

James E. Green

JUDICIAL. James E. Green received a bachelor of arts degree from the University of Akron in Ohio in 1980 and earned a juris doctor degree from Ohio State University in 1984. He served as an assistant prosecuting at-

torney from 1984 to 1989. He was an instructor at Columbus State Community College from 1987 to 1995 and was an administrator of Clients Security Fund of Ohio from 1989 to 1995. He was appointed a judge to the Franklin County Municipal Court in Columbus, Ohio, in 1994 and was elected to the court, where he currently serves.

LeRoy Green, Jr.

LAW ENFORCEMENT. LeRoy Green, Jr., is a native of Kansas City, Kansas. He attended schools on both sides of the river. After graduating from Bishop Ward High School he later attended Kansas City Kansas Community College. Green is the son of a professional boxer and later became a Golden Gloves champion as well as a professional boxer himself, claiming the title of Midwest Middleweight Champion. He began his career with the Wyandotte County Sheriff's Office in 1978 when he was employed as a detention deputy. In 1982, Green commanded the Wyandotte County Tag Enforcement Unit. In 1985, he was promoted to the rank of sergeant and remained at that rank until 1995, when he was appointed by Sheriff Mike Dailey to be his undersheriff. When Sheriff Dailey resigned, Green made history when he was appointed sheriff of Wyandotte County in 1999 and became the first African American sheriff in the state of Kansas. Green was elected sheriff of Wyandotte County in April 2001 with sixty-four percent of the votes and re-elected in 2005 with seventy-eight percent of the votes.

Samuel Green

MILITARY. Samuel Green is a native of Goodman, Mississippi. He is a graduate of Long Creek High in Sallis, Mississippi. He earned a bachelor of science degree from Embry Riddle University in Daytona Beach, Florida. His military courses include warrant officer aviation basic, rotary wing qualification, fixed wing multi-engine qualification, AH-1 aircraft maintenance officer test pilot, warrant officer senior, Aircraft Repairman-Mechanic School, and Noncommissioned Officer Academy.

Green's military career began on July 30, 1969, when he was drafted into the United States Army. He completed basic training at Fort Bragg, North Carolina, and advance individual training at Fort Eustis, Virginia. His career includes tours of duty in Vietnam in 1970 and part of 1973. He served in Germany from 1976 to 1978 and returned to the United States. His second tour in Germany was from 1983 to 1986. He served in Operations Desert Shield and Desert Storm in 1990 and 1991, and in Korea in 1992–1993. Green's military awards include the Legion of Merit, Bronze Star Medal, Air Medal 6th award , Meritorious Service Medal, Army Commendation Medal, and many others.

Tomie Zean Turner Green

JUDICIAL. Tomie Zean Turner Green was educated in the Jackson (Mississippi) Public Schools. After completing the 11th grade at Jim Hill High School, she entered Tougaloo College, where she obtained her bachelor of arts degree. She earned a master of science degree from Jackson State University and a juris doctor from the Mississippi College School of Law. Green is a graduate of the National Judicial College at the University of Nevada in Reno.

She practiced law for 15 years. She served as a judicial law clerk for federal judge Henry T. Wingate; as an assistant district attorney for Hinds and Yazoo City, Mississippi; and as an adjunct law professor at the Mississippi College School of Law. She served in the Mississippi House of Representatives from 1992 to 1998. Green was the first woman ever elected judge to the Mississippi Hinds County Circuit Court; she took the oath of office on January 4, 1999.

Walter M. Green

JUDICIAL. Walter M. Green received a bachelor of arts degree in psychology from Boston University in 1985. He earned his juris doctor from the University of Florida in 1988. He has served as an Alachua County Court Judge since 2005. He serves in the County Family and Civil Justice Center in Gainesville, Florida. (See photograph on page 86.)

Kevin Greenaugh

ENGINEERING. Kevin Greenaugh received a bachelor's degree in mechanical engineering from Mercer University in Macon, Georgia, in 1977, and he went to Los Alamos National Laboratory to develop non-destructive techniques for analysis of weapons-related radioactive materials. While there, he obtained master's degrees in nuclear engineering and public policy. He designed a nuclear research reactor for Howard University, where he has taught a course in energy engineering since 1987.

He moved in 1990 to the Mitre Corporation to develop a plan to extend the life of the strategic petroleum reserve and conduct studies for the Defense Nuclear Facility Safety Board on radiation protection and fire safety at reactors. Five years later, Greenaugh was selected to run a billion-dollar program for the Department of Energy, Air Force, Navy Strategic Command and Department of Defense to maintain the safety and reliability of the nation's nuclear weapons stockpiles. In 1998, he became the first African American to receive a doctorate in nuclear engineering from the University of Maryland.

Clayton Greene, Jr.

JUDICIAL. Clayton Greene, Jr., is a native of Glen Burnie, Maryland, and a graduate of Northeast High School in Pasadena, Maryland. He received a bachelor of arts degree from the University of Maryland in College Park in 1973 and earned his juris doctor from the University of Maryland School of Law in 1976.

Greene served as an assistant county solicitor for Anne Arundel County from 1977 to 1978; in private law practice from 1977 to 1988; as an assistant public defender from 1978 to 1985; and as deputy public defender, 1985 to 1988. He served as a member of District 7 Anne Arundel County Education Committee, 1989 to 1994; as an administrative judge, District Court of Maryland, District 7, Anne Arundel County, from 1990 to 1995 (associate judge, March 1988 to October 1995); as an administrative judge, Anne Arundel County Circuit Court, 5th Judicial Circuit, from November 1996 to January 4, 2002. Then from January 2002 to January 2004, he was a judge on the Maryland Court of Special Appeals, 5th Appellate Circuit. Since January 2004, Judge Greene has served on the Maryland Court of Appeals, 5th Appellate Circuit.

Karyn Greer

MEDIA. Karyn Greer is a native of Chicago, Illinois. She received a bachelor's degree in broadcast journalism from the University of Illinois at Champaign in 1984. Greer began her broadcast career in September 1983 when WCIA-TV in Champaign hired her as weekend assistant director. In December 1984, she worked for WICD-TV, also in Champaign, as weekend anchor and reporter. She then spent three years at WCSC-TV in Charleston, South Carolina, where she was the solo anchor and reporter and hosted many station events. From WCSC, she moved to WGNX-TV in Atlanta, Georgia. In January 1989, when WGNX launched *News at Ten*, Greer became weekend anchor and medical reporter before serving as the main anchor. She joined 11Alive News in August 1999. She serves the station as a reporter for 11Alive's Special Projects Unit as well as an anchor for *11Alive Weekend*.

Wilton D. Gregory

MINISTRY. Wilton D. Gregory is a native of Chicago, Illinois. He attended Catholic schools in Chicago. He became attracted to the priesthood before he converted to Catholicism, which he did at 11. He studied at Archbishop Quigley Preparatory Seminary, Niles College, and St. Mary of the Lake Seminary before being ordained as a priest on May 9, 1973, by Cardinal John Cody. He received a Ph.D. in sacred liturgy from the

Pontifical Liturgical Institute in Rome in 1980. He holds doctorates of humane letters from Spring Hill College in Mobile, Xavier University in Cincinnati, McKendree College in Lebanon, Lewis University in Romeoville, and Saint Louis University in St. Louis.

Gregory was appointed auxiliary bishop of Chicago and titular bishop of Oliva on October 31, 1983. He received his Episcopal consecration on December 13, 1983. He remained in Chicago until December 29, 1993, when he was appointed the seventh bishop of Belleville; he was installed on February 10, 1994. In 1998, he was elected vice president of the National Conference of Catholic Bishops and in November 2001, he was elected as its president. He is the first African American to serve as president of the National Conference of Catholic Bishops. Pope John Paul II named Bishop Gregory the seventh archbishop of Atlanta on December 9, 2004, and his installation took place on January 17, 2005. He is the second African American to serve as archbishop in Atlanta.

Wendell Griffen

JUDICIAL. Wendell Griffen is a native of Prescott, Arkansas, and grew up near Delight (Pike County), Arkansas. He graduated in 1968 from Delight High School. He received a bachelor of arts degree in political science from the University of Arkansas in 1973 and earned his juris doctor from the University of Arkansas School of Law in 1979. Griffen served in the U.S. Army from 1973 to 1976, attaining the rank of first lieutenant before his honorable discharge. After graduation from law school he worked in private law practice. On April 15, 1985, Governor Bill Clinton appointed him chairman of the Arkansas Worker's Compensation Commission, and Griffen served in that position until February 1987. He returned to private law practice until December 1995, when Governor Jim Guy appointed him a judge on the Arkansas Court of Appeals; he began his judicial service on January 1, 1996.

Stanley Griffin

LAW ENFORCEMENT. Stanley Griffin has over twenty-five years of service with the Louisiana State Police. He embarked on his law enforcement career after receiving his associate degree in criminal justice in 1977 from Southern University in Baton Rouge. He joined the department on January 4, 1981, after serving two years with the Baton Rouge City Police Department. He has attended numerous law enforcement related schools to advance his knowledge and experience in the criminal justice field. On September 8, 2000, he completed the 202nd Session of the FBI National Academy in Quantico, Virginia.

Griffin has served with Troop L in Covington and Troop A in Baton Rouge as a road trooper for approximately eleven years. In March 1992, he accepted assignment in the Video Gaming Section as an investigator, progressing through the ranks to lieutenant to command the section. In November 2000 he achieved the rank of captain of the Narcotics Section, where he commanded approximately ninety employees responsible for enforcing the federal and state drug laws. He was appointed deputy superintendent of support in January 2004, and in June 2006, he was selected to serve as deputy superintendent–chief of staff for the Louisiana State Police. On July 19, 2007, Colonel Griffin was promoted to superintendent of Louisiana State Police and deputy secretary of the Department of Public Safety.

Dorothea Grimes-Frederick

ENGINEERING. Dorothea Grimes-Frederick received a bachelor of science degree in physics from Southern University. She earned a master of science degree and a Ph.D. in science education psychology from Rutgers University. She is also a graduate of the executive education programs from Northwestern University and Duke University. After joining a world-renowned telecommunication research laboratory, Grimes-Frederick became the first African American woman promoted to a senior technical position in that organization's 100-year history. During her 20-year career in Fortune 500 companies, she has led major initiatives

from research and development to operations. She is the president and founder of NuLeaders, Inc., an organization whose focus is cultivating, inspiring and uplifting leaders.

Marlin N. Gusman

LAW ENFORCEMENT. Marlin N. Gusman is a native of New Orleans. He received a bachelor of science degree and a bachelor of arts degree from the University of Pennsylvania, Wharton School of Finance and Commerce and earned his juris doctor degree from Loyola University in New Orleans. He is also a graduate of the New Orleans Chamber Regional Leadership Institute and the Harvard University Kennedy School of Government Program for Senior Executives in State and Local Government.

Gusman has served in private law practice and was a regional tax attorney for the Louisiana Department of Revenue and Taxation handling tax litigation and appeals; between 1994 and 2000, he was the chief administrative officer of the City of New Orleans in the administration of Mayor Marc H. Morial. In his first run for public office in October 2000, he was elected to fill the vacant City Council District D seat in a first primary victory from a field of six candidates. He was re-elected in February 2002. Gusman was elected criminal sheriff of Orleans Parish on November 2, 2004, nine months before Hurricane Katrina made landfall. He was re-elected to a four-year term in the April 2006 primary.

Lloyd "Vic" Hackley

EDUCATION. Lloyd "Vic" Hackley is a native of Roanoke, Virginia. He received a bachelor's degree in political science from Michigan State University in 1965 and a doctorate in international relations from the University of North Carolina at Chapel Hill in 1976. Hackley served as an officer in the U.S. Air Force, retiring in 1978. He joined the University of North Carolina general administration as an assistant vice president and later associate vice president for academic affairs.

In 1981, he left the state to serve as a tenured professor and chancellor of the University of Arkansas at Pine Bluff. In 1985, he was recruited back to the University of North Carolina general administration to become vice president for student services and special programs. Three years later, the unc Board of Governors tapped Hackley to serve as chancellor of Fayetteville State University, a post he held from 1988 to 1995. He is past president of the North Carolina Community College System. He served as the interim deputy chancellor of North Carolina Agricultural and Technical State University until the summer of 2007.

Willie Hagan

EDUCATION. Willie Hagan holds a master of fine arts degree from the University of California Los Angeles and earned a doctorate in psychology from the University of Connecticut. He served as a lobbyist for the University of Connecticut and the Connecticut Board of Governors for Higher Education at the state and federal level. He was associate vice president for administration at the University of Connecticut. In August 1996, he joined Cal State Fullerton as vice president for administration, overseeing the university's administrative functions and providing increased levels of services to the university during a period of unprecedented growth. From July 2000 through 2003, he also served as interim vice president of university advancement and was instrumental in the reorganization of that division. Effective April 1, 2005, Hagan assumed responsibility for university financial operations, serving as the chief financial officer.

John M. Hairston

EDUCATION. John M. Hairston received a bachelor of science degree in English from Bluefield State College in Bluefield, West Virginia, and earned a master's degree in educational administration from Cleveland State University. He has completed courses at John F. Kennedy's School of Public Policy in Cambridge, Massachusetts, Kent State University, and Case Western Reserve University. He spent 27 years with the Cleveland City School Sys-

tem. He held a series of responsible positions there, including English teacher, special project center director, assistant education program manager, staff development director and chief of the community relations department.

He now serves as director of the external programs at the National Aeronautics and Space Administration's John H. Glenn Research Center. He was appointed to this position in June 1991. He is responsible for the development and implementation of outreach, educational and informational programs that contribute to scientific literacy and strengthen awareness and participation of target groups in the center's mission and vision.

Sophia Hall

JUDICIAL. Sophia Hall is a native of Chicago, Illinois. After attending a parochial school, she went to the University of Chicago Laboratory School, a high school program for gifted students. She received a bachelor of arts degree in history from the University of Wisconsin in 1964 and earned her juris doctor degree from Northwestern University School of Law in 1967. Hall worked in private law practice until she was elected a Cook County judge in 1980. In 1983, she became the first female judge to serve in the Criminal Court of Cook County in twenty years. In 1992, she served as the presiding judge of the juvenile division and later the presiding judge of juvenile justice and child protection assigned to the Chancery Division. In 1998, President Bill Clinton appointed Judge Hall to serve on the Board of the State Justice Institute.

Tanya Forrest Hall

SPORTS. Tanya Forrest Hall is a graduate of Syracuse University; she holds a degree in retailing and has also completed courses in sports marketing and management at New York University. Hall worked for four years for Newark Sports and Entertainment, a wholly owned subsidiary of YankeeNets owned by the New Jersey Nets, New York Yankees, New Jersey Devils and the yes Network. She also worked as assistant manager of marketing and operations for Empire Sports and Entertainment and for Bloomingdale's Department Stores as a buyer and manager.

She served with American Urban Radio Networks, more than 475 radio stations nationwide with an estimated 25 million listeners. As marketing and promotions manager, she was responsible for generating sales, managing major events, radio remotes and national promotional campaigns, development and placement of media, and the creation of marketing materials. She joined the Atlanta Braves, a division of Turner Broadcasting System and Major League Baseball's winningest franchise since 1991, as the senior manager of multicultural marketing, responsible for all projects related to the organization's commitment to reaching out to a more diverse fan base.

Edith Amos Hambie

SCIENCE. Edith Amos Hambie received a bachelor of science degree in biology from Georgia State University and a master of science degree in microbiology from Atlanta University. Hambie is a health scientist and research microbiologist for Centers for Disease Control and Prevention and was a member of the Decatur Board of Education from 1976 to 1998, also serving as chair. She is a member of the American Society for Microbiology, the Scientific Research Society of North America, in Georgia.

Carolyn Hamilton-Evans

MILITARY. Carolyn Hamilton-Evans is a native of Shreveport, Louisiana. Her military career spans 26 years. During this time she has held numerous supervisory and leadership positions, including as a supply squadron commander at MacDill Air Force Base in Tampa, Florida. She currently serves as the Defense Supply Center Philadelphia's assistant deputy commander and chief of staff. She is the principal staff assistant and advisor to Defense Supply Center Philadelphia's commander and deputy commander.

Delon Hampton

ENGINEERING, EDUCATION. Delon Hampton received several degrees from Purdue University and the New Jersey Institute of Technology. He received his master's degree in civil engineering in 1958 from the University of Illinois, his Ph.D. in civil engineering in 1961 and an honorary doctorate from Purdue University.

Hampton was president of the American Society of Civil Engineers from 1999 to 2000, the first and only African American to serve in this position. He has been actively involved in university teaching and research for approximately 25 years. He has published over 40 papers in professional and technical journals. He has also served as an assistant professor at Kansas State University in its civil engineering department. While on leave from Kansas State University, he was head of soil mechanics research at the University of New Mexico's Eric H. Wang Civil Engineering Research Facility in Albuquerque, New Mexico. He took a position as senior research engineer at iit Research Institute in Chicago, Illinois. Hampton then became managing partner in a firm named Gnaedinger, Baker, Hampton and Associates, devoted to providing geotechnical engineering services in the metropolitan Washington, D.C., area.

Robert L. Hampton

EDUCATION. Robert L. Hampton received a bachelor of arts degree from Princeton University. He earned master of arts and Ph.D. degrees from the University of Michigan. Hampton has served as a professor of sociology, as an associate provost for academic affairs and as dean for undergraduate studies at the University of Maryland in College Park, Maryland. He served as president and professor, Department of Social Sciences, at York College of the City University of New York. Hampton is provost and executive vice president at Tennessee State University. He also served in the United States Army Reserve from 1972 to 1996 and retired as a lieutenant colonel.

Cecil D. Haney

MILITARY. Cecil D. Haney is a 1978 graduate of the United States Naval Academy, where he received a bachelor of science degree in ocean engineering. He earned a master's degree in engineering acoustics and system technology from the Naval Post Graduate School and a master's degree in national security strategy from the National Defense University.

He has had assignments aboard the USS *John C. Calhoun* (SSBN 630) in various division officer assignments and aboard the USS *Frank Cable* (AS 40), where he completed surface warfare qualifications while serving as radiological controls officer. He served as engineer aboard the USS *Hyman G. Rickover* (SSN 709), as executive officer aboard the USS *Asheville* (SSN 758), and as assistant squadron deputy at Submarine 8 before taking command of the USS *Honolulu* (SSN 718) in June 1996. He commanded Submarine 1 from June 2002 to July 2004.

Haney's shore duty tours include administrative assistant for enlisted affairs at naval reactors, and congressional appropriations liaison officer for the Office of the Secretary of Defense (Comptroller). His most recent assignment was deputy chief of staff of plans, policies and requirements, U.S. Pacific Fleet. Admiral Haney currently is the commander of Submarine Group 2.

Charlotte Hardnett

JUDICIAL. Charlotte Hardnett received a bachelor's degree in English from Cheyney University in Pennsylvania and a master's degree in library science from Atlanta University. She earned her juris doctor from the University of Idaho. Hardnett began her legal career as an assistant attorney general, Office of the Attorney General, State of Washington. After returning to the East Coast, she was hired as a staff attorney with the Region III Office of the Chief Counsel, Department of Health and Human Services. She advanced to the positions of supervisory attorney, special assistant to the regional chief counsel, acting regional chief counsel, and regional chief counsel in Region

III before transferring to the Social Security Administration as its regional chief counsel when the administration became independent of Department of Health and Human Services in 1995. She was principal deputy general counsel, senior advisor to the general counsel, and acting general counsel. She was appointed an administrative law judge for the Social Security Administration. Hardnett was sworn in as an administrative law judge at the Federal Energy Regulatory Commission in May 2005.

Lisa White Hardwick

JUDICIAL. Lisa White Hardwick is a native of Kansas City, Missouri. She received a bachelor's degree in journalism from the University of Missouri at Columbia in 1982 and a juris doctor from Harvard Law School in 1985. Her professional career began in private law practice in 1985. She was twice elected to the Jackson County, Missouri, Legislature, serving as an at-large representative from 1993 to 2000. From January 2000 to April 2001, she was a trial court judge on the Jackson County Circuit Court in Missouri. She has served as a judge on the Missouri Court of Appeals for the Western District since May 2001. Her current judicial duties include serving as chair of the Missouri Supreme Court's Appellate Practice Commission.

Lubbie Harper, Jr.

JUDICIAL. Lubbie Harper, Jr., is a native of New Haven, Connecticut. He attended local public schools, graduating from Wilbur L. Cross High School. He received a bachelor of science degree from the University of New Haven in 1965 and a master's degree from the University of Connecticut School of Social Work. He earned his juris doctor from the University of Connecticut School of Law in 1975. He has worked in private law practice and as president of the Harper Neighborhood Development Corporation, a not-for-profit corporation created to develop low-income housing for New Haven residents. He also served as president of the Board of Directors of the New Haven Legal Assistance Association, Inc., for twelve years.

Harper was nominated to the Connecticut Superior Court bench in 1997. He served in the Hartford, Fairfield and New Haven judicial districts. In 2005, Governor M. Jodi Rell nominated Judge Harper for elevation to the Connecticut Appellate Court, and on January 26, 2005, he took the oath of office as an appellate court judge.

Sara J. Harper

JUDICIAL. Sara J. Harper is the first African American woman to graduate from Case Western Reserve University Law School; the first woman to serve on the judiciary of the United States Marine Corps Reserve; and to co-found the first victims' rights program in the country.

Harper ran for her first political office, state representative, in 1954. In 1980, she ran as the endorsed Republican candidate for chief justice of the Ohio Supreme Court, the first African American woman to do so. In 1990, Harper and another African American woman became the first women to win seats on the Ohio Court of Appeals. In 1992, she sat by assignment on the Ohio Supreme Court, another first for an African American woman.

Judge Harper is the recipient of many awards, including the Ohio Supreme Court's Excellent Judicial Service Award, the NAACP's Unsung Heroine Award and Raymond Pace Alexander Award. She is a member of the Ohio Veterans Hall of Fame and the National Bar Association Hall of Fame. The Sara J. Harper Library in the Outhwaite Homes housing project is named in her honor.

Carol D. Harris

MEDICINE. Carol D. Harris received her medical doctor degree from the University of Mississippi Medical Center in Jackson, Mississippi. After receiving her medical degree, Dr. Harris completed an internship as well as a residency in anesthesiology at Loyola University in Maywood, Illinois. She completed a pain fellowship at Texas Tech University Health Science at Lubbock, Texas.

Dr. Harris has

been practicing medicine since 1995, serving most recently as an associate anesthesiologist at St. Joseph Provena Hospital in Joliet, Illinois. He treats acute, chronic cancer and post-operative pain patients and pain disorders. Dr. Harris joined the Central Mississippi Medical Center staff and is affiliated with Advanced Diagnostic Pain Center in Jackson, Mississippi. Dr. Harris is board certified in pain management and anesthesiology.

Gloria Harris

MEDICINE. Gloria Harris is a native of Columbia, Georgia. She completed her graduate level work at the Department of Clinical and Health Psychology at the University of Florida, where she received master of science and doctor of philosophy degrees in clinical psychology with a concentration in clinical neuropsychology. She completed an internship at the Psychology Training Consortium at the University of Alabama in Birmingham, where she broadened her training in the areas of geropsychology, acquired brain injuries, and geriatric and adult neuropsychology. She returned to the Department of Clinical and Health Psychology at the University of Florida to complete a postdoctoral fellowship in child neuropsychology and child psychology.

Dr. Harris spent 2000 to 2007 as an independent contractor in Columbus, Georgia, at Columbus Psychological Associates. She serves as part of the Women's Health at Water's Edge with her husband, Dr. J. David Harris, and Dr. Kimberly Fields. Her practice includes comprehensive neuropsychological and psychological assessment of children and adults.

James "Jimmy Jam" Harris III

MUSIC. James "Jimmy Jam" Harris III is a native of Minneapolis, Minnesota. While attending high school in Minneapolis he met Terry Lewis and formed a band called Flyte Tyme, which evolved into The Time. In 1981, they were joined by Morris Day and toured with Prince as Morris Day and the Time. As members of The Time they recorded three of the group's four albums (*The Time, What Time Is It?* and *Pandemonium*. The first two albums are said to have shaped early eighties rhythm and blues music (featuring "Cool," "Get It Up," "The Walk," "777-9311" and "Gigolos Get Lonely Too"). Harris and Lewis were fired from the tour because a blizzard left them unable to rejoin after a short break to produce The SOS Band. However, one of the tracks they produced for The SOS Band, "Just Be Good to Me,"' became a big hit and made their reputation, as well that of the SOS Band.

After working with other artists like Gladys Knight and Luther Vandross, Harris and Lewis were introduced to Janet Jackson and produced her breakthrough album *Control* in 1986, for which the duo won a Grammy Award. The collaboration on her next album, 1989's *Rhythm Nation 1814*, was even more successful. They founded Perspective Records and worked with artists including Jordan Knight, Alexander O'Neal, Patti Austin, Usher, Boyz II Men, Michael Jackson, the Human League, Mariah Carey, Sounds of Blackness, Karyn White, Ralph Tresvant, Mint Condition, Vanessa L. Williams, Yolanda Adams, TLC, Mary J. Blige, Bryan Adams, Cheryl Lynn, and Mya and Utada Hikaru. Harris was selected to serve as chairman of the National Academy of Recording Arts and Sciences.

Leroy Harris

MILITARY. Leroy Harris received a bachelor of science in engineering technology from Savannah State University in Savannah, Georgia, in 1973; earned a master of science in administration and management from Georgia College and State University in Milledgeville in 1988; and earned a second master of science, this one in national security strategy, from the National War College at the National Defense University in Fort McNair, Washington, D.C., in 2002. He has undertaken other studies in the fields of computer science and military leadership.

Harris began his federal service at Robins Air Force Base in Georgia in 1979 with engineering assignments. At the materiel management directorate at Warner Robins Air Logistics Center, Robins Air Force Base, he was electronics engineer (September 1985 to May 1986); chief engineer, item management division (May 1986 to July 1987); chief, Special Operations Forces Helicopter and Fixed Wind Aircraft Engineering Section, System Program Office Division (July to November 1987); chief, Technical Advisor Engineering Branch, Electronic Warfare Management Division (November 1987); and chief, Radar Warning Receiver Branch, Engineering Division (April 1988).

Also at Warner Robins, he was chief, F-15, F-11, and ARL-69 Electronic Warfare Tactical Engineering Branch, Electronic Warfare Management Directorate in June 1992; in April 1995, chief of the Joint Surveillance Target Radar System Software Production Branch, Space and Special Systems Management Directorate, Warner Robins; and in March 1997, chief of Machinery, Materials and Tools, Weapons, Computers, and Bare Base Systems Division, Space and Special Systems Management Directorate.

In February 2001 he was deputy program executive officer, fixed wing aircraft acquisition, Special Operations Command at McDill Air Force Base in Florida. From October 2002 to July 2003, he served as deputy director for space and special systems management directorate at Warner Robins. He was selected as the deputy director for the Intelligence, Surveillance And Reconnaissance Directorate there in July 2003.

Zelema Harris

EDUCATION. Zelema Harris received a bachelor's degree from Prairie View A&M University in Prairie, Texas. She earned a master's degree and Ph.D. in education from the University of Kansas. She was honored with a place in the university's Women's Hall of Fame in 1988. Harris was hired as president of Parkland College in Champaign, Illinois, in 1990. She is the recipient of numerous awards, including President of the Year by the American Association of Women in Community Colleges.

Michael T. Harrison, Sr.

MILITARY. Michael T. Harrison, Sr., received a bachelor of arts degree in English from Howard University and a master of science in administration from Central Michigan University. He earned a master of science in strategy from the United States Army War College. His military education includes Infantry officer basic and advance courses; U.S. Army Command and General Staff College; Armed Forces Staff College; and the U.S. Army War College.

Harrison was commissioned into the U.S. Army on May 28, 1980, through the Reserve Officer Training Corps program. His military assignments include numerous leadership and management positions, serving as a company commander; aide-de-camp to the chairman of the Joint Chiefs of Staff in Washington, D.C.; small groups instructor; logistics officer; operations officer, Counternarcotics Division; battalion commander; brigade commander; chief, Dominant Maneuver Division; executive officer to the deputy chief of staff; chief, Joint Requirements and Assessments Division, Office of the Deputy Chief of Staff; and deputy commanding general (programs), Combined Security Transition Command — Afghanistan, Operation Enduring Freedom. General Harrison is the deputy commanding general (support), 10th Mountain Division (Light), at Fort Drum, New York.

Beverly J. Harvard

LAW ENFORCEMENT. Beverly J. Harvard is a native of Macon, Georgia. She received a bachelor of arts degree in sociology from Morris Brown College in Atlanta, Georgia. She earned a master of science degree in urban government and administration from Georgia State University and holds two honorary doctorate of law degrees from Morris Brown and the University of South Carolina. She is a graduate of the Atlanta Police Academy and the Federal Bureau of Investigation National Academy in Quantico, Virginia. She is also a graduate of the FBI National Executive Institute.

Harvard began her career with the Atlanta Police Department in 1973 as a patrol officer. She has been executive protection officer, breaking ground as the first woman to serve in the male-dominated unit; director of public affairs; and deputy chief of police for the Career Development Division, the Criminal Investigation Division and the Administrative Services Division.

Harvard was appointed chief of police by Mayor Bill Campbell and confirmed by the Atlanta City Council in October 1994. As police chief, she was responsible for the overall operation of the largest municipal law enforcement agency in the state of Georgia with 2,300 police officers and civilian employees and a budget of over $100 million. She was the first African American woman in the nation and many parts of the Western world to run a major police department.

Mark A. Harvey

MILITARY. Mark A. Harvey received an associate degree from Central Texas College and a bachelor of science degree in human services from Thomas Edison

State College, and he is currently pursuing a master's degree in environmental policy management from the University of Denver. He has completed all levels of the noncommissioned officer education system and has completed the courses for graduate of the battle staff, first sergeant, master fitness trainer, drill sergeant, instructor training, safety officer, environmental compliance officer, and battalion intelligence and operations sergeants, plus the Airborne School, Air Assault School, and the U.S. Army Sergeants Major Academy (Class 52).

Harvey entered the U.S. Army in June 1979 as a chemical, biological, radiological and nuclear operations specialist. He served in numerous leadership positions ranging from squad leader, platoon sergeant and first sergeant to battalion command sergeant major. His most recent leadership position was command sergeant major for the 82nd Chemical Battalion, Fort Leonard Wood, Missouri. He currently serves as the Fort Irwin Garrison command sergeant major.

William J. Harvey

BUSINESS. William J. Harvey is a native of Portsmouth, Virginia. He received a bachelor of science degree from Virginia Commonwealth University and earned a master of business administration from the University of Virginia. Harvey joined the DuPont Corporation in 1977 in the polymers department as a product specialist in Wilmington, Delaware. After numerous assignments of increasing responsibility and authority, in February 2002, he was appointed vice president and general manager of the advanced fiber businesses. In November 2002, he assumed the additional responsibility for Personal Protection, a new business focused on growing DuPont's position in worker protection. He was named vice president of DuPont corporate operations in June 2007.

Leroy Rountree Hassell, Sr.

JUDICIAL. Leroy Rountree Hassell, Sr., is a native of Norfolk, Virginia, and a graduate of Norview High School. He received a bachelor's degree from the University of Virginia in 1977 and earned his juris doctor degree from Harvard University Law School in 1980. Hassell has served in private law practice in Richmond, Virginia; he worked as counsel to the Richmond Redevelopment and Housing Authority; he was chosen as the chairman of the Richmond School Board and director for the Carpenter Center for the Performing Arts. He was nominated by Governor Gerald L. Baliles and elected by the Virginia General Assembly to the Virginia Supreme Court in 1989. His fellow justices honored him in voting him in as chief justice in 2002. He is the first African American chief justice of the Virginia Supreme Court.

Alcee Lamar Hastings

JUDICIAL, FEDERAL GOVERNMENT. Alcee Lamar Hastings is a native of Altamonte Springs, Florida, and graduated from Crooms Academy, Sanford, Florida, in 1953. He received a bachelor of arts degree from Fisk University in Nashville, Tennessee. He attended Howard University School of Law in Washington, D.C., and earned a juris doctor from Florida Agricultural and Mechanical University, Tallahassee, in 1963. Hastings has served in private law practice and as a judge of the Circuit Court of Broward County, Florida (1977 to 1979). He was appointed a U.S. District judge for the Southern District of Florida, 1979 to 1989. Hastings was elected as a Democrat to the 103rd and to the seven succeeding Congresses (January 3, 1993, to present).

Emile H. Hawkins

MINISTRY, MILITARY. Emile H. Hawkins received a bachelor's degree in professional studies from Barry University and a master's of theology in church history and Pentecostal-charismatic studies from Oral Roberts University. He also earned a Ph.D. in strategic leadership from Regent University. Hawkins serves as chair of the Division of Business at Oklahoma Wesleyan University, a four-year Christian university of the liberal arts and sciences. He is also employed by the Oklahoma Air National Guard. He is a major serving as chaplain for over twelve hundred men and women.

Grant W. Hawkins

JUDICIAL. Grant W. Hawkins received his juris doctor degree from Indiana University in Indianapolis, Indiana. He served in private law practice for 27 years before he was elected a Marion County Superior Court judge in 2000. During his time on the bench, he has

presided over hundreds of trials in felony court, personal injury cases and hundreds of divorce cases. He has been a member of the Indianapolis and Marion County Bar Association for over 30 years and served as a vice-president of the Indianapolis Bar Association.

Judith Warren Hawkins

JUDICIAL. Judith Warren Hawkins received a bachelor's degree in home economics from Andrew University and her master's degree from the Ohio State University. She earned her juris doctor from Florida State University in 1984 and was admitted to the Florida bar in 1985. Hawkins established her law firm in 1987. In 1996, she was elected a judge for Florida's 2nd Judicial Circuit, Leon County, in Tallahassee. She is the first woman elected to the county bench without being appointed by a governor. She was re-elected in September 2000.

Larry Hawkins

BUSINESS. Larry Hawkins received a bachelor's degree from the University of Houston, Texas, in 1974 and is a graduate of Southwestern Graduate School of Banking at Southern Methodist University. Hawkins serves as president and chief executive officer of Houston's Unity National Bank, a minority-owned bank serving primarily a low-income population. He began his banking career in 1970 as a part-time teller while attending college. He has worked for such banking endeavors as First City National Bank, Republic Bank and First Republic Bank. He resigned in 1989 to become executive vice president of Unity National Bank, and then was named president and chief executive officer in November 1990. Hawkins is active in numerous organizations, including the Greater Houston Partnership, Independent Bankers Association of Texas, American Red Cross, Boy Scouts of America and ymca. He joined the Community Advisory Committee in 2002 and serves on the consumer credit committee and the depository and delivery systems committee.

Muriel Hawkins

EDUCATION. Muriel Hawkins received a bachelor of science degree in radiological sciences from Chicago Medical School and a master of education in counseling from The Citadel. She has also earned a Ph.D. in curriculum and instruction from Loyola University of Chicago. Hawkins has held positions in administration, teaching and clinical practice at Chicago State University, Medical University of South Carolina, Meharry Medical College, and Malcolm X College. She has been named a Kellogg Fellow. Hawkins is the assistant vice chancellor for academic support and diversity at the University of Wisconsin Oshkosh.

Walter L. Hawkins

LAW ENFORCEMENT, AUTHOR. Walter L. Hawkins was born in Atlanta, Georgia. He graduated from South Fulton High in East Point, Georgia, in 1967. He attended DeKalb College and the University of Georgia. He has also completed numerous military courses, police courses and training through the U.S. Postal Service.

His military assignments began in 1969 with Supply Point 39, 8th Army, in Korea, continuing with promotions and various duties in the U.S. In March 1998, he was selected to serve as the command sergeant major for the 75th Combat Support Hospital in Tuscaloosa, Alabama, which has three units with nearly 528 soldiers assigned in Alabama and Mississippi. He began his law enforcement career as a police cadet in June 1968 with the Atlanta Police Department at the age of 19. He entered the U.S. Army in De-

cember 1968. Beginning in January 1971 he was employed with the Atlanta Police Department as a police officer, police narcotic detective and internal investigator. In 1975 he became one of the first four black police officers in the Fulton County Police Department. He later became its first African American sergeant. He has also worked with the Fulton County Sheriff's Department. In 1990 he was appointed postal police officer and in 1997 promoted to postal police sergeant. He was appointed chief of the Postal Police Atlanta Division and later the Southeast Area, including Georgia, Alabama, Mississippi and Tennessee. He has also served as the diversity coordinator for the Southeast Area of the U.S. Postal Inspection Service.

For over 20 years, Hawkins has been publishing reference books on African American history makers, from the famous to the obscure. His first was *African American Biographies: Profiles of 558 Current Men and Women*, published in 1992. Subsequent books have focused on generals and flag officers, military leaders, and additional varied profiles. His books are used in black studies programs at major U.S. colleges and universities.

His awards include proclamations from the City of Atlanta and Fulton County, Georgia, naming April 30, 1994, Walter L. Hawkins Day. His military awards and decorations include the Army Meritorious Service Medal, Army Commendation Medal (with oak leaf clusters), Armed Forces Expeditionary Medal (Korea), and others. He is employed with the U.S. Postal Service in Atlanta, Georgia.

Carla D. Hayden

LOCAL GOVERNMENT. Carla D. Hayden received a bachelor's degree from Roosevelt University. She earned her master of arts and Ph.D. degrees from the Graduate Library School of the University of Chicago. Her professional career includes serving as the library services coordinator at the Museum of Science and Industry in Chicago and as an assistant professor in the School of Library and Information Science of the University of Pittsburgh. Hayden is the executive director of the Enoch Pratt Free Library in Baltimore, Maryland. She is a member of the American Library Association, serving as president for 2003–2004.

Cecil Hayes

INTERIOR DESIGN. Cecil Hayes is a native of Fort Lauderdale, Florida. She received a bachelor of arts degree in arts education from Florida A&M University in 1967 and earned a design degree from the Art Institute of Fort Lauderdale in 1973. Hayes taught art at Alma High School in Alma, Georgia, from 1967 to 1971 and was employed from 1973 to 1975 at Santa Stevens Interior Design. In 1975 she created Cecil's Designers Unlimited and quickly became the first African American interior designer to be recognized worldwide. In 2002, she founded the Mikala Collection, her signature luxury furniture line consisting of case goods (consoles and tables) and upholstery. Her awards include being named to *Architectural Digest*'s list of the 100 top interior designers and architects worldwide, the Visionary Design Award from the Design Center of the Americas; an NAACP Hall of Fame Award, induction into the Smithsonian Institute's Cooper-Hewitt Design Museum, and induction into the History Makers video archival program.

Hayes' signature work can be seen in the celebrity homes of Samuel L. Jackson, Wesley Snipes, Ty Law, Derek Brown, P.J. Brown, Jamaal Mashburn, and music mogul Tim Mosley ("Timbaland"), among others. Her award-winning décor has been featured in *Architectural Digest*, the *New York Times*, the *Washington Post*, the *Robb Report*, *Florida Design*, and *Southern Living*. She is the founder and CEO of the Cecil Hayes Companies.

Mark Hayes

TELEVISION. Mark Hayes is a native of New York, New York. He received a bachelor of arts in communications from Howard University in 1989. He has been a journalist with WBAL-TV in Baltimore, Maryland; KMGH-TV in Denver, Colorado; and work in Rochester, New York; he also worked as an anchor at WXYZ-TV in Detroit, Michigan. In April 2002, Hayes was named co-host of Fox 5 morning news show *Good Day Atlanta*.

George W. Hayman

LAW ENFORCEMENT. George W. Hayman received an associate degree from Wayne County Community College. He received a bachelor of arts degree in social work and earned a master of science degree from Rutgers University. Hayman joined the New Jersey State

Department of Corrections in 1983 as a social worker. During his 25 years of service, he has held numerous positions: principal procedures analyst; director, special medical unit; hospital administrator; administrator, central medical and transportation; and assistant director, Division of Operations.

He was appointed assistant commissioner, Division of Operations, in June 2003. In that capacity, he supervised the overall management of all state correctional facilities, satellites and specialized units as well as creating a series of innovative programs through which objectives were set to establish quality programming for staff and inmates. Hayman assumed his duties as acting commissioner for the New Jersey Department of Corrections in January 2006. He was confirmed as commissioner on January 8, 2007, by the New Jersey Senate.

Samara P. Heaggans

BUSINESS. Samara P. Heaggans received a bachelor of science degree in chemical engineering from Hampton University in 1991 and a master's degree in biochemical engineering and virology from Johns Hopkins University in 1993. Heaggans served with DuPont Merck Pharmaceutical Company and later with Frito-Lay, Inc. She is project manager in process research and development for Campbell Soup Company in Camden, New Jersey.

Marian L. Heard

PUBLIC SERVICE. Marian L. Heard received an associate degree from the University of Bridgeport and a bachelor's degree from the University of Massachusetts at Amherst. She earned a master's degree from Springfield College and has completed the executive leadership program at the University of Michigan. She has been executive director of Inner-City Children's Center in Bridgeport, Connecticut, a moderator at wicc radio in Bridgeport, and owner of Heard Typing Services. She has served 17 years with United Way of Eastern Fairfield County in Bridgeport, spending her last three years as president and chief executive officer. In 1992, she was selected as president and chief executive officer of the United Way of Massachusetts Bay and chief executive officer of the United Ways of New England.

In 1997, she accepted an appointment by former President Bill Clinton to serve as chief executive officer of the steering committee of Presidents Clinton and Bush chaired by retired General Colin Powell, the largest gathering for domestic issues in the country's history. She is the recipient of 12 honorary doctorate degrees and numerous local, regional and national awards.

Clarence A. Hedge

ARTS. Clarence A. Hedge received an associate in science degree from Coffeyville Community College in Coffeyville, Kansas, and a bachelor of science degree from Northeastern State University. He earned a master's in education from the University of Central Oklahoma and his doctor of education degree from Oklahoma State University. Hedge has served as chairman of the Department of Technology at Langston University since 1988. He was appointed by Governors Frank Keating and Brad Henry to serve six year terms on the Oklahoma Arts Council and has served on the council's executive and nominating committees. In 2004, Hedge was elected vice-chair of the council. He was honored by Oklahoma Governor Brad Henry at the 31st Annual Governor's Arts Awards. He received the Marilyn Douglass Memorial Award, which recognizes an outstanding arts council member.

Anthony M. Henderson

MILITARY. Anthony M. Henderson was born in Washington, D.C. He graduated from Southern University and A&M College at Baton Rouge, Louisiana, in 1989 with a bachelor of arts degree in history and in 1993 with a juris doctor degree. He is a licensed attorney in the State of Louisiana. His military schools include the Basic School, Amphibious Warfare School, the

Navy Command and Staff College, and the Naval War College in Newport, Rhode Island. He has served as the company grade infantry officer monitor from May 1999 to July 2001. In June 2002, he was assigned as executive officer, Third Battalion, Seventh Marines, First Marine Division, Twenty-nine Palms, California.

He deployed with the battalion to Operation Enduring Freedom in January 2003. He served with the battalion in Operation Iraqi Freedom during major combat operations to destroy anti–Iraqi forces and capture Baghdad. He completed the battalion's deployment and returned to the United States in September 2003. He again deployed with the battalion to Iraq in February 2004. Continuing to serve as the Third Battalion, Seventh Marines' executive officer, he led counter-insurgency, stability and reconstruction operations along the Iraqi-Syrian border until September 2004. From January 2005 until June 2005 he was the current operations officer, Seventh Marine Regiment. On September 1, 2006, he was promoted to lieutenant colonel.

Thelton Henderson

JUDICIAL. Thelton Henderson is a native of Shreveport, Louisiana, and graduated from Jefferson High School in Los Angeles. He received a bachelor of arts degree in political science from the University of California at Berkeley in 1956 and earned his juris doctor degree from at the University of California at Berkeley Boalt Hall School of Law in 1962.

Henderson served two years in the U.S. Army as a clinical psychology technician. After receiving his law degree he was an attorney in the Civil Rights Division of the U.S. Department of Justice from 1962 to 1963. He served in private law practice and was the directing attorney of the East Bay Shore Neighborhood Legal Center in the East Palo Alto–East Menlo Park area. In 1976, he became an assistant dean of the Stanford University School of Law, and also taught law at the Golden State University of Law in San Francisco. Henderson was appointed to the United States District Court on June 30, 1980, and became chief judge of the U.S. District Court of the Northern California District in 1990, becoming the first African American to reach that position. He assumed senior status on November 28, 1998.

Sharon M. Henry

MEDICINE. Sharon M. Henry received her medical degree from the University of Maryland School of Medicine and completed her surgical residency at the State University of New York Health Sciences Center in Brooklyn, where she also served as assistant professor of surgery. She completed her surgical critical care fellowship at the University of Minnesota. Dr. Henry is a trauma surgeon, associate professor of surgery, and chief of the Division of Wound Healing and Metabolism at the R. Adams Cowley Shock Trauma Center, University of Maryland Medical Center. She conducts research in the management of complex wounds and critical illness. She is the first African American woman elected as a member of the American Association for the Surgery of Trauma.

Willie W. Herenton

LOCAL GOVERNMENT. Willie W. Herenton is a native of Memphis, Tennessee, and a graduate of Booker T. Washington High School. He received a bachelor's degree from LeMoyne Owen College and a master's degree from the University of Memphis. He earned his doctorate degree at Southern Illinois University. He has also received honorary doctor of humanities degrees from Rhodes and Christian Brothers colleges. Herenton served as a teacher and principal in the Memphis City School System before becoming superintendent of Memphis City Schools. He made history as the first African American to be elected mayor of the City of Memphis, on October 3, 1991. Sixteen years later on October 4, 2007, he made history again as the first Memphis mayor to be elected to five consecutive terms.

Wayne Hester

MILITARY. Wayne Hester joined the staff of the United States Military Academy Band in June of 2000 and served until May 2004 as associate bandmaster and director of the Jazz Knights. Under his leadership, the Jazz Knights spread patriotism, entertained audiences and inspired students at a wide range of events. Highlights of his four years with the band include performances of newly commissioned jazz compositions for the academy's bicentennial, appearances at music festivals in Colorado and Virginia, and educational outreach clinics for developing jazz students. With Hester at the helm, the band performed with such world renowned guests as the Vanguard Jazz Orchestra, drummer Steve Houghton, vibraphonist Emil Richards, saxophonist James Carter, bassist John Clayton and clarinetist Eddie Daniels. Chief Warrant Officer Hester is the commander of the 4th Infantry Division Band at Fort Hood, Texas.

Paul B. Higginbotham

JUDICIAL. Paul B. Higginbotham is a native of Philadelphia, Pennsylvania. He received both a bachelor of arts degree in 1981 and a juris doctor degree in 1985 from the University of Wisconsin Madison. Higginbotham began his career as a staff attorney for Legal Aid Society of Milwaukee from 1985 to 1986. From 1986 to 1988, he served in private law practice. From 1988 to 1992, he was the Dane County minority affairs coordinator. In 1993, he was appointed a City of Madison Municipal Court judge. From 1993 to 1994, he was acting executive director, Madison Equal Opportunities Commission. From 1994 to 2003, he served as a Circuit Court judge. In 2003, he was appointed an appellate judge, District IV Court of Appeals in Madison, Wisconsin.

Judith M. Hightower

JUDICIAL. Judith M. Hightower received a bachelor of arts degree in comparative literature (Spanish) from the University of Washington and earned her juris doctor degree from Seattle University School of Law in 1983. She was admitted to the bar in Washington State in 1984. She worked in private law practice from 1984 to 1990. Since 1991, she has served as a judge on the Municipal Court of Seattle. She has also served as member of the National Bar Association Judicial Council and as a University of Washington Law School mentor.

Curtis T. Hill, Jr.

LOCAL GOVERNMENT. Curtis T. Hill, Jr., is a native of Elkhart County, Indiana. He received a bachelor of science degree in marketing from Indiana University School of Business and a doctor of jurisprudence from the Indiana University School of Law. Hill first joined the Elkhart County Prosecuting Attorney's Office in 1988. He was a part-time deputy prosecuting attorney while maintaining a private law practice in the City of Elkhart. Since January 1, 2003, Hill has served as Elkhart County prosecuting attorney. Now in his second term, he has transformed the office of the prosecuting attorney into a model for professional prosecution enforcement. Under Hill's leadership, the office has implemented the most sweeping changes in the history of the Elkhart County criminal justice system and has been recognized throughout the state of Indiana as a leader in aggressive law enforcement and child support collections.

Victor Hill

LAW ENFORCEMENT. Victor Hill is a native of Charleston, South Carolina, where he received a public education and later attended Trident Technical College. He is a martial arts enthusiast who began studying martial arts at age 14 and attained a first degree black belt at age 20. Hill joined the Clayton County, Georgia, Police Department in July 1992. He was promoted to detective in 1995. In 1996 he became the first African American hostage negotiator for the Clayton County Police Department.

In 2002, he was elected to the Georgia House of

Representatives for District 81. He was the first police detective to serve in the General Assembly while still an active law enforcer. As a Georgia state representative he served on the public safety, special judiciary, and game, fish, and parks committees. In July 2004 he was elected the 20th sheriff of Clayton County. He is the first African American ever elected in the history of Clayton County, Georgia.

Wyllstyne D. Hill

BUSINESS. Wyllstyne D. Hill received a bachelor of science in math from Tuskegee University in Tuskegee, Alabama. She also earned a 1992 executive program certificate from the University of Arizona's Karl Eller Graduate School of Management, and a 1995 executive management certification from the University of Southern California. Hill joined Hughes Aircraft Company in 1971 as a general clerk. When Raytheon acquired Hughes, Hill was managing a center. After the merger she was named deputy to the director of the information technology organization. She now serves as vice president of information technology and chief information officer of Raytheon Missile System in Tucson, Arizona.

Enrique X. Hines

MILITARY. Enrique X. Hines was born in the Republic of Costa Rica and raised in Bronx, New York. He entered the Marine Corps in June of 1979. He graduated from Company F, 2nd Recruit Training Battalion, at Parris Island, South Carolina. Hines' military career includes serving as a drill instructor and senior drill instructor in Company B, 1st Recruit Training Battalion, at the Marine Corps Recruit Depot at San Diego, California. In June 1990, he served as a gunnery sergeant and later platoon sergeant with Company B, 1st Combat Engineer Battalion, 1st Marine Division.

He then was instructor of the noncommissioned officer basic course (assigned June 1991); training chief and staff noncommissioned officer in charge of the sappers leaders course with the 1st Marine Division; first sergeant for Headquarters Battery, 11th Marine Regiment, 1st Marine Division (June 1997); and first sergeant of Headquarters and Service Company, 3d Assault Amphibian Battalion (June 2000). In 2002, he was sergeant major for the 9th Communication Battalion, where he participated in support of combat Operations Enduring Freedom and Iraqi Freedom.

In January 2004, Hines was assigned as the Support Battalion Sergeant Major for Recruit Training Regiment, Marine Corps Recruit Depot in San Diego. He is currently assigned as sergeant major, 13th Marine Expeditionary Unit — Special Operations Capable.

Melvin "Kip" Holden

MEDIA, LOCAL GOVERNMENT. Melvin Holden was born in New Orleans and graduated from Scotlandville Senior High School, Baton Rouge, Louisiana, in 1970. He received a bachelor of arts degree in journalism from Louisiana State University in 1974 and a master's degree in journalism from Southern University in 1985. He earned a juris doctor from Southern University School of Law in 1998 and was given an honorary doctor of public policy from Southern University. He was also invited to study at the Oxford University Round Table in England in 2002.

Holden was news director at WXOK radio in Baton Rouge, Louisiana, from 1975 to 1977; a reporter at WWL radio in New Orleans from 1977 to 1978; a reporter at WBRZ in Baton Rouge from 1978 to 1979; public relations specialist for the United States Census Bureau in Baton Rouge; public information officer for Baton Rouge City Police; and law clerk at the Louisiana Department of Labor Office of Workers Compensation, Baton Rouge. From 1984 to 1988, he was a councilman for Baton Rouge Metro Council District 2; from 1988 to 2001, he was a state representative, Louisiana House of Representatives District 63.

Since 1991 he has served as an adjunct professor of Law at Southern University School of Law. He also worked in private law practice in Baton Rouge and was elected a Louisiana state senator for District 15. He was elected mayor-president, City of Baton Rouge Parish of East Baton Rouge and was inaugurated on January 3,

2005. He is the first African American mayor of Baton Rouge.

Eric Himpton Holder, Jr.

JUDICIAL. Eric Himpton Holder, Jr., is a native of New York City, and his parents have roots in Barbados. He attended Stuyvesant High School in Manhattan and earned a Regents Scholarship. He attended Columbia University, where he played freshmen basketball and earned a Bachelor of Arts degree in American history in 1973. He received his juris doctor degree from Columbia Law School and joined the Department of Justice in Washington, D.C., as part of the attorney general's honors program. Holder was assigned to the newly formed Public Integrity Section in 1976 to investigate and prosecute official corruption on the local, state and federal levels. In 1988, he was nominated by President Ronald Reagan to become an associate judge of the Superior Court of the District of Columbia. He was confirmed by the Senate and received his commission in October 1988. In 1993, President Bill Clinton nominated Holder as U.S. attorney for the District of Columbia. He was confirmed later that year and served as the head of the largest U.S. Attorney's office in the nation for nearly four years. He was the first African American to serve in that position. In 1997, President Clinton appointed Judge Holder to serve as deputy attorney general, the number two position in the U.S. Department of Justice. He was first African American to serve in that post. He served under President George W. Bush as acting attorney general pending the confirmation of Attorney General John Ashcroft.

In November 2008, President-elect Barack Obama selected Holder to serve as the United States attorney general. Mr. Holder's confirmation made him the first African American U.S. attorney general in American history.

George W. Holifield

JUDICIAL. George W. Holifield is a native of Seattle, Washington. He attended Garfield High School, received a bachelor of arts degree from Whitman College, and earned his juris doctor degree from American University School of Law. Holifield worked full time as a staff assistant to Senator Warren G. Magnuson in Washington, D.C., while in law school. He was an underwriter for Safeco Insurance Company, as well as a supervisor with the Washington State Human Rights Commission. He also worked as an attorney for the Public Defender Association and as director of Social Health Services (the largest agency in state government). In addition, he has extensive civil and criminal trial experience. Holifield has served as a Seattle Municipal Court judge for 28 years and has been elected seven times.

Marcella A. Holland

JUDICIAL. Marcella A. Holland is a native of Baltimore, Maryland. She received a bachelor of arts degree in political science from the University of Maryland, Baltimore County, in 1980. She earned her juris doctor from the University of Maryland School of Law in 1983 and was admitted to Maryland Bar Association in 1983. She was an assistant state's attorney for Baltimore City from 1984 to 1997. On September 18, 1997, she was appointed an associate judge for the Maryland Circuit Court in Baltimore. From 2001 to 2003, she was the judge in charge of Family Division. Since November 8, 2003, she has served as the Maryland Circuit Administrative judge, Baltimore City Circuit Court, 8th Judicial Division.

Tameika N. Hollis

ENGINEERING. Tameika N. Hollis received a bachelor's degree in mechanical engineering from Florida A&M University and earned her master's degree in mechanical engineering from the University of Michigan. Hollis joined Northrop Grumman Electronic Systems as a systems engineer. After only two months, she was named integrated product team leader for systems engineering and integration and testing for her program. She is responsible for the development of all systems engineering tasks and budgets as well as system test activities. In addition to her technical contributions, Hollis was a part of a task force chartered with streamlining all the systems engineering processes at the company. She serves as first chair of the Northrop Grumman Society of Women Engineers at the company's Baltimore facilities.

Sanford Eugene Holman

MILITARY. Sanford Eugene Holman received a bachelor of science degree from the United States Military

Academy. He earned a master of science degree in operations research from the Florida Institute of Technology and a master of science degree in national security strategy from the National Defense University. He is also a graduate of the operations research systems analysis military application course; the Combined Arms and Services Staff School; U.S. Army Command and General Staff College; the National War College; and the armor officer, military police officer and quartermaster officer advanced courses.

His key military assignments include serving in 1979 as student evaluation officer in the Office of the Secretary, U.S. Army Infantry School at Fort Benning, Georgia; in 1990 as combat operations analyst, U.S. Army Training and Doctrine Analysis Command, White Sands Missile Range, New Mexico; in 2002, as commander, 1st Brigade (Initial Entry Training), with the 80th Division (Institutional Training), at Fort Meade, Maryland; and in October 2004, division advisor support team leader, Detachment 6, 98th Division, Mosul, Iraq. In November 2005, he was the assistant division commander, 98th Division (Institutional Training), in Rochester, New York. Since March 2007, he has served as the deputy commander, Combined Joint Task Force, Djibouti, Horn of Africa.

Jan Bromell Holmes

JUDICIAL. Jan Bromell Holmes is a native of Horry County, South Carolina. She received a bachelor of arts degree in English and political science magna cum laude from Fisk University in Nashville, Tennessee. She earned her juris doctor from North Carolina Central School of Law in Durham, North Carolina, in 1995. While in law school, she was a member of the Moot Court Board, and her two-member team won the Moot Court Board championship in 1994. Holmes returned to Georgetown, South Carolina, after law school and entered private practice. In 1997, she formed her own practice and was a sole practitioner. She handled cases in various areas of law until her election to the position of family court judge for the Fifteenth Judicial Circuit, Seat 1, on February 7, 2007.

Rhonda Holt

ENGINEERING. Rhonda Holt, daughter of an Army command sergeant major, excelled in the schools she attended moving around the country and overseas as her father changed assignments. She ended up in Florida, where she graduated with straight A's from high school and won two scholarship offers to go to the University of Florida. She held a part-time job at the U.S. Agriculture Department during the summer of her junior year. Working for a research scientist, collecting field research data and entering it into the office computers for the summer got her fascinated with the machines. She was hired by IBM in Boca Raton, Florida, as a summer intern while in college and at graduation in 1986 she was hired as an associate programmer.

Holt received a bachelor of science degree in computer science from the University of Florida. She serves on the advisory board to the dean of the university's College of Engineering and the computer science department. After working as an associate programmer, she soon was assigned to work on operating systems and became an expert in OS/390 and IBM's Unix variant, aix. She rose rapidly at IBM, and six years after she began her career, she was promoted to manager and moved to product development teams. She moved to California in 1994 and began developing fault-tolerant storage arrays.

Holt joined Sun Microsystems in 1996 as a senior program manager. From 1997 to January 2001, she was director of the Solaris cluster product. In February 2001, at age 36, she was selected to serve as vice president of storage systems engineering, becoming one of the youngest top executives at Sun. From January 2003 to February 2005, she was vice president of enterprise systems management software for Dell, Inc. She returned to Sun Microsystems in March 2005 as vice president for the grid engineering program office, where she is responsible for providing program management governance, cost engineering support, and operational support to the grid engineering program team.

Charles N. Hood

PUBLIC SAFETY. Charles N. Hood received a bachelor of science degree in fire service management from Ottawa University. He has more than 23 years of fire and emergency service experience with the Phoenix Fire Department. His tenure included high ranking

management positions as a division chief, battalion chief, as deputy chief and assistant chief. He also serves as an adjunct faculty member at Texas A&M University at College Station, Texas, in the national Emergency Response and Rescue Training Center.

Hood has served on national deployments including Hurricane Katrina in 2005, the 2004 Democratic National Convention, the 2003 Columbia Space Shuttle incident and the 2002 Winter Olympics in Salt Lake City, Utah. On April 16, 2007, the San Antonio (Texas) City Council confirmed Charles N. Hood as the city's fire chief. He became the first African American fire chief in the history of San Antonio.

Denise Page Hood

JUDICIAL. Denise Page Hood is a native of Columbus, Ohio, and attended high school at the Columbus School for Girls. She received a bachelor of arts degree from Yale University in 1974 and earned her juris doctor from the Columbia University School of Law in 1977. Hood served as an assistant corporation attorney for the City of Detroit Law Department after law school. In 1982, she was appointed judge to Detroit's 36th District Court, Recorder's Court and Wayne County Circuit Court. She was nominated by President Bill Clinton and confirmed by the Senate in 1994 to the United States District Court for the Eastern District of Michigan. In 1993, she became the first African American female president of the Detroit Bar Association.

Melvin Andre Hooks

BUSINESS. Melvin Andre Hooks is a native of Birmingham, Alabama, and graduated from Ullman High School in 1959 at the age of 16 as a member of the National Honor Society. After working as a dishwasher for $20 a week at an upscale hotel and being told by his supervisor he would never make it in college, he attended Alabama A&M University in Huntsville, Alabama, and received a bachelor of science degree with honors in 1964. His career began as a high school science instructor in Tuscaloosa, Alabama, and in Atlanta, Georgia, for several years. In 1969, he began his career as a real estate developer in Atlanta, Georgia, before moving to Los Angeles, California, in 1974. In Los Angeles, Hooks developed single family homes, condominium complexes, residential housing tracts and commercial shopping centers. One of the gems in his real estate development career was Washington Village, a 28 unit condominium project in South Los Angeles, the first new development of its kind to be built in the area in more than twenty years. Currently, in 2008, he is developing real estate projects on 60 acres valued at approximately $300 million. Hooks has lectured at the University of Southern California on the real estate development process. He is the recipient of numerous civic awards and the founder of the Association of Minority Real Estate Developers, a nonprofit organization established in 1981.

Charles Wayne Hooper

MILITARY. Charles Wayne Hooper received a bachelor's degree from the United States Military Academy at West Point and a master of public administration degree with honors from Harvard University. He earned a master of science degree from the U.S. Army War College. He is also an honor graduate of the Defense Language Institute and British Ministry of Defense Chinese Language School, and is fluent in the Mandarin dialect of Chinese, the national language of China. Hooper is an infantry officer who has served in command and staff positions with the 25th Infantry and 82nd Airborne Divisions, and has commanded a U.S. Army recruiting battalion. He has served as deputy division chief and Asia-Pacific strategist, War Plans Division army staff, and assistant army attaché, Defense Office, U.S. Embassy in Beijing. He was the senior country director for China, Taiwan, and Mongolia in the Office of the Secretary of Defense (2001–2003).

Hooper coordinated and executed the first post–9/11 senior-level security dialogue between the United States and China, and negotiated a series of bilateral activities with the Chinese military that will increase their transparency and the United States' understanding of China's military intentions. From 2003 to 2005, he served as chief of U.S. Army International Affairs and structured a senior-level bilateral Army staff talks program that became the capstone Army forum for the management of bilateral security cooperation and coalition interoperability projects with 13 key U.S. allies and partners. General Hooper is Army chairman/foreign area officer for training development at the Center for Contemporary Conflict.

Christina Hopper

MILITARY. Christina Hopper received a bachelor of arts degree with honors in psychology from the University of Texas at Austin in May 1998. She received her commission as the distinguished graduate from the U.S. Air Force Reserve Officer Training Corps program. Shortly after graduation, she attended undergraduate pilot training at Vance Air Force Base in Enid, Oklahoma, and earned Air Force pilot wings in April 2000. Following pilot training, she attended F-16 training at Luke Air Force Base in Arizona.

Hopper received her first operational assignment in June 2001, flying F-16s at Cannon Air Force Base in New Mexico as part of the 524th Fighter Squadron, known as the "Hounds of Heaven." She was the first African American female to fly an Air Force jet into combat. She logged over 800 hours as an F-16 "Fighting Falcon" pilot. She logged over 50 combat and combat support missions during the Iraq War. She now instructs young pilots.

Gerry House

EDUCATION. Gerry House received a bachelor's degree in English education from North Carolina A&T State University in Greensboro and a master of science degree in counseling from Southern Illinois University. She earned her doctorate in education administration from the University of North Carolina at Chapel Hill. She has received honorary doctor of humanities degrees from Rhodes College and Lemoyne Owen College, both in Memphis, Tennessee. She served for 15 years as school superintendent in Memphis, Tennessee, and in Chapel Hill, North Carolina.

She is currently is president and chief executive officer of the Institute for Student Achievement in New York, a nonprofit organization that partners with high schools to transform them into academically rigorous and personalized small schools and small learning communities that graduate students prepared for success in college. House was the 1999 American Association of School Superintendents' national Superintendent of the Year. In 2000 she was the first recipient of the Alumni Leadership Award from the University of North Carolina at Chapel Hill School of Education.

Lillie Howard

EDUCATION. Lillie Howard received a bachelor's degree from the University of South Alabama. She earned her master's degree and Ph.D. from the University of New Mexico. She was associate provost for academic affairs at Wright State from 1987 to 1999 and associate provost for academic affairs and dean of University College from 1999 until her promotion to vice president. She was named vice president for curriculum and instruction and dean of the University College at Wright State University. She was inducted into the Consortium of Doctors in San Francisco, a national professional organization that recognizes the achievements of African American women with earned doctorates.

Cheryl Howard-Young

MEDICINE. Cheryl Howard-Young holds a bachelor of science in nursing and a master of public and institutional administration. She earned a medical doctor degree from Western University of Health Sciences and completed her residency training at the University of Medicine and Dentistry at New Jersey and Michigan State University's St. Joseph Hospital. Before entering medical school, Dr. Howard-Young worked as a charge nurse in obstetrics at the Nix Medical Center in San Antonio, as well as flight nurse for the U.S. Air Force Reserve and at Brooks Army Medical Center in San Antonio.

Freeman A. Hrabowski III

EDUCATION. Freeman A. Hrabowski III is a native of Birmingham, Alabama. He received a bachelor's degree in mathematics with highest honors at age 19 from

Hampton Institute. He earned a master of arts degree in mathematics and a Ph.D. in higher education administration and statistics from the University of Illinois at Urbana-Champaign. Hrabowski worked as a consultant to the National Science Foundation, the National Institutes of Health, the U.S. Department of Education, and universities and school systems nationally. He has served as president of the University of Maryland, Baltimore County, since May 1992.

Vera Hughes

MILITARY. Vera Hughes enlisted in the U.S. Navy through the delayed entry program in February 1979 and entered active duty in May 1979. For the past twenty-four years, her duty stations have included Naval Hospital Philadelphia, Naval Hospital Guantanamo Bay, Cuba, and Naval Hospital Bethesda, Maryland, where she attended Advanced Laboratory Technician School, Naval Hospital Lemoore, California, and Naval Medical Center San Diego.

In October 1991, as a petty officer first class, she attended Field Medical Service School and was assigned to the 1st Force Service Support Group, Camp Pendleton, California. Hughes took on the arduous task of running the hazardous materials laboratory and conducting the osha safety inspections and training for the 1st Force Service Support Group. In January 1994, began instructing at the Naval School of Health Sciences San Diego, where she earned an associate faculty position from George Washington University and her master training specialist designator. She was promoted to the rank of chief petty officer.

In April 1998, she reported to Naval Hospital Sigonella, Italy, as the leading chief petty officer for ancillary services departments. She served in that capacity until December 2000, when she transferred to Field Medical Service School Camp Pendleton. There she held multiple positions, including senior military advisor, staff development coordinator, master training specialist coordinator, physical fitness coordinator and the academics alpha. She was promoted to the rank of senior chief petty officer. In September 2003, she was transferred to 3D Force Service Support Group, now known as 3D Marine Logistics Group. She was S3 training executive officer and headquarters and service company senior enlisted leader, and currently is command master chief.

James P. Humphrey

MILITARY. James P. Humphrey was born in Paris, France, and raised in Columbia, South Carolina. He graduated from recruit training at Parris Island, South Carolina, in February 1985. He reported to Naval Air Station Millington, Tennessee, to become an aviation ground support equipment technician. Humphrey has held numerous key leadership positions, including quality assurance representative, senior noncommissioned officer in charge of the Support Equipment Division at Marine Corps Air Station New River in North Carolina. He served as the squadron gunnery sergeant for Marine Aviation Logistics Squadron 26. In September 2000, he reported to Marine Aviation Logistics Squadron 24, Marine Aircraft Group 24, at Marine Corps Air Station Kaneohe Bay, Hawaii, as the senior noncommissioned officer in charge of the Support Equipment Division. In February 2004, he was promoted to first sergeant for 1st Battalion, 12th Marines, Battery C, at Kaneohe Bay. In July 2004, First Sergeant Humphrey and Battery C were attached to Battalion Landing Team 1/3, 31s Marine Expeditionary Unit, and participated in operations Phantom Fury and Al Fjar, the siege of and rebuilding of Fallujah, Iraq. Upon his return from Iraq in May 2005, Humphrey was transferred back to 1st Battalion, 12th Marines, Battery A. In May 2007 he was transferred to Headquarters Battery. He was promoted to sergeant major in March 2007 and is the sergeant major of the Marine Wing Support Squadron at Marine Corps Air Station Cherry Point, North Carolina.

Rosalind Hunt

EDUCATION, BUSINESS. Rosalind Hunt received a master's degree in mathematics and physics from Hunter College, City University of New York, and earned her Ph.D. in psychology from Columbia University. She has served as the director of human resources at Telcordia Technologies, part of the AT&T Bell System. Her work for Telcordia focused on organizational consulting and human resources strategy and development. Since retiring from Telcordia she has a private practice in psychotherapy and continues to consult for industry. She is chairman of the Board for the Children's Home Society of New Jersey and an adjunct professor at several New York universities, including the State University of New York, City University of New York, Long Island University and Columbia University.

Shirley Ann Hunt

MILITARY. Shirley Ann Hunt is a native of Mullins, South Carolina. She received a bachelor of social science

degree from Excelsior College. She is currently enrolled in Touro University pursuing a master's degree in logistics. Her military education includes all the noncommissioned officer education system courses, Drill Sergeant School, first sergeant course, and the U.S. Army Sergeants Major Academy (Class 53).

Hunt has served as a squad leader, section leader, platoon sergeant, drill instructor, first sergeant and battalion command sergeant major. Her duty assignments include the 92nd Medical Detachment in Hanau, Germany; 121st Evacuation Hospital in Korea; 16th Medical Logistic Battalion in Korea; 44th Medical Brigade at Fort Bragg, North Carolina; 32nd Medical Logistics Battalion at Fort Bragg; 158th Infantry Brigade, 4th Training Support Battalion, Orlando, Florida; 1st Medical Brigade at Fort Hood, Texas; 147th Medical Logistics Battalion at Fort Sam Houston, Texas; and 421st Medical Evacuation Battalion, Wiesbaden Army Airfield, Germany. She is the command sergeant major for the 115th Combat Support Hospital at Fort Polk, Louisiana.

Ted E. Imes

ENGINEERING. Ted E. Imes received a bachelor's degree from Loyola College in Maryland and a master's degree in technical management from the Johns Hopkins University. He is director of the strike and weapons program operations at Northrop Grumman Electronic Systems in Baltimore. His responsibility includes program management for transmit-receive module development and the knowledge aided sensor signal processing and expert reasoning program. His technical expertise in avionics systems contributed to the establishment and training of European and Pacific Rim subsidiaries. He managed the international subcontracts for the Airborne Warning and Control System radar system improvement program, which required the coordination of five companies in five countries across two continents.

Kym Ingram

MILITARY. Kym Ingram received a bachelor of arts degree in education from Southern Illinois University and a master of science degree in strategic studies from the U.S. Army Command and General Staff College. She is a graduate of the Naval War College. Her assignments have included administrative and legal officer, Naval Ocean System Center Command, Point Loma, California; bachelor and enlisted quarters officer and assistant officer in charge, Broadened Opportunity for Officer Selection and Training (BOOST) program, Service Schools Command, San Diego, California; officer in charge, Fleet Activities Yokohama Detachment, Yokohama, Japan; director, Officer Performance Branch, Bureau of Naval Personnel, Arlington, Virginia; officer in charge, Personnel Support Detachment, Great Lakes, Illinois; and director, Base Operations, Recruit Training Command at Great Lakes, Illinois. She serves as the officer programs officer, Navy Recruiting Region South.

Roderick L. Ireland

JUDICIAL. Roderick L. Ireland earned his bachelor of arts degree from Lincoln University and a juris doctor degree from Columbia University Law School. His legal career began in 1969 as a Neighborhood Legal Service attorney, and then he worked as a public defender from 1971 to 1973 with the Roxbury Defenders Committee, first as chief attorney, then deputy and executive director. From 1975 to 1977 he was assistant secretary and chief legal counsel for the Massachusetts Executive Office of Administration and Finance. In 1977 he was chairman of the Massachusetts Board of Appeals on Motor Vehicle Liability Policies and Bonds.

He was an adjunct faculty member at Northeastern University. Justice Ireland served on the Boston Juvenile Court for almost thirteen years and the Massachusetts Appeals Court for seven years. He was appointed an associate justice of the Massachusetts Supreme Justice Court in 1997, and is the first African American to sit on this bench in its over three-hundred year history.

388. Wanda E. Irving

PUBLIC SERVICE. Wanda E. Irving received a bachelor of arts degree in English from Dartmouth College in 1975, as one of two African Americans in the first class of women. Irving was a consultant to the Private Industry Council. She designed and taught a job readiness training program to offer job alternatives for youth at risk of gang involvement. Her work with the Portland Bureau of Housing and Community Development involved assessing community demographics, needs and expectations.

She served as director of public relations for Volunteers of America; as president, National Political Con-

gress of Black Women, Inc.; as community relations director for Region X, U.S. Department of Agriculture; and as assistant program manager for social entrepreneurship at the University of Notre Dame's Mendoza College of Business. Irving worked with a diverse clientele in both the Pacific Northwest and Midwest. She accepted a position with the National Urban Fellows as director of public relations.

Cheryl Boone Isaacs

BUSINESS, FILM. Cheryl Boone Isaacs began her career in 1977 as a publicist at Columbia Pictures. She was an adjunct professor at the University of Southern California's Cinema and Television School's Peter Stark Producing Program teaching motion picture marketing. She joined Paramount Pictures in 1984 as director, publicity and promotion, West Coast, and was promoted to executive director one year later. Between 1986 and 1990, she worked at the Motion Picture Group of Paramount Pictures as vice president for publicity. From 1990 to 1994, she was senior vice president for publicity. During her tenure at Paramount she publicized the launch of such blockbusters as *First Wives Club*, *Mission: Impossible*, *The Firm*, *Ghost*, *The Addams Family*, *Coming to America*, *Fatal Attraction*, and the *Beverly Hills Cop* trilogy.

Isaacs also served as director of advertising and publicity for the Ladd Company, where she worked on *The Right Stuff*, *Police Academy* and *Once Upon a Time in America*. Prior to that, she spent five years at Melvin Simon Productions (*The Stunt Man*, *Love at First Bite*, *Porky's*), where her last position was vice president, worldwide advertising and publicity. In 1997, Isaacs joined New Line Cinema as president of theatrical marketing. She developed and executed the campaigns for *Austin Powers: The Spy Who Shagged Me*, the company's highest grossing film at that time, and such critically acclaimed motion pictures as *Wag the Dog*, *Boogie Nights* and *American History X*. Largely through the efforts of Isaacs and her marketing team, New Line was one of only two studios to have four films—*Lost in Space*, *Blade*, *Rush Hour*, and *Pleasantville*—open at number one at the box-office in 1998. *Rush Hour*'s $33 million opening was, at the time, the largest in company history. In 1997 and 1998, Isaacs was profiled in the *Hollywood Reporter*'s special issue *Women in Entertainment, The Power 50*.

Isaacs was the first African American woman to run a studio marketing department, overseeing creative advertising, publicity, media-buying, co-op advertising, product placement and market research. She was also the first African American woman elected to the Board of Governors of the Academy of Motion Pictures Arts and Sciences and the first African American woman named to the board of the Motion Picture and Television Fund.

Alphonso Jackson

FEDERAL GOVERNMENT. Alphonso Jackson is a native of Texas and grew up in south Dallas. He received a bachelor's degree in political science and a master's degree in education administration from Truman State University. He earned his juris doctor degree from Washington University School of Law. Jackson was selected to serve as the director of public safety for the City of St. Louis in 1977. He has served as executive director of for the St. Louis Housing Authority; director of consultant services for a certified public accounting firm; and assistant to the chancellor and assistant professor at the University of Missouri.

From January 1989 to July 1996, he was president and CEO of the Housing Authority of the City of Dallas, Texas. He was appointed director of the Department of Public and Assisted Housing in Washington, D.C., and also served as chair for the District of Columbia Redevelopment Land Agency Board. In June of 2001, he joined the George W. Bush Administration as the deputy secretary and chief operating officer of the U.S. Department of Housing and Urban Development (HUD). In 2004, he was nominated by President Bush as the department's secretary. The U.S. Senate unanimously confirmed Jackson as the nation's 13th secretary of hud on March 31, 2004.

Curtis James Jackson III

MUSIC. Curtis James Jackson III is a native of the South Jamaica neighborhood of Queens in New York, New York. His mother was 15 when she gave birth to him. He grew up without a father and his mother was murdered at the age of 23. He moved in with his grandmother and eight aunts and uncles. He attended Andrew Jackson High School. Jackson started rapping in a friend's basement using turntables to record over instrumentals. In 1996, a friend introduced him to Jam

Master Jay of Run DMC, who was organizing his label, Jam Master Jay Records. It was the first time he entered a studio. Jay taught him how to count bars, write choruses, structure songs, and make a record.

Jackson chose the name "50 Cent." His first official appearance was on a song titled "React" with the group Onyx on their 1998 album *Shut 'Em Down*. He credited Jam Master Jay as an influence who helped him improve his ability to write hooks. He produced "50 Cent's" first album. On May 24, 2000, an assailant walked up to Jackson and shot him nine times with a 9mm pistol at close range. While in the hospital, he signed a publishing deal with Columbia Records. But Columbia dropped him from the label and "blacklisted" him in the recording industry after it was discovered he was shot. He traveled to Canada, where he recorded over thirty songs for mixtapes, including *Guess Who's Back?*

In 2002, Eminem introduced Jackson to Dr. Dre, who signed him to a million dollar record deal. Jackson released the mixtape *No Mercy, No Fear*. On February 6, 2003, his commercial debut album, *Get Rich or Die Tryin'*, was released. Interscope granted Jackson his own label, G-Unit Records, in 2003. The Game was later signed under a joint venture with Dr. Dre's Aftermath Entertainment. On March 3, 2005, his second commercial album, *The Massacre*, was released. It sold 1.14 million copies in the first four days. He is the second richest black recording artist and record company executive.

Hue Jackson

SPORTS. Hue Jackson is a native of Los Angeles, California. He played quarterback at the University of the Pacific in 1985 to 1986, throwing for 2,544 yards and 19 touchdowns in his career. He also lettered in basketball in 1986. Jackson began his coaching career in 1987 at the University of the Pacific. After three years there, he moved on to Cal State Fullerton from 1990 to 1991, Arizona State (1992 to 1995) and California in 1996. At California, he was offensive coordinator and helped lead the Golden Bears to an Aloha Bowl appearance.

He picked up his first year's experience in pro football in 1991 as the running backs, special teams and wide receivers coach for the London Monarchs of the World League. He also had three NFL summer internships, working with the Los Angeles Rams in 1990, the Arizona Cardinals in 1992 and the Redskins in 1995. He was the running backs coach from 2001 to 2002 and then the offensive coordinator with the Washington Redskins. In 2004, he joined the Cincinnati Bengals as a wide receivers coach. In 2007, Coach Jackson joined the Atlanta Falcons as an offensive coordinator.

Janet E. Jackson

JUDICIAL. Janet E. Jackson received a bachelor of arts degree in history from Wittenberg University in 1975 and earned her juris doctor degree from the National Law Center at George Washington University in 1978. She was an assistant attorney general for the state of Ohio. She served as a Franklin County Municipal Court judge. She was the first African American judge in Franklin County. She also was the first woman ever elected Columbus city attorney in Ohio. Judge Jackson was appointed on January 13, 2003, to head the Columbus Ohio United Way, the 14th largest United Way organization in the nation.

Jesse L. Jackson, Jr.

FEDERAL GOVERNMENT. Jesse L. Jackson, Jr., is a native of Greenville, South Carolina. He received a bachelor of science degree from North Carolina Agricultural and Technical State University in Greensboro, North Carolina, in 1987 and a master of arts degree from Chicago Theological Seminary in Chicago, Illinois, in 1989. He also earned a juris doctor degree from the University of Illinois College of Law in Chicago in 1993. Jackson has served as secretary for the Democratic National Committee's Black Caucus and as national field director for the National Rainbow Coalition from 1993 to 1995. Jackson was elected as a Democrat to the 104th Congress to fill the vacancy created by the resignation of Rep. Mel Reynolds, then was reelected to the six succeeding Congresses (December 12, 1995, to present).

Jesse Louis Jackson, Sr.

MINISTRY. Jesse Louis Jackson, Sr., is a native of Greenville, South Carolina. He received a bachelor of arts degree in sociology and economics from North Carolina A&T State University. He has received numerous honorary doctor degrees. In 1966, he and others were the founders of Operation Breadbasket, a joint project of the Southern Christian Leadership Conference, in Chicago, Illinois. In 1967, he was named national director of Operation Breadbasket. In 1968, he was ordained a Baptist minister. He left the conference in 1971 and founded this own organization, Operation push (People United to Save Humanity). On November 3, 1983, he announced that he was a candidate for the presidency of the United States of America. He gained enough delegates and support to go into the Democratic National Convention as a strong voice in the construction of the 1984 Democratic platform. In 1987, he was on the road with a new campaign for the Democratic nomination for president of the United States. This time he had a vision of a Rainbow Coalition. At the 1988 Democratic National Convention in Atlanta, The Rev. Jackson gave a 49-minute, nationally televised speech and received a 15-minute ovation at its conclusion.

In September 1990, The Rev. Jackson traveled to Baghdad, Iraq, and Kuwait City, Kuwait. He met Iraqi President Saddam Hussein and left Kuwait with 500 freed hostages. In 2005, he was enlisted as part of the United Kingdom's Operation Black Vote, a campaign to encourage more of Britain's ethnic minorities to vote in political elections ahead of the May 2005 general election. During 2007, he was involved in a variety of protests, including the Jena 6 in Louisiana. In June 2007 he was arrested in connection with a crowd protesting at a gun store in Riverdale, a poor suburb of Chicago, Illinois. The Rev. Jackson was protesting the fact that the gun store allegedly had been selling firearms to local gang members and was contributing to the decay of the community.

Paula Jackson

SPORTS. Paula Jackson is a native of Baton Rouge, Louisiana. She received a bachelor's degree in broadcast and print journalism, with a minor in public relations, from Southern Louisiana University in 1986. While there, she was a member of the cheerleading squad. She earned her master of business administration from Clark Atlanta in 1991.

Jackson joined the Savannah State University administrative staff from Morehead State University, where she served as an assistant athletics director and senior women's administrator. She held the same positions at Clark Atlanta University from June 2001 to May 2003. Jackson is the assistant athletic director of compliance and senior women's administrator at Savannah State University. As the director of compliance, her responsibilities include certifying that the athletics program adheres to all NCAA (National Collegiate Athletic Association) regulations, which includes eligibility, recruitment, the NCAA Clearinghouse, playing and practice seasons, reporting potential violations and financial aid. As the senior women's administrator, she is the liaison for all gender equity and minority related issues in the Savannah State University athletics department.

Stanley Jackson

LOCAL GOVERNMENT, EDUCATION. Stanley Jackson received a bachelor's degree from the University of North Carolina at Fayetteville and has done graduate work in business administration at Howard University. He has completed the senior executive training course at Harvard University's John F. Kennedy School of Government. Jackson joined the District of Columbia government in 1981 as a management analyst at the Office of Tax and Revenue, where he later became division manager, chief tax enforcement officer, and chief of Assessment Services Division. From 1995 until his appointment as chief of staff, Jackson worked as the Office of Tax and Revenue's director of customer service administration. He served as chief of staff to the District of Columbia chief financial officer from May 2000 to July 2001. He was director of the Department of Community and Housing Development. Jackson was named acting president of the University of the District of Columbia in July 2007.

Yvonne R. Jackson

BUSINESS. Yvonne R. Jackson is a native of Los Angeles, California. She is a graduate of Jordan High School. She received a bachelor of arts degree in history from Spelman College and is vice chairman of the Spelman Board of Trustees. She received a certificate in management development from Harvard Business School in 1985.

Jackson has served as a personnel manager for Sears Roebuck and Company. In 1979, she became an executive recruiter for Avon Products, Inc. From 1980 to 1983, she was a manager of employee relations and staffing. In 1989, she became Avon Products' vice-president of human resources for the North American division. She

worked for the Burger King Corporation in 1993, and in 1999, with Compaq Computers. She served as the senior vice president for human resources and a member of the Pfizer Leadership Team, the company's senior executive governing body. As the senior vice president for human resources, she oversaw human resources for the 130,000 employees of Pfizer, Inc., around the world. She currently is head of her own management and human resources consulting firm, Beecher Jackson.

Yvonne T. Jackson

FEDERAL GOVERNMENT, ENGINEERING. Yvonne T. Jackson received a bachelor of science degree in industrial engineering from the University of Alabama in Tuscaloosa and a master of science degree in management from the Florida Institute of Technology. She earned a master of science degree in science and technology commercialization from the University of Texas. Her military education includes the advanced program manager's course, Defense Systems Management College at Fort Belvoir, Virginia; sustaining base leadership and management, Army Management Staff College at Fort Belvoir; Senior Service College and Army War College fellowship, Center for Professional Development, University of Texas in Austin; Leadership for a Democratic Society, Federal Executive Institute in Charlottesville, Virginia; defense leadership and management program; and Senior Executive Service Federal Candidate Development Program.

Jackson began her career as an intern with the Department of the Navy at the Naval Facilities Engineering Command in 1986. She transferred to the Department of the Army, where she served in a number of positions of increasing responsibility at the U.S. Army Missile Command. These included senior engineer, assistant program manager for survivability for the Javelin weapon system, and assistant program executive officer for survivability and advanced technology for peo tactical missiles. In 1998, Jackson was selected by the acquisition program manager's board as the product manager for the U.S. Army Small Computer Program at Fort Monmouth, New Jersey. She was one of the first civilians selected to a product manager position. Jackson served on the Headquarters United States Army staff in the Office of the Assistant Secretary of the Army in a number of positions from senior acquisition management specialist to acting director for enterprise development in the Office of the Undersecretary of Defense for Acquisition Technology and Logistics.

Jackson joined Headquarters U.S. Air Force in July 2005 as the assistant peo for combat and mission support. She also was the special assistant for energy conservation to the undersecretary of the Air Force prior to her appointment to the Senior Executive Service in August 2006 as deputy peo, Combat and Mission Support, Office of the Assistant Secretary of the Air Force for Acquisition.

Adrienne C. James

EDUCATION. Adrienne C. James received a bachelor of arts degree in Spanish and secondary education from Wittenberg University and a master's in elementary education from Xavier University. She earned a doctor of education in curriculum and instruction from the University of Cincinnati and completed undergraduate studies from the University of Madrid. James has served over 22 years with the Sycamore Community Schools and four years with the Worthington School District. She worked as the assistant principal at Blue Ash Elementary and was promoted to principal in 1992. In August 2006, the Board of Education named James the superintendent of Sycamore Community Schools. She is the first African American superintendent of Sycamore Community School District. She also served as the president of the Cincinnati Chapter of Links, Inc., 2005–2007.

George E. James

MILITARY. George E. James enlisted in the United States Marine Corps on September 12, 1986, and attended recruit training at the Marine Corps Recruit Depot, Parris Island, South Carolina, followed by engineer training at Courthouse Bay, Camp Lejeune, North Carolina. He is a graduate of the Drill Instructor School at Marine Corps Recruit Depot Parris Island. He is also a graduate of the Marine Security Guard School and the U.S. Army Airborne School.

James has held numerous key leadership positions during his 20-plus year career, including serving in December 1990 with the Marine Security Guard Detachment at the American Embassy in Lisbon, Portugal. In February 1992, he was reassigned to Marine Security Guard Detachment at the American Consulate in Karachi, Pakistan, as the assistant detachment commander. In June 1993, he reported to the 1st Marine Division, Camp Pendleton, California, where he was assigned to the 11th Marine Regiment. James participated in numerous desert firing exercises and Operation Wild Fire in Wenatchee National Forest in the state of Washington. In April 1995, he re-

ported to the 3rd Marine Division for duty with the 12th Marine Regiment on Okinawa, Japan. He was a drill instructor, senior drill instructor, series chief drill instructor, and battalion drill master with the 3rd Recruit Training Battalion.

In August 1999, he reported to the 3rd Force Service Support Group, where he was assigned as the engineer chief, 3rd Transportation Support Battalion. In January of 2000, he assumed the duties of company gunnery sergeant, Support Company, 3rd Transportation Support Battalion. In February 2001, he deployed to Tandem Thrust/Freedom Banner 01 in Australia as the group gunnery sergeant, Brigade Service Support Group 3, 3rd Marine Expeditionary Brigade. In October 2002, he reported to Marine Wing Support Squadron 273 for duty as the engineer chief and was deployed to Kuwait and Iraq in January 2003 with Marine Wing Support Squadron 272 to participate in Operations Enduring Freedom and Iraqi Freedom. He served as the first sergeant of Company B, 2nd Light Armored Reconnaissance Battalion, 2nd Marine Division, and participated in combat operations in Operation Secure Tomorrow on the island of Haiti during 2004, and in Operation Iraqi Freedom 4-6 in Iraq during 2005. Selected to his present rank in November 2006, James was assigned as the sergeant major of Marine Helicopter Training Squadron 302 during May 2007.

Synthia Saint James

ARTIST. Synthia Saint James is a native of Los Angeles, California. She attended Los Angeles Valley College; Dutchess Community College, Poughkeepsie, New York; Inner City Cultural Center, Los Angeles, California; and H&R Block, Los Angeles, California (certified tax practitioner). James is a self-taught artist and author and an internationally recognized fine artist. Her first commissioned paintings were in 1969 in New York; her first one-woman show was in 1977 at the Inner City Cultural Center in New York. She participated in a group exhibition in Paris, France, at the Musee des Duncans in 1980 and the House of Seagram commission for Black History Month in 1989. She designed the cover art for Terry McMillan's *Waiting to Exhale*, international edition, 1992.

Since 1990, she has completed over 50 commissions for major organizations, corporations and individual collectors, including Brigitte Matteuzzi's School of Modern Jazz Ballet (Geneva, Switzerland), the Mark Taper Forum, the Los Angeles Women's Foundation, Kayser-Roth/Maybelline, *Essence* magazine's 25th Anniversary, the American Library Association, unicef, Dance Africa, the Girl Scouts of the USA's 85th Anniversary, Attorney Johnnie L. Cochran, Jr., and the U.S. Postal Service, which commissioned her to create the first Kwanzaa stamp, made available on October 22, 1997. She was also commissioned by Coca-Cola for the Lady of Soul Awards for the American Dance Legacy Institute in honor of Donald McKayle's ballet *Rainbow Round My Shoulder*, along with the Natural History Museum of Los Angeles, the International Association of Black Professional Fire Fighters and many more non-profit organizations.

James has 13 children's picture books currently on the market, three of which she wrote. Her architectural designs include a tile mural for Ontario International Airport, six elevator doors for the East End Complex in Sacramento, California, and three stained glass windows for the West Tampa Library, Tampa, Florida. She also created an original 3 by 6 foot painting for Glendale Memorial Hospital in Glendale, California.

Leon N. Jamison

JUDICIAL. Leon N. Jamison received a bachelor of arts degree and his juris doctor degree from the University of Arkansas at Fayetteville in 1970 and 1975. Jamison served in the United States Army from 1970 to 1973. He worked in private law practice in Pine Bluff, Arkansas, from 1976 to 1992. He has served as a judge for Jefferson and Lincoln counties since 1993. The Arkansas Supreme Court appointed him to the Judicial Discipline and Disability Commission in February 1997. He was a member of the Army Reserve or Arkansas Army National Guard from 1974 to July 1997. He retired from the Arkansas Army National Guard with the rank of lieutenant colonel.

Michael T. Jamison

JUDICIAL. Michael T. Jamison received a bachelor of science degree from Washington University in St. Louis, Missouri, and earned his juris doctor degree from St. Louis University. Jamison served in private law practice from 1992 to 1994. He worked for Anheuser-Busch Companies as an associate general counsel in the Labor Law Section of the Legal Department from 1994 to 1997. He was appointed an associate circuit judge on May 8,

1997. On August 12, 2005, he was appointed a Missouri State Circuit Court judge for Division 10 by Missouri Governor Matt Blunt.

Charlene Drew Jarvis

EDUCATION. Charlene Drew Jarvis is a native Washingtonian. She received a bachelor of arts degree from Oberlin College and a master of science degree from Howard University. She earned a doctor of philosophy degree in neuropsychology from the University of Maryland and has conducted brain research at the Institute of Mental Health. Jarvis is the daughter of Dr. Charles R. Drew, the noted blood bank pioneer. In July 1996, she was selected to serve as the ninth president of Southeastern University and is the first woman to hold this position. In 2007, she began serving as chair of the Consortium of Universities of the Washington Metropolitan Area.

Erich D. Jarvis

SCIENCE. Erich D. Jarvis is a native of Harlem, New York, and attended the High School of the Performing Arts in New York, where he studied dance, majoring in ballet. He received a bachelor of arts degree in biology and mathematics from Hunter College in Manhattan, New York. He earned a Ph.D. in molecular neurobiology and animal behavior from the Rockefeller University in 1995. He was one of only 52 African Americans out of more than 4,300 biologists to earn a doctorate.

Jarvis has received numerous awards for his work, which combines molecular, behavioral, electrophysiological, and computational tools to decipher vocal learning, using learning in birds as a model system. He is using his Pioneer Award to test a hypothesis about the genetic machinery underlying vocal learning that could pave the way for repairing vocalization disorders in humans. Jarvis serves as an associate professor in the Department of Neurobiology at Duke University Medical Center in Durham, North Carolina.

Mabel M. Jasper

JUDICIAL. Mabel M. Jasper received a bachelor of science degree from Kent State University and her juris doctor degree from Cleveland Marshall Law School. She began her legal career in private law practice, which included general counsel for a local savings and loan association. She later served as an assistant attorney general and as a trial attorney for the Bureau of Worker's Compensation for three years. She was then appointed a general trial referee for Cuyahoga County Court of Common Pleas Domestic Relations Division for four years, after which she was elected judge to the Cleveland Municipal Court. She is a member of many civic and professional organizations, including the Ohio State Bar Association.

Vera Jean-White

LOCAL GOVERNMENT. Vera Jean-White is a native of Winsboro, Louisiana, and a graduate of Franklin Parish Training School. She received a bachelor's degree in religious education from the United Bible College and Seminary in 1988, and has also received specialized management certification from Elizabethtown College. Jean-White's career began in 1968 with the Commonwealth of Pennsylvania's Department of Health, serving as program administrator for the Bureau of Basic Education Fiscal Administration Child Nutrition Unit. She was appointed executive director of the Harrisburg School District's first after school program. She currently serves as the parent educator for the Tri-County Opportunities Industrialization Center. In 1992, she was elected a councilwoman to the City Council of Harrisburg, Pennsylvania.

Mildred F. Jefferson

MEDICINE. Mildred F. Jefferson is a native of Pittsburg, Texas, and attended public schools in East Texas. She received a bachelor of arts degree summa cum laude from Texas College in Tyler, Texas, and a master of science degree from Tufts University in Medford, Massachusetts. She earned a medical doctor degree and became the first African American woman to graduate from Harvard Medical School in 1951. She has been awarded 28 honorary degrees by American colleges and universities. Dr. Jefferson served as a general surgeon with the former Boston University Medical Center and assistant clinical professor of surgery at Boston University Medical School for many years. She helped establish the National Right to Life Committee and served three times as its president. She was elected president of the Massachusetts Citizens for Life.

Wallace B. Jefferson

JUDICIAL. Wallace B. Jefferson is a native of San Antonio, Texas. He received a bachelor's degree from James Madison College at Michigan State University and earned his juris doctor degree from the University of Texas School of Law in 1988. Jefferson first served as an attorney in private practice in San Antonio. He was appointed to the Texas Supreme Court in 2001 by Governor Rick Perry and won an election the following year. He is the first African American to serve on the Texas Supreme Court. He was appointed chief justice and confirmed by the Texas Senate in March 2005. He was elected to the chief justice position in 2006.

Carolyn Jefferson-Jenkins

EDUCATION. Carolyn Jefferson-Jenkins received a master's degree in education administration from John Carroll University and a Ph.D. in urban education and administration from Cleveland State University. She also earned an education specialist (Ed.S.) degree from Kent State University.

Jefferson-Jenkins has served as executive director for instructional support services of Douglas County School District in Castle Rock, Colorado. She was the 15th president of the League of Women Voters of the United States and chair of the League of Women Voters Education Fund. As the first woman of African American descent to head the 80-year old organization, Jefferson-Jenkins placed a high priority on issues such as increased citizen participation in the electoral process, campaign finance reform, voting and health care. She is a recognized authority on the voting rights of African Americans and is the author of *The Road of Black Suffrage* and *One Man One Vote: The History of the African American Vote in the United States.*

Carol Jenkins

MEDIA. Carol Jenkins received a bachelor's degree from the University of New York and honorary doctorates from the College of New Rochelle and Marymount Manhattan College. She has served for 23 years at WNBC-TV, where she co-anchored the pivotal 6 P.M. newscast. She was most identified with her reporting of national political stories, including from the floor of Democratic and Republican national conventions that yielded Presidents Carter, Reagan, Bush, and Clinton. She hosted her own talk show, *Carol Jenkins Live*, on WNYW-TV. She is the founding chair of the Board of Greenstone Media, the talk radio network for women. Jenkins is the author, with her daughter Elizabeth Gardner Hines, of *Black Titan: A.G. Gaston and the Making of a Black American Millionaire.* It was selected by the Black Caucus of the American Library Association as one of the best non-fiction books of 2004. She is an executive producer of the pbs documentary *What I Want My Words to Do to You*, which won the Freedom of Expression Award at the Sundance Film Festival in 2003.

Esther J. Jenkins

EDUCATION. Esther J. Jenkins received a bachelor of arts degree from Northwestern University in Evanston, Illinois. She earned a master of arts and Ph.D. from the University of Michigan in Ann Arbor. Jenkins serves as a professor of psychology at Chicago State University in Chicago, Illinois, where she formerly was chair of the Department of Psychology. She currently serves as research director for the Community Mental Health Council of Chicago. She is a member of the American Psychological Association, Homicide Research Working Group and International Society.

Martin J. Jenkins

JUDICIAL. Martin J. Jenkins is a native of San Francisco, California. He received an associate degree from City College of San Francisco in 1973 and a bachelor of arts degree from Santa Clara University in 1976. He earned a juris doctor degree from the University of San Francisco School of Law in 1980. Jenkins served as a law clerk in the Alameda County District Attorney's Office in California; as deputy district attorney from Alameda County District Attorney's Office from 1981 to 1983; and as a trial attorney, Civil Rights Division, U.S. Department of Justice.

From 1985 to 1989, he worked in private law practice; from 1989 to 1992, he was a judge of the Oakland-Piedmont-Emeryville Municipal Court, California. He was a judge for the Alameda County Superior Court, California, from 1992 to 1997. Judge Jenkins was nominated by President Bill Clinton in July 1997 to a seat on the U.S. District Court for the Northern

District of California. He was confirmed by the U.S. Senate on November 9, 1997, and received his appointment and commission on November 12, 1997.

Robert R. Jennings

EDUCATION. Robert R. Jennings earned his bachelor of arts degree in sociology from Morehouse College in Atlanta, Georgia, in 1972. He earned a master of arts degree in educational psychology (1974) and a master of education science degree in interrelated learning (1979) from (Clark) Atlanta University. In 1982, he earned a doctor of education degree in education administration and policy studies from Clark Atlanta University. In 1978, he was a Fulbright-Hays fellow assigned to the Institute of Pernambuco in Recife, Brazil.

Jennings was executive vice president and chief operating officer of Future Focus 2020 at the Babcock Graduate School of Management at Wake Forest University in Winston-Salem, North Carolina. He has also served as an associate professor in the Education and Psychology Department of Morris Brown College in Atlanta, Georgia; as vice president for development and president of the foundation at Norfolk State University in Virginia (1988–1991); as vice president for institutional advancement at Albany State University (1991–1997); and vice chancellor for development and university relations at North Carolina A&T State University, 1997–1998. He was appointed the 10th president of the 130-year old Alabama A&M University in January 2006.

Renaldo M. Jensen

BUSINESS. Renaldo M. Jensen received a bachelor's degree in mechanical engineering from Howard University in Washington, D.C., in 1958, and a master's degree in aerospace engineering from the Air Force Institute of Technology in Dayton, Ohio, in 1963. He earned a Ph.D. in aerospace mechanical engineering from Purdue University in 1970. He served for over 20 years as a United States Air Force officer, and during this time he held several command and staff positions at the Pentagon. In addition, he was an assistant professor of aerospace–mechanical engineering at Howard University. He had attained the rank of lieutenant colonel when he left the service in 1978 to join Ford Motor Company.

Jensen joined Ford Motor Company's Design Center in 1978 as a principal design engineer in the Aerodynamics Department. He was a supervisor of advanced concepts and the advanced engineering design staff. In 1987, he was appointed director of the Ford Motor Company minority supplier development program, created to revitalize and expand the company's business relationships.

Patricia Coats Jessamy

LOCAL GOVERNMENT. Patricia Coats Jessamy was the seventh of eight children raised on a farm in the Mississippi Delta. She graduated from high school in Hollandale, Mississippi, in 1966. She received a bachelor's degree in history and political science from Jackson State University in 1970 and earned her juris doctor degree from the University of Mississippi School of Law in 1974.

Jessamy began her legal career in 1974 in Cleveland, Mississippi. She moved to Maryland in 1985 and served as an assistant state's attorney. In 1986 she was appointed chief of the Economic Crimes Division. In 1987, State's Attorney Stuart Simms appointed Jessamy as deputy state's attorney for administration. In 1995, the Maryland Circuit Court unanimously appointed her as state's attorney when Simms resigned following his appointment as state secretary of juvenile services. She was elected to her second term in November 1998 and re-elected to her third term in November 2002. Jessamy currently serves as Baltimore City state's attorney, the first woman in this post.

Jaicy John

PUBLIC SERVICE. Jaicy John received a bachelor's degree in psychology from Barnard College. She earned a master's degree from New York University and a Ph.D. in social psychology from the City University of New York. John leads New York Life Foundation Girl Scouts Scholars, a college and ca-

reer-oriented program for girls from grades seven through twelve held at Barnard every Saturday throughout the school year. Because the aim of the Girl Scouts is to prepare girls for higher education and professional careers, John, as program administrator, believes the college environment is an ideal place to help them explore their dreams.

Anthony D. Johnson

MILITARY. Anthony D. Johnson received a bachelor of science degree in electrical engineering from the University of South Florida in Tampa. His military education includes Squadron Officers School, Air Command and Staff College, Air War College, Officer Training School, and Pilot Training at Columbus Air Force Base. Johnson received his commission from Officer Training School in April 1979. He is a command pilot with more than 4,000 hours in fighter aircraft. He graduated from undergraduate pilot training at Columbus Air Force Base in Mississippi in May 1980. He flew the RF-4 from 1980 to 1985, logging approximately 1,200 hours. Colonel Johnson transitioned to the A-10 in 1985 and has flown more than 2,900 hours and has served in Operations Deny Flight, Decisive Endeavor, Northern Watch, Iraqi Freedom and Enduring Freedom. He has approximately 70 combat missions and more than 200 combat hours.

In March 2005, he was assigned as commander of the 442nd Operations Group at Whiteman Air Force Base in Missouri. In May 2007, he was selected to serve as the vice commander of the 442nd Fighter Wing at Whiteman. He is an international first officer for American Airlines in his civilian occupation. Before assuming his current position in May 2007, he was the commander of the 442nd Operations Group.

Arthur E. Johnson

BUSINESS. Arthur E. Johnson received a bachelor of arts degree from Morehouse College in Atlanta, Georgia. He joined Lockheed Martin Corporation from IBM in 1994. In 1996, he was elected vice president of Lockheed Martin Corporation and named president of Lockheed Martin Federal Systems. In 1997, Johnson was named president and chief operating officer of Lockheed Martin's information and services sector. In October 1999, he was named senior vice president, corporate strategic development.

Carol R. Johnson

EDUCATION. Carol R. Johnson received a bachelor's degree in elementary education from Fisk University in Nashville, Tennessee. She earned both her master of science and Ph.D. degrees from the University of Minnesota. Johnson worked as superintendent of Minneapolis Public Schools, where she was named Superintendent of the Year, and as superintendent of the Memphis City Schools in Tennessee. She garnered national praise for her work in Memphis, where she was named the Tennessee Superintendent of the Year by the Tennessee Parent Teacher Association for her commitment to family and community engagement as a key priority for improving student achievement. In August 2007, Johnson began her career as the superintendent of the Boston Public Schools. She received a five-year contract through June 2012.

Earvin Effay Johnson, Jr. (Magic)

SPORTS. Earvin Effay Johnson, Jr., known as Magic Johnson, was born in Lansing, Michigan. He attended Everett High School, where he joined the school's basketball team. He had a triple-double at age 15, scoring 36 points, 16 rebounds and 16 assists. After this, a sports writer called him "Magic" for the first time. As a senior, Johnson led Everett to a 27–1 record and the Michigan state title while averaging 28.8 points and 16.8 rebounds. He attended Michigan State University, where he helped the college's basketball team win the NCAA college basketball championship in 1979.

Having won everything possible at the college level, Johnson declared himself eligible for the 1979 National Basketball Association draft. The Los Angeles Lakers drafted Johnson and signed him for a salary of $600,000 a year. His pro career includes playing for the Los Angeles Lakers from 1979 to 1991 and in 1996. During this time he was a three-time NBA most valuable player (MVP) (1987, 1989 and 1990); five-time NBA cham-

pion (1980, 1982, 1985, 1987, 1988); three-time NBA finals MVP (1980, 1982, 1987); 12-time All-Star (1980–1992); two-time All-Star MVP (1990, 1992); and 1992 Olympic gold medalist. He was named to the NBA's 50th anniversary All-Time Team in 1997and the Hall of Fame in 2002. In his career he scored 17,707 points, 5,559 rebounds and 10,141 assists.

Johnson hosted a short-lived late night talk show on Fox called *The Magic Hour* in 1998. He is the founder, president and chief executive officer of Magic Johnson Enterprises, which specializes in urban business development with a variety of ventures. It oversees the daily operations of the Magic Johnson brand and partnerships including 24 Hours Fitness, Burger King, Cadbury Schweppes, Magic Johnson Travel Group, SodexhoMagic and TNT, Starbucks Coffee and Magic Johnson Theaters.

Edward L. Johnson

MILITARY. Edward L. Johnson received a bachelor of science degree in business administration from Trinity College and University. His military education includes completion of the first sergeant course, standard property book system course, master fitness course, instructor training course, drill sergeant course, the United States Army Sergeants Major Academy, and the command sergeants major course.

Johnson enlisted in the U.S. Army in March 1985. He received his basic combat training at Fort Leonard Wood, Missouri. He has served in numerous leadership positions, including unit supply sergeant, property book noncommissioned officer, drill sergeant, platoon sergeant, 92Y senior career advisor, first sergeant, brigade S-3 sergeant major, and command sergeant major.

Among other assignments, he has served with the 3rd Infantry Division in Aschaffenburg, Germany, and in Korea on two tours. He was deployed during Operation Desert Shield, Operation Desert Storm and Operation Provide Comfort from December 1990 to May 1991 with 3rd Infantry Division. Most recently he was deployed to Operation Iraqi Freedom IV from July 2005 to July 2006 with the 101st AA Division. He serves as the command sergeant major of the 498th Combat Sustainment Support Battalion Command in Korea.

Faith Johnson

JUDICIAL. Faith Johnson is a native of Atlanta, Georgia. She received a bachelor of arts degree in psychology and her master's of education in community counseling from Georgia State University. She earned a juris doctor degree from the Thurgood Marshall School of Law at Texas Southern University in 1980. Johnson has worked as psychological counselor, attorney, as an assistant district attorney, and chief felony prosecutor of a child abuse unit. In 1989, she was appointed by Governor Bill Clements as a state Criminal District Court judge in Dallas County. She was the first African American female in the state of Texas to be appointed to the position. She was also the first African American female to attain the highly regarded status of chief felony prosecutor in the Dallas County District Attorney's Office. Her tenure at the district attorney's office spanned over seven years and her tenure on the bench spanned 17 years.

Frederick J. Johnson

MILITARY. Frederick J. Johnson received a bachelor of arts degree in music and education from South Carolina State University in 1976. He earned a master of science in strategic studies from the United States Army War College. Johnson was commissioned second lieutenant in the U.S. Army Reserve in December 16, 1976 from ROTC at South Carolina State University. He entered active duty in January 1977 at Fort Knox, Kentucky, and was assigned to the armor officer basic course. He served in various active duty assignments from 1977 to 1988. In 1990, General Johnson entered the Alabama Army National Guard, where he served in numerous staff level positions in operations, training, and intelligence and later as the assistant chief of staff at Headquarters, 62nd Troop Command. He has served with distinction as the commander of the 3rd Battalion 200 Leadership Regiment; 167th Materiel Management Command; and the 621st Troop Support Command. Upon his promotion to brigadier general in October 26, 2005, he was assigned as the assistant adjutant general, Army Joint Forces Headquarters, Alabama Army National Guard.

Grindley Johnson

STATE GOVERNMENT. Grindley Johnson is a native of Chesapeake, Virginia. She received a bachelor's degree in accounting from Norfolk State University. She has held positions with Siemens in community and public relations, media relations, human resources and accounting. She was a 1995 fellow for the American Swiss Young Leaders and a 1996 fellow for the Sorenson Institute of Political Leadership. Johnson currently is the Virginia Commonwealth Transportation Commission's chief of equal business and employee opportunity. Her primary area of responsibility is to lead the Civil Rights Division within Virginia Department of Transportation. Her charge is to ensure that equal access is provided to protected classes of employees, contractors and patrons in terms of employment, business opportunities, and physical access.

Hank Johnson

FEDERAL GOVERNMENT. Hank Johnson is a native of Washington, D.C. He received a bachelor of arts from Clark College (Clark Atlanta University), Atlanta, Georgia, and earned his juris doctor from Thurgood Marshall School of Law, Texas Southern University, Houston, Texas, in 1979. Johnson has worked in private practice; as a member of the DeKalb County, Georgia, board of commissioners from 2001 to 2006; and as a judge in DeKalb County Magistrate Court. He was elected as a Democrat to the 110th Congress (January 3, 2007).

Jack Johnson, Jr.

MILITARY. Jack Johnson, Jr., received an associate in arts degree in communications application technology from the Community College of the Air Force at Maxwell Gunter Air Force Base in Alabama. He earned a bachelor of science degree in global business management and a master of science degree in security management from Bellevue University in Bellevue, Nebraska. His military education includes completion of the Noncommissioned Officer Academy at Kadena Air Base in Japan; the Air Force First Sergeants Academy at Maxwell Air Force Base; the Air Force Senior Noncommissioned Officer Academy at Maxwell; joint senior noncommissioned officer correspondence course from the National Defense University in Washington, D.C.; and the U.S. Air Force senior leadership course from the Center for Creative Leadership, San Diego, California.

Johnson entered the U.S. Air Force in October 1984. His primary specialty is as an intelligence superintendent. He has had a variety of assignments at squadron, group, wing, agency, center, combatant command and air staff levels. Prior to his current assignment, he was the first sergeant special duty manager, Office for the Chief Master Sergeant of the Air Force, Headquarters U.S. Air Force in Washington, D.C. He is the command chief master sergeant for the largest war-fighting wing in the U.S. Air Force, the 18th Wing, Kadena Air Base, Okinawa, Japan.

Jim Johnson

EDUCATION. Jim Johnson received a bachelor of science from North Carolina Central University and a master of science from the University of Wisconsin at Madison. He received a Ph.D. from Michigan State University. He serves as the William R. Kenan, Jr., distinguished professor of entrepreneurship and director of the Urban Investment Strategies Center at the University of North Carolina Chapel Hill. He is co-director of the Center for Sustainable Enterprise.

Johnson's research interests include community and economic development, the effects of demographic changes on the U.S. workplace, interethnic minority conflict in advanced industrial societies, urban poverty and public policy in urban America, and workforce diversity issues. With support from the Russell Sage Foundation, he is researching the economic impact on U.S. metropolitan communities of the September 11, 2001, terrorist attacks.

Justin Morris Johnson

JUDICIAL. Justin Morris Johnson received a bachelor of arts degree and a juris doctor degree from the University of Chicago. He has attended the graduate program for judges at the University of Virginia. His active military duty (1954–1959) and his reserve duty (1963–1973), including two active duty flights into Vietnam during 1971, were with the U.S. Air Force as an aircraft commander. From 1977 until his appointment to the bench he was a member of the Pennsylvania Crime Commission. He was appointed judge to the State Superior Court of Pennsylvania in 1980.

He also sat on the Permanent Judicial Commission of the General Assembly, Presbyterian Church (USA), from 1981 to 1989. Johnson completed a six-year term on the Advisory Committee on the constitution of that national, churchwide body in June 1996. In 1989, he completed twenty years of service on the Pennsylvania Board of Law Examiners, the last six as its chairman. In August 1993, he was appointed to a two-year term on the newly established Court of Judicial Discipline by Acting Governor Mark S. Singel. He also served five years as an adjunct professor at Duquesne University School of Law.

Mamie Bush Johnson

MINISTRY, JUDICIAL. Mamie Bush Johnson received a bachelor's degree in 1985 and earned a juris doctor degree from Texas Southern University. She served as a municipal court judge from 1990 to 1993 and Tarrant County Criminal Court judge from 1994 to 1997. Johnson was involved in missionary work while on the bench and in 1999 became the full-time minister at Rising Star Baptist Church in Fort Worth.

Melvin N. Johnson

EDUCATION. Melvin N. Johnson received a bachelor's degree in economics from North Carolina A&T State University and a master of arts in economics from Ball State University. He earned a master of business administration and doctor of business administration in business economics and public policy from Indiana University. He taught at the U.S. Air Force Academy and served in the U.S. Air Force as a lieutenant colonel. He served in senior academic roles at North Carolina A&T State University. He was provost and vice chancellor for academic affairs at Winston-Salem State University and tenured professor of economics since July 2000. Johnson was named the seventh president of Tennessee State University on March 10, 2005.

Michael K. Johnson

ENGINEERING. Michael K. Johnson received a bachelor's degree in electrical systems technology at the University of Central Florida, with post-baccalaureate studies in statistical communication theory at the University of California Los Angeles. He is a Six Sigma black belt at Northrop Grumman Space Technology. In recent assignments, Johnson was deputy integration and test manager of the Space Tracking and Surveillance System program. He also served as section captain for the Mars Reconnaissance Orbiter proposal, managing inputs for various engineering functions. He was field integration and test manager for the Tactical High Energy Laser program, where he orchestrated more than 40 high-energy-laser missions, including the first single-rocket shootdown.

Norman S. Johnson

MINISTRY. Norman S. Johnson is a native of Little Rock, Arkansas. He has been in the Christian ministry since 1973 and was ordained in 1979. He was associate minister of the Greater Bethlehem Baptist Church in Dallas, Texas, from 1975 to 1979. He was pastor of two other Los Angeles Baptist churches, Greater Faith (1980 to 1985) and Galilee (1985 to 1988). The Rev. Johnson has served as pastor of the First New Christian Fellowship Missionary Baptist Church in Los Angeles since 1988. He was also the executive director of the South Christian Leadership Conference, Los Angeles Chapter.

Otis Johnson

EDUCATION, LOCAL GOVERNMENT. Otis Johnson was the first African American from Savannah, Georgia, to earn a bachelor's degree from the University of Georgia in 1967. He earned a master of social work degree from Atlanta University and a Ph.D. in social wel-

fare from Brandeis University, Waltham, Massachusetts. Johnson began his career with the Economic Opportunity Authority and the Model Cities Program before joining Savannah State College as a professor. He was elected to the Savannah City Council in 1982. In 1988, he resigned from the City Council and tenured faculty position at Savannah State to become executive director of the Youth Futures Authority, a collaborative of agencies that help children and families fight drug use, teen pregnancy, dropping out of school and other social problems.

In 1998, he became dean of the College of Liberal Arts and Social Sciences at Savannah State; he was elected without opposition to the Savannah-Chatham Board of Education. In May 2002, he retired from the dean's position at Savannah State University. He was elected mayor of the City of Savannah in November 2003.

Robert Johnson

MILITARY. Robert Johnson was commissioned in the infantry upon graduation from the United States Military Academy with a bachelor's degree in 1975 and earned a master of arts in clinical psychology from the University of Tennessee. His military education includes infantry officer basic course; Airborne School; Air Assault School; Ranger School; infantry mortar platoon leader course; infantry officer advance course; the Pathfinder course; the Marine Command and Staff College; and the Naval War College, where he earned a master's degree in national security and strategic studies in 1994.

He initially served as a company grade officer at the 101st Airborne Division (Air Assault) at Fort Campbell from June 1976 to December 1979. He commanded Alpha Company, 1st Battalion, 503rd Infantry Regiment, 101st Airborne Division. From August 1982 to June 1985, he served on the staff and faculty at West Point as a cadet counselor and tactical officer. He departed West Point and went to Korea, where he was a battalion S-3 and battalion executive officer for 1st Battalion, 38th Infantry Regiment, 2nd Infantry Division. He was the regimental executive officer with the 3rd United States Infantry (the Old Guard) from 1990 to October 1991. He was selected to serve as the battalion commander, 1st Battalion, 503rd Infantry Regiment, 2nd Infantry Division, in Korea. He returned to West Point as the deputy director of admissions in November 1995, a position he held until October 2004, when he was appointed the director of admissions for the U.S. Merchant Marine Academy at Kings Point.

Robert S. Johnson

MILITARY. Robert S. Johnson is a native of St. Petersburg, Florida, where he graduated from Gibbs High School in 1946. He received a bachelor of arts in natural science (emphasis in biology) from Paine College in Augusta, Georgia, in 1950, and a master's in education (emphasis in science education) from Atlanta University (now Clark Atlanta University). He studied at the University of Georgia, Louisiana State University and Florida State University under National Science Foundation grants. His military education includes: clerical typing and procedure course; Leadership School, Non-Commissioned Officer (NCO) School, Senior Noncommissioned Officer School, senior personnel sergeant course, advanced personnel course, Chemical Biological and Radiological course, 71L non-commissioned officer education systems course, Academy of Health basic courses, and basic personnel officers course (10 series).

Johnson joined the Organized Reserve Corps in 1950 and entered active military service in 1952. His key military assignments include basic and advanced training at Fort Jackson, South Carolina; operations NCO with the 802nd Engineer Aviation Battalion in Korea and Japan; training NCO with the 1st Special Troops at Fort Benning, Georgia; company clerk, 928th Engineers at Albany, Georgia; personnel records chief, 2300 Augmentation Group, Atlanta, Georgia; and personnel management supervisor, 461st Personnel Service Company, East Point, Georgia. He was assigned as the operation and readiness NCO, G-1, at the Third U.S. Army at Fort McPherson, Georgia; as manpower analyst for the U.S. Army Manpower Requirement and Document Agency at Fort Belvoir, Virginia; and as an instructor of personnel management courses for the Knoxville, Tennessee, and Harrisburg, Pennsylvania, U.S. Army Reserves Schools.

He was also an instructor for the 81st Army Reserve Command NCO Academy at Fort Indiantown Gap, Pennsylvania. In September 1982 Johnson became the first black promoted to sergeant major in the 81st Army

Reserve Command. He is also the first African American photographer for the Atlanta Bureau of the Associated Press and United Press. He served as a high school biology teacher in Florida and Georgia. He taught at Price High School in Atlanta from 1957 to 1987.

Sandra K. Johnson

ENGINEERING. Sandra K. Johnson received a bachelor of science in electrical engineering summa cum laude from Southern University in 1982. She earned a master of science degree in electrical engineering from Stanford University and a Ph.D. in electrical engineering from Rice University. She is a member of the Morgan State University School of Engineering Advisory Board. Johnson is a senior technical staff member and the chief technology officer for global small and medium business at IBM Systems and Technology Group.

Her previous assignments include working as the Linux performance architect at the IBM Linux Technology Center in Austin, Texas, and managing the Linux performance team at the IBM Linux Technology Center, the WebSphere Database Development team at the IBM Silicon Valley Laboratory and the Java server performance (JASPER) team within IBM Research. She has conducted research in a number of high-end computer related areas and was part of the design team that developed the prototype for the IBM Scalable Parallel Processor (SP2), the base machine for "Deep Blue," IBM's world famous chess machine.

Johnson is a member of the prestigious IBM Academy of Technology, which consists of the top 300 of IBM's over 195,000 technical professionals. This academy drives IBM's technical strategy and provides input to IBM's executives regarding future technologies. She is a research division master inventor with thirteen patents and eight pending. She has authored and co-authored over 80 publications, is editor-in-chief of the book *Performance Tuning for Linux Servers*, and has published a book of words of wisdom titled *Inspirational Nuggets*.

Sterling Johnson, Jr.

JUDICIAL. Sterling Johnson, Jr., is a native of Brooklyn, New York. He received a bachelor of arts from Brooklyn College in 1963 and earned an LL.B. degree from Brooklyn Law School in 1966. Johnson served in the United States Marine Corps from 1952 to 1955. He was a police officer, New York City Police Department, 1956 to 1967; assistant United States attorney, Southern District of New York, 1967 to 1970; and executive director, Civilian Complaint Review Board, New York City Police Department, 1970 to 1974.

In 1974 he was executive liaison officer, U.S. Drug Enforcement Administration. From 1975 to 1991, Johnson was special narcotics prosecutor for New York City, and from 1999 to 2003 he was commissioner, United States Sentencing Commission. Johnson was nominated judge by President George H.W. Bush on May 17, 1991, to a seat on the U.S. District Court for the Eastern District of New York. He was confirmed by the U.S. Senate on June 27, 1991, and received his commission on July 2, 1991. He assumed senior status on June 1, 2003.

Sylvester M. Johnson

LAW ENFORCEMENT. Sylvester M. Johnson attended Philadelphia Community College, Temple University, the Senior Management Institute for Police at Harvard University, Pennwalt Corporation's targeted management training, the U.S. Secret Service dignitary protection training, the Federal Bureau of Investigation's (FBI) National Academy Class 172, and the FBI National Executive Institute.

Johnson joined the Philadelphia Police Department in 1964. During his long and distinguished career, he served in a wide variety of assignments, including the Highway Patrol Unit, Police Radio/Communications Unit, East Detective Division, Homicide Unit, Northwest Detective Division, North Central Detective Division, Dignitary Protection Unit/Mayor's Security and the Headquarters Investigation Unit. In 1998, he was appointed deputy commissioner of operations, the second highest-ranking officer in the department with responsibility for all front-line police operations. On January 4, 2002, he was named the 13th police commissioner of the City of Philadelphia.

Wayne Johnson

CULINARY ARTS. Wayne Johnson's culinary adventures started in high school, working as a dishwasher and prep cook. He attended the University of Northern Colorado to study accounting and spent the next three and a half years cooking his way through college. He has special training in the foods of Spain and studied at Greystone, located in Napa Valley.

In 1981, Johnson moved to Vail, Colorado. At the Marriott Hotels and Resorts he went from cook to banquet chef from 1981 to 1990. In 1990, he took his first executive chef position and later became the executive chef at the four diamond rated Renaissance Parc 55 Hotel in San Francisco. In 1999, Johnson was named the executive chef of the Mayflower Park Hotel in downtown Seattle and the well loved Andaluca Restaurant and Bar. In 2002, he cooked at the James Beard House and under his supervision Andaluca won many awards, including "Seattle's Best Mediterranean Restaurant." He was named one of the United States' top African American chefs.

William Johnson

JUDICIAL. William Johnson received a bachelor of arts from Rollins College in 1970 and earned his juris doctor degree from the University of Miami in 1973. He served in private practice from 1971 to 1977 and as a judge of compensation claims for the State of Florida, District K. He currently serves as a Florida Circuit Court judge for the Juvenile Division.

C. Darnell Jones II

JUDICIAL. C. Darnell Jones II is a native of Philadelphia, Pennsylvania. He received a bachelor of science degree from Southwestern College in 1972 and earned his juris doctor degree from American University in 1972. He served as an attorney from 1972 to 1987. In 1987, he was first appointed a judge to the Pennsylvania Court of Common Pleas by Governor Robert Casey. He was an adjunct professor of law at the University of Pennsylvania Law School and has taught there since 1993, and is a senior faculty member of the National Judicial College, where he teaches state trial judges and U.S. military judges death penalty litigation and evidence. He has been commissioned by the Pennsylvania Supreme Court to teach Pennsylvania common pleas judges death penalty jurisprudence.

Darryl Jones

PUBLIC SAFETY. Darryl Jones received a bachelor's degree from Carlow College and earned a master's degree from Carnegie Mellon University. He has served as a squad leader for the Pennsylvania Urban Search and Rescue Strike Team, and also worked as an emergency medical technician in Bridgewater prior to joining the Aliquippa Fire Bureau. After serving 12 years as Aliquippa's fire chief, he joined the City of Pittsburgh Fire Department as an assistant chief. In July 2007 Mayor Luke Ravenstahl appointed Jones the fire chief for the City of Pittsburgh, Pennsylvania. He became the first African American to serve as that city's fire chief.

Deneese L. Jones

EDUCATION. Deneese L. Jones received a bachelor's degree from Texas Woman's University. She earned her master's degree and Ph.D. from Texas A&M University. She was a first grade teacher at Fannin Elementary in Bryan, Texas, and has served as chair of the President's Commission on Diversity and associate dean of the graduate school at the University of Kentucky. She currently is professor and dean of Longwood University's College of Education and Human Services in Farmville, Virginia. Through Jones' efforts, the university is one of only five in the nation participating in the Call Me Mister program that aims to recruit minority males into the elementary teaching profession.

Elijah Jones, Jr.

MILITARY. Elijah Jones, Jr., is a native of Chicago, Illinois. His military education includes all the noncommissioned officer courses, Special Weapons School, Master Fitness School, Airborne School, Drill Sergeant School, Cadet Command Course, first sergeant course, and the sergeants major course (Class 55). Jones entered the U.S. Army on December 5, 1978, as a field artillery cannon crewman. He attended basic training and advanced individual training (one station unit training) at Fort Sill, Oklahoma. During his career he has served in many leadership positions, including platoon sergeant, senior drill sergeant, chief instructor for artillery training, first sergeant, and operations sergeant major.

He has served as chief instructor of artillery at Fort Sill; first sergeant, 3rd Battalion, 18th Field Artillery, Fort Sill; First Sergeant, 1st Battalion, 19th Field Artillery, Fort Sill; University of Oklahoma chief instructor, HHB 21D Fires Brigade; and division fires and effects sergeant major. Jones assumed duties as the Battlefield Coordination Detachment — Korea sergeant major in July 2006.

Emanuel Jones

STATE GOVERNMENT, BUSINESS. Emanuel Jones is a native of Atlanta, Georgia, and graduated class valedictorian from West Fulton High School in Atlanta in 1977. He received a bachelor of science degree in electrical engineering from the University of Pennsylvania in 1981 and a master of business administration in finance and accounting from Columbia University in 1986.

Jones served in 1980 the U.S. Army Corps of Engineers and rose to the rank of captain. From 1981 to 1984 he was with IBM and from 1986 to 1988 with Arthur Anderson and Co. In 1988, he entered the automobile business as president and owner of Legacy Ford of McDonough, Georgia, Legacy Toyota of Union City, Georgia, Legendary Ford-Mercury of Marion, North Carolina, Legacy Goodyear Tire Center of McDonough, Georgia, and ANSA Automotive of Macon, Georgia, and Los Angeles, California.

Jones was first elected to the Georgia State Senate from the 10th District in 2004. He serves parts of DeKalb and Henry counties.

Michael F. Jones

MILITARY. Michael F. Jones graduated from Lakewood High School in June 1983 and reported for recruit training at Marine Corps Recruit Depot at Parris Island, South Carolina, in July 1983. He also completed the marine artillery scout observers course at Fort Sill, Oklahoma. His leadership positions have included liaison chief, scout observer, forward observer, fire support coordination chief, drill instructor, senior drill instructor, security chief, enlisted career counselor, first sergeant, and sergeant major.

Jones participated in Operation Desert Storm in 1991. He participated in several exercises, including combined arms exercises at Palms, California, and deployed to Southwest Asia in support of Operations Enduring Freedom and Iraqi Freedom from February to July 2003. In August 2003, he was assigned to the 3rd Marine Division as the battalion sergeant major for Combat Assault Battalion. In December 2003, he was transferred within the 3rd Marine Division as the Headquarters Battalion and camp sergeant major for Camp Courtney. In May 2004, he was transferred to Marine Corps Base, Camp Butler, to serve as director of the Senior Noncommissioned Officer Academy in Okinawa, Japan. In August 2006, he was transferred to his current assignment as the regimental sergeant major of the 10th Regiment, 2nd Marine Division.

Nathaniel R. Jones

JUDICIAL. Nathaniel R. Jones is a native of Youngstown, Ohio. He received a bachelor of arts degree in 1951 and his LL.B. degree in 1956, both from Youngstown State University. Jones served with the U.S. Air Force during World War II. He worked in private law practice; as executive director of the Fair Employment Practices Commission; and as an assistant U.S. attorney for the Northern District of Ohio in Cleveland. He held that position until his 1967 appointment as assistant

general counsel to President Lyndon Johnson's National Advisory Commission on Civil Disorders (the Kerner Commission).

In 1969, he was asked to serve as general counsel of the NAACP by executive director Roy Wilkins. For the next ten years, Judge Jones directed all NAACP litigation. On May 17, 1979, President Jimmy Carter nominated Jones to the U.S. Court of Appeals for the Sixth Circuit. He received his commission and appointment on October 15, 1979, and currently is a senior judge on that court.

Richard A. Jones

JUDICIAL. Richard Jones is a native of Settle, Washington. He received a bachelor's degree in public affairs from Seattle University in 1972 and earned his juris doctor from the University of Washington in 1975. He has served as a deputy prosecutor for King County, Washington; from 1979 to 1983, he was a staff attorney for the Port of Seattle; from 1983 to 1987, he worked in private law practice; from 1988 to 1994, he was an assistant U.S. Attorney in the Western District of Washington; and from 1994 to 2007, he was a judge on the King County Superior Court in Washington. Jones was nominated by President George W. Bush on March 9, 2007, as a federal judge on the U.S. District Court in the Western District of Washington. He was confirmed by the U.S. Senate on October 4, 2007.

Samuel L. Jones

LOCAL GOVERNMENT. Samuel L. Jones is a native of Mobile, Alabama. He is a graduate of Central High School and attended Florida Junior College and Jacksonville University in Jacksonville. He attended Alabama Interdenominational Seminary and was awarded an honorary doctorate. Jones served nine years in the U.S. Navy, during which time he was a flight deck troubleshooter for A-7 aircraft aboard U.S. Navy aircraft carriers and an equal opportunity officer. He served as executive director of Mobile Community Action, Inc., from 1980 to 1987, supervising 240 employees and a $5 million annual budget. Before being elected mayor, he was a four-term county commissioner for the state's second largest county. He helped pioneer the city-county partnerships evident in the construction of Metro Jail and Mobile Government Plaza.

Theodore T. Jones, Jr.

JUDICIAL. Theodore T. Jones, Jr., is a native of Brooklyn, New York, and attended public schools in New York City. He received a bachelor of arts degree in history and political science from Hampton University in Hampton, Virginia, in 1965 and earned his juris doctor degree from St. Johns University School of Law in 1972. He served as a criminal defense attorney with the Legal Aid Society. He was law secretary to Justice Howard A. Jones, New York State Court of Claims. He then entered private practice in Brooklyn, New York. He was elected to the New York Supreme Court with a term beginning 1990. Jones was elected to the State Supreme Court in Brooklyn in 1989 and re-elected in 2003, eventually serving as administrative judge of the court's civil term. On February 13, 2007, Jones was sworn in as the newest judge on New York State's highest court, the Court of Appeals, by Governor Eliot L. Spitzer. He was confirmed by the New York State Senate on February 12, 2007.

Voresa Jones

MILITARY. Voresa Jones received a bachelor's degree in business administration from Lane College in May 1981 and enlisted in the United States Navy in February 1983. She earned a master's degree in systems management from the Naval Postgraduate School.

Following boot camp and Personnelman "A" school, she was selected for Officer Candidate School in Newport, Rhode Island, and was commissioned in March 1985. Her military education includes Navy Legal Justice School, senior legal course, Navy Drug and Alcohol Abuse Counselor School, Navy rights and responsibilities instructor course, total quality leadership instructor course, and manpower analyst course.

Commander Jones has served as a legal officer and security manager, commander with Training Squadron Ten; officer programs officer, commander, Navy Recruiting District Seattle; manpower analyst, commander, U.S. Atlantic Fleet; officer-in-charge, Personnel Support Activity Detachment Oceana; commanding officer, Tampa Military Entrance Processing Station; chief, Navy and Marine Corps Personnel and Navy Element Commanding Officer; and commander, United States Special Operations Command. She currently serves as the executive officer, Navy Recruiting District, in Nashville, Tennessee.

Pandora Jones-Glover

JUDICIAL. Pandora Jones-Glover is a native of Charleston County, South Carolina. She received a bachelor of arts degree in history and political science from Clemson University in 1995 and earned her juris doctor degree from the University of Arkansas School of Law in 2000. Jones-Glover began her legal career as the law clerk for the Honorable Clifton B. Newman of Third Judicial Circuit. In March 2002, she began working as an assistant solicitor for the First Judicial Circuit. She was promoted to first assistant solicitor in February of 2004. On July 1, 2004, Jones-Glover was appointed by Governor Mark Sanford to fill the unexpired term of Judge Vivian Ross-Bennett. She was sworn in as Orangeburg County probate judge on July 9, 2004, by the Honorable Clifton Newman, Circuit Court, 3rd Judicial Circuit.

Claudia J. Jordan

JUDICIAL. Claudia J. Jordan is a native of Raleigh, North Carolina. She attended segregated schools until high school. She received a bachelor's degree from the University of North Carolina at Charlotte and earned her juris doctor degree from the University of Colorado School of Law. Judge Jordan's legal career includes serving as a trial attorney for the Colorado State Public Defender. In 1987, she opened her own law practice in the heart of Denver. In 1994, she was appointed a Colorado District Court judge for Denver County.

Diane Jordan

LOCAL GOVERNMENT. Diane Jordan is retired from Delta Airlines and is currently employed by gem Technologies, Inc., as director of public relations. In 1994 she became the first African American woman to be elected to the Knox County, Tennessee, Commission. She was re-elected in 1998 and 2002. She serves on the finance committee as well as the Knox County Board of Zoning Appeals and the Knox County Insolvency Board. She led the fight for the creation of a Citizens' Review Board for the Knoxville Police Department. Jordan is also deeply involved in the ministry of her husband, John, the pastor of Peace and Goodwill Baptist Church.

Linus Jordan, Jr.

MILITARY. Linus Jordan, Jr., is a native of Eunice, Louisiana. He received an associate degree in applied science, instructor technology and military science from Community College of the Air Force. He earned an occupational instructor certificate from the same institution. His military education includes all the noncommissioned officers courses; the U.S. Air Force Academic Instructor School at Maxwell Air Force Base; Airman Leadership School instructor course at Maxwell; U.S. Air Force Senior Noncommissioned Officer Academy at Maxwell; chief leadership course at Maxwell; Army transportation senior leader course, Fort Eustis, Virginia; basic combat convoy course at Camp Bullis, Texas; and Army combat skills training at Fort Sill, Oklahoma.

Jordan entered the U.S. Air Force in July 1988. His assignments took him to base, numbered Air Force, and major command positions in Louisiana, Japan, Florida, Korea, Germany, Virginia and Texas. He led transportation support of humanitarian relief missions during Operation Enduring Freedom and deployed to Southwest Asia in support of Operations Desert Thunder and Iraqi Freedom, including two combat tours executing theater convoys with the U.S. Army. From April 2005 to July 2006, he served as vehicle management flight chief with the 1st Logistics Readiness Squadron at Langley Air Force Base; from July 2006 to July 2007 he was superintendent of the 37th Mission Support Group at Lackland Air Force Base in Texas. In July 2007 he became command chief master sergeant, 374th Airlift Wing, Yokota Air Base in Japan.

Jethro Joseph

BUSINESS. Jethro Joseph received a bachelor of arts degree from Morris Brown College and earned a master of business administration degree from Wayne State University. He has also conducted studies at the University of Michigan and Walsh College. In his professional career he has served as financial controller at three of DaimlerChrysler's facilities — Mt. Elliott Tool and Die, Sterling Stamping and Warren Truck Assembly. He was appointed senior manager, diversity supplier development, at DaimlerChrysler Corporation on July 1, 1996.

Tom Joyner, Sr.

MEDIA. Tom Joyner is a native of Tuskegee, Alabama, and a graduate of Tuskegee (Institute) University, with a bachelor of science in sociology. He began his broadcasting career in Montgomery at WRMA-AM immediately after graduation.

In the mid–1980s Joyner accepted a position as "morning drive man" at Chicago's WGCI while still working in Montgomery. Flying every day between the two cities to work eventually earned Joyner national recognition, the nickname "Fly Jock," seven million frequent flyer miles, syndication and undoubtedly the largest audience of any urban radio program. The Tom Joyner Foundation assists African-American students in historically black colleges and universities across the nation. The foundation has raised more than $14 million to date. In 1999, Tom Joyner was inducted into the Radio Hall of Fame. Every day more than seven million listeners in more than 120 radio markets listen to the *Tom Joyner Morning Show*.

Damon Jerome Keith

JUDICIAL. Damon J. Keith is a native of Detroit, Michigan. He received a bachelor of arts degree from West Virginia State College in 1943 and an LL.B. degree from Howard University in 1949. He earned an LL.M. degree from Wayne State University Law School in 1956. Keith served in the United States Army from 1943 to 1946. He worked from 1950 to 1967 in private law practice.

He was nominated by President Lyndon B. Johnson in September 1967 as a federal judge and was confirmed by the U.S. Senate in October 1967. He received his commission and appointment on October 12, 1967, to serve as a judge on the U.S. District Court for Eastern District of Michigan. He served as chief judge from 1975 to 1977. Keith was nominated by President Jimmy Carter in September 1977 to a seat on the U.S. Court of Appeals for the Sixth Circuit. He was confirmed by the Senate on October 20, 1977, and received his commission on October 21, 1977. He assumed senior status on May 1, 1995.

LeVerne W. Kelley

ENGINEERING. LeVerne W. Kelley received a bachelor of science degree from Morgan State University and went to grad school at the Johns Hopkins University. She completed her master's studies at the University of the Redlands in California. Kelley serves as vice president of human resources, environmental health and safety, and security at SanDisk Corporation, the world's largest supplier of flash data storage card products. She is responsible for global human resources, overseeing compliance with the regulations that protect the employees, and the company's physical and intellectual property.

William E. Kennard

FEDERAL GOVERNMENT; MEDIA. William E. Kennard is a native of Los Angeles, California. He graduated from Hollywood High School in Hollywood, California. He received a bachelor of arts degree in communications from Stanford University in 1978 and earned his juris doctor degree from Yale Law School in 1981. Kennard has worked in private law practice as a partner and

member of the board of directors of a Washington, D.C., law firm. He served with the Federal Communication Commission as a general counsel from 1993 to 1997. In 1997, he was named chairman of the U.S. Federal Communication Commission, becoming the first African American to serve in that position. When his term expired in 2001, he was hired by the Carlyle Group as managing director of Global Telecom and Media Group.

C. Ray Kennedy

BUSINESS. C. Ray Kennedy is a native of Newton, North Carolina, and was one of nine children. He was educated in the segregated public school system (Central High School), received a bachelor of science degree from the University of Maryland Eastern Shore, and earned a master of business administration from North Carolina Central University. His education also includes the Louisiana State University Graduate School of Banking of the South and the University of North Carolina Chapel Hill executive program of professional management education. Kennedy is most distinguished as an innovative entrepreneur. He owns Ramsey-Peele Corporation (three university child development centers and three currency exchange financial centers) and is founder and majority shareholder of American Product Distributors, Inc.

Nathelyne A. Kennedy

ENGINEERING, BUSINESS. Nathelyne A. Kennedy was the first woman to receive a bachelor of science degree in architectural engineering from Prairie View A&M University. She is a registered professional engineer in Texas, with more than 37 years of experience as a design engineer and project manager. Kennedy is the founder and president of Nathelyne A. Kennedy and Associates, a professional civil and structural consulting engineering firm in Houston.

Paul Killpatrick

EDUCATION. Paul Killpatrick received a bachelor's degree in social studies and a Ph.D. in post-secondary education from Oregon State University. He earned his master's degree from Western Oregon State University. He has worked in senior administrative positions at Yakima Valley Community College in Yakima, Washington. He served as the vice president of instruction and the vice president of instructional support and community at Mt. Hood Community College in Gresham, Oregon. Killpatrick assumed the presidency of Great Basin College in June 2002. Since then Great Basin College has shown steady growth. Enrollments increase at an average of 7 percent each year and the college has secured millions of dollars in grant awards during his tenure.

Walter M. Kimbrough

EDUCATION. Walter M. Kimbrough is a native of Atlanta, Georgia, and a graduate of Benjamin E. Mayes High School and Academy of Math and Science as the salutatorian and student body president. He received a bachelor of science degree in biology from the University of Georgia in 1989. He earned a master of science degree in college student personnel services in 1991 and a Ph.D. in higher education from Georgia State University in 1996 in Atlanta, Georgia. Kimbrough, at age 39, was named the 12th president of Philander Smith College in Little Rock, Arkansas, becoming the first college president from the hip-hop generation.

Bernard Kincald

EDUCATION, LOCAL GOVERNMENT. Bernard Kincald received a bachelor of arts degree from Miles College in 1970 and a master of arts degree from Miami University in Oxford, Ohio, in 1971. He earned his Ph.D. from the University of Alabama in Tuscaloosa in 1980 and a juris doctor from Birmingham School of Law in 1994. Kincald was a youth counselor, Program Center, Social Security Administration, Birmingham, Alabama, from 1970 to 1971. From 1971 to 1995, he served as assistant professor and assistant to the dean for cultural diversity and minority affairs, School of Health Related Professions. From 1996 to 1997, he was an educational consultant and worked at Miles College as a contract director of development.

In 1997, he was elected to the Birmingham City Council from District 8, and in 1999, was elected mayor of the City of Birmingham.

Leslie D. King

JUDICIAL. Leslie D. King is a native of Greenville, Mississippi, and a graduate of the Greenville public school system. He received a bachelor's degree in political science from the University of Mississippi. He was among the first class of African Americans to begin and complete undergraduate degree requirements at Ole Miss in 1970. He earned his juris doctor degree from Texas Southern University School of Law in Houston.

King worked in private law practice in Greenville until 1994. He served as a Mississippi state representative from Washington County from 1980 to 1994 in the Mississippi House. While a legislator, he was vice chairman of the ways and means and conservation and water committees. He was selected to serve as a judge on the Mississippi State Court of Appeals in 1995. He was a presiding judge from 1999 to 2004, when he was appointed to fill the vacancy of chief judge. He was appointed to a full four-year term in the position by state Supreme Court Chief Justice James W. Smith, Jr.

Tim K'Nuckles

LAW ENFORCEMENT. Tim K'Nuckles is a native of Pine Bluff, Arkansas. He is a 1997 graduate of the Northwestern University Traffic Institute, School of Police Staff and Command. He joined the Arkansas State Police in 1985 as a trooper assigned to Chicot County. He has served as a post sergeant in Troop F (Union County) between 1995 and 1998 and was promoted to lieutenant in August 1998. He was reassigned as an administrative assistant to the commander of the Highway Patrol Division. Subsequently he spent two years assigned as an administrator within the director's office before he was promoted to captain and assigned as commander of Highway Patrol, Troop E, at Pine Bluff. He served as chief of staff to the director of the Arkansas State Police. Lieutenant Colonel K'Nuckles was appointed the deputy director of the Arkansas State Police.

Shiriki K. Kumanyika

PUBLIC HEALTH. Shiriki K. Kumanyika is a native of Baltimore, Maryland. She received a bachelor of arts in psychology degree from Syracuse University in 1965 and a master of science degree in social work from Columbia University in 1969. She earned a Ph.D. in human nutrition from Cornell University in 1978 and a master of public health degree with emphasis on epidemiology from the Johns Hopkins University School of Hygiene and Public Health in 1984. She is also a senior fellow in Penn's Leonard Davis Institute of Health Economics and the Institute on Aging.

Kumanyika was a social caseworker and community organizer in the areas of foster care and adoption services, child mental health services, and chronic disease care; she joined the Cornell University faculty teaching community nutrition in both classroom and field settings; from 1984 to 1991, she served as a professor and researcher in nutritional epidemiology at the John Hopkins University School of Hygiene and Public Health.

Kumanyika has served as principal investigator or co-investigator of numerous major studies, including several clinical trials of dietary behavior change for health improvement in underserved and minority populations. Her recent studies involved the development and evaluation of culturally appropriate interventions to prevent or treat obesity among African Americans in clinical or community based settings. She served as the principal investigator and director of the Penn-Cheyney export (Excellence in Partnerships for Community Outreach, Research on Health Disparities and Training) Center for Health. The center is a collaboration between the University of Pennsylvania and the Cheyney University of Pennsylvania. She currently serves as associate dean for health promotion and disease prevention, founding director of the graduate program in public health studies, professor of epidemiology in biostatistics and epidemiology and in pediatrics (nutrition), and senior scholar in the Center for Clinical Epidemiology and Biostatistics, all at the University of Pennsylvania School of Medicine.

Linda Lacey

EDUCATION. Linda Lacey received a bachelor's degree in social science from the University of California at Berkeley. She earned a master's degree and Ph.D. in city and regional planning from Cornell University. She was associate dean of the graduate school at the University of North Carolina at Chapel Hill and a professor of city and regional planning and a research fellow of the Carolina Population Center at UNC Chapel Hill. As a professor of city

and regional planning, she has worked in 12 countries consulting on development plans for population and health issues. Since 1998, she has worked to promote distance education programs in Thailand and Ghana under a grant from the Andrew W. Mellon Foundation. Lacey was appointed dean of the graduate school at New Mexico State University.

Ronald N. Langston

FEDERAL GOVERNMENT. Ronald N. Langston holds degrees from the University of Iowa, the City University of New York (national urban/rural fellow) and Harvard University's John F. Kennedy School of Government. He was appointed by President George W. Bush as the head of the Minority Business Development Agency on March 19, 2001. He is the first individual to officially hold the title of national director.

Wright Lassiter

EDUCATION. Wright Lassiter received a bachelor's degree in business administration from Alcorn State University in Mississippi. He earned a master's degree in business administration from Indiana University and a Ph.D. in education from Auburn University in Alabama. Lassiter has served as director of auxiliary enterprises and business manager at Tuskegee University (then Tuskegee Institute) in Tuskegee, Alabama, and as vice president for finance and administration at Morgan State University (Baltimore).

He was appointed president of Schenectady County Community College (New York) and was president of Bishop College (Dallas). Lassiter joined the Dallas County Community College District as president of El Centro College in August 1986. In 2002, he was nominated by President George W. Bush and confirmed by the U.S. Senate to serve as a member of the National Advisory Council to the National Endowment for the Humanities. The Dallas County Community College District board of trustees named Lassiter chancellor of the district in 2006.

Risa J. Lavizzo-Mourey

MEDICINE. Risa J. Lavizzo-Mourey is a native of Seattle. She earned her medical doctor degree from Harvard Medical School and completed her internship and residency at Brigham and Women's Hospital in Boston. In 1984 she was named a Robert Wood Johnson clinical scholar at the at the University of Pennsylvania, and she received a master of business administration degree in health care administration from the University of Pennsylvania's Wharton School of Business in 1986. Her career combines geriatric medicine and health policy, focusing on disease, disability prevention, and health care issues among minorities. She served as deputy administrator of the federal Agency for Health Care Policy and Research from 1992 to 1994. She was appointed president and chief executive officer of the Robert Wood Johnson Foundation. She is the first woman and first African American to hold the post.

LaDawn Law

EDUCATION. LaDawn Law received a bachelor of arts in education from California State University in Los Angeles and a master's in social science from Azusa Pacific University. She earned a Ph.D. in education from Claremont Graduate University. Law has served as an elementary school principal, a consultant for the Consortium on Reading Excellence, as assistant superintendent of the child development program for the San Francisco Unified School District, and as assistant superintendent of curriculum and instruction in a large urban district and a small suburban district. In August 2004, she was hired as superintendent of the Ravenswood City School District.

Howard N. Lee

EDUCATION. Howard N. Lee received a bachelor of arts degree in sociology from Fort Valley State College and a master's degree in social work from the University of North Carolina at Chapel Hill. He has served as a member of Southern Regional Education Board and the Education Commission of the State of North Carolina. He was a member of the North Carolina Utili-

ties Commission and a former senior advisor with the James B. Hunt, Jr., Institute for Educational Leadership and Public Policy. In addition to owning several businesses, he served in the North Carolina State Senate and is former mayor of Chapel Hill, North Carolina. He was appointed to the State Board of Education by Governor Michael F. Easley in May 2003 to fill an unexpired term. He was unanimously elected chair of the board by its members. Lee is the first African American to hold that post.

Beverly Leedom

MILITARY. Beverly Leedom joined the United States Navy in 1984 as a non-designated striker. After completing basic training, she was assigned commander-in-chief, U.S. Pacific Fleet, Pearl Harbor, Hawaii. Leedom attended Dental "A" School in 1986, where she excelled as the class leader. While serving aboard the USS *Camden* (AOE 2), she was selected as chief petty officer. In her following tour at the Construction Battalion Center in Port Hueneme, she was selected senior chief petty officer. She became master chief petty officer while at Navy Medical Education and Training Command as the Dental "C" School program manager. Leedom transferred to the U.S. Naval Hospital Yokosuka in August 2005 and was the senior enlisted advisor of the seven detachments located throughout the Pacific Rim. She assumed the duties as the command master chief in April 2006.

Valeria A. Lemmie

STATE GOVERNMENT. Valeria A. Lemmie received a bachelor's degree in political science and urban society from the University of Missouri and earned a master's degree in urban affairs and public policy planning from Washington University. She was a scholar-in-residence at Kettering Foundation, a research organization focused on democracy and the strengthening of public life. She has been an adjunct professor in public administration at the University of Dayton and senior fellow at the Center for Excellence in Municipal Management at George Washington University. She was appointed city manager for Cincinnati and Dayton, Ohio. She also served as the city manager for Petersburg, Virginia. She was appointed a commissioner to the Public Utilities Commission of Ohio by Governor Bob Taft in 2006.

Tammy Bass-Jones LeSure

JUDICIAL. Tammy Bass-Jones LeSure is a native of Mineral Wells, Texas. She received a bachelor of arts degree in political science from the University of Oklahoma and earned her juris doctor degree from the University of Oklahoma College of Law. Her legal career began at the Oklahoma County Public Defender's Office as a staff attorney. She left the public defender's office and entered private law practice. In 1997, she was sworn in as a special judge for Oklahoma City. On November 3, 1998, LeSure became one of the first African American females elected District Court judge in the history of Oklahoma County and the state of Oklahoma.

Audre Levy

EDUCATION. Audre Levy received a bachelor's degree in public speaking from Michigan State University, three master's degrees (master of arts in education from the University of Michigan; master of science in educational psychology from California State University at Long Beach; and master of science from California State University, Dominguez Hills). In 1991, she graduated with a doctoral degree in institutional management from Pepperdine University, and in June 2004 she earned her fourth master's degree, this one in divinity. She has served in all levels of education: elementary, junior high school, senior high school, adult school, community college, and four-year university. She has been an instructor teaching English, reading, and public speaking for over 12 years. She was a junior high, senior high,

and community college counselor for seven years and an administrator for over 15 years.

Her administrative assignments at the post-secondary level have included as director of several state and federal programs, vice president of student services, executive vice president, provost, and president of Los Angeles Southwest College. She has held positions of leadership at Los Angeles Community College District and San Jose Evergreen Community Colleges. In May 2006, the Glendale Community College Board of Trustees appointed Levy to the position of superintendent and president of the college district. She is the first woman to serve in the position in the 78-year history of the institution.

Aylwin B. Lewis

BUSINESS. Aylwin B. Lewis is a native of Houston, Texas. He received a bachelor's degree in business management and English literature from the University of Houston. He earned a master of business administration from the University of Houston. He has worked as a director of Sears Holdings Corporation and Halliburton Co. In 1996 he was appointed chief operating officer of Pizza Hut and from 2000 to 2003 as chief operating officer of yum! Brands. He has served with KFC, Long John Silver, Taco Bell and A&W. In October 2004, he was named president and chief executive officer of Kmart. He is currently president and chief executive officer of Sears Holdings Corporation, a nationwide retailer.

Casandra Lewis

JUDICIAL. Casandra Lewis began her legal career as an intern at the United States Attorney's Office. She served as an assistant state's attorney and was an instructor at the National Institute for Trial Advocacy at Loyola Law School. She was a trial lawyer for 12 years; she now serves as a Circuit Court judge in Cook County, Illinois. In 2007, Lewis ran for justice of the Illinois Appellate Court.

David B. Lewis

JUDICIAL. David B. Lewis is a native of Ardmore, Oklahoma. He received a bachelor's degree in business economics from the University of Oklahoma and earned his juris doctor from the University of Oklahoma Law School in May 1983. He worked in private law practice from 1984 to 1987. In 1987, he joined the district attorney's office of Comanche County as an assistant at the courthouse in Lawton, Oklahoma. From January 1991 to April 1999, he was a special district judge for Comanche County. On April 2, 1999, he was appointed district judge of Comanche, Stephens, Cotton, and Jefferson counties. In 2004, he served as president, Oklahoma Judicial Conference.

Grover C. Lewis

MILITARY. Grover C. Lewis is a native of Minden, Louisiana, and attended Northeast Louisiana University, where he graduated with a bachelor of business administration degree in May 1981 and a master's degree in national resource strategy from the Armed Forces in Washington, D.C., in June 2003. He was commissioned a second lieutenant upon graduation from Officer Candidate School in December 1982. Following completion of the basic school in June 1983, he attended the infantry officer course in Quantico, Virginia. He is a graduate of the Marine Command and Staff College at Quantico. His served in 1989 as the logistics officer for Marine Security Forces Battalion at Mare Island Naval Shipyard in Vallejo, California. Following this tour, he was assigned to 1st Battalion, 8th Marine Regiment, at Camp Lejeune, North Carolina, where he was the battalion landing team logistics officer and deployed as part of the 22nd Marine Expeditionary Unit.

In 1994, he was the Headquarters Battalion logistics officer. In August 1998, he was selected to serve as the aide-de-camp for the assistant commandant of the Marine Corps. In August 1999, he was assigned to G-3 Operations section with the 2nd Force Service Support Group. On June 13, 2000, he assumed command of Marine Wing Support Squadron 171 in Iwakuni, Japan. He served as deputy director of Asian-Pacific affairs in the Office of the Secretary of Defense, International Security Affairs, in 2003. He was assigned to the Marine Corps Combat Service Support School.

John R. Lewis

FEDERAL GOVERNMENT. John R. Lewis is a native of Troy, Alabama. He received a bachelor of arts from the American Baptist Theological Seminary in Nashville, Tennessee, in 1961 and a bachelor of arts degree from Fisk University in Nashville in 1967. During the height of the Civil Rights Movement from 1963 to 1966, he served as chairman of the Student Nonviolent Coordinating Committee. He was director of action, a federal volunteer agency from 1977 to 1980. He was community affairs director, National Consumer Co-op Bank, Atlanta, Georgia, and elected a member of the Atlanta City Council, 1982 to 1986. He was elected as a Democrat to the 100th and to the ten succeeding Congresses (January 3, 1987, to present).

Juan C. Lewis

MILITARY. Juan C. Lewis received an associate in applied science degree in hotel and restaurant management and certified hotel administrator license from the American Hotel and Lodging Education Institute. He earned a bachelor of applied science degree in management studies and a personal trainer license from Coopers Institute. He is a graduate of the Senior Noncommissioned Officer Academy at Maxwell Air Force Base in Alabama. Lewis has held key management and leadership positions in the services career field, including joint billets at Joint Task Forces and the North Atlantic Treaty Organization.

He was chief enlisted manager for the 48th Mission Support Group at the Royal Air Force Base in Lakenheath, England. In addition, he has served as the honor guard superintendent. Lewis is the 95th Air Base Wing command chief master sergeant. He is responsible for advising the wing commander on the welfare, utilization, recognition and progression of the 630 enlisted men and women assigned to the Air Base Wing at Edwards Air Force Base, California.

Marvin Lewis

SPORTS. Marvin Lewis is a native of McDonald, Pennsylvania, near Pittsburgh. He received a bachelor's degree in physical education from Idaho State University in 1981 and earned his master's in athletic administration from Idaho State University in 1982. He was inducted into Idaho State's Hall of Fame in 2001, having earned All Big Sky Conference honors as a linebacker with the Idaho State University Bengals for three consecutive years (1978–1980).

Lewis never played in the National Football League, but he was both a player and a coach at the college level. He was head coach of his alma mater, Idaho State University (1981–1984), and a linebackers coach at Long Beach State (1985–1986), the University of New Mexico (1987–1989), and the University of Pittsburgh (1990–1991).

In 1992, Coach Lewis was hired by the Pittsburgh Steelers as a linebackers coach. He was hired as the defensive coordinator for the Baltimore Ravens in 1996. In 2000, the Ravens won the Super Bowl, defeating the New York Giants 34–7. In 2002, he was hired as the Washington Redskins' defensive coordinator. In 2003, he became head coach of the Cincinnati Bengals. Lewis is the only Bengal head coach not to experience a losing season. Taking over after the 2002 club had posted a franchise-worst 2–14 record, he led a pair of 8–8 finishes before breaking through to claim the division title.

Yvonne Lewis

JUDICIAL. Yvonne Lewis received a bachelor of science degree from State University of New York, College of Geneseo, in 1967 and earned her juris doctor degree from the University of Buffalo School of Law in 1973. She was an assistant clinical professor of law at Hofstra Law School; in 1986, she became the first African American female judge to serve on the Civil Court in Kings County, New York. She has served as a Supreme Court justice for the 2nd Judicial District in New York since 1991. She was still serving on the Supreme Court in 2008.

Delice Liggon

MILITARY. Delice Liggon is a native of Greenville, Mississippi. She received a bachelor of science degree in management from Columbia College and is currently pursuing a master's degree in business management at Webster University. Her military education includes all the noncommissioned officer courses; instructor training course; small group leader training course; Training and Doctrine Command cadre training course; equal opportunity course; Drill Sergeant School; first sergeant course; the U.S. Army Sergeants Major Academy; and the command sergeants major course at Fort Bliss, Texas.

Liggon entered the U.S. Army on December 5, 1983. She completed base combat training at Fort Dix, New Jersey. Her leadership assignments include serving as petroleum dispatch supervisor, 19th Materiel Management Center, Wiesbaden, Germany; drill sergeant, 262nd Quartermaster Battalion, Fort Lee, Virginia; senior drill sergeant and operations sergeant, 23rd Brigade at Fort Lee; first sergeant for the national support element in Tazar, Hungary; first sergeant for the 565th Quartermaster Company at Fort Hood, Texas; sergeant major for the Petroleum Division, 19th Theater Support Command at Camp Henry, Korea; and as the command sergeant major, 559th Quartermaster Battalion, Hunter Army Airfield, at Fort Stewart, Georgia. Sergeant Major Liggon was deployed in support of Operation Iraqi Freedom with the Division Support Brigade, 3rd Infantry Division, Camp Taji, Iraq.

Sam Lindsay

JUDICIAL. Sam Lindsay is a native of San Antonio, Texas, and was raised in South Texas. He received a bachelor's degree in history and government magna cum laude from St. Mary's University in 1974 and earned his juris doctor degree from the University of Texas School of Law in Austin, Texas, in 1977. Lindsay began his career in the Dallas City Attorney's Office, Prosecution Division, in May 1979. He worked in the federal litigation section for 10 years, served as executive assistant city attorney from 1990 to 1991, as first assistant city attorney for 10 months, acting city attorney for six months and finally took the top job in May 1992, becoming the first African American city attorney for Dallas.

He held the post until his appointment as a federal judge for the Northern District of Texas. Judge Lindsay was nominated by President William J. Clinton on November 8, 1997, to a new seat created by legislation. He was confirmed by the Senate on March 11, 1998, and received his commission on March 17, 1998. He is the first African American federal judge appointed to the Northern District of Texas.

Samuel Lloyd

LOCAL GOVERNMENT. Samuel Lloyd is a native of Baltimore, Maryland, and a graduate of Paul Laurence Dunbar High School. He received a bachelor's degree from Morgan State University and a law degree from Catholic University. His professional career started at the Rouse Company in the legal department in 1973. A unique opportunity took him to Charles Center–Inner Harbor Management from 1975 to 1977. In 1977 he was executive director of the Maryland Human Relations Commission. From 1978 to 1982, he was assistant secretary for economic development in the then Maryland Department of Economic and Community Development. From 1986 to 1989, he served as vice president and general manager for American Cable Systems of California. From 1989 to 1999, he held the positions of sale vice president for wireless national accounts in AT&T's Government Markets organization and director of national accounts and government services in the AT&T Wireless Services organization. Lloyd spent two years at historic Fisk University in Nashville, Tennessee, as chief of staff and senior vice president to President Carolynn Reid-Wallace. After spending almost 25 years away from the city in various business and academic pursuits, he returned home to serve the mayor and city of Baltimore.

Benjamin H. Logan II

JUDICIAL. Benjamin H. Logan II is a native of Dayton, Ohio, where he graduated from Chaminade High School in 1961. He received a bachelor of arts in accounting and history from Ohio Northern University and earned his juris doctor degree from Ohio Northern University Law School in 1972. He was with the Legal Aid Soci-

ety of Kent County, 1972–1974; an evening instructor at Davenport College, 1973–1975; in general practice of law, 1974–1988; instructor at Grand Valley State University, 1975–1977; and arbitrator, American Arbitration Association, 1981–1988.

Logan was elected judge to the 61st District Court in Grand Rapids, Michigan, on November 6, 1988, when the first write-in election in Kent County's history yielded the first black judge on the 61st District Court, serving a six-year term. The Grand Rapids community has only an eight percent black population. Logan has served as chair of the Judicial Council National Bar Association. On August 10, 1994, he was sworn in as chair of the Judicial Council National Bar Association in Seattle, Washington. Judge Logan has won every election since 1988, with no opposition in 1994 and 2000.

Yolanda J. Lomax

MILITARY. Yolanda J. Lomax began her military career in the United States Army Reserve in August 1979. She received training in the 45B career management field, small arms repairman. She has completed all facets of the military schooling and is a graduate of the U.S. Army Sergeants Major Academy.

Her leadership assignments have included small arms section leader, 602nd Maintenance Company at Fort Hood, Texas; small arms shop foreman, 123rd Maintenance Company, Furth, Germany; drill sergeant, basic combat training, Fort Jackson, South Carolina; armament maintenance platoon sergeant and shop foreman, 54th Forward Support Battalion, Friedberg, Germany; convoy commander, in charge of 20 vehicles and 41 personnel during Operations Desert Shield and Desert Storm; armament shop foreman, maintenance control supervisor, and S-3 operations sergeant, 324th Forward Support Battalion at Fort Benning, Georgia; armament maintenance supervisor, 501st Corps Support Battalion, Camp Red Cloud, Republic of Korea; first sergeant, 187th Ordnance Battalion, Fort Jackson, South Carolina; first sergeant, 2nd Battalion, 39th Infantry Regiment (Basic Combat Training), Fort Jackson, South Carolina; and operations sergeant major, 100th Area Support Group, Grafenwoehr, Germany. She was selected to serve as the command sergeant major for the 417th Base Support Battalion in Kitzingen, Germany.

Eddie L. Long

MINISTRY. Eddie L. Long is a native of North Carolina and received a bachelor's degree in business administration from North Carolina Central University. He earned a master of divinity degree from Atlanta's Interdenominational Theological Center and a Ph.D. in pastoral ministry from the International College of Excellence, an affiliate of Life Christian University in Tampa, Florida. Additionally, he received honorary doctorate degrees from North Carolina Central University, Beulah Heights Bible College of Atlanta, and the Morehouse School of Religion. He first served as a pastor in 1987 for a congregation consisting of just over 300 members. He now serves as bishop of the New Birth Missionary Baptist Church Lithonia, Georgia, with a membership of over 25,000.

Alfred Davis Lott

LOCAL GOVERNMENT. Alfred Davis Lott was born in Detroit and grew up in Mobile, Alabama. After graduating from Williamson High School in 1972, he received a bachelor of science degree in political science from Tuskegee University in 1976. He earned a master of science degree in public administration from the University of Central Texas. He received training as a pilot at Tuskegee. He was a distinguished military graduate of Tuskegee's Army ROTC program. In 2004, he received his certified public manager's credentials from George Washington University and the Metropolitan Washington Council of Governments.

He has served in the U.S. Army as an infantrymen, aviator (helicopter pilot), commander, and public affairs officer for 22 years, retiring as a lieutenant colonel. In local government service, Lott has been assistant city manager of the City of College Park, Maryland; public works director of the City of Takoma Park, Maryland; and currently is the city manager of Albany, Georgia. He has served as the Albany's city manager since September of 2005.

Darlene A. Lovell

MILITARY. Darlene A. Lovell entered the United States Navy in May 1977. She completed basic military training at Recruit Training Center, Orlando, Florida, and Cryptologic Technician "A" School at Naval Technical Training Center, Pensacola, Florida. She received an associate in science degree in mid-management from Harold Washington College and a bachelor of science degree in criminal justice from National University.

She completed the Command Career Counselor's School in 2000 and is a graduate of the Navy Senior Enlisted Academy at Newport, Rhode Island.

Lovell has held a variety of leadership positions: in January 1995, she was a recruiter in charge and leads supervisor at Navy Recruiting District in San Francisco; she was department head of administration at the Naval Security Group Activity Imperial Beach, California; and from May 2000 to March 2001, she was aboard the USS *Peleliu* as the public affairs officer and site television leading chief petty officer. As command master chief of the USS *Shiloh*, homeported in San Diego, she was deployed to the Arabian Gulf in support of Operations Southern Watch, Enduring Freedom and Iraqi Freedom. After a successful tour aboard the USS *Shiloh*, she assumed duties as command master chief, Naval Security Group Activity San Diego, in September 2003. In May 2005, Lovell assumed duties as command master chief, USS *Hopper*.

Donna Lowry

MEDIA. Donna Lowry received a bachelor of arts degree in communications administration and management from Chatham College in Pittsburgh, Pennsylvania, and a master of science in journalism from Northwestern University near Chicago. After a short stint in radio, in 1981, she served with WEEK-TV in Peoria, Illinois; in 1983, she worked for WESH-TV in Orlando–Daytona Beach, Florida. Lowry joined WXIA-TV 11 Alive News in Atlanta in 1986. During her tenure she has covered the entire spectrum of news stories and has won praise and awards, including Emmys, for her coverage of everything from child abuse and domestic violence to daycare and educational issues.

Sammie L. Lymon

MILITARY. Sammie L. Lymon graduated from high school in 1979 in Greenwood, Mississippi. He enlisted in the U.S. Navy on July 20, 1979. He completed recruit training at Naval Recruit Training Center, Orlando, Florida, followed by fireman apprenticeship training. His was instructor at Machinist's Mate "A" School at Service School Command Great Lakes and was named Sailor of the Quarter and Sailor of the Year. He was selected as engineering department leading chief petty officer and division officer for Main Propulsion Division on the USS *Cape Cod*, homeported in San Diego, California.

He then reported to Recruit Training Command San Diego, California. He transferred to Recruit Training Command Great Lakes in October 1993 as a recruit division commander and ship's leading chief petty officer. He received orders to the USS *Ponce* as engineering department leading chief petty officer and division officer for main propulsion. He reported to Expeditionary Warfare Training Group Atlantic in August 1998 as instructor and course supervisor for fuels testing and bulk petroleum. While assigned to Expeditionary Warfare Training Group Atlantic, he was advanced to master chief petty officer and selected for the command master chief program. He served as command master chief for the USS *Gunston Hall* and the USS *Battaan* (LHD5). On January 29, 2007, he assumed the duties as Assault Craft Unit Four command master chief.

Alphonso C. Mack, Jr.

MILITARY. Alphonso C. Mack, Jr., is a native of Florence, South Carolina. He graduated from West Florence High School in 1979. He enlisted in the U.S. Marine Corps on May 26, 1983. In October 1983, he graduated from Camp Geiger at Camp Lejeune, North Carolina. He also completed Advanced Noncommissioned Officer School, the substance abuse counseling officer course, force protection officer course, and the first sergeant course.

His most recent assignments include as first sergeant for the 2nd Battalion, 4th Marines, company first sergeant for Weapons Company. He deployed with 2nd Battalion 4th Marines in support of Operation Iraqi Freedom II; in April 2005 First Sergeant Mack redeployed to Okinawa, Japan, with 2nd Battalion, 4th Marines, as a part of the 31st Marine Expeditionary Unit. On June 23, 2006, he was assigned as the sergeant major for Marine Heavy Helicopter Squadron 362.

DeLores Mack

EDUCATION. DeLores Mack is a native of Bolton, Mississippi, and a graduate of Sumner Hill School in 1969. She is a 1971 graduate of Utica Junior College and received a bachelor's degree in elementary education from Alcorn State University. She earned a master's degree in elementary education from Jackson State University. She received a specialist's degree in deaf education from New York University in 1986 and specialist's degree in special education from Jackson State University in 1989. Mack earned a doctorate in early childhood education and curriculum instruction from Jackson State University in 2000. She has also earned a specialist's degree from Jackson State University in administration and supervision and leadership. In addition, she has studied at Smith College in North Hampton, Massachusetts, the University of London in London, England, and the University of Manchester, Manchester, England.

Mack has over 33 years of experience in education, serving as a teacher assistant, librarian, elementary teacher, middle school teacher, curriculum coordinator, elementary principal, and secondary principal. The Mississippi State Board of Education appointed Mack as the superintendent of the Mississippi School for the Deaf in April 2005. She is the first African American to serve in this position.

Tracy Mack

ENGINEERING. Tracy Mack received a bachelor of science degree in mechanical engineering from Rensselaer and is pursuing her master's in engineering at Purdue. Her professional career began in computer aided engineering at General Motors, where she received recognition for creative innovation and high performance. She serves as a harmony engineer with the Harmony and Human Factors Department at General Motors.

Carolyn R. Mahoney

EDUCATION. Carolyn Mahoney received a bachelor of science degree in mathematics from Siena College in Memphis, Tennessee. She earned a master of science degree and a Ph.D. in mathematics from the Ohio State University. Mahoney served 10 years at California State University in San Marcos as one of 12 founding faculty members, chairperson of the Department of Mathematics, and interim vice president for academic affairs. She also has served as program director in the Office of Systemic Reform at the National Science Foundation. She was dean of the Elizabeth City State University School of Mathematics, Science and Technology. Mahoney was selected to serve as vice chancellor of academic affairs and provost of Elizabeth City State University. She was appointed the first woman to serve as president of Lincoln University of Missouri.

Shirley Malcom

SCIENCE. Shirley Malcom received a bachelor's degree with distinction in zoology from the University of Washington and a master's degree with distinction in zoology from the University of California at Los Angeles. She earned a Ph.D. in ecology from Pennsylvania State University and received 14 honorary degrees. Malcom serves as head of the directorate for Education and Human Resources Programs of the American Association for the Advancement of Science. The directorate includes programs in education, activities for underrepresented groups, and public understanding of science and technology. In 2006 she was named co-chair of the National Science Board Commission on 21st Century Education in Science, Technology, Engineering and Mathematics (STEM). She has served on numerous other boards, including the Howard Heinz Endowment and the H. John Heinz III Center for Science, Economics and the Environment. She has been honorary trustee of the American Museum of Natural History; regent of Morgan State University; trustee of Caltech; trustee of the Carnegie Corporation of New York; a member of the National Science Board, the policymaking body of the National Science Foundation; and on the President's Committee of Advisors on Science and Technology.

Mark Mallory

LOCAL GOVERNMENT. Mark Mallory is a native of the West End of Cincinnati, Ohio. He is a graduate of

the Cincinnati Academy of Math and Science. He received a bachelor of science degree in administrative management from the University of Cincinnati. Mallory served in the Ohio General Assembly for nearly eleven years. In 1994, he was elected to his first of two terms in the Ohio House, replacing his father, who retired after three decades in the legislature.

In 1998, he defeated an incumbent to be elected to the Ohio Senate. He served in leadership for most of his tenure in the legislature and rose to the position of assistant minority leader of the Senate. Mallory was sworn in as the 68th mayor of the City of Cincinnati on December 1, 2005. Mayor Mallory's election marks the first time in over 70 years that Cincinnati has elected a mayor who was not previously a member of the City Council.

Gerald Malloy

STATE GOVERNMENT. Gerald Malloy is a native of Chesterfield, Colorado. He received a bachelor of science degree from the University of South Carolina in 1984 and his juris doctor degree from the University of South Carolina in 1988. Malloy served in private law practice and as past president of the South Carolina Trial Lawyers Association. He was chosen to serve in the South Carolina Legislature in a special election on November 5, 2002. He is currently a South Carolina Senator for District 29, Chesterfield, Darlington, Lee and Marlboro counties.

Beverly Malone

NURSING. Beverly Malone received a bachelor's degree in nursing from the University of Cincinnati in 1970. She earned a master's degree in psychiatric nursing and a doctorate in clinical psychology in 1981. Malone's career has mixed policy, education, administration and clinical practice. She has worked as a surgical staff nurse, clinical nurse specialist, director of nursing and assistant administrator of nursing. During the 1980s she was dean of the School of Nursing at North Carolina Agricultural and Technical State University. In 1996 she was elected for two terms as president of the American Nurses association, representing 180,000 nurses in the U.S. In 2000 she became deputy assistant secretary for health within the U.S. Department of Health and Human Services, the highest position so far held by any nurse in the U.S. government. In February 2007, Malone was appointed chief executive officer of the National League for Nursing in New York.

Sharon Malone

MEDICINE. Sharon Malone received a bachelor's degree cum laude from Harvard University in 1981 and earned her medical doctor degree from Columbia University College of Physicians and Surgeons in New York City. She then completed her residency at the George Washington University in obstetrics and gynecology. Malone began her professional career as a systems engineer with IBM for three years before attending medical school. She has been in private practice with Foxhall Ob/Gyn since 1992.

508. Craig Manson

FEDERAL GOVERNMENT. Craig Manson received a bachelor's degree from the United States Air Force Academy and a juris doctor from the University of the Pacific Law School. He was an officer in the U.S. Air Force from 1976 to 1989, and from 1989 to 1993, he worked in private law practice. In 1993, he served as the general counsel in the California Department of Fish and Game. In 2001, he was selected to serve as a judge on the Superior Court of California for the County of Sacramento. He currently serves as the assistant secretary of the interior for fish and wildlife.

Herman Marable, Jr.

JUDICIAL. Herman Marable, Jr., is a native of Flint, Michigan. He received a bachelor of arts in American public policy with emphasis in metropolitan studies from James Madison College at Michi-

gan State University. He earned a juris doctor degree from the Ohio State University College of Law. Marable served as an assistant district attorney in Pittsburgh–Allegheny County. He has also served as a law clerk with the UAW-GM legal service and as an assistant prosecuting attorney of Genesee County in Flint, Michigan. He currently serves as Genesee County 68th District Court judge.

Jonathan D. Mariner

BUSINESS. Jonathan D. Mariner received a bachelor of science degree in accounting from the University of Virginia and a master of business administration from Harvard Business School. He is a former certified public accountant. Mariner served as chief operating officer and chief finance officer of Charter Schools USA, one of the nation's leading and fastest growing charter school development and management companies. In this role, he was responsible for overseeing all of the company's day-to-day activities, including curriculum development, education and school operations, marketing and public relations, finance, technology, and human resources.

Mariner was executive vice president and chief financial officer for the Florida Marlins Baseball Club, and in that post was responsible for directing all of the club's financial and administrative activities, including financial reporting, budgeting, payroll, and cash management, as well as the human resources, information technology, and risk management functions. He currently serves as executive and chief financial officer of Major League Baseball in the Office of the Commissioner. In addition to his daily responsibilities of overseeing Major League Baseball's central office budgeting, financial reporting, and risk management activities, Mariner's duties include administering the organization's $1.5 billion league-wide credit facility.

John Marks

LAW, LOCAL GOVERNMENT. John Marks received a bachelor of science degree from the Florida State University School of Business and earned his juris doctor degree in 1972 from the Florida State University College of Law. He served four years in the United States Air Force as a judge advocate, and then in private law practice. In 1979, Florida Governor Bob Graham appointed him to serve an eight year term on the Florida Public Service Commission, the last two years as chairman. Marks is the managing partner of the Tallahassee office of Adorno and Yoss. He was elected mayor of the City of Tallahassee, Florida, on February 25, 2003.

Nikki Marr

JUDICIAL. Nikki Marr is a native of Kirkwood, Missouri, located in the suburbs of St. Louis, where she attended elementary and high school. She received a bachelor of science degree in education from Northeast Missouri State Teachers College (which has been renamed Truman University). She earned master of science degree in educational counseling from the University of Missouri in St. Louis in 1976 and a juris doctor degree from Georgia State University in 1990.

In her professional career she has served as a high school English teacher and guidance counselor. She has worked in private legal practice, specializing in family law, adoptions and juvenile defense. She served seven years as an associate judge of the Juvenile Court of DeKalb County, Georgia. She has returned to private practice, focusing her work on adoptions and mediations, and has become an advocate for children.

Carl Martin

SPORTS. Carl Martin is a native of Highland Park, Michigan, where at the age of 15 he began training in the art of isshinryu karate in 1968. After attending Eastern Michigan University, he was promoted to sho dan in November 1978 by Grand Master Willie Adams in Detroit, Michigan, and promoted to nana dan (7th degree black belt) in September 2003 by Adams.

Martin has competed extensively in the eastern United States, most notably winning grand championships in kumite, kata, weapons and self-defense. A few of these include: Orlando World Championship team fighting Grand Champion Detroit team in 1978; the North American Karate

Championships kumite grand champion in 1979; New Jersey Open Karate Tournament black belt kumite champion in 1980; Lake Erie Shore Open Karate Tournament heavy weight black belt kumite champion in 1986; the 17th Annual AOKA Grand Nationals kata and weapons champion, in 1991; and May Day Mayhem Tournament kata and self-defense grand champion.

Martin established the Tradition Okinawan Karate Institute (TOKI) in 1983 in Norristown, Pennsylvania, and relocated the school to West Chester, Pennsylvania, in 1990, where it remains. A satellite location was established at the Delco Training Gym in Woodlyn, Pennsylvania, in 1994.

Joshua Martin

LAW, BUSINESS. Joshua Martin received a bachelor's degree in physics from Case Institute of Technology. He earned his juris doctor from Rutgers University School of Law and completed the Wharton School executive development program. He was a physicist at the DuPont Company in 1966; in private law practice from 1974 to 1982; from 1978 to 1982, he served on the Delaware Public Service Commission; from 1982 to 1990, he was a judge on the Delaware Superior Court; and in 1990, he joined Verizon's predecessor serving as vice president, general counsel and secretary. Martin has served as president and chief executive officer of Verizon Delaware since 1996.

Mable Martin-Scott

JUDICIAL. Mable Martin-Scott received a bachelor of science degree from the University of Illinois in 1980 and earned her juris doctor degree from the University of Iowa Law School in 1983. Martin-Scott has served as the Indiana state purchasing director as well as general counsel for the Indiana Department of Administration. She was an adjunct business law professor for the Indiana Vocational Technical College. She was appointed administrative appeals judge and was an assistant city attorney for the city of Evansville, Indiana. She also worked in private law practice in Indiana.

Martin-Scott was appointed the chief administrative law judge for the State of Indiana's Unemployment Insurance Review Board. She joined Thomas M. Cooley Law School as an associate professor. She belongs to the state bars of Michigan and Indiana and is admitted to practice before the U.S. District Court, Southern District Indiana.

Kedar Massenburg

ENTERTAINMENT. Kedar Massenburg is a native of Brooklyn, New York. He graduated from college and earned a juris doctor degree from the University of North Carolina Law School at Chapel Hill, North Carolina. He was a district manager for PepsiCo and with SmithKline Beecham Clinical Labs Pharmaceuticals. In 1991, he formed Kedar Entertainment, an artist-management firm. He later diversified the company into various musical activities and made Kedar Entertainment a recording label in 1995. He signed and promoted artist Erykah Badu and D'Angelo in 1996. Massenburg was named president of the Motown label and senior vice president of parent company Universal Records in 1999.

After a six-year stint in the top position at Motown Records, in 2005, he reopened Kedar Entertainment as an independent label. He expanded his reach into the fashion industry with the launch of Sneakerluxe, a couture sneaker line. Kedar Entertainment also encompasses a management arm, a beverage company with French wine called Korus and plans to develop television and film properties.

Donald J. Massey

MILITARY. Donald J. Massey enlisted in the United States Navy through the delayed entry program on January 27, 1987. He completed recruit training at Navy Recruit Training Command, Great Lakes. He is a graduate of the Senior Enlisted Academy. He earned his master training specialist and was responsible for developing the aviation warfare apprentice training course. Massey has served in aviation maintenance and earned the enlisted aviation warfare specialist pin; he served as a Navy recruiter and recruiter in charge, as the quality assurance division officer, and the command managed equal opportunity officer. Massey was deployed to Atsugi, Japan, where he served as the quality assurance division officer aboard the USS *Kitty Hawk*. He is the command master chief for Navy Recruiting District Miami.

Kevin E. Masters

LAW ENFORCEMENT. Kevin E. Masters received a bachelor of arts degree in communication arts and journalism from Park College in Parkville, Missouri. He is a graduate of the FBI National Academy 201st Session, June 2000, and the Department of Justice School of Command Organizational Leadership for Executives. Masters is the Kansas City Police Department's deputy chief for executive services bureau commander.

Janet T. May

LOCAL GOVERNMENT. Janet T. May is a native of Anniston, Alabama, and a graduate of Anniston High School in 1972. She received a bachelor's degree in communications from the University of Alabama and also attended the university's executive master of business administration program. May is president of Thomas-May and Associates, Inc., a marketing, advertising and public relations agency in Montgomery, Alabama. In 2000 and 2004 she won a delegate seat to the Democratic National Convention from 7th Congressional District. In November 2003, she beat the incumbent by a 55 to 45 percent margin to represent District 3 on the Montgomery City Council.

Joseph F. Mayfield

MILITARY. Joseph F. Mayfield is a native of Greenville, South Carolina. He received an associate degree in human resources from Trinity College and an associate degree in criminal justice from Vincennes Community College. His military education includes all levels of the noncommissioned officer education system courses; Drill Sergeant School; battle staff noncommissioned officer course; master fitness course; the first sergeant course; the U.S. Army Sergeants Major Academy at Fort Bliss, Texas; and the U.S. Army command sergeants major course.

Mayfield has served in every field artillery leadership position: howitzer section chief, drill sergeant, platoon sergeant, fire support sergeant, senior enlisted advisor, first sergeant, senior career management noncommissioned officer, joint operational fires and effects sergeant major, and battalion command sergeant major. He was deployed in support of Operation Iraqi Freedom and served as the joint operational fires and effects sergeant major at Fort McPherson, Georgia. He was selected as the command sergeant major for 3rd Battalion, 320th Field Artillery (Red Knight Rakkansans), 3rd Brigade, 101st Airborne Division (Air Assault), Fort Campbell, Kentucky.

W. Dwayne Maynard

JUDICIAL. W. Dwayne Maynard received a bachelor of arts degree from Brown University in 1980 and earned a juris doctor degree from the Ohio State University in 1985. He was the night director and hearing officer at the city attorney's office for the City of Columbus, Ohio, from 1983 to 1985. He served as the director of the bad checks program at the city attorney's office from 1985 to 1987. He was appointed assistant city attorney for the Criminal Division, City of Columbus, from 1987 to 1993. In 1993, he was appointed judge to the Franklin County Municipal Court in Columbus.

Barry Mayo

BUSINESS, MEDIA. Barry Mayo received a bachelor of arts in radio from Howard University and served as the first general manager of the student-run WHBC. From 1988 to 1995, he was co-founder and president of Broadcasting Partners, Inc., where he used his programming and management background to lead numerous radio stations to success. Under his leadership, Broadcasting Partners, Inc., originally a five-station group, grew to a nine-station publicly traded radio company with stations in New York, Dallas, Detroit, Chicago and Charlotte. Broadcasting Partners, Inc., grew to 11 stations before it was sold to Evergreen Media (now part of Clear Channel) for $243 million in 1995.

Mayo then owned his own consulting firm, Mayomedia. He was hired as senior vice president and market manager of Emmis Communications New York's

WQHT-FM, WRKS-FM, and WQCD, a position he held from December 2002 to June 2006. He now serves as president of Mayomedia, a boutique media consulting firm.

Helen T. McAlpine

EDUCATION. Helen T. McAlpine received a bachelor's degree from Talladega College and a master's degree from Jacksonville State University. She earned a Ph.D. from the University of Alabama. She is a graduate of the Huntsville–Madison County leadership program. Her teaching experience includes serving at the secondary and post-secondary levels, including Jacksonville State University in Jacksonville, Alabama. She was an assistant superintendent of the Huntsville City School System and at the Gadsden City School System. On October 26, 2000, McAlpine was named the third president of J.F. Drake State Technical College. She is first female to serve as president of that institution.

William E. McAnulty

JUDICIAL. William E. McAnulty is a native of Indianapolis, Indiana. He received a bachelor of science degree from Indiana University. He earned a master's degree and his juris doctor degree from the University of Louisville in Kentucky. Justice McAnulty has served at all four levels of the Kentucky state court system. He began his judicial career on the Jefferson County Juvenile Court in 1975. He was elected to Jefferson District Court in November 1977, where he served until his election to Jefferson Circuit Court in November 1983. He briefly returned to private practice in January 1990, and then returned to the Circuit Court in 1993.

In 1998, he served as chief judge of the Jefferson Circuit Court until he was elected to the Kentucky Court of Appeals in November 1998 to represent the 4th Appellate District. Justice McAnulty was appointed to the Supreme Court bench on June 28, 2006, to fill the position vacated by a retiring justice. He was elected to the state's highest court, the Supreme Court of Kentucky, in November 2006 to represent the 4th Supreme Court District, which consists of Jefferson County. He is the first African American to serve on the Supreme Court of Kentucky.

Gloria S. McCall

BUSINESS, EDUCATION. Gloria S. McCall received a bachelor's degree in speech pathology and audiology from South Carolina University and a master's degree in education from Western Kentucky University. She earned her doctorate in education, adult and community college, from North Carolina State University. McCall has held a number of positions in both the academic and business worlds, affording her diverse experiences in dealing with the public.

She has served as a speech therapist for nine years for students K through 12 and as a project manager developing and delivering training programs at AT&T. McCall re-entered academia to become the executive assistant to the vice president of student services and director of special projects at Midlands Technical College in Columbia, South Carolina. She has served as interim director for grants development and dean of enrollment management services at Allen University in Columbia, South Carolina. She was the dean of student affairs for Cuyahoga Community College in Cleveland, Ohio. McCall was named vice chancellor of the Kentucky Community and Technical College System in June 2006 with administrative responsibilities for student services, global studies, enrollment management, student financial aid, transfer, and developmental education.

Joseph S. McClain

MILITARY. Joseph S. McClain was born at Offutt Air Force Base, Omaha, Nebraska. The son of a career Army officer, he enlisted in the United States Navy in 1977, attending the Naval Academy Preparatory School in Newport, Rhode Island. He graduated from the U.S. Naval Academy in 1982 with a bachelor of science degree in engineering. He holds a master of arts degree in history from the University of Alabama and a

master of arts in national and strategic studies from the Naval War College. After completion of Flight School, he earned his wings in October of 1983 and reported to VS-41 for training in the S-3A Viking, and has also completed the S-3B transition training.

Captain McClain is a career naval aviator; his key leadership and command positions include serving on the staff of commander, Naval Air Force U.S. Pacific Fleet as the S-3B/ES-3A readiness officer, later serving as the air wing programs officer, responsible for Pacific Fleet Carrier Air Wing readiness and requirements. Captain McClain reported to the "Blue Wolves" of VS-356 in 1998 as executive officer, then commanding officer, completing two cruises on the USS *Abraham Lincoln* (CVN-72). While he was commanding officer, the squadron won the Battle "E," the Golden Wrench for Maintenance Excellence, and the Pacific Fleet Retention awards. After his command tour, Captain McClain was the North Africa–Mid East Branch chief for the director, plans and policy, U.S. European Command in Stuttgart, Germany, from 2001 to 2004, with duties focusing on political-military affairs and counterterror planning and operations. He currently serves as the commander of Sea Control Wing for the U.S. Atlantic Fleet.

Garry McClure

MILITARY. Garry McClure enlisted in the U.S. Navy under the delayed entry program in July of 1981 after graduating from high school. He completed basic training at the Recruit Training Command at Great Lakes, Illinois, in March 1982 and went on to attend airman apprenticeship training at Great Lakes, Illinois. He is a graduate of the Naval Senior Enlisted Academy (Class 109 Khaki Group) and the command master chief course (Class 25 in 2006). He then qualified as an S3-A Viking plane captain and commenced his career in naval aviation maintenance.

McClure has held numerous leader positions, including line division chief; flight deck coordinator; and maintenance control supervisor in Strike Fighter Squadron One Nine Five based in Atsugi, Japan, and deployed on board the USS *Kitty Hawk*. He completed his sea duty aviation maintenance career as the leading chief petty officer and deployed for Detachment Three in Helicopter Anti-Submarine Squadron Light Five One based in Atsugi, Japan. He was assigned as recruit division commander and military training evaluator at Recruit Training Command at Great Lakes, Illinois, where he earned his certification as master training specialist. He reported to Strike Fighter Squadron Two Seven in April 2006 and assumed the duties as the Royal Maces command master chief.

Teri Plummer McClure

BUSINESS. Teri Plummer McClure is a native of Kansas City, Kansas. She received a bachelor's degree in marketing and economics from Washington University in St. Louis, Missouri, and a juris doctor degree from Emory University School of Law in Atlanta. McClure began her legal career in 1985 practicing labor and employment law in Atlanta, Georgia. She joined ups in 1995 as employment counsel for the Corporate and Employment Practice Group and assumed responsibility for office management and technology administration for the Legal Department. In 2003, McClure was named vice president of operations for the Central Florida District at United Parcel Service.

Alice O. McCollum

JUDICIAL. Alice O. McCollum received a bachelor of arts degree in mathematics from the University of North Carolina at Greensboro and earned her juris doctor degree from the University of Cincinnati College of Law. McCollum served as the director of the pre-law program at Wilberforce University. In 1977, she became an assistant professor of law and assistant director of clinical legal studies at the University of Dayton Law School. She served in the Probate Division in Montgomery County. She was the first and only woman elected judge to the Dayton Municipal Court. Judge McCollum is the first woman to serve in the Montgomery County Court of Common Pleas Probate Division.

William S. McCoy

MILITARY. William S. McCoy entered the United States Marine Corps on April 24, 1983, at Marine Corps Recruit Training at Parris Island, South Carolina. He attended infantry training school at Camp Geiger and graduated as company honorman. His key leadership positions include serving as a fire team

leader, squad leader, platoon guide, platoon sergeant, platoon commander, and instructor at squad leader school, combat instructor trainer and a martial arts instructor trainer. In 2001, he was assigned to division schools at Camp Margarita at Camp Pendleton as the chief instructor of the martial arts instructor course. In May 2002, he was selected as first sergeant and with 1st Light Armored Reconnaissance Battalion. In January 2003, he deployed to Operation Iraqi Freedom aboard the USS *Tarawa* with the 15th Marine Expedition Unit/Special Operations Capable, Battalion Landing Team 2/1. In March of 2004, he again received orders for inspector-instructor duty in New Haven, Connecticut. He served as the inspector-instructor first sergeant for the Marine Reserve Unit of the 4th Marine Logistic Group, 6th Motor Transport Battalion, Companies A and B Direct Support, 1st Truck Platoon. In December 2005, McCoy was promoted to sergeant major and, in April 2006, was assigned to his current position with the Marine Wing Squadron 272, Marine Wing Support Group 27.

Warren E. McDaniels

PUBLIC SAFETY. Warren E. McDaniels entered the New Orleans Fire Department on October 19, 1969, as a firefighter. He has served in almost every rank of the department. On April 1, 1993, he was appointed to the highest rank in the department, superintendent of fire. Chief McDaniels made history by being the first African American to hold that office.

Darren W. McDew

MILITARY. Darren W. McDew received a bachelor of science degree in civil engineering from Virginia Military Institute in Lexington, Virginia, and a master of science degree in aviation management from Embry-Riddle Aeronautical University. His military schools include the Squadron Officer School at Maxwell Air Force Base; Air Command and Staff College; and national security studies, Maxwell School of Citizenship and Public Affairs at Syracuse University, New York. He was a secretary of defense corporate fellow with Sun Microsystems at Palo Alto, California.

McDew was commissioned in 1982 following his graduation from Virginia Military Institute. From October 1982 to October 1983 he was a student in undergraduate pilot training at Williams Air Force Base in Arizona. He began his flying career at Loring Air Force Base in Maine. His staff assignments include serving as a member of the Air Force Chief of Staff Operations Group, Air Force aide to the president, and chief of the U.S. Air Force Senate Liaison Division, Washington, D.C. He has commanded at the squadron, group, and wing levels. Additionally, he has deployed in support of ongoing operations in Central and Southwest Asia as an air expeditionary group commander and later as the director of mobility forces. He served as vice commander of 18th Air Force at Scott Air Force Base in Illinois. He currently is the director of public affairs, Office of the Secretary of the Air Force, the Pentagon, Washington, D.C. He was promoted to brigadier general on September 2, 2006.

Anita D. McDonald

EDUCATION. Anita D. McDonald received a bachelor of philosophy in mathematics and a master's degree in secondary mathematics from Wayne State University. She earned a Ph.D. in education from St. Louis University and attended Harvard's Management and Leadership Institute. McDonald was an American Council on Education fellow for 1992–1993. She served as dean of the Evening College, director of summer sessions, and assistant professor of education studies in the Department of Mathematics and Computer Science at the university. She is the Penn State DuBois Campus executive officer.

Regina M. McDuffie

LOCAL GOVERNMENT. Regina M. McDuffie is a native of Macon, Georgia. She received a bachelor's degree in psychology and communications from Mercer University in Macon and attended graduate school majoring in business administration at the University of Georgia in Athens. McDuffie has served in the local government in Macon for over 19 years, with her longest position as budget director for the City of Macon. She was appointed as the general manager of the Macon Centreplex in August of 1997 after serving in an interim capacity for eight months. She was the first African American to serve as general manager of the Macon Centreplex, one of the largest such facilities in the state of Georgia with a 9,000-seat arena, a convention facility with more than 100,000 square feet of meeting space, and a multi-use theater facility that seats up to 2,700.

Frances E. McGee

JUDICIAL. Frances E. McGee received a bachelor of arts degree from Howard University in 1978 and earned her juris doctor degree from the Ohio State University College of Law in 1981. McGee worked in the legal department of the former Winters National Bank, now known as Chase Bank, from 1981 to 1983. From 1983 to 2007, she was employed by the Montgomery County

Prosecutor's Office. She was appointed a judge on the General Division of Montgomery County Common Pleas Court in 2007. She serves on the judicial appointments, civil practice, jury management and security committees.

James D. McGee

FEDERAL GOVERNMENT. James D. McGee is a native of Chicago, Illinois. He received a bachelor's degree from Indiana University. He served in the United States Air Force from 1968 to 1974 and completed Vietnamese language studies at the Defense Language Institute in Monterey, California. McGee began his career in the foreign service in 1981 and served as third secretary and vice consul at the American Embassy in Lagos, Nigeria, from 1982 to 1984. From 1984 to 1986, he served as administrative officer at the American Consulate General in Lahore, Pakistan. He was second secretary and supervisory general services officer at the American Embassy in The Hague, the Netherlands, from 1986 to 1989.

From 1989 to 1991, he was administrative officer at the American Consulate General in Bombay, India. He volunteered for duty from 1991 to 1992 at the American Embassy in Bridgetown, Barbados, where he served as administrative counselor from 1992 to 1995. He was administrative counselor at the American Embassy in Kingston, Jamaica, from 1995 to 1998, and at the American Embassy in Abidjan, Cote d'Ivoire, from 1998 to 2001. From 2002 to 2004, he was the ambassador to Swaziland and from 2004 to 2007 the ambassador to the Republic of Madagascar. He was nominated by President George W. Bush to serve as the U.S. ambassador to Zimbabwe. He was confirmed by the U.S. Senate on October 26, 2007, and was sworn in on November 6, 2007.

Yolanda Y. McGowan

JUDICIAL. Yolanda Y. McGowan received a bachelor of science degree in political science from the University of Wisconsin Whitewater and earned her juris doctor from the University of Wisconsin Madison. McGowan was appointed an administrative law judge for social service agencies in Milwaukee, Wisconsin. She also serves as an instructor with Believers in Christ School of Excellence in Milwaukee.

Aaron McGruder

AUTHOR, ARTIST. Aaron McGruder is a native of Chicago, Illinois, and attended a Jesuit school from grades two to nine, followed by public high school at Oakland Mills High School and the University of Maryland, from which he graduated with a degree in African American studies.

His career began as a cartoonist best known for writing and drawing "The Boondocks," which debuted in the campus newspaper. The Universal Press Syndicate comic strip is about two young African American brothers from inner-city Chicago now living with their grandfather in a sedate suburb. Through Huey and his younger brother Riley, a gangsta-wannabe, the strip explores issues involving African American culture and American politics. McGruder created the comic while working at the presentation graphics lab on campus. At the time, he was also a disc jockey on the *Soul Controllers Mix Show* on WMUC. McGruder lives in Los Angeles, California, where his projects include the *Boondocks* animated TV series. He is also the co-author, with Reginald Hudlin, of a 2004 comic novel, *Birth of a Nation.*

Saundra Yancy McGuire

EDUCATION. Saundra Yancy McGuire received a bachelor of science degree magna cum laude in chemistry from Southern University in Baton Rouge, Louisiana, and a master of arts in chemistry from Cornell University in Ithaca, New York. She earned a Ph.D. in chemical education from the University of

Tennessee at Knoxville. McGuire is the author of numerous publications, including the "Problem Solving Guide and Workbook," "Study Guide," and "Instructor's Teaching Guide" for Russo and Silver's *Introductory Chemistry*, third edition. She has been teaching chemistry for the past 36 years and has previously held academic appointments at the State University of New York, Brockport; the University of Tennessee, Knoxville; and Alabama A&M, Huntsville. She spent eleven years at Cornell University, where she served as acting director of the Center for Learning and Teaching and senior lecturer in the Department of Chemistry. She joined Louisiana State University in 1999 and currently is the director, Center for Academic Success, adjunct professor, chemistry, and associate dean, University College.

Calvin W. McLarin

MEDICINE. Calvin W. McLarin is a native of Atlanta, Georgia. He is a graduate of Atlanta public schools and entered Morehouse College in Atlanta at age 16. He received a bachelor of science in biology from Morehouse College in 1968 and earned his medical doctor degree from Emory University School of Medicine in Atlanta in 1972. Dr. McLarin completed his internship in internal medicine in 1973 and his residency for internal medicine in 1975 at Emory University School of Medicine.

He served in the United States Army from 1975 to 1977 as a major at Fort Myers, Virginia. After receiving an honorable discharge from the Army, he served from 1977 to 1980 in an Emory University affiliated hospital fellowship in cardiology. In 1980, Dr. McLarin co-founded Metropolitan Atlanta Cardiology Consultants, PC. He also serves as a clinical associate professor, Morehouse School of Medicine, and was chairman of the board of the Association of Black Cardiologists from 2002 to 2004.

Rhine McLin

LOCAL GOVERNMENT. Rhine McLin is a native of Dayton, Ohio. She received a bachelor of arts in sociology and secondary education from Parsons College in Iowa and earned a master of education in guidance counseling from Xavier University in Cincinnati. She earned an associate degree in mortuary science from Cincinnati College of Mortuary Science. She is a licensed funeral director and embalmer for McLin Funeral Home in Dayton.

She served for six years in the Ohio House of Representatives, from 1988 to 1994, and was then elected senator for the 5th Ohio Senate District, serving Montgomery and Miami counties. When elected in 1994, she became the first African American woman to serve in the Ohio Senate. In 1998, she was elected by her peers to serve in leadership as the minority whip. Two years later, she was elected minority leader. McLin became the first female mayor of Dayton when she was elected to the city commission for the term beginning January 7, 2002. She is Dayton's 67th mayor and the third African American in that post. She was re-elected mayor in November 2005.

Brenda Salter McNeil

MINISTRY. Brenda Salter McNeil received a bachelor's degree from Rutgers University. She earned a master of divinity from Fuller Theological Seminary and a Ph.D. in ministry from Eastern Baptist Theological Seminary, now named Palmer Theological Seminary. McNeil is a powerful, prophetic preacher and thought leader in the field of racial and ethnic reconciliation. She founded Overflow Ministries, Inc., a nonprofit, faith-based organization devoted to the ministry of racial and ethnic reconciliation, in 1995. She continues this work through Salter McNeil and Associates, a racial and ethnic reconciliation-focused speaking, training, consulting, and leadership development firm based in Chicago, Illinois.

Sheila McNeil

LOCAL GOVERNMENT. Sheila McNeil is a native of San Antonio, Texas, and graduated from Sam Houston High School. She received a bachelor's degree in social work and urban studies from Oakwood College and earned a master's degree in public administration from the University of Texas in San Antonio. McNeil was an aide to a former San Antonio councilwoman and spent four years operating behind the scenes for District 2. She also acquired another level of governmental experience working for State Rep. Ruth Jones McClendon. McNeil is self-employed as a contractor with the State of Texas doing court-ordered adoption home studies. She is serving her first term as a member of the San Antonio City Council.

Walter McNeil

LAW ENFORCEMENT. Walter McNeil holds a master's degree in criminal justice from St. Johns University in Springfield, Louisiana. He has completed graduate work toward his master of business administration at Nova Southeastern University School of Business and a master's degree in criminal justice from the University of Virginia. He is an adjunct college instructor at Florida A&M University. He has also served as an adjunct professor there.

He began his law enforcement career in 1979 as a Tallahassee police officer. In his 28-year career with the Tallahassee Police Department, he rose through the ranks to become, in 1997, the first black police chief. He served as chief of the Tallahassee Police Department for 10 years. In 2007, he was appointed secretary of the Florida Department of Juvenile Justice.

Irving Pressley McPhail

EDUCATION. Irving Pressley McPhail is a native of New York. He received a bachelor's degree in sociology from Cornell University, a master's degree in reading from Harvard University and doctor of education degree in reading and language arts from the University of Pennsylvania. He was an American Council on Education fellow in academic administration and is a graduate of Harvard's Institute for Educational Management and the President's Academy of the American Association of Community Colleges.

McPhail's professional career includes serving in faculty, administrative and research posts at Delaware State University, Morgan State University, the Johns Hopkins University and the University of Maryland at College Park. He was provost of Pace University and dean of arts and sciences at Wayne County Community College. He has served as the president of St. Louis Community College at Florissant Valley and LeMoyne-Owen College in Memphis, Tennessee. He was appointed chancellor of the Community College of Baltimore County in February 1998. While serving as the chief executive officer of Community College of Baltimore County Community College system, he was responsible for three campuses at Catonsville, Dundalk and Essex, and extension centers at Owings Mills, Hunt Valley, Towson and White Marsh.

Sidney A. McPhee

EDUCATION. Sidney A. McPhee received a bachelor of arts (with highest honors, summa cum laude) from Prairie View A&M University and a master's degree from the University of Miami in Coral Gables, Florida. He earned a doctorate degree in applied behavioral studies in education from Oklahoma State University. He is also a graduate of the Harvard University Management Development Program and has completed professional development programs at St. Mary's University of San Antonio, Texas, and Colorado College in Colorado Springs, Colorado.

McPhee has completed a five year term on the ncaa (National Collegiate Athletic Association) Division I Board of Directors and a three-year term on the ncaa Executive Committee. In 2002, President George W. Bush appointed him to serve on the National Council for the Humanities, and the U.S. Senate confirmed him. In May 2005, he was appointed to the ncaa Presidential Commission on the Future of Intercollegiate Athletics. He currently serves as president of the Sun-Belt Conference athletics league and chairman of the league's CEO executive committee.

McPhee has served in various administrative capacities at several major universities, including Oklahoma State University, the University of Louisville and the University of Memphis. In May 2007, McPhee was conferred the honorary professor title at China Agricultural University in Beijing, China. He has served as the executive vice chancellor at the Tennessee Board of Regents in Nashville and as chief academic officer and interim chancellor for the Tennessee Board of Regents. McPhee currently is the tenth president of Middle Tennessee State University.

Bernard C. McPherson

MILITARY. Bernard C. McPherson received a bachelor of arts degree in liberal arts from Excelsior University. His military education includes all levels of the non-commissioned officer education system; Drill Sergeants School; the instructor training course; the military police physical security course; the nuclear security course; the first sergeant's course; and the U.S. Army Sergeants Major Academy.

McPherson entered the United States Army in November 1979. He has held numerous staff and command assignments, including as a military policeman, team leader, squad leader, game warden, section security non-commissioned officer, drill sergeant, desk sergeant, provost marshal operations sergeant, platoon sergeant, readiness group senior enlisted adviser, company operations sergeant, first sergeant, battalion operations sergeant major, and command sergeant major. He was command provost sergeant major for Headquarters and Headquarters Company, Headquarters Command, Training and Doctrine Command, at Fort Monroe, Virginia. He is now the command sergeant major for the 18th Military Police Brigade.

Cherry A. McPherson

MILITARY. Cherry A. McPherson enlisted in the United States Marine Corps in March 1980 and reported to recruit training at Marine Corps Recruit Depot Parris Island, South Carolina. Upon graduation, she was assigned to the Engineer Equipment School at Fort Leonard Wood, Missouri. McPherson has held numerous key leadership assignments, including with the Marine Corps Detachment at Quantico, Virginia, where she was squad counselor for Noncommissioned Officer's School, then sergeant instructor at Officer Candidate School, and then engineer equipment operator. As gunnery sergeant for with the 2nd Marine Air Wing at Cherry Point, North Carolina, she participated in Operations Desert Shield and Desert Storm; in May 1995, she was selected to serve as the first sergeant for the Communication Company at Headquarters and Service Battalion. She was first sergeant for Service Company at Marine Corps Recruit Depot, Parris Island, June 1996, and later first sergeant, 4th Battalion, Marine Corps Recruit Depot Parris Island. In 2004, she was the base sergeant major at Marine Corps Logistics Base in Albany, Georgia; in 2005, she was transferred to 2nd Marine Logistics Group and was the sergeant major of 2nd Transportation Battalion and Combat Logistics Regiment 27. McPherson is currently serving as sergeant major, 2nd Marine Logistics Group, at Camp Lejeune, North Carolina.

Vanzetta Penn McPherson

JUDICIAL. Vanzetta Penn McPherson is a graduate of the Alabama State College Laboratory School. She received a bachelor's degree from Howard University. She earned a master of law degree and a juris doctor from Columbia University School of Law. She worked for 15 years in private law practice before she was appointed a United States magistrate judge for the Middle District of Alabama in April of 1992. She retired from the bench in 2006. Judge McPherson is currently a member of the Alabama State Council on the Arts and the board of directors of the Alabama Shakespeare Festival.

Sharon Meadows

ENGINEERING. Sharon Meadows earned a bachelor's and master's degrees in engineering from the University of Southern California. She is a systems engineer at Northrop Grumman Space Technology, where she develops and utilizes her digital-processing expertise at multiple program levels and serves as the lead responsible system engineer (RSE) for the Advanced Extreme High Frequency program's configurable on-board router (COR). Under her leadership, the COR SE team has supported several successful unit and subsystem design reviews. Meadows supported the Milstar program for many years in various RSE, verification RSE, and launch- and on-orbit operations roles.

Tyrone E. Medley

JUDICIAL. Tyrone E. Medley received a juris doctor degree from the University of Utah College of Law in 1977. He has served as a research attorney for the Third District Court and a deputy attorney for Salt Lake County. He worked in private law practice. Medley was appoint to the Third Circuit Court in July 1984 by Governor Scott M. Matheson and was appointed to the Third District Court in December 1992 by Governor Norman H. Bangerter. He serves Salt Lake, Summit and Tooele counties.

Kendrick B. Meek

FEDERAL GOVERNMENT. Kendrick B. Meek is a native of Miami, Florida. He received a bachelor of science degree from Florida A&M University in Tallahassee in 1989. Meek was a member of the Florida House of Representatives from 1994 to 1998 and served in the Florida State Senate from 1998 to 2002. He was elected as a Democrat to the 108th and two succeeding Congresses (January 3, 2003, to present).

Andrea Nelson Meigs

ENTERTAINMENT. Andrea Nelson Meigs is a native of Bellflower, California, and spent her teen years in Palos Verdes before moving to Boston. She received a bachelor's degree in English and Spanish in 1990 after studying as an exchange student at Spelman College in Atlanta University Center, Atlanta, Georgia, and at the Universidad Autonoma de Madrid, Spain. She earned a juris doctor degree from Duke University in 1994. Meigs began her career in show business as a child actor. From the age of six she appeared in several internationally aired commercials for products such as Mattel Toys, Burger King, and Kellogg's Sugar Smacks. She also appeared in television sitcoms and was a child model.

She has served as an assistant with the Los Angeles

District Attorney's Office. Having expected to become an entertainment lawyer, she realized that her legal background would be invaluable as a talent agent, a job that is contracts-based, demands acute negotiation skills, and is also highly creative. She spent four years learning the business at Creative Artists Agency before becoming an agent in 2000. Her first client was Cedric the Entertainer, co-star of the *Steve Harvey Show*, who at the time was trying to break out of television comedy into film. In 2004, she became a member of the Steering Committee for the American Black Film Festival, and in April of 2006, she was featured in the Hollywood issue of *Essence* magazine as a "Woman on Top" in her field.

Frank E. Melton

STATE AND LOCAL GOVERNMENT. Frank E. Melton is the 50th mayor of the City of Jackson, Mississippi. He also serves as chairman and chief executive officer of the TV-3 Foundation in Jackson. He was CEO of WLBT TV-3, Inc. from 1984 to 2002, guiding the NBC affiliate to become the leader in local broadcasting. Lt. Governor Eddie Briggs appointed Melton to serve on the Mississippi State Board of Education. His leadership transcends political and geographic boundaries. Four Mississippi governors and two Texas governors have recognized Melton for his leadership abilities. Most recently he served as director of the Mississippi Bureau of Narcotics, appointed by Governor Ronnie Musgrove in December 2002. Shortly after his election, Governor Kirk Fordice appointed Melton to chair the Governor's Criminal Justice Task Force.

Harold Melton

JUDICIAL. Harold Melton was born in Washington, D.C., and grew up in East Point and Marietta, Georgia. He received a bachelor of science degree from Auburn University and earned his juris doctor from the University of Georgia in 1991. Melton has served in the office of Alabama Governor Guy Hunt as assistant attorney general in the Fiscal Affairs Division. He later was the senior assistant attorney general in 1997 and section leader in the Tax Division. In 1998, he was selected as assistant to the governor for youth affairs. From 1998 to 2003, he served as a section leader over the Consumer Interest Division in the Georgia Department of Law in Atlanta. In January 2003, he was appointed executive counsel to Georgia Governor Sonny Perdue to represent the governor on legal issues. On July 1, 2005, at age 38, he was appointed to the Supreme Court of Georgia.

Lloyd Miles

MILITARY. Lloyd Miles received a bachelor of science degree from the United States Military Academy and a master of science in strategy studies from the U.S. Army War College. He is a graduate of the infantry officer basic and advanced courses and the U.S. Army Command and General Staff College.

Miles has held numerous staff and command assignments, including his most recent, from July 2002 to May 2005, as commander, 2nd Brigade Combat Team, with the 25th Infantry Division (Light) at Schofield Barracks in Hawaii and with Operation Iraqi Freedom, Iraq. From June 2005 to July 2006, he served as executive officer to the commander of the U.S. Southern Command in Miami, Florida. From July 2006 to September 2007, he was executive officer to the chief of staff of the Army in Washington, D.C. In September 2007, he was appointed deputy commander and assistant commandant, U.S. Army Infantry Center and School at Fort Benning, Georgia. Miles was promoted to brigadier general on February 1, 2008.

Malinda Miles

LOCAL GOVERNMENT. Malinda Miles received a bachelor of science degree in history and government with a minor in political science from St. Augustine College. She earned a master's degree from Howard University in 1976 and a master's degree from Antioch School of Law in 1978, focusing on administrative management and labor law. She has worked as employment manager, National Education Association; director of human resources, Woodbourne Center; and executive director, Prisoners Aid Association of Maryland,

Inc. In 1987, she was the first Black Woman elected to Mount Rainier's Council and won three additional terms. Miles was elected mayor of Mount Rainier, Maryland, in 2004. She is now serving a four year term from 2005 to 2009.

Brian S. Miller

JUDICIAL. Brian S. Miller received a bachelor's degree from the University of Central Arkansas and earned his juris doctor degree from Vanderbilt University. He began his career in private law practice. He served as the city attorney for Helena, Arkansas; Edmonson city attorney; Lakeview city attorney; Holly Grove city judge; and as Phillips County deputy prosecuting attorney. He currently is an Arkansas Supreme Court justice.

Juanita D. Miller

LOCAL GOVERNMENT. Juanita D. Miller received a bachelor's degree in education and psychology from the District of Columbia Teacher's College. She earned a master's degree in special education and a Ph.D. in leadership and policy management from George Washington University. She also pursued post-graduate studies at American University, the University of Maryland, College Park, and Trinity University. Miller has been a professor at Bowie State University and served on the Board of Visitors for the University of Maryland, College Park, African American Studies Department, and the Advisory Board for the Prince George's County Family Crisis Center. In 1989, she was elected to the Maryland General Assembly, representing the 25th Legislative District for four years. Miller was appointed as a Washington suburban sanitary commissioner from Prince George's County in October 2005. She is a special education administrator with the Prince George's County School System.

Larry Miller

BUSINESS. Larry Miller is a native of Philadelphia, Pennsylvania. He received a bachelor's degree in accounting from Temple University and earned a master of business administration from La Salle University. He has served as an executive for Jantzen, Inc., and has held a variety of executive positions at Nike, Inc., most recently in 2006 as vice president and general manager, basketball. In 1999, he was president of the Jordan Brand. He is currently president of the Portland Trail Blazers National Basketball Association franchise, having been hired for the position on June 20, 2007.

Sifu Larry Miller

MARTIAL ARTS. Sifu Larry Miller has been involved in the martial arts for over 25 years. He briefly studied tae kwon do under Mike Uselton and later studied peishaolin kung fu under then Sifi John Wong (now grand master). After a few setbacks, he went on to study traditional aikido under Sensei Josef Birdsong (aikido of Austin) and later earned his shodan in aikido under Sensei Gary Shabo (aikido of Houston). He is currently studying and training under Professor Moses Williams of the Fire Dragon Martial Arts Institute. He holds a black belt in kajudenbo and has earned his black sash in spiritual kung-fu tiger crane. He won his division in the 1st Annual Fire Dragon Tournament of Champions in 2003.

Lawrence Miller

MILITARY. Lawrence Miller is a native of South Carolina. He graduated from Lake City High School, Lake City, South Carolina, and is working toward a bachelor's degree in civil engineering. His military education includes courses in platoon confidence training, mountaineering, instructor trainer, amphibious warfare training, jungle warfare training, marksmanship trainers, air assault, master fitness trainer, drill sergeant, all levels of the noncommissioned officer education system, and command sergeants major designee, along with the U.S. Army Sergeants Major Academy. Miller enlisted in the United States Army on January 15, 1980. He has served in every leadership position from corporal to command sergeant major. He is the command sergeant major of the 1st Armored Division Engineers.

Jimmy L. Mincey

MILITARY. Jimmy L. Mincey is a native of Twin City, Georgia. He enlisted into the United States Marine Corps in November 1977 and graduated from recruit training at Parris Island, South Carolina, in January 1978. After this and Infantry Training School at Camp Pendleton, California, he was assigned to Marine Barracks Rota, Spain, for two years. In May 1982, he attended Drill Instructor School at Parris Island. Mincey has served as a drill instructor at Marine Corps Recruit Depot in San Diego, California. In November 1989, he was assigned as the assistant Marine officer instructor at Florida A&M University in Tallahassee. In November 1993, he was assigned to the 3rd Battalion, 2nd Marine Division, at Camp Lejeune, North Carolina. He was assigned to 2nd Combat Engineers at Camp Lejeune in May 1997 as Headquarters and Support Company first sergeant.

In April 1998, he became inspector-instructor first sergeant for D Company, 8th Tank Battalion, in Columbia, South Carolina. In May 2001 he was made battalion sergeant major and received orders to 3rd Medical Battalion, 3rd Force Service Support Group. In December 2004, he was assigned to Marine Aircraft Group 36, 1st Marine Air Wing, as squadron sergeant major. In April 2005, Mincey received orders to his present command as group sergeant major for Marine Aircraft Group 17, 1st Marine Air Wing.

William D. Missouri

JUDICIAL. William D. Missouri received a bachelor of science degree from Bowie State University in 1975 and earned his juris doctor degree from the University of Maryland Law School in 1978. He served as an assistant state attorney for Prince George's County in Maryland from November 1978 to July 1985. He was appointed an associate judge for the District Court of Prince George's County. From October 1987 to January 1988, he was an administrative judge for the District Court for the same county. From January 1988 to October 1992, he was an associate judge at the State Circuit Court, then was county administrative judge at the Circuit Court in 1992, and circuit administrative judge at the State Circuit Court since May 1997, all for Prince George's County.

Edward W. Mitchell

MILITARY. Edward W. Mitchell is a native of Richmond, Virginia. He received an associate degree in general studies from Central Texas College and a bachelor of science in human resources and occupation training and development from the University of Louisville. He earned a master of science in computer information systems from the University of Phoenix. His military education includes the battle staff course, first sergeants course, the Bradley master gunner course, Drill Sergeant School, scout platoon leader course, pathfinder course, the air assault course and the U.S. Army Sergeants Major Academy.

Mitchell enlisted in the U.S. Army in 1986 and attended One Station Unit Training in D Troop, 6th Cavalry, at Fort Knox, Kentucky. He has served in numerous leadership positions, including as a squadron operations sergeant major, squadron and troop master gunner, tank company first sergeant, platoon sergeant, and section sergeant. He currently serves as command sergeant major for the 1st Battalion, 66th Armor Regiment, at Fort Hood, Texas.

Keith Moncrief

MILITARY. Keith Moncrief received a bachelor of science degree in political science and pre-law from Baylor University in Waco, Texas, and a master of science degree in education from Troy State University in Troy, Alabama. He earned a master of arts degree in air mobility at the Air Mobility Warfare Center, Air Force Institute of Technology, Wright-Patterson Air Force Base in Ohio, and a master of arts degree in national security and strategic studies, Naval War College in Newport, Rhode Island. His military schools include Squadron Officer School at Maxwell Air Force Base in Alabama, and Air War College Seminar, Travis Air Force Base, California.

Moncrief was commissioned into the U.S. Air Force in May of 1982. His military assignments include serving as a squadron instructor navigator, squadron safety officer, squadron chief, Tactics Division; squadron training flight instructor navigator; joint force plans officer; aide-de-camp to commander-in-chief, United Nations Command/Combined Forces Command/U.S. Forces Korea; and squadron commander. From June 2003 to May 2004, he was deputy commander, 715th Air Mobility Operations Group at Hickam Air Force Base, Hawaii. From June 2004 to January 2006, he served as commander, 730th Air Mobility Squadron at Yokota Air Base in Japan. In February 2006, he was assigned as the commander of the 97th Mission Support Group, Altus Air Force Base in Oklahoma. In April 2007, he was also assigned as the commander of the 64th Air Expeditionary Group in Eskan Village, Saudi Arabia. Colonel Moncrief is a master navigator with over 1,800 hours.

Charlene Monk

MINISTRY. Charlene Monk is a native of Baltimore, Maryland. She received a bachelor of science degree in management science from Coppin State College in June 1981. She earned a master's degree from the Howard University School of Divinity in May 1985 and a Ph.D. from the Howard University School of Divinity in 1988. Monk served as pastor of Douglas Memorial United Methodist Church in Washington, D.C., from July 1986 to September 2005. On June 12, 2004, she opened the New Horizon Christian Faith Outreach Center in Mount Rainier, Maryland, a 767 seat, theater style edifice as a venue for live Christian services, entertainment, concerts, and educational programs. On September 15, 2005, Monk became pastor and founder of the New Horizon Christian Faith Church.

Lester P. Monts

EDUCATION, MUSIC. Lester P. Monts received a bachelor of arts degree in music education from Arkansas Polytechnic College and a master of music degree in trumpet performance from the University of Nebraska Lincoln. He earned a doctor of philosophy degree in musicology from the University of Minnesota. He has served on the faculties of Edinboro University; the University of Minnesota; Case Western Reserve University; and the University of California, Santa Barbara. From 1988 to 1993, he was dean of undergraduate affairs in the College of Letters and Science and in the role directed Santa Barbara's undergraduate honors programs. As an orchestral trumpeter, he has performed with the Minnesota Orchestra, the St. Paul Chamber Orchestra, the Omaha Symphony, the Erie Philharmonic, the Santa Barbara Symphony, and the Santa Barbara Chamber Orchestra.

Over a fifteen year period, he served as principal trumpet for the Allegheny Summer Music Festival and the Music Festival of Arkansas. Monts has served as an academic administrator and professor of music at the University of Michigan since 1993. He currently is the senior vice-president and assists the provost and executive vice president for academic affairs at the University of Michigan.

Bruce T. Moore

LOCAL GOVERNMENT. Bruce T. Moore received a bachelor of science degree from Henderson State University and a master of public administration degree from Arkansas State University. In 2003, he completed the senior executive in state and local government program at the John F. Kennedy School of Government at Harvard University. Moore has served as the lead city staff person for the development of William Jefferson Clinton Presidential Center and Park in downtown Little Rock. In the spring of 2000, he was selected by the United States/Japan Foundation as one of twenty Americans to participate in a two-year business and cultural exchange program with Japan.

He was appointed as Little Rock city manager on December 17, 2002, after having served as assistant city manager since April 1999. He is the chief administrative officer appointed by the mayor and board of directors, and is the principal adviser to the governing body on all operational matters pertaining to the direction and administration of municipal government.

David T. Moore

LAW ENFORCEMENT. David T. Moore was selected to serve as the police chief of the Rochester, New York, Police Department. Chief Moore's staff consists of more than 800 diverse sworn and nonsworn men and women

who reflect the Rochester community. He reports directly to the mayor.

Eddie N. Moore, Jr.

EDUCATION. Eddie N. Moore, Jr., is a native of Philadelphia, Pennsylvania. He received a bachelor of science degree in accounting from the Pennsylvania State University and a master of business administration from the University of Pittsburgh. He is a certified public accountant in both Texas and Virginia. He holds an honorary doctor of humane letters for leadership in public service from Virginia State University.

Moore began his career in the private sector in 1971 with Gulf Oil Corporation. During his 14-year tenure, he rose through the ranks to direct major components of the corporation's accounting and budgeting functions. He entered the public sector in 1985 as the assistant comptroller for accounting and reporting for the Commonwealth of Virginia. In 1988, he was selected to serve concurrently as the university comptroller for the College of William and Mary and the treasurer of its endowment association. In 1990, Moore was appointed state treasurer by Governor Lawrence Douglas Wilder. As the state treasurer, he was the head of the Department of the Treasury and served on fifteen state boards and authorities with oversight of over $20 billion of the Commonwealth's assets. Moore assumed his position as the twelfth president of Virginia State University on June 1, 1993.

Lori Moore

MEDICINE. Lori Moore received a bachelor's degree from Stanford University and earned her doctor of medicine degree from the University of California at San Francisco Medical School. After completing her residency in ophthalmology, Dr. Moore performed specialty fellowship training in cornea and refractive surgery at the prestigious Kresge Eye Institute in Detroit. She is a board certified ophthalmologist with specialty fellowship training in cornea refractive surgery.

Dr. Moore has been in private practice since 1991. She is the founder, president, and chief surgeon of NuVision Laser. She has personally selected and trained her staff members to focus on providing each patient optimal vision after surgery, using the latest in laser technology. She is also a cataract implant surgeon using the "no stitch" surgical technique. The newest in intraocular lens technology is used, including procedures that simultaneously correct for reading and distance vision.

Thomas Hill Moore

FEDERAL GOVERNMENT. Thomas Hill Moore earned a bachelor of science degree in accounting from Jacksonville University in 1971 and a juris doctor degree from the University of Florida College of Law in 1974. He is a member of the Florida Bar Association, the District of Columbia Bar Association and the Communications Bar Association.

Moore served from 1974 to 1977 as assistant dean of the University of Florida College of Law, where he directed the law school's programs for minority students. He served as a government relations consultant and legislative affairs director at Allen, Rovin and Associates, and staff attorney at the National Consumer Law Center, where he developed legislative policy on consumer credit issues. He was an executive vice president at the National Medical Association, where he supervised a 12-member staff in congressional and federal relations, conference planning, fund raising, and corporate and community relations. He served as legislative counsel to U.S. Senator John Breaux from 1988 to 1995.

Moore began his first term as a commissioner of the U.S. Consumer Product Safety Commission in May of 1995, having been appointed by President Bill Clinton. He was appointed by President Clinton to a second term, which expired on October 26, 2003. President George W. Bush appointed him to a new seven-year term through October 26, 2010.

Charles Alexander Moose

LAW ENFORCEMENT. Charles Alexander Moose is a native of New York, New York, and grew up in Lexington, North Carolina. He received a bachelor of arts degree in U.S. history from the University of North Carolina at Chapel Hill in 1975 and a master of public administration degree from Portland State University in 1984. He has also earned a Ph.D. in urban studies and criminology from Portland State University in 1993. He has completed numerous police academies, including Montgomery County, Maryland, and the Honolulu Police Academy.

Moose served as the 15th Montgomery County, Maryland, police chief from August 2, 1999, to June 18, 2003, when he resigned to write a book about the Beltway sniper attacks that occurred during his time as chief. During October 2002, he became internationally known as the primary official in charge of the efforts to apprehend the Beltway snipers. Chief Moose led the high-profile manhunt for the snipers who killed 10 people and terrorized the Washington, D.C., region. In

September 2003, he released a book titled *Three Weeks in October: The Manhunt for the Serial Sniper.*

Moose now serves with the Honolulu Police Department. Until 2005, he was the squadron commander of the 113th Security Forces Squadron, District of Columbia Air National Guard, United States Air Force. While with that unit, he deployed to Operation Katrina and served as military liaison and advisor to the New Orleans Police Department in the wake of Hurricane Katrina. Moose was promoted to lieutenant colonel and was a security forces officer in Hawaii.

Michael Morgan

MUSIC. Michael Morgan is a native of Washington, D.C., where attended public schools and began conducting at the age of twelve. While a student at Oberlin College Conservatory of Music, he spent a summer at the Berkshire Music Center at Tanglewood, where he was a student of Gunther Schuller and Seiji Ozawa and first worked with Leonard Bernstein. In 1980, he won first prize in the Hans Swarowsky International Conductors Competition in Vienna and became assistant conductor of the St. Louis Symphony Orchestra under Leonard Slatkin.

His operatic debut was in 1982 at the Vienna State Opera in Mozart's *The Abduction from the Seraglio.* In 1986, Sir Georg Solti chose him to become the assistant conductor of the Chicago Symphony Orchestra, a position he held for seven years. His debut conducting a regular subscription concert of the Chicago Symphony came in 1987 when he stepped in to replace the ailing Maestro Solti with no rehearsal and to critical acclaim. During his tenure in Chicago he was also conductor of the Civic Orchestra of Chicago (training orchestra of the Chicago Symphony) and the Chicago Youth Symphony Orchestra. In 1986, he was invited by Leonard Bernstein to make his debut with the New York Philharmonic. He served as artistic director of the Oakland Youth Orchestra, music director of the Oakland East Bay Symphony, and artistic director of the Festival Opera in Walnut Creek. He was honored as one of the ten most influential African Americans in the Bay Area in 2000 at *CityFlight* news magazine's second annual awards gala.

Morgan is music director of the Sacramento Philharmonic. He has also conducted the New York City Opera, the National, Haifa, Baltimore, Houston, Seattle, Detroit and Vancouver symphonies, and the Royal Flanders, Los Angeles and Warsaw philharmonics and the Philadelphia Orchestra. He was also a guest conductor for the Atlanta, Kansas City, San Antonio, New Jersey, and Cincinnati symphonies.

Bernadette A. Morris

MEDIA. Bernadette A. Morris received a bachelor of arts degree in English and communications from Stetson University and the University of North Florida and a master of public administration from Florida International University. Morris has worked as a broadcast journalist for PBS-NPR and as a producer of children's programming. She served as associate dean and division director of public affairs at Miami-Dade Community College, the largest community college in the nation. She is the founder and chairman of Sonshine Communications, a public relations, marketing and advertising firm based in Miami, Florida, and with a bureau office in Tallahassee.

Morris is a senior partner of Hispanic Public Relations Wire. She is also the president, owner and founder of Black Public Relations Wire, Inc., a news distribution service for black media in the United States and the Caribbean. Black PR Wire has a list of over 1,000 black owned media, media executives, community leaders and journalists.

Yolonda T. Moses

EDUCATION. Yolonda T. Moses received an associate degree from San Bernardino College in 1966 and a bachelor's degree in sociology with honors from California State College in San Bernardino in 1968. She earned both her master's and Ph.D. degrees with highest honors in anthropology from the University of California at Riverside in 1976. From 1982 to 1988 she was dean of the College of the Arts and professor of social science (anthropology) at California State University in Pomona; from 1988 to 1993, she was vice-president for academic affairs and professor of anthropology at California State College. She served as president of the City College of New York from 1993 to 1999. Then from 2000 to 2003, Moses was the president of the American Association for Higher Education, the oldest national organization dedicated to the advancement of higher education, based in Washington, D.C.

Otis Moss, Jr.

MINISTRY. Otis Moss, Jr., is a native of LaGrange, Georgia. He received a bachelor of arts from Morehouse College in 1956 and a master of divinity from Morehouse School of Religion and Interdenominational Theological Center in 1959. He conducted special studies at Interdenominational Theological Center (1960–1961) and earned a doctor of ministry degree from the United Theological Seminary in Dayton, Ohio. His honorary degrees include: doctor of divinity from Temple Bible College in 1970, Morehouse College in 1977, and LaGrange College in 2004; and doctor of humane letters from Shorter College in North Little Rock, Arkansas, in 1988 and Cleveland State University in 1997.

Moss began his ministry as the pastor of Old Mt. Olive Baptist Church in La Grange in 1954, and in 1956 he served as pastor of Provident Baptist Church in Atlanta, Georgia. From 1961 to 1975 he was pastor of Mt. Zion Baptist Church in Lockland (Cincinnati), Ohio. He served in 1971 as co-pastor to Martin Luther King, Sr., at Ebenezer Baptist Church in Atlanta, Georgia. He has served as the pastor for Olivet Institutional Baptist Church in Cleveland, Ohio, since 1975. Moss was an adjunct faculty member at United Theological Seminary in Dayton, Ohio. In 1994, he was first elected chairman of Board of Trustees at Morehouse College in Atlanta.

Moss has received numerous awards and honors: he was a guest on *The Oprah Winfrey Show* in 1986; special guest at Taegu University in Taegu, South Korea, in 1985; consultant to President Jimmy Carter at Camp David in 1979; and honored by Ohio House of Representatives resolutions.

Timothy A. Mullins

MILITARY. Timothy A. Mullins is a native of the foothills of Martinsville, Virginia. He received an associate degree in general studies from Central Texas College in Killen, Texas, and a bachelor's degree in management and human resources from Park University, Parkville, Mississippi. He has earned a master's degree in human resource management and human resource development at Webster University, Webster Groves, Mississippi. His military education includes the courses for: noncommissioned officer, first sergeant, battle staff, airborne, air assault, ranger, anti-armor, advanced marksmanship, sniper, basic recruiter, infantry company cold weather orientation, and the U.S. Army Sergeants Major Academy.

Mullins entered the U.S. Army on June 7, 1983. His leadership assignments include serving as a team leader, a scout platoon leader, first sergeant, operations sergeant, and command sergeant major. He deployed to Saudi Arabia in support of Operation Desert Shield and Desert Storm and in support of Operation Enduring Freedom, and later to Iraq in support of Operation Iraqi Freedom. He was the called by Training and Doctrine Command to serve as the brigade command sergeant major of 3rd Base Training Brigade at Fort Leonard Wood, Missouri. He assumed the duties as command sergeant major for Joint Task Force Bravo, Soto Cano Air Base, Honduras, on February 6, 2006.

Allegra Webb Murphy

LOCAL GOVERNMENT. Allegra Webb Murphy received a bachelor's degree in vocational home economics from Tuskegee University and earned a master's degree from the University of Georgia and a certification in administration and supervision from Florida Atlantic University. Murphy was an educator and county administrator for the Broward County School Board. She is past president of the Florida Home Economics Association. She has served as a commissioner for the City of Oakland Park and was the first African American to serve as mayor of the City of Oakland.

Leonard Murray

JUDICIAL. Leonard Murray received a bachelor of science in economics from St. Francis College and earned his juris doctor degree from Northwestern University Law School. Murray, prior to receiving his law degree, served in the Foreign Service of the U.S. Army from 1968 to 1970. He worked in private law practice until 2007. He was appointed associate judge of the Circuit Court of Cook County, Illinois, in April 2007.

Linda Rae Murray

MEDICINE. Linda Rae Murray is a native of Cleveland, Ohio, where she graduated from Collinwood High School in 1966. She received a bachelor of science degree in mathematics in 1973 and her medical doctor degree in 1977, both from the University of Illinois at Chicago. She also received a master of public health from the University of Illinois School of Public Health in 1980 and a Ph.D. in public health from the University of Michigan School of Public Health. She completed her residency in internal medicine and occupational therapy at Cook County Hospital.

Dr. Murray has served at Bethany Hospital in

Chicago; in 1983, she was named the medical director of the Manitoba Federation of Labour in Winnipeg, Canada; in 1985, she served as a teacher at Meharry Medical College in Chicago. In 1987 she joined the Chicago Department of Health. She was named the medical director of the Near North Health Services Corporation in 1992. Dr. Murray currently is the medical officer of primary care and community health, which includes the Ambulatory and Community Health Network of Cook County.

C. Anthony Muse

MINISTRY. C. Anthony Muse received a bachelor of arts degree in history from Morgan State University and a master of divinity from Wesley Theological Seminary. He has also earned a doctorate of ministry in church and community development from Howard University in Washington, D.C. Muse is the founder and senior pastor of the over 3,000 member Ark of Safety Christian Church of Upper Marlboro, Maryland. He has been an ordained minister for more than twenty-five years and is one of Prince George's County's most prominent pastors. The Ark of Safety opened Victory House in Fort Washington, Maryland, a shelter for victims of domestic violence and abuse. In 2003, Muse was bestowed the highest honor in the Christian church with his election to the Joint College of Pentecostal Bishops based in Cleveland, Ohio. In 2006, Bishop Muse was elected a state senator for the Maryland 26th legislative district.

C. Ray Nagin

LOCAL GOVERNMENT. C. Ray Nagin is a native of New Orleans, Louisiana, and a graduate of O. Perry Walker High School in 1974. He received a bachelor of science degree in accounting from Tuskegee University in Tuskegee, Alabama, in 1978 and a master of business administration from Tulane University in 1994. Nagin has served as a manager and vice president of Cox Communications, a cable company and subsidiary of Cox Enterprises. In 2002, was elected mayor of New Orleans, Louisiana. In August 2005, Mayor Nagin ordered the first ever mandatory evacuation hours before landfall of Hurricane Katrina, a powerful category five storm that directly hit New Orleans. In 2006, he won a second term as mayor.

Cynthia Nance

EDUCATION. Cynthia Nance received a bachelor's degree in economics from Chicago State University and a master of arts in finance from the University of Iowa. She earned a juris doctor degree with distinction and completed coursework for a Ph.D. in industrial relations, both from the University of Iowa. She is licensed to practice law in Iowa. Nance was a labor educator at the University of Iowa Labor Center and was selected as a faculty fellow in the College of Law. In 1994, she joined the University of Arkansas School of Law. In May 2006, she was named dean of the University of Arkansas School of Law, effective July 1, 2006. She is the first woman to serve as dean and the first African American dean.

Bettye Henderson Neely

STATE GOVERNMENT. Bettye Henderson Neely received a bachelor of science in English from Mississippi Valley State University and a master of science in elementary education from Jackson State University, an education specialist in administration and supervision from Delta State University, and a doctor of philosophy in curriculum and instruction from Mississippi State University. Neely is an administrative assistant in the Grenada School District, where she is federal programs coordinator, curriculum coordinator (6–12), district test coordinator, substitute teacher coordinator and district reading specialist. Neely was appointed to the board by Governor Ronnie Musgrove in June 2000 to represent the former Fourth Congressional District for a term to expire May 7, 2012.

Evelyn M. Nelson

MEDICINE. Evelyn M. Nelson holds a doctor of dental medicine degree and a certificate in general dentistry from the University of Medicine and Dentistry of New Jersey, and a master of public health degree from Yale University School of Epidemiology and Public Health. Dr. Nelson has served as an assistant professor of general dentistry and hospital dentistry at the University of Medicine and Dentistry of New Jersey and was appointed assistant professor of general dentistry and management science and of epidemiology and health promotion. Dr. Nelson is currently working with Dr. Ralph V. Katz, professor and chairman of the Department of Epidemiology and Health Promotion on the Tuskegee Legacy Project, and with Dr. Joan A. Phelan, professor and chairperson of the Department of Oral Pathology, on the Women's Interagency HIV Study.

William L. Nelson

MILITARY. William L. Nelson is a native of Pittsburg, California. After completion of the Navy's Broaden Opportunity for Selection and Training program, he earned a bachelor of science degree in computer science from the University of Idaho and was commissioned an ensign via the Reserve Officer Training Corps (ROTC) program in December 1987. He reported to Pensacola, Florida, for flight training and was designated a naval aviator in August 1989.

Nelson's first naval assignment was in March 1990, with Patrol Squadron Nine at Naval Air Station Moffett Field in California, flying the P-3C Orion. He completed deployments and detachments to Misawa, Japan; Adak, Alaska; and Panama. He was next assigned to Navy Recruiting District Buffalo, New York, in April 1993, where he served as officer programs officer. In May 1996, he reported to the USS *Independence* (CV-62) stationed in Yokosuka, Japan, as a catapult and arresting gear officer and V-2 division officer. As part of the Forward Deployed Battle Group, he completed multiple cruises throughout Southeast Asia and the Arabian Gulf. In August 1998, he reported to staff of commander, Patrol and Reconnaissance Wing Ten at Whidbey Island, Washington, and served as the safety/naval air training and operating procedures standardization officer. He then reported to Patrol Squadron One in October 1999, where he was instructor pilot, mission commander, patrol plane commander, Safety/NATOPS officer, officer in charge of Detachment Kadena, Japan, and maintenance officer. In November 2001, he reported to Washington Headquarters Service, Executive Services and Communications Directorate, Cables Division, as the deputy division chief of the secretary and deputy secretary of defense's communications center. In April 2003, he was designated the division chief until his detachment in January 2005. Commander Nelson reported to Navy Recruiting District Ohio in April 2005 to serve as executive officer with a follow-on tour as commanding officer.

Charles W. Nesby

FEDERAL GOVERNMENT. Charles W. Nesby is a former United States Navy captain and Air Wing commander; he retired from the Navy in 1997. He is a second-generation fighter pilot and is named after his father, Charles Nesby, Sr., one of the original Tuskegee Airmen of World War II. Nesby reported to Aviation Officer Candidate School in Pensacola, Florida, in June of 1973 and received his wings as a naval aviator in January 1975. Following deployment to the Western Pacific and Mediterranean, he completed pilot training for the Navy F-14A Tomcat Fighter. From August 1978 to September 1981, he completed two deployments onboard the USS *America* (CV-66). During this tour, he graduated from the U.S. Navy Fighter Weapons School (Topgun) and was a distinguished graduate in the maritime air superiority syllabus (Topscope).

He served as an instructor pilot, operations officer and readiness officer from 1981 to 1989. A distinguished graduated from the Industrial College of the Armed Forces at Fort McNair in Washington, D.C., he assumed command of Strike Training Squadron Twenty-Two at Naval Air Station Kingsville, Texas, in 1992. Under his command, the squadron flew more than 114,000 mishap-free flight hours and was named best training squadron in the Naval Air Training Command. In September 1993, he assumed dual duties as director of Air Force and Navy requirements, Joint Primary Aircraft Training System, and director of the Joint Cockpit Officer/Wright Laboratories, Wright-Patterson Air Force Base in Ohio. He served as commander, Strike

Training Air Wing Two in Kingsville, Texas, from September 1995 until his retirement in 1997.

In November 2001, he was appointed director of the Department of Veterans Affairs Center for Minority Veterans. As director, he is the principal advisor to the secretary of veterans' affairs on policies and programs affecting minority veterans. Prior to his appointment, he managed a computer-based training project for D.P. Associates of San Diego, California. He was responsible for developing software and hardware components to support a flight training program for Navy and Marine Corps combat aircrews.

Patricia A. Newby

SCIENCE. Patricia A. Newby received a bachelor's degree in computer science and a master of business administration in management from Loyola College in Maryland. She also completed the executive finance program at the Wharton School of the University of Pennsylvania and the general manager program at Harvard Business School. Newby serves as president of Xetron Corporation, a wholly owned subsidiary of Northrop Grumman. At Xetron, she is responsible for management of all resources, personnel and equipment involved in the design, development and manufacture of sophisticated, secure-communications equipment for a variety of U.S. military applications. Newby has been honored by *U.S. Black Engineer and Information Technology* magazine.

Clifton B. Newman

JUDICIAL. Clifton Newman is a native of Kingstree, South Carolina. He was raised in Greeleyville, South Carolina, where he graduated valedictorian of Williamsburg County Training School in 1969. He received a bachelor's degree from Cleveland State University, where he served as the president of student government and earned his juris doctor degree from Cleveland-Marshall College of Law in 1976. Newman began his legal career in private law practice in Cleveland, Ohio, and later returned to South Carolina in private law practice. He was appointed assistant solicitor for Williamsburg County in 1983. In 1994, he returned to private law practice. After 24 years as a practicing attorney and 17 years as an assistant solicitor, he was elected Circuit Court judge by the South Carolina General Assembly on May 24, 2000.

Bruce W. Nichols

MILITARY. Bruce W. Nichols is a native of Philadelphia, Pennsylvania. He received a bachelor of arts degree in English from Franklin and Marshall College. He performed graduate studies at Villanova University before joining the Navy in 1981. He earned a master of arts degree in National Security from the Naval War College. He received his commission from Officer Candidate School in April 1982 and completed the Surface Warfare Officer School Command, Coronado, California.

Captain Nichols' key command and staff assignments include: serving as the engineer officer on board the USS *Oldendorf* (DD 972) in the Arabian Gulf, participating in Desert Shield and Desert Storm; as commanding officer of the USS *O'Bannon* (DD 987) deployed to Central and South America, conducting unitas and counter narcotic operations; and on the staff of commander, Cruiser Destroyer Group Three, in the USS *Abraham Lincoln* (CVN 72) as the battle group operations officer. The *Abraham Lincoln* Carrier Battle Group completed a historic ten month deployment, including three combat operations: Operation Enduring Freedom, Operation Southern Watch, and Operation Iraqi Freedom. Captain Nichols then served as senior naval advisor to the U.S. Department of State in the Office of International Security Operations.

Samuel Thomas Nichols, Jr.

MILITARY. Samuel Thomas Nichols, Jr., received bachelor of science and master of science degrees in education from Mississippi State University. His military education includes military police officer basic and advanced courses; engineer officer advanced course; adjutant general officer basic course; Combined Arms and Services Staff School; the U.S. Army Command and General Staff College; and Senior Service College fellowship.

Nichols began his military career in August 1977 as a second lieutenant in the U.S. Army Reserves. He has held numerous staff and command assignments, including his most recent: from September 1997 and July

2000 as chief, Secretariat for Department of the Army Selection Boards (Reserve Components), Personnel Command, Saint Louis, Missouri; from June 2001 to June 2003, Senior U.S. Army Reserve representative (Defense Integrated Military Human Resource System), Army Reserve Support Center, Arlington, Virginia; from July 2003 to August 2004, senior policy board advisor, Office of the Secretary of Defense/Reserve Forces Policy Board, Washington, D.C.; and as commander, 3rd Personnel Command in Jackson, Mississippi. He has been commander, Regional Support Group East in Birmingham, Alabama, since August 2007. He was promoted to brigadier general on January 7, 2008.

Jeanne Nizigiye

MEDICINE. Jeanne Nizigiye obtained a doctor of medicine degree from the University of Mississippi Medical Center in Jackson, Mississippi, where she completed a residency in psychiatry and behavior science. She also has a doctor of medicine degree from the University of Burundi School of Medicine in Burundi, East Africa. Dr. Nizigiye joined the medical staff of Central Mississippi Medical Center at the Mississippi Neuroscience Center. She is certified by the American Board of Psychiatry and Neurology, Inc. Dr. Nizigiye came to Central Mississippi Medical Center from East Mississippi State Hospital in Meridian.

Eucharia E. Nnadi

EDUCATION. Eucharia E. Nnadi received a bachelor of science degree in pharmacy, cum laude, from Creighton University in Nebraska in 1977. She earned a master of science in hospital pharmacy in 1978 and a Ph.D. in social and administrative pharmacy from the University of Minnesota in 1982. She received a juris doctor with high honors from the College of Law at Florida State University in 1993, and has received training in dispute resolution using mediation, total quality management, and leadership training.

Nnadi is an experienced and accomplished teacher, researcher and prolific writer. She has taught numerous courses to graduate and undergraduate students. She served as principal or co-investigator of grants totaling more than a million dollars. She began her academic career as an assistant professor of pharmacy administration at the College of Pharmacy and Pharmaceutical Sciences, Florida A&M University in Tallahassee, Florida, in 1981. She became the first African American female dean of a United States school of pharmacy in 1994. She served as the dean of the College of Pharmacy and Pharmaceutical Sciences at Howard University. She next was vice president for academic affairs at the University of Maryland Eastern Shore from February 1997 to December 2002. Nnadi was named vice president for academic affairs and program planning at the University of Southern Nevada.

Flemming L. Norcott, Jr.

JUDICIAL. Flemming L. Norcott, Jr., is a native of New Haven, Connecticut, and a graduate of Taft School in 1961. He received a bachelor of arts degree from Columbia University in 1965 and earned his juris doctor degree from Columbia University School of Law in 1968. He also received an honorary LL.D. degree from the University of New Haven in 1993, and an honorary doctor of humane letters from Albertus Magnus College in 2004. Norcott worked as a Peace Corps volunteer in Nairobi, Kenya, where he was a lecturer in the faculty of law at the University of East Africa. He then served on the Bedford Stuyvesant Restoration Corporations legal staff in New York City and later as an assistant attorney general in the U.S. Virgin Islands.

He was the co-founder and executive director of the Center for Advocacy, Research and Planning, Inc., in New Haven. Prior to his appointment to the bench, he also served as a hearing examiner for the Commission on Human Rights and Opportunities. He currently is an associate fellow of Calhoun College at Yale and serves as a lecturer there. Norcott was nominated to the Superior Court in 1979 and remained there until his appointment to the Appellate Court in 1987. In 1992, he was elevated to his current position as an associate justice of the State of Connecticut Supreme Court.

Beverly Wilkes Null

MINISTRY. Beverly Wilkes Null received a bachelor of science from Murray State University in Murray, Kentucky, in 1981 and a master of divinity from Saint Paul School of Theology in Kansas City, Missouri, in 1989. She earned a doctor of ministry from the United Theological Seminary Dayton, Ohio, in 2003.

Null served in the Missouri National Guard as a commissioned officer in 1987. From 1989 to 1992, she was pastor of Sharon United Methodist Church in Decatur, Illinois; in 1991, she was ordained elder at the former Central Illinois United Methodist Church Conference (presently the Illinois Great Rivers Conference). From 1992 to 1994, she was associate pastor of Morton United Methodist Church in Morton, Illinois; from 1995 to 1997, Null was Protestant chaplain at Millikin University in Decatur, Illinois. She was pastor of Springfield Grace United Methodist Church in Springfield, Illinois, from 1997 to 2002. In 2002, she was named Mississippi River district superintendent, United Methodist Church.

Cheryl L. Nunez

EDUCATION. Cheryl L. Nunez received a bachelor of arts degree in English from Harvard University and a master of education in educational foundations from the University of Cincinnati. Nunez has served in various professional capacities for the Cincinnati public schools, *N.I.P.* magazine, the American Jewish Committee, the Council on Opportunity in Graduate Management Education, the Procter and Gamble Company, and as director for affirmative action and multicultural affairs at Northern Kentucky University for nine years. On May 2, 2005, Cheryl Nunez became the first vice provost for diversity at Xavier University, Cincinnati, Ohio.

Barack Obama

FEDERAL GOVERNMENT. Barack Obama is a native of Honolulu, Hawaii, and obtained his early education in Jakarta, Indonesia, and Hawaii. He continued his education at Occidental College in Los Angeles, California, and Columbia University in New York City. He earned his juris doctor from Harvard University in 1992, where he became the first African American president of the Harvard Law Review. Senator Obama was a lecturer on constitutional law at the University of Chicago; elected to the Illinois State Senate (1997–2004); and elected as a Democrat to the U.S. Senate in 2004 for term beginning January 3, 2005. On January 20, 2009, he was sworn in as 44th president of the United States and the first black American and non-white to serve as president in the history of this country.

Beverly J. O'Bryant

EDUCATION, HEALTH. Beverly J. O'Bryant is director of the doctoral program in educational leadership, assistant professor and coordinator of the research component of the Minority Male Health Project, and former professor in the Department of Counseling at Bowie State University in Bowie, Maryland. She is president and chief executive officer of Counseling and Training System, Inc., and a senior fellow with the Center for Health Behavioral Change. O'Bryant is past president of the 80,000 member American Counseling Association (the second African American president elected in its 57 year history). She is a past president of the 30,000 member American School Counselor Association.

Harris Odell

LOCAL GOVERNMENT. Harris Odell received a bachelor of science in psychology and a master of science in guidance and counseling, a master of public health and health care administration, and a juris doctor degree. Odell has worked as business manager at Meharry Medical College; director of human resources at Memorial Medical Center, and as a corporate trainer. He has been in private law practice for 23 years. Odell joined the Board of Chatham County Commissioners in Savannah, Georgia, in 1995. He has served the community as former president of Frank Callen Boys and Girls Club, former president of Savannah Trial Lawyers Association, and former president of the Port City Bar Association.

Angela M. Odom

MILITARY. Angela M. Odom is a native of Mississippi. She is a 1988 U.S. Army Reserve Officer Training Corps distinguished graduate from the University of Southern Mississippi, where she was homecoming queen, received a bachelor of science degree in personnel management, and was commissioned an Adjutant General's Corps second lieutenant. She earned a master's degree in human resources management from Cen-

tral Michigan University. Her military education includes Command and General Staff College, Combined Arms Services and Staff School, and adjutant general's advanced and basic courses.

Odom has held numerous management and leadership positions, including in the Strategic Plans Analysis and Readiness Branch; Enlisted Personnel Management Directorate; Human Resources Command; executive officer to the Central Command's J5, where she was deployed in support of Operation Enduring Freedom, strength manager at Fort Carson; officer manager at Army Central Command; commander at Fort Wainwright, Alaska; personnel and supply officer at Montgomery, Alabama, Recruiting Battalion; and various personnel related positions at Fort Bragg, North Carolina, where she deployed in support of Hurricane Andrew and Operations Desert Shield and Desert Storm. She has been commander of the 15th Personnel Services Battalion since October 12, 2006.

Janet Bell Odom

MINISTRY. Janet Bell Odom received a bachelor of arts degree in sociology from the University of Houston and a master of divinity degree from Southern Methodist University Perkins School of Theology, Dallas, Texas. She earned a doctor of ministry degree from Southern Methodist University Perkins School of Theology in Dallas with a concentration in urban ministry.

Odom is an ordained elder of the North Texas Conference of the United Methodist Church. She began her pastoral experience as an assistant pastor at St. Luke Community United Methodist Church under the leadership of Zan W. Holmes, Jr., senior pastor. She was assistant chaplain at Southern Methodist University and senior pastor at Lambuth United Methodist Church and Owenwood United Methodist Church, both in Dallas. Odom and her spouse, Reverend Elzie D. Odom, Jr., are co-founding pastors of the New Jerusalem Fellowship United Methodist Church in Lewisville, Texas. She is currently senior pastor of Camp Wisdom United Methodist Church in Dallas, Texas.

Elizabeth A. Okoreeh-Baah

MILITARY. Elizabeth A. Okoreeh-Baah's father is a native of Ghana, North Africa, and she grew up in Memphis, Tennessee. She enlisted in the United States Marine Corps through the delayed entry program and received a bachelor's degree from the U.S. Naval Academy, in Annapolis, Maryland. Okoreeh-Baah spent the first five and a half years of her career in the Marine Corps as a CH-46E "Sea Knight" pilot, but when Marine Medium Helicopter Squadron 263 began transitioning to the Osprey program while she was stationed there, she became one of the first female pilots to begin training on the controls of the tiltrotor aircraft. She was the first female selected on the V-22 transition conversion board. She spent her first three months with VMMT-204 training on the flight simulators at Marine Aircrew Training Systems Squadron. On March 13, 2006, she made history when she became the first female to pilot the MV-22 Osprey, Marine Medium Tiltrotor Squadron 263, at Marine Corps Air Station New River, North Carolina.

Charles H. Oldham

MILITARY. Charles H. Oldham enlisted in the United States Marine Corps on June 6, 1979, and attended boot camp at Marine Corps Recruit Depot Parris Island, South Carolina. He also completed the U.S. Army Airborne school at Fort Benning, Georgia, and the redeye-stinger gunner's course at Marine Corps Detachment, Fort Bliss, Texas. He is also a graduate of the Marine Security Guard School in Quantico, Virginia.

His other military assignments include serving in May 1985 as an instructor for the redeye-stinger gunner course at Fort Bliss; in January 1990, he reported to Marine Corps Recruit Depot in San Diego, where he served as a drill instructor. Next he was at Camp Pendleton, California, as a platoon sergeant and battery gunnery sergeant with Alpha Battery, 3rd Low Altitude Air Defense Battalion.

At the American Embassy, Riyadh, Saudi Arabia, he was detachment commander; in July 1977 he reported to the 1st Force Service Support Group at Camp Pendleton, California, where he was first sergeant. In August 2001, he was assigned as squadron sergeant major at Marine Corps Air Station Miramar, California, Marine Aircraft Group 11, 3rd Marine Aircraft Wing. During this assignment, he was forward deployed and participated in Operation Iraqi Freedom. In July 2005, Oldham assumed the post of inspector instructor sergeant major for the 14th Marine Regiment, 4th Marine Division, Naval Air Station Joint Reserve Base, Fort Worth, Texas.

Eugene Oliver, Jr.

JUDICIAL. Eugene Oliver, Jr., is a native of New York. He received a bachelor of arts degree from Middlebury College in Vermont in 1970 and earned a juris doctor from Fordham University School of Law in 1977. Oliver is a former company commander of the United States Army Reserves and served as an executive assistant district attorney with the Bronx District Attorney's Office. He is a founding member of the Black Bar Association of Bronx County.

Oliver was appointed to the bench in August 1990 by Mayor David Dinkins. He has served as supervising judge to Bronx Criminal Court and New York County Criminal Court. He served in the Criminal Court until February 1994, when he was elevated to acting Supreme Court judge in Bronx Supreme Court. Judge Oliver is deputy administrative judge of the Criminal Division, Bronx Supreme Court.

Ernest Stanley O'Neal

BUSINESS. Ernest Stanley O'Neal is a native of Wedowee, Alabama. He received a bachelor's degree in industrial administration from General Motors Institute (later known as Kettering University) and earned a master of business administration from Harvard Business School in 1978.

O'Neal worked as an analyst for General Motors and within three years he was a director in the treasury division. He joined Merrill Lynch in 1986, working in the junk bond department, which he was heading three years later. By the early 1990s, he was running Merrill's leveraged finance division. After serving as global head of capital markets and co-head of the corporate and institutional client group, he spent two years as chief financial officer from 1998 to 2000. He then briefly served as president of Merrill's U.S. private client group before becoming president of the firm in 2001. By 2003, he was CEO and chairman. He retired in October 2007. He served as a member of the board of directors of General Motors from 2001 to 2006.

Rodney O'Neal

BUSINESS. Rodney O'Neal received a bachelor's degree from Kettering University and earned a master's degree from Stanford University. He began his career at General Motors in 1971 as a student. In 1976, he joined the Inland Division, where he held a number of engineering and manufacturing positions in Dayton, Portugal and Canada. He was named director of industrial engineering for the former Chevrolet-Pontiac-GM of Canada Group in 1991 and the following year became a director of manufacturing for Delphi. He was named general director of warehousing and distribution for General Motors Service Parts Operations in 1994. In 1997, he was elected a General Motors vice president and named general manager of Delphi Interior Systems. He was elected a Delphi vice president and president of Delphi Interior Systems in November 1998. In 2000, O'Neal was named executive vice president of the former Safety, Thermal and Electrical Architecture Sector. In January 2005, he was named president and chief operating officer. On January 1, 2007, O'Neal was appointed chief executive officer and president of Delphi Corporation.

Clarence Otis, Jr.

BUSINESS. Clarence Otis, Jr., is a native of Vicksburg, Mississippi, and grew up in Watts neighborhood in Los Angeles, California. He received a bachelor of arts degree magna cum laude from Williams College in 1977 and earned a juris doctor degree from Stanford Law School in 1980. He was vice president of First Boston Corp. from 1987 to 1990, then was managing director of Giebert Municipal Capital. He was vice president of Chemical Securities, Inc., from 1991 to 1992 and managing director from 1992 to 1995.

He was recruited by Darden Restaurants in Orlando for the post of treasurer and later promoted to vice president, 1995 to 1997, senior vice president for finance, 1997 to 1999, and chief financial officer, 1999 to 2004. In 2003, he was appointed president of Smokey Bones unit and was Darden Restaurants' chief executive officer in 2004. He faced numerous challenges as Darden CEO: the company's flagship Red Lobster and Olive Garden chains matured, and each suffered from flat sales at times. Otis was able to boast of strong sales increases for those two chains in 2005. In the 2000s African Americans remained rare as chief executives of Fortune 500 companies — the 500 largest companies in the United States. When Otis was named CEO of Darden Restaurants in December of 2004, he was one of just seven.

Alan C. Page

JUDICIAL. Alan C. Page is a native of Canton, Ohio. He received a bachelor of arts degree from the University of Notre Dame in 1967 and earned his juris doc-

tor degree from the University of Minnesota in 1975. Page played professional football with the Minnesota Vikings from 1967 to 1978, and from 1978 to 1981, he played for the Chicago Bears. He was named an All-Pro defensive tackle ten times and a member of professional football's Hall of Fame in 1988. In 1971 he was the first defensive player in the history of the NFL to receive the Most Valuable Player Award.

Page's legal career began in private law practice. He had prepared twice to run for a seat on the Minnesota State Supreme Court, only to be thwarted by eleventh-hour appointments by governors Rudy Perpich and Arne Carlson. Page took Carlson to court, the Minnesota Supreme Court, over the last maneuver. The entire court excused itself, naming seven retired judges to serve in its stead. This judicial tribunal invalidated Governor Carlson's appointment, clearing the way for an election for the court seat. Justice Page was overwhelmingly elected to the Minnesota State Supreme Court in November 1992. On January 4, 1993, after three of his four children helped him don his robe and the fourth read from the speeches of Robert F. Kennedy, he became the first African American justice in the history of the Minnesota Supreme Court.

Felton Page

FEDERAL GOVERNMENT. Felton Page is a native of Buffalo, New York. He received a bachelor of science degree from Central State University, Wilberforce, Ohio. He was honored as an ROTC distinguished military graduate and commissioned as a second lieutenant.

He was Airborne and Ranger qualified, which afforded him numerous challenging assignments. Those assignments included serving as company commander; intelligence officer (S-2) of Special Forces Battalion; and operations officer (S-3). He pursued his advanced degree in criminal justice from Wichita State University, Wichita, Kansas. Page began his equal opportunity career while on active duty as a race relations officer. He is a graduate of the Defense Equal Opportunity Management Institute, the premier Department of Defense school for race relations.

In July 1987, he joined the National Guard Bureau Headquarters as an equal employment opportunity specialist. In 1991, he was selected as the special emphasis programs manager. He has successfully had the National Guard recognized and included as a member of the Department of Defense, Joint Services, Diversity Education/Special Emphasis Program Planning Group. He successfully planned, coordinated and supervised the National Guard's hosting of all military events as Department of Defense's lead service during the 83rd and 90th NAACP Conventions and the 21st and 28th National Image Conventions.

He is the director, Office of Equal Opportunity and Civil Rights, for the National Guard bureau, with responsibility for equal opportunity and equal employment opportunity policy and regulatory guidance affecting all Army and Air National Guard, military and civilian personnel in the 54 states and territories.

Marcia L. Page

SCIENCE. Marcia L. Page received a bachelor of science degree in business administration from the University of Nebraska and has completed the executive education program at Harvard University and the University of Indiana. Page has more than 22 years of experience in marketing support and organization development. She has held positions in computer science, technical services and marketing. She has held key management positions with Xerox Corporation in Rochester, New York, and Union Pacific Railroad Company in Omaha, Nebraska. She joined Texas Instruments in October 1995 as director of business excellence in the Semiconductor Group, the company's largest business group. As vice president of Texas Instruments' worldwide mass marketing she was responsible for providing strategic development and direction for all sales and marketing initiatives that serve the mass marketing customer base in the Americas, Asia Pacific, Japan and Europe.

Page joined the Foundation for Community Empowerment in Dallas, Texas, in February 2005. She serves as a loaned executive from Texas Instruments. She assumed the position of president and chief executive officer in September 2006. She is responsible for the foundation's strategic direction and the alignment and implementation of its core initiatives: community building, institutional and systemic change, and research.

Charles Parent

PUBLIC SAFETY. Charles Parent joined the New Orleans, Louisiana, Fire Department in 1982. He advanced through the ranks of to become a fire captain in 1990, district chief in 1995, and acting deputy chief in August 2002. He was named superintendent of the New Orleans Fire Department.

Linda V. Parker

STATE GOVERNMENT. Linda V. Parker is a native of Detroit, Illinois. She received a bachelor's degree from the University of Michigan and earned a juris doctor from the National Law Center at George Washington

University in Washington, D.C. Parker was executive assistant U.S. attorney for the Eastern District of Michigan from 1994 to 2000. She was a private attorney in Detroit and chair of New Steps, an organization committed to providing services for economically disadvantaged new mothers in substance abuse recovery. She also served as a volunteer attorney with the Women's Justice Center, where she provided legal counseling for women who were being physically or emotionally abused.

Parker was appointed as director of the Michigan Department of Civil Rights in November 2003. Under her leadership, the Michigan Civil Rights Commission was awarded the 2006 Champions of Choice Award by the Michigan Abortion Rights Action League. Recently, the Michigan Department of Civil Rights was awarded 2007 Victims of Crime Act grant from the Crime Victim Service Commission to enhance victim support through its competency programs.

Mamie Parker

FEDERAL GOVERNMENT. Mamie Parker was among the first African American students to attend integrated schools in Wilmot, Arkansas. She attended the University of Arkansas at Pine Bluff and earned advanced degrees in fish and wildlife management, culminating in a Ph.D. in limnology. Parker, a fishery biologist and avid angler, rose to become the assistant director of the U.S. Fish and Wildlife Service, the first Arkansan and first African American to do so, and did it by starting at the bottom, as a fishery biologist at a national fish hatchery in Wisconsin. She supervises fish culture throughout the nation, including three Arkansas national fish hatcheries, and has addressed serious conservation needs by leading the efforts in creating a U.S. Fish and Wildlife Service field office in Conway, Arkansas. She was also the first African American to serve as a deputy regional director and regional director in the U.S. Fish and Wildlife Service.

Toney C. Parks

EDUCATION, MINISTRY. Toney C. Parks is a native of Birmingham, Alabama. He received a bachelor's degree in criminal justice from the University of South Carolina in 1980. He earned a master's degree in divinity from Erskine College and Theological Seminary and a doctorate degree in counseling from Westminster Theological Seminary. Parks is an assistant professor of biblical counseling at Erskine Theological Seminary. He is the 2nd vice moderator of the Enoree River Baptist Association, president of the Greenville Congress of Christian Education and 2nd vice president of the South Carolina Congress of Christian Education. The governor appointed him a Commissioner on Women for the state of South Carolina. He serves as chaplain of the Greenville City Police Department and is the president and co-founder of Family Outreach Community Services in Greenville. Parks serves as co-host of the 107.3 *Vital Link* morning radio show dealing with community issues relating to the family. He is the pastor of Mt. Sinai Missionary Baptist Church in South Carolina.

Vallerie Parrish-Porter

BUSINESS. Vallerie Parrish-Porter received a bachelor of science degree from Southern University in Baton Rouge, Louisiana, and earned a master's of business administration from the University of Miami. She served for 18 years with Schlumberger before joining Compaq in 1999 as vice president worldwide for sales and services and information management. She has also served as vice president–group information officer for Hewlett-Packard.

Parrish-Porter joined Sprint Nextel as vice president for enterprise services for Sprint, a position she assumed in October 2004. In this role, she was responsible for achieving customer-focused success in all functional areas within enterprise services — computer operations, engineering, mailing services and desktop operations and support. She also oversaw company-wide business continuity efforts. She now is the chief information officer at Sprint Nextel Corporation, Local Telecommunications Division.

David Alexander Paterson

STATE GOVERNMENT. David Alexander Paterson was born in Brooklyn, New York, with no sight in his left eye and severely limited vision in his right. He is the son

of Basil Paterson, former New York secretary of state, who was the first African American deputy mayor of New York City and the first African American to run for statewide office in New York. He received a bachelor of arts degree in history from Columbia University in 1977 and earned his juris doctor from Hofstra Law School.

Paterson began his career with the Queens District Attorney's Office, but failed the New York bar examination, and so did not become an attorney at law. In 1985, he joined the campaign staff of David Dinkins for Manhattan borough president. That year, after the death of Senator Leon Bogues, he won a highly competitive New York County (Manhattan) Democratic Party Committee appointment for the rest of Bogues' term as senator for the 29th District. The following year, 1986, he won the seat for his first full term representing the 29th District. Paterson was elected Senate minority leader in 2002, becoming both the first nonwhite state legislative leader and the highest ranking black elected official in the history of New York State. In November 2006, he was elected lieutenant governor and assumed office on January 1, 2007. On March 17, 2008, he assumed the office of governor of the State of New York after Governor Eliot Spitzer. Paterson became the first African American governor to serve the State of New York and the first legally blind governor in the United States.

Deval Patrick

State Government. Deval Patrick is a native of Chicago, Illinois, and graduated from the Milton Academy in Boston, Massachusetts. He received a bachelor's degree from Harvard University in 1978 and spent a post-graduate year working on a United Nations youth training project in the Darfur region of Sudan. He returned to Cambridge to attend Harvard Law School in the fall of 1979. He received his juris doctor from Harvard Law School.

Patrick began his professional career as a law clerk to a federal appellate judge before joining the NAACP Legal Defense and Education Fund. In 1986, he entered private law practice. In 1994, President Bill Clinton appointed Patrick assistant attorney general for civil rights, the nation's top civil rights post. At the Justice Department, he worked on a wide range of issues, including prosecution of hate crimes and abortion clinic violence, employment discrimination, and enforcement of fair lending laws and the Americans with Disabilities Act. During his tenure, he led the largest criminal investigation prior to September 11, 2001, coordinating state, local and federal agencies to investigate church burnings throughout the South in the mid–1990s.

In 1997, he returned to private law practice. In 2001, he joined the Coca-Cola Company as executive vice president and general counsel. He was elected to the additional role of corporate secretary in 2002 and served as part of the company's senior leadership team as a member of the Executive Committee. Patrick was elected governor of Massachusetts in November of 2006, the first African American in that post.

Tina Patterson

Public Policy. Tina Patterson received a bachelor's degree from Brown University and earned a graduate certificate in advanced studies in alternative dispute resolution from Southern Methodist University. She is fluent in Spanish, Portuguese and French, and has a working knowledge of Arabic and German. Patterson is the first African American female president of the United Nations Association, Dallas chapter. She serves on the advisory board of the American Center for International Policy Studies and is the Texas Bureau chief for the International Public Policy Institute. She is an arbitrator and a facilitator for the community and specializes in issues of finance and securities, human trafficking and literacy.

Barbara Buckles Paxton

Local Government. Barbara Buckles Paxton was born in Montezuma, Georgia. She graduated from Fulton High School in Atlanta, Georgia, in 1979. In December 1989, she graduated from Atlanta Technical College at the top of her class with a certificate in cosmetology and barbering as well as accounting. She is a licensed master cosmetologist and master barber.

She begin her career with the United States government as a clerk at the Office of Personnel Management, a secretary at Internal Revenue Service, a receptionist at the Minority Small Business Development Agency, and a secretary with the Bureau of Prisons at the Atlanta Federal Penitentiary. In August 1998 she started her ca-

reer at the United States Postal Service. Her first postal assignment was as parcel post distribution clerk at the Atlanta Bulk Mail Center. In October 1999 Paxton entered the Postal Service's Associate Supervisor's Program, and was promoted to supervisor of distribution operations at the Atlanta Postal Air Mail Center. In January 2001 she was promoted to supervisor of customer services at the Griffin, Georgia, Post Office. In August 2002 she was assigned to the Union City, Georgia, Post Office as supervisor of customer services. In January 2005 she served as officer in charge at the Union City Post Office.

On May 27, 2006, Barbara Buckles Paxton was promoted to postmaster of the Union City Post Office. This appointment made her the first African American female to hold this position in the history of the Union City Post Office.

Donald Milford Payne

FEDERAL GOVERNMENT. Donald Milford Payne is a native of Newark, New Jersey, and a graduate of Barringer High School in 1952. He received a bachelor of arts degree from Seton Hall University in South Orange, New Jersey, in 1957. He was served as a teacher, insurance executive, president of the Young Men's Christian Association of the United States, and a member of Essex County, New Jersey, Board of Chosen Freeholders from 1972 to 1978. He was an unsuccessful candidate for nomination to the Ninety-seventh Congress in 1980; he was elected a member of the Newark Municipal Council from 1982 to 1988. Payne was elected as a Democrat to the 101st and to the ten succeeding Congresses (January 3, 1989, to present).

Jeff Payton

JUDICIAL. Jeff Payton earned his juris doctor degree from the Cleveland Marshall College of Law and has been a practicing attorney for 30 years. He has served as judge of Mansfield Municipal Court for the past 18 years. During his tenure on the bench, he has instituted a victim's assistance program, intensive probation supervision, local and regional drug court, driver intervention program, and community service work program. He also has been appointed by the chief justice of the Ohio Supreme Court to serve on two statewide commissions, the Ohio Criminal Sentencing Commission and the Ohio Courts Futures Commission.

Monica Pearson

MEDIA. Monica Pearson received a bachelor's degree from the University of Louisville in Kentucky. In 1969, she participated in the summer program for minority groups later called the Michelle Clark Fellowship, at the Graduate School of Journalism, Columbia University, in New York. Pearson began her career in Louisville as a reporter with the *Louisville Times* for four years. She worked in public relations for Brown-Forman Distillers before joining WHAS-TV in Louisville as a reporter and anchor for two years. She moved to Atlanta and joined WSB-TV Channel 2 to serve as the 5, 6, and 11 P.M. *Action News* anchor. She joined the Channel 2 staff in August 1975 and was still serving in that position in 2008. She has received numerous awards and honors in her 40-year career in journalism.

Andrea C. Peeples

JUDICIAL. Andrea C. Peeples received a bachelor of arts degree from Miami University in Ohio in 1991 and earned her juris doctor from the Ohio State University College of Law in 1994. She was a legal intern for the Columbus City Prosecutor's Office from 1994 to 1995 and an assistant prosecutor for the Columbus City Prosecutor's Office, juvenile, grand jury and trial staff from 1998

to 1999. From 1999 to 2005, she was counsel at the Columbus City Attorney's Office Civil Division. She was elected judge on the Franklin County Municipal Court, General Division, in Columbus, Ohio.

Buddie J. Penn

FEDERAL GOVERNMENT. Buddie J. Penn is a native of Peru, Indiana. He received his bachelor of science degree from Purdue University, West Lafayette, Indiana, and his master of science from George Washington University, Washington, D.C. He has also received certificates in aerospace safety from the University of Southern California and in national security for senior officials from the Kennedy School, Harvard University.

Penn began his career as a naval aviator. He amassed over 6500 flight hours in sixteen different types of aircraft. He was EA-6B Pilot of the Year in 1972. Significant leadership assignments include: executive officer and commanding officer VAQ 33; battalion officer at the U.S. Naval Academy (including officer-in-charge of the plebe detail for the class of 1983); air officer in the USS *America*; special assistant to the chief of naval operations; commanding officer of Naval Air Station North Island, California; and deputy director of the Navy Office of Technology Transfer and Security Assistance.

Prior to becoming the assistant secretary of the Navy (installations and environment), he was the director of industrial base assessments from October 2001 to March 2005, responsible for the overall health of the U.S. defense industrial base, the department's policies and plans to ensure existing and future industrial capabilities can meet the defense missions, guidelines and procedures for maintaining and enhancing and transformation of the defense industrial base, industrial base impact assessments of acquisition strategies of key programs, supplier base considerations, and offshore production.

On March 1, 2005, he was appointed assistant secretary of the Navy (installations and environment). Penn is responsible for formulating policy and procedures for the effective management of Navy and Marine Corps real property, housing, and other facilities; environmental protection ashore and afloat; occupational health for both military and civilian personnel; and timely completion of closures and realignments of installations under base closure laws.

Richard J. Pennington

LAW ENFORCEMENT. Richard J. Pennington received a bachelor's degree from American University and a master's degree from the University of the District of Columbia. His law enforcement education includes the FBI National Academy, the FBI National Executive Institute, and the senior executive program at Harvard University's John F. Kennedy School of Government. Pennington's career began in the Metropolitan Washington, D.C., Police Department, where he rose to the rank of assistant chief. In 1994, he was hired as the chief of police for New Orleans, Louisiana. In 2002, Pennington was selected to serve as police chief for the City of Atlanta, Georgia.

James E.C. Perry

JUDICIAL. James E.C. Perry is a native of New Bern, North Carolina, and a graduate of J.T. Barber High School. He received a bachelor of arts in business administration and accounting. After serving in the United States Army as a first lieutenant, he went on to Columbia Law School, where he earned his juris doctor degree in 1972. Perry worked in private law practice prior to his election as judge. He now serves as the chief judge of the Eighteenth Judicial Circuit in Seminole County, Sanford, Florida. He is married to Adrienne M. Perry, the former mayor of Longwood, Florida.

Matthew James Perry, Jr.

JUDICIAL. Matthew James Perry, Jr., is a native of Columbia, South Carolina, and a graduate of Booker T. Washington High School. He received a bachelor of science degree from South Carolina State College in 1948 and earned a doctor of law degree from South Carolina State College in 1951. He was in the United States Army during World War II from 1943 to 1946. During the 1950s, 1960s and 1970s, he was the leading civil rights attorney in the state of South Carolina. Perry was appointed by President Gerald Ford as judge on the U.S. Court of Military Appeals in 1976. He was the first African American attorney from the Deep South to be appointed to the bench. He was nominated by President Jimmy Carter on July 5, 1979, to serve as a U.S. District Court judge in a new seat created by legislation for the District of South Carolina. He was confirmed by the U.S. Senate on September 19, 1979, and received his commission on September 20, 1979. He assumed senior status on October 1, 1995. Judge Perry is the first African American U.S. District Court judge in South Carolina history.

Russell Perry

BUSINESS. Russell Perry, after being associated with an Oklahoma City newspaper for several years, started his own publication, the *Black Chronicle*, in 1979. Today, the *Black Chronicle* is the largest weekly paid newspaper in Oklahoma. He owns the controlling interest in a small Oklahoma City bank. Governor Frank Keating appointed Perry his secretary of commerce, the first African American to serve in that position.

In 1993, Perry made his first radio acquisition, purchasing a daytime AM station, now krmp in Oklahoma City, and later a 50,000 watt FM station in Tulsa, Oklahoma. He has also purchased stations in Lawton, Duncan, Anadarko, and an additional station in Tulsa. kvsp was added to the Oklahoma City market. Perry Publishing and Broadcasting is the largest independently owned radio group in Oklahoma. Its network of eleven stations reaches 99 percent of the African American community in Oklahoma with urban radio. In 2004, Perry Publishing and Broadcasting built a 2,000 foot tower, the tallest radio or television tower in Oklahoma. It also produces a weekly cable TV show, *The Urban Outlet*, which is seen in Oklahoma City, Tulsa and Lawton.

Stephen A. Perry

BUSINESS. Stephen A. Perry is a 1963 graduate of Timken High School in Canton, Ohio. He received a bachelor of science degree in accounting from the University of Akron. He completed the executive management program at the University of Michigan School of Business Administration and earned a master of science degree in management from Stanford University. Perry has served as a member and chairman of a hospital's board of directors and as the president and executive director of the Pro Football Hall of Fame; he has a distinguished professional, public and community service record. He was the 17th administrator of the U.S. General Services Administration from March 2001 to October 2005. He is a former executive of the Timken Company, concluding his 37 year career in 2001 as senior vice president for human resources, purchasing and communications. From 1991 to 1993, Perry was appointed to Ohio Governor (now U.S. Senator) George V. Voinovich's cabinet as director of the Department of Administrative Services.

Tyler Perry

THEATER, ENTERTAINMENT. Tyler Perry is a native of New Orleans, Louisiana. He was one of four children; he grew up in poverty and was physically abused. He was once homeless and lived in his car for three months. After years of intense anger and deep resentment, Perry was inspired to write letters about his painful childhood. These letters eventually became his plays. When Perry's work failed at the box office, he was left penniless. Perry is now said to have found that because he had allowed so much anger from his turbulent past to build inside of him, he always found a way to self-sabotage his ventures.

Perry saved $6,000, moved to Atlanta in 1992, and struggled until *I Know I've Been Changed* had its his first success in 1998, first at the House of Blues and later at the Fox Theatre. His following play, a staging of Bishop T.D. Jakes' book *Woman Thou Art Loosed*, was an immediate hit, grossing over $5 million in five months. A film version was later created starring Kimberly Elise and Loretta Devine, released in theaters in 2004. His work is aimed at a primarily African American audience. He ultimately created a successful touring theater company. By March 2005, Perry's plays had grossed over $75 million in ticket and DVD sales. Perry's other highly successful plays include *Diary of a Mad Black Woman, I Can Do Bad All by Myself, Madea's Family Reunion* and *Madea's Class Reunion*.

He also wrote and created the hit play *Why Did I Get Married?* featuring rhythm and blues singer Kelly Price, and another titled *Meet the Browns*. In 2005, he returned to the stage with another successful hit, *Madea Goes to Jail*. Another play, *What's Done in the Dark*, which Perry wrote and directed but does not appear in, went on tour beginning in September 2006. His other films include *Madea's Family Reunion, Daddy's Little Girls*, and *Why Did I Get Married?* He produced a television show titled *Tyler Perry's House of Payne*, and on June 6, 2007, the first two episodes ran on TBS.

Ewaul B. Persaud, Jr.

MEDICINE. Ewaul B. Persaud, Jr., is a native of New York, where he began his quest for success in the medical field at age 16, when he left Brooklyn to attend Xavier University in New Orleans. Upon graduating from college in 1990, he earned his medical doctor degree from the Morehouse School of Medicine in Atlanta, Georgia. He completed his residency at the Georgia Baptist Family Practice Program in 1997. He is a board certified family physician.

Dr. Persaud served as a medical doctor with the Southside Medical Care for nine years south of Atlanta, Georgia. In July 2006, he founded the Premier South Medical Group in Southwest Atlanta. Dr. Persaud has become of one of the leading medical providers in the City of Atlanta. In addition to his daily duties as a physician, he has participated in many community events and has been a preceptor for numerous medical students. He has shared his expertise on various local radio and television productions.

Joseph C. Persaud

MILITARY. Joseph C. Persaud joined the United States Navy in July 1977. Upon completion of recruit training at Great Lakes, Illinois, he reported to the USS *Proteus*, home ported in Guam. He graduated from the Senior Enlisted Academy in April 2001 and was named Class 096 honor graduate. He completed the command master chief course.

His leadership positions include serving in support during Operation Desert Shield and Desert Storm; in March 1998, he volunteered to go aboard the USS *Supply* during her summer deployment to the Persian Gulf and the Mediterranean, ultimately receiving orders there. Persaud served in the capacity of refueling at sea equipment leading chief petty officer and division officer. In March 1999, he was advanced to senior chief petty officer and was assigned duties as deck leading chief petty officer with an impeccable safety record during his 28-month tenure. He was also command master chief, Strike Fighter Squadron 81, Virginia Beach, Virginia, and command master chief, Naval Recruiting District in New York.

Karyn Pettigrew

EDUCATION. Karyn Pettigrew received a bachelor of arts degree in economics from Wellesley College and earned master of business administration with a concentration in marketing from Harvard University. She has held executive positions with People's Energy, the Illinois State Lottery, and Quaker Oats through myriad marketing, communication and corporate strategy initiatives. She serves on the board of directors for the Chicago Chapter of the National Association of Women Business Owners. She founded KPConsulting, a firm helping businesses to readily and successfully apply intuition to traditional business principles.

Michael E. Phelps

MILITARY. Michael E. Phelps received a bachelor of science degree in business management and accounting in 1982 and a master's degree in public administration, both from Troy State University. His military education includes: Squadron Officer School at Maxwell Air Force Base in Alabama; comptroller staff officer course, Maxwell; Air Command and Staff College; Department of Defense Professional Military Comptroller School at Maxwell; and Air War College.

Phelps enlisted in the United States Air Force in 1975. He served in accounting and finance and was commissioned as a second lieutenant in August 1982 through the Reserve Officer Training Corps program. His career has spanned all levels of Air Force Comptrollership in command and staff capacities, including assignments as an accounting and finance officer, budget officer, major command budget officer, plans staff officer, executive officer, Air Staff budget officer, comptroller squadron commander, and military assistant to the assistant secretary of the Air Force (financial management and comptroller) at the Pentagon in Washington, D.C.

From July 2004 to June 2006 he was as chief of the Budget Division, Directorate of Comptroller, Headquarters Air Mobility Command, at Scott Air Force Base in Illinois. In July 2006, he was assigned as the comptroller at Headquarters Air Combat Command at Langley Air Force Base in Virginia. He is the chief financial officer for the largest operational command in the Air Force and the principal financial advisor to the commander.

Audre F. Piggee

MILITARY. Audre F. Piggee is a native of Stamps, Arkansas. He received a bachelor of science degree in biology from the University of Arkansas at Pine Bluff and a master of science degree in material acquisition management at the Florida Institute of Technology. He earned a master's degree in military strategy from the United States Army War College. His military education includes the quartermaster officer basic course; the ordnance officer advance course; Combined Arms Staff Services School; the logistics executive development course; and the Command and General Staff College.

Piggee's numerous command and staff management positions include serving as maintenance officer, 16th Corps Support Group, Hanau, Germany; commander, 77th Maintenance Company in Babenhasen, Germany; assistant chief of staff for logistics (G-4) with the 1st Cavalry Division; (G-3) plans officer, 13th Corps Support Command, and support operation officer, 544th Maintenance at Fort Hood, Texas; logistics operations officer; chief, Executive Services Office; chief, Leader Development Branch, Combined Arms Support Command at Fort Lee, Virginia; commander, 15th Forward Support Battalion; and assistant chief of staff (G-4) for logistics, 1st Cavalry Division, Fort Hood, Texas. From August 2004 to April 2005 he was commander, 1st Cavalry Division Rear Detachment at Fort Hood; from May 2005 to July 2005 he served as the chief of staff, 1st Cavalry Division. Colonel Piggee is the commander, 15th Support Brigade, 1st Cavalry Division, at Fort Hood.

Timothy Mark Pinkston

ENGINEERING. Timothy Mark Pinkston received a bachelor of science degree in electrical engineering from the Ohio State University in 1985. He earned a master of science degree in electrical engineering in 1986 and a Ph.D. in electrical engineering from Stanford University in 1993. Pinkston has served as an electrical engineer with the technical staff at Bell Laboratories. He was a doctoral fellow at Hughes Research Laboratory and a visiting researcher at IBM T.J. Watson Research Laboratory. He joined the faculty at the University of Southern California in 1993. He currently serves as a professor in the Electrical Engineering–Systems Department, director of the Computer Engineering Division, and chair of the faculty of the Viterbi School of Engineering at the University of Southern California.

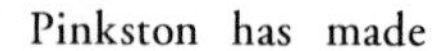

Pinkston has made fundamental research contributions on different aspects of computer system interconnection networks covering multiple levels, from solid theories on deadlock-free network routing to design and implementation of high-performance router chips. He has co-authored over 100 technical publications, with several of his works being widely cited in the literature. The SMART Interconnects Research Group, headed by Pinkston, has produced publicly available and widely used interconnection network simulators.

Myrtle Potter

BUSINESS. Myrtle Potter received a bachelor of arts degree from the University of Chicago. She worked 14 years for Merck before joining Bristol-Myers Squibb in 1996 as vice president for strategy and economics. She was promoted to group vice president, Worldwide Medicines Group, and then to senior vice president of sales, U.S. Cardiovascular/Metabolic, before becoming president of that business. Potter joined Genentech in 2000 as executive vice president and chief operating officer. In 2004, she was promoted to president, commercial operations, which included sales, marketing, managed care, business development, product distribution, customer service, and commercial operations functions. She also co-chaired Genentech's product portfolio committee and served as a member of the executive committee.

Colin Luther Powell

FEDERAL GOVERNMENT. Colin Luther Powell is a native of New York City, South Bronx, where he graduated from Morris High School in 1954. At the City College of New York he majored in geology and got his first taste of military life as a cadet in the ROTC. In 1971, he earned a master of business administration degree from George Washington University. In 1972, he was selected to be a White House fellow and served his fellowship year as special assistant to the deputy director, Office of the President.

As one of the more than 16,000 American military advisers sent to South Vietnam by President John F. Kennedy, Powell was assigned from October 1962 to January 1963; he was assigned as South Vietnam Self Defense Corps Training Center advisor, 2d Infantry Division, I Corps, Military Assistance Advisory Group. From January 1963 to November 1963, he was senior battalion advisor, Unit Advisory Branch, and later assistant G-3 (operations) advisor, 1st Infantry Division, Army of the Republic of Viet Nam, Military Assistance Advisory Group.

While marching through a rice paddy one day in 1963, he stepped into a Punji-stick trap, impaling his foot on one of the sharpened stakes concealed just below the water's surface. He was given a Purple Heart, and in that same year he was awarded the Bronze Star. In 1968, Powell returned for a second Vietnam tour of duty with infantry as a battalion executive officer and division operation officer. He was injured a second time in a helicopter crash landing.

In 1973, he assumed command of the 1st Battalion, 32nd Infantry, in Korea. Upon completion of the National War College in 1976, he assumed command of the 2ND Brigade, 101st Airborne Division (Air Assault), Fort Campbell, Kentucky. In 1977, Powell went to Washington to serve in the Office of the Secretary of Defense. Over the next three years, he was senior military assistant to the secretary of energy. In 1981, he became the assistant division commander for operations and training, 4th Infantry Division (Mechanized), Fort Carson, Colorado. In 1983, he returned to Washington as senior military assistant to Secretary of Defense Caspar Weinberger.

In July 1986, he assumed command of the V United States Army Corps, Frankfurt, Germany. In January 1987, Powell returned to the White House as deputy assistant to National Security Adviser Frank Carlucci. A military man at heart, he had to be persuaded to accept the job by his commander in chief, President Ronald Reagan. After the Iran-Contra scandal, Powell distinguished himself by reorganizing the National Security Council according to the recommendations of the Tower Commission. He also proved invaluable as the chairman of the interagency review group that coordinated the activities of the cia, the State Department, the Defense Department, and other agencies. When Carlucci took over as secretary of defense in 1989, Powell became assistant to President Reagan on national affairs (military matters), the first African American to hold this position.

In April 1989, Powell assumed command of the U.S. Army Forces Command, which directs operations and training for all active and reserve troop units in the continental United States as well as all Army National Guard units in the 48 continental states, Alaska, Puerto Rico, and the Virgin Islands. Powell became the first black general in this post, his first four-star assignment. In August 1989, he was nominated as chairman of the Joint Chiefs, the first black general nominated for the top post in the armed forces, chosen over 30 other four star generals, most of them more senior. In October 1989, General Powell was confirmed by the U.S. Senate as chairman of the Joint Chiefs of Staff, the principal military adviser to the president, the National Security Council, and the secretary of defense, and as a member of the Pentagon Executive Committee established by Defense Secretary Dick Cheney.

In 1991, as chairman of the Joint Chiefs of Staff under President George H.W. Bush, he became a national figure during the Desert Shield and Desert Storm operations that expelled the Iraqi army from Kuwait. In 1994, he joined former President Jimmy Carter and Senator Sam Nunn on a last-minute peace-making expedition to Haiti, which resulted in the end of military rule and the peaceful return to power of the elected government of that country.

Powell was nominated by President George W. Bush on December 16, 2000, as secretary of state. After being unanimously confirmed by the U.S. Senate, he was sworn in as the 65th secretary of state on January 20, 2001. On November 15, 2004, he announced his resignation from that position. On January 5, 2006, he participated in a meeting at the White House of former secretaries of defense and state to discuss United States foreign policy with Bush administration officials. Also in 2006, he began appearing as a speaker at a series of motivational events called Get Motivated, along with former New York Mayor Rudy Giuliani.

Tanya Walton Pratt

JUDICIAL. Tanya Walton Pratt received a bachelor's degree from Spelman College in Atlanta, Georgia, and earned her juris doctor degree from Howard University School of Law in Washington, D.C. She was a public defender in Marion County Superior Court, Criminal Division Room Two, for five years. She worked in private law practice in Indianapolis, Indiana. From 1994 to 1996, she served as the master commissioner in Marion County Superior Court, Room One, where she is now the presiding judge. She was elected Marion County

Superior Court judge on November 5, 1996. She has served as presiding judge of Superior Court, Criminal Division, Room One, since January 1, 1997.

Orlando A. Prescott

JUDICIAL. Orlando A. Prescott received a bachelor of arts degree from Rutgers University in 1981 and earned his juris doctor degree from the University of Florida in 1984. He was an assistant state attorney from 1984 to 1991 and assistant U.S. attorney from 1991 to 2000. In 2000, he was appointed a Miami-Dade County judge in Florida.

Cheryl Price

LAW ENFORCEMENT. Cheryl Price received a bachelor's degree from Huntingdon College in Montgomery. After graduating from college she enrolled in the Alabama Correctional Officer's Training Program in 1982. She worked through the ranks to successively higher positions. With the department over 20 years, Price is now warden of an intermediate security prison in Brent, Alabama, for inmates predominantly incarcerated for drug violations.

Deborah Pryor

BUSINESS. Deborah Pryor received a bachelor of science degree in chemical engineering from the University of Southern California. With 30 years of professional experience, she manages the assessment and remediation of former and current underground storage tank sites in Southern California and Nevada for Shell Oil Company. She also directs Shell's California state reimbursement program and leads the Environmental Services Department Minority/Women Business Enterprise Team.

Debra Pryor

PUBLIC SAFETY. Debra Pryor attended Stanford University's pre-hospital care program and became a firefighter and paramedic. Early career promotions included apparatus operator, lieutenant, and assistant fire marshal in Berkeley, California. By 1993, Pryor was promoted to fire captain and soon thereafter was the department training officer. In 1996 she was promoted to assistant fire chief and on October 19, 1998, Pryor was sworn in as Berkeley's deputy fire chief.

Pryor left the Berkeley Fire Department in October 2002 to join the Palo Alto Fire Department, where she initially served as the fire marshal and then as departmental operations chief. In December 2004, Debra Pryor returned to the Berkeley Fire Department as the city's first female fire chief and the nation's second African American fire chief.

Carla M. Pugh

MEDICINE. Carla Pugh received her undergraduate degree in neurobiology at the University of California Berkeley and her medical degree at Howard University School of Medicine. Upon completion of her surgical training at Howard University Hospital, she went to Stanford University and obtained a Ph.D. in education. Her thesis was titled "Evaluating Simulators for Medical Training: The Case of the Pelvic Exam Simulator." Dr. Pugh holds a patent on the method of simulation used to design the pelvic exam simulator and is currently engaged in the design of other simulators using similar technology.

Dr. Pugh is assistant professor of surgery and associate director of the Center for Advanced Surgical Education at Northwestern University. She also holds an appointment in the School of Education at Northwestern. She is working with the National Board of Medical Examiners to support their interest in using her simulators in the licensing examinations for U.S. physicians. Dr. Pugh has a broad interest in the use of technology for medical and surgical education, and is especially interested in how medical professionals learn. In addition to her appointments at Northwestern, Dr. Pugh also holds an appointment at the Telemedicine and Advanced Technology Research Center as special assistant to the director. At the center, Dr. Pugh manages the advanced distributed learning portfolio and the medical skills proficiency area.

Edna J. Ragins

EDUCATION. Edna J. Ragins received a bachelor of science degree in management from Hampton Univer-

sity and a master of science degree in marketing from the University of Wisconsin Madison. She earned a Ph.D. in marketing from Florida State University. She joined the North Carolina Agricultural and Technical State University faculty as an associate professor in 1990. In 2004, Ragins was named interim chair and later chair of the Department of Business Administration, School of Business and Economics, at North Carolina A&T State University.

Willie Larry Randolph

SPORTS. Willie Larry Randolph is a native of Holly Hill, South Carolina. His family moved to the Brownsville section of Brooklyn when he was a child. He graduated from Samuel J. Tilden High School in Brooklyn before Pittsburgh Pirates drafted him in the 7th round of the 1972 draft. Randolph made his major league debut in 1975 and was, at age 20, the sixth youngest player in the National League. He was traded to the New York Yankees in December 1975. He spent 13 of his 18 seasons as a player with the New York Yankees (1976–1988), and also played for the Pittsburgh Pirates (1975), Los Angeles Dodgers (1989–1990), Oakland Athletics (1990), Milwaukee Brewers (1991), and New York Mets (1992).

He played more games at second base (1,688) than any other player in Yankees' history, and also played the sixth most career major league games at second base (2,152) and turned the third most double plays (1,547) in baseball history among second basemen. He ranks among all-time Yankees leaders in games (1,694), at-bats (6,303), runs (1,027), hits (1,731), doubles (249), triples (58) and stolen bases (251). He won two World Championships as a player (1977 and 1978) and four more as a coach (1996, 1998, 1999 and 2000).

In 1993, Randolph was named an assistant general manager of the Yankees. From 1994 to 2004, he was a coach with the New York Yankees, serving as third base coach, and was the bench coach in 2004. In 2004, he was named manager of the New York Mets for the 2005 season. In 2006, Randolph managed the Mets to a league-best record of 97–65, and the National League East Division title (the team's first division championship since 1988). He came in second place in the 2006 National League Manager of the Year voting. On January 24, 2007, he signed a three year, $5.65 million contract extension with Mets. In 2007, he coached the Mets to lead the National League East for most of the season.

Johnnie B. Rawlinson

JUDICIAL. Johnnie B. Rawlinson is a native of Concord, North Carolina. She received a bachelor of science degree in psychology from North Carolina A&T State University in 1974 and earned her juris doctor degree from the University of the Pacific at McGeorge School of Law in 1979. From 1979 to 1980 she worked in private law practice in Las Vegas, Nevada; in 1980, she served as a staff attorney at Nevada Legal Services in Las Vegas. From 1980 to 1998, she served with the Office of the District Attorney in Las Vegas, first as a deputy district attorney, then as chief deputy district attorney and as assistant district attorney.

Rawlinson was nominated by President William J. Clinton on January 27, 1998, to serve as a United States District Court judge for the District of Nevada. She was confirmed by the U.S. Senate on April 2, 1998, and received her commission on April 7, 1998. She was nominated by President Clinton on February 22, 2000, to the U.S. Court of Appeals for the Ninth Circuit. She was confirmed by the U.S. Senate on July 21, 2000, and received her commission on July 26, 2000. She is the first African American woman to serve on the Ninth Circuit Court of Appeals.

Charles A. Ray

FEDERAL GOVERNMENT. Charles A. Ray is a native of Center, Texas. He received a bachelor's degree from Benedictine College in Atchison, Kansas, and a master of science degree at the University of Southern California in Los Angeles. He also received a master's degree from the National Defense University in Washington, D.C. Ray served in the United States Army for twenty years and obtained the rank of major in 1982. He joined the Department of State in 1982 and held several positions, such as deputy

chief of the U.S. Embassy in Freetown, Sierra Leone. He also served in the U.S. Consulate General offices in Guangzhou and Shenyang, China. He was consul general in Ho Chi Minh City in Vietnam.

He was confirmed by the White House in 2002 and sworn in as the U.S. ambassador to the Kingdom of Cambodia, where he served until 2005. He has also served as the diplomat in residence at the University of Houston. Ambassador Ray was appointed in September 2006 as deputy assistant secretary of defense for prisoners of war (POW) and missing personnel. He is responsible to the secretary of defense for policy, control and matters pertaining to missing personnel.

Monica Ray

LAW ENFORCEMENT. Monica Ray is a native of Hammond, Indiana. She received a bachelor of arts degree from Marquette University in 1979 and a master's degree in public service and justice administration from Marquette University. She is a graduate of the FBI National Academy in Quantico, Virginia.

Ray's career began with the Milwaukee Police Department on April 16, 1984. In 1990, she was promoted to detective and to a detective lieutenant in 1993, becoming the first female supervisor in the history of the Criminal Investigation Bureau. She was promoted to captain in 1995 and deputy inspector in 1996. She currently holds the rank of deputy chief of the Special Operations Bureau, where she directs the daily operations of the Criminal Intelligence Division, Vice Control Division, Patrol Support Division, Special Assignment Division and Planning and Operations Units.

Lewis Reed

LOCAL GOVERNMENT. Lewis Reed attended Southern Illinois University on a wrestling scholarship. There he majored in mathematics and computer science, a field he would go into professionally. Reed is director of networks and telecommunications for the Edison Brothers Stores' world wide operations, developing and managing an annual budget in excess of $3 million, managing staff and renegotiating multi-million dollar world-wide contracts, reducing cost and increasing production. Reed was elected a St. Louis, Missouri, city alderman for the 6th Ward. On April 3, 2007, he was elected president of the St. Louis Board of Aldermen. He is the first African American elected to this position.

Sarah Reeder

MEDICINE. Sarah Reeder received her bachelor of science in nursing from Howard University. She earned a master of science degree in nursing and a Ph.D. from the University of Maryland. Reeder's clinical background is in critical care nursing and includes over 22 years of service in the U.S. Army Reserve Nurse Corps, where she achieved the rank of lieutenant colonel. Her academic appointments include the University of Pittsburgh and Tuskegee University. Reeder has served on the faculty of the College of Nursing since 2002, teaching both graduate and undergraduate students. She is also a faculty advisor to the new Villanova chapter of Chi Eta Phi nursing sorority for minority students.

Jerry Reese

SPORTS. Jerry Reese is a native of Tiptonville, Tennessee. He received a bachelor's degree in health and physical education and a master's degree in education administration and supervision from the University of Tennessee at Martin. In the fall of 1995, he was inducted into the University of Tennessee Martin Hall of Fame. His career began in 1988 as a coach of the football secondary at the University of Tennessee at Martin. He moved to coaching the receivers and assumed the assistant head coach title in January 1993.

He joined the NFL's New York Giants scouting department on December 15, 1994. In the spring of 1999, he was appointed an assistant in the pro personnel department. In that position, he scouted the Giants' upcoming opponents and evaluated NFL players. Reese was promoted to director of player personnel on May 1, 2002. He was named the New York Giants' senior vice president and general manager on January 16, 2007. He is the third African American general manager in the history of the National Football League.

Antonio "L.A." Reid

ENTERTAINMENT. Antonio Reid is a native of Cincinnati, Ohio. He and Kenneth Edmonds, both members of the 1980s rhythm and blues band The Deele, founded LaFace Records in 1989 and issued their product through Arista Records. LaFace went on to become a highly dominant and successful label throughout the 1990s, responsible for producing popular artists such as TLC, Toni Braxton, OutKast, P!nk, Usher, Goodie Mob, Ciara, Sean Soltys, Donell Jones and Cee-Lo. In 2000, LaFace was merged into Arista Records with Reid being promoted to president and chief executive officer of Arista. Following his stint at Arista, he was appointed as chairman of the Island Def Jam Music Group in 2004. Reid appointed rapper Jay-Z as president of Def Jam Recordings and guided singer Mariah Carey's comeback with her 2005 hit album, *The Emancipation of Mimi*. He serves as chairman and chief executive officer of Hitco Music Publishing, a division of Windswept.

Inez Smith Reid

JUDICIAL. Inez Smith Reid was born in New Orleans, Louisiana, and raised in Washington, D.C. She received a bachelor of arts degree magna cum laude from Tufts University and a juris doctor from Yale Law School. She earned a master of arts degree from the University of California at Los Angeles, a Ph.D. from Columbia University, and master of laws in the judicial process from the University of Virginia School of Law.

Reid has worked in private law practice. She served as inspector general counsel for the Environmental Protection Agency, as general counsel for the New York State Division for Youth, and deputy general counsel for regulation review for the former federal Department of Health, Education and Welfare. She has taught at several universities and is a prolific author of scholarly writings in the areas of constitutional law, environmental law, African politics and African American history. In 1995, President William Jefferson Clinton appointed Reid to the District of Columbia Court of Appeals. She has served as chair of the District of Columbia Courts' Standing Committee on Fairness and Access to the District of Columbia Courts.

Samuel R. Reid, Jr.

SCIENCE. Samuel R. Reid, Jr., received a bachelor's degree with honors in computer science from the University of Maryland, Baltimore County, and earned a master's degree in computer science from the Johns Hopkins University. Reid is a software engineer in the Test Engineering Systems department at Northrop Grumman Electronic Systems and began his career in the professional development program as a software engineer. Through the course of solving difficult technical problems, Reid garnered a patent disclosure and two trade secret awards.

Wilhelmina Reuben-Cooke

EDUCATION. Wilhelmina Reuben-Cooke was one of the first three African American students admitted to Duke's Women's College, where she received a bachelor's degree in 1967. She attended Harvard University as a Woodrow Wilson scholar and received a juris doctor degree from the University of Michigan as a John Hay Whitney fellow. Reuben-Cooke was elected as a Duke trustee in 1989, becoming the first African American woman to serve in that capacity. She served on the board until 2001. She chaired the trustees' academic affairs committee and served on the executive committee.

Phillip S. Rhoda

MILITARY. Phillip S. Rhoda received an associate in applied science degree in aerospace technology from the Community College of the Air Force and a bachelor's degree in organizational management from Colorado Christian University at Lakewood, Colorado. His military education includes all the noncommissioned officer courses, the U.S. Air Force Senior Noncommissioned Officer Academy at Gunter Air Force Base in Alabama, and the chief leadership course at Gunter.

Rhoda is a native of Elizabethtown, North Carolina, and entered the U.S. Air Force on December 14, 1982. His background includes duties such as noncommissioned officer in charge of standards and evaluations, headquarters, North American Aerospace Defense Command; superintendent of C41 voice systems at Headquarters Air Combat Command; noncommissioned officer in charge of the mobile training team, U.S. Joint Forces Command; and superintendent of the 437th Airlift Wing Command Post, Charleston, South Carolina. He assumed his current position in May 2006 as the senior enlisted leader, U.S. Pacific Command, J3, Camp Smith, Hawaii.

Tynia D. Richard

JUDICIAL. Tynia D. Richard received a bachelor of science degree in business administration at Washington University in St. Louis in 1984 and a juris doctor degree from Harvard Law School in 1990. She was a law clerk for Judge Leon Higginbotham of the U.S. Court of Appeals for the Third Circuit in the summer of 1988. In the summer of 1989, she served as a human rights intern for the Legal Resource Center in Zimbabwe. From 1990 to 1991, she was a law clerk for Judge Constance Baker Motley in the U.S. District Court in the Southern District of New York. From 1991 to 1993, she was a senior staff attorney at Planned Parenthood Federation of America, Inc. From 1994 to 1997, she worked in private law practice in New York. She was an assistant attorney general in the New York State Attorney General's Office from 1997 to January 2003, with stints in the Civil Rights Bureau and the Charities Bureau. Since January 2003, she has served as an administrative law judge at the Office of Administrative Trials and Hearings, called upon to fulfill important decision-making roles in city government. She interprets and applies policies and directives for many different agencies of New York.

Fredrick D. Richardson, Jr.

LOCAL GOVERNMENT. Fredrick D. Richardson, Jr., is a native of Conecuh County, Alabama. He is the fifth of 12 children and a graduate of Conecuh County Public Schools. He attended Carver State Vocational College, Bishop State Community College and the University of South Alabama, where he earned a bachelor of arts degree in political science and history. He did further study at the University of South Alabama toward a master's degree in history.

Richardson served with the U.S. Postal Service from 1961 to 1992. He was manager of station and branch operations in both the Loop and Bel Air post offices. While working and attending school, Richardson found time to do research and write. His first book, *The Genesis and Exodus of NOW*, was published in 1978. It documented social and political change in Mobile from 1965 to 1975, as a direct result of now (Neighborhood Organized Workers). A second edition was published in February of 1996. Richardson was appointed to fill a vacancy on the City Council for District 1 of Mobile, Alabama, in 1997. He currently serves as councilman for District 1.

Jeffrey L. Richardson

MILITARY. Jeffrey L. Richardson received an associate degree in liberal arts from Chicago City-wide College and a bachelor of arts degree in psychology from Chapman University in Orange, California. He earned a master's degree in public administration at Troy State University, Troy, Alabama, and an associate degree in applied science (health science) at the Community College of the Air Force. His military courses include all the noncommissioned officer courses, survival, water survival non-parachuting, independent duty medical technician, advanced battle field trauma and surgical skills, intermediate executive skills, chief mentor, Air Force chief master sergeants leadership, U.S. senior leadership at the Center for Creative Leadership, Greensboro, North Carolina, and U.S. Air Force senior leadership at Gettysburg Leadership Experience, Gettysburg College.

Richardson entered the Air Force in July 1978. He has held numerous leadership positions, including his most recent assignments: superintendent, Group Medical Operation, and chief, Medical Plans, Programs and Resources, 352nd Special Operations Group in the United Kingdom; from January 1998 to June 1999, superintendent of Aeromedical-Dental Squadron, 314th Medical Group; superintendent, Flight Medicine, 59th Aerospace Medicine Squadron, Wilford Hall Medical Center; command manager, Aerospace Medicine Division, Air Education and Training Command; group superintendent, chief enlisted for medicine, 52nd Medical Group; command chief master sergeant, 352nd Special Operations Group in the United Kingdom; and since January 2007, command chief master sergeant, 1st Special Operations Wing, Hurlburt Field, Florida.

Laura Richardson

FEDERAL GOVERNMENT. Laura Richardson is a native of Los Angeles, California. She received a bachelor's degree in political science from the University of California, Los Angeles, in 1984 and earned a master of business administration from the University of Southern California. She has also studied in China at Hong Kong, Beijing, and Shanghai.

Richardson joined the Xerox Corporation in 1987 and worked there for 14 years. From 1996 to 1998, she was field deputy for Congresswoman Juanita Millender-McDonald. She served on the Long Beach City Coun-

cil from 2000 to 2006. In 2004, she won a second term outright on the first ballot. From 2001 to 2006, she served as the Southern California director for Lt. Governor Cruz Bustamante. She served from 2006 to 2007 in the California State Assembly, for the 55th Assembly District. The district encompasses the inland section of Long Beach, Carson and most of Lakewood. In 2007, she was elected to the U.S. Congress as a Democrat from the 37th California District.

Warren J. Riley

LAW ENFORCEMENT. Warren J. Riley received an associate in arts degree in criminal justice from Delgado University of New Orleans, Louisiana. He earned bachelor of science and master of arts degrees in criminal justice from Southern University of New Orleans. He has attended the Senior Management Institute for Police Executives at Harvard's Kennedy School of Government, as well as other management courses. Riley has served as a New Orleans patrolman in the 6th Police District and as an undercover detective in the vice crimes and major case narcotics sections of the Special Investigations Division and the Internal Affairs Division. He was platoon sergeant in the 5th Police District.

After his promotion to lieutenant he was the executive commander of the 6th District and commanded the department's Community Oriented Policing Squad (cops). As a captain of police, Riley commanded the 5th Police District, which includes the lower 9th Ward, and as assistant superintendent he commanded the Policy, Planning and Training Bureau. Prior to his appointment as superintendent, he was the deputy superintendent and held the number two position in the department as the chief operation officer. On September 27, 2005, 28 days after Hurricane Katrina, he was appointed interim superintendent. He was officially sworn in as superintendent of police on November 24, 2005.

Wayne Joseph Riley

EDUCATION. Wayne Joseph Riley received a bachelor of arts degree in medical anthropology at Yale University in New Haven, Connecticut, and a master of public health degree in health systems management from the Tulane University School of Public Health and Tropical Medicine in New Orleans. He earned his medical doctor degree from the Morehouse School of Medicine in Atlanta, Georgia, and a master of business administration from Rice University's Jesse H. Jones Graduate School of Management for Executives program.

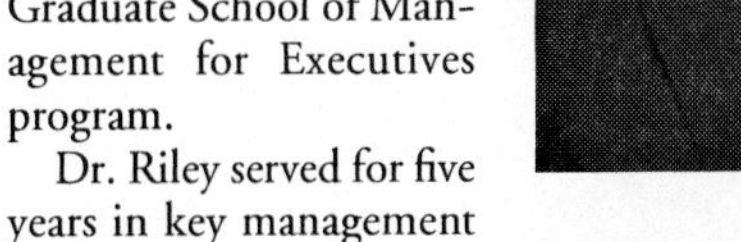

Dr. Riley served for five years in key management and policy positions to New Orleans' late legendary Mayor Ernest N. Morial, including serving as executive assistant to the mayor for intergovernmental relations. He was an adjunct professor of management at Rice University's Jesse H. Jones Graduate School of Management and co-faculty director of the Baylor College of Medicine/Jones Graduate School of Management Certificate in Medical and Healthcare Management program. Dr. Riley was assistant director of the Baylor Internal Medicine Consultant's General Internal Medicine Teaching Service at the Methodist Hospital and director of the Baylor Travel Medicine Service. He was the assistant dean for education from 2000 to 2004. Dr. Riley was appointed the 10th president of Meharry Medical College in Nashville, Tennessee. He assumed that post on January 1, 2007.

James B. Rivers

LAW ENFORCEMENT. James B. Rivers began his career at the City of Stone Mountain, Georgia, in 1956 with the Public Works Department. After moving to the Stone Mountain Police Department, he ascended through the ranks to become chief of police in 1988. Rivers was the first African American to serve in this position. After retirement in 1995, he served on the command staff of the Stone Mountain Park Police.

Neriah Roberts

EDUCATION. Neriah Roberts is a retired deputy superintendent of Polk County Schools in Florida. Roberts was re-appointed to another four-year term on

Polk Community College's District Board of Trustees. He will serve from August 3, 2007, to May 31, 2011. Roberts was elected chairman of the District Board of Trustees. He is also the director of the Association of School Based Administrators and an educational advisor for the Lakeland Housing Authority. In addition, he is a past director for Lakeland Regional Medical Center.

Jon Robertson

EDUCATION, MUSIC. Jon Robertson enjoys a distinguished career as a pianist, conductor and academician. His career as a concert pianist began at age nine with his debut in Town Hall, New York. As a child prodigy and a student of the renowned pianist and teacher Ethel Leginska, he continued to perform throughout the United States, the Caribbean and Europe. He was awarded full scholarship six consecutive years to the Juilliard School of Music, where he earned a bachelor of music degree, a master of science degree, and doctorate of music arts degree in piano performance as a student of Beveridge Webster.

He was chair of the Department of Music at Oakwood College in Huntsville, Alabama. In 1972, he was chair of the Thayer Conservatory of Music at Atlantic Union College in Massachusetts. From 1979 to 1987, he was the conductor and music director of the Kristiansand Symphony Orchestra in Norway. He appeared in Redlands, California, as guest conductor in the spring of 1982. Maestro Robertson became the conductor and music director of the Redlands Symphony Orchestra in the fall of that year and is currently in his twenty-second successful season with that ensemble. For 12 years, 1992–2004, Robertson was chair of the Department of Music at the University of California Los Angeles. He was the principal guest conductor of the Armenian Philharmonic Orchestra in Yerevan from 1995 to 1998. He has also conducted the Bratislava Chamber Orchestra at the Pianofest Austria at Bad Aussee, Austria, and most recently in South Africa, at the University of Stellenbosch International Festival. Robertson is currently the music director and conductor at Lynn University in Boca Raton, Florida.

Adam M. Robinson, Jr.

MILITARY. Adam M. Robinson, Jr., is a native of Louisville, Kentucky. He earned a doctor of medicine degree from the Indiana University School of Medicine, Indianapolis, through the Armed Forces Health Professions Scholarship Program. Following completion of his surgical internship at Southern Illinois University School of Medicine, Springfield, he was commissioned into the United States Navy in 1977.

Robinson's first assignment was as a general medical officer, Branch Medical Clinic, Fort Allen, Puerto Rico, before reporting to the National Naval Medical Center, Bethesda, Maryland, in 1978 to complete a residency in general surgery. Subsequent duty assignments included staff surgeon, U.S. Naval Hospital, Yokosuka, Japan, and ship's surgeon, USS *Midway* (CV-41). After completing a fellowship in colon and rectal surgery at Carle Foundation Hospital at the University of Illinois School of Medicine, he reported to the National Naval Medical Center in Bethesda as the head of the colon and rectal surgery division.

Dr. Robinson has been acting deputy assistant secretary of defense for health affairs, Clinical and Program Policy, and in July 2004, was commander of the National Naval Medical Center, Bethesda. He assumed the duties as commander, Navy Medicine National Center Area Region, in October 2005. In 2007, he was appointed the Navy's Medical Corps' Surgeon Corps surgeon general and chief of bureau of medicine and surgery. He is the first African American to serve as the surgeon general in the history of the United States Navy.

Nicole R. Robinson

EDUCATION. Nicole R. Robinson received a bachelor of arts and a master of arts in music education from North Carolina Central University in Durham and a doctor of philosophy in music education from Florida State University in Tallahassee. She began her professional career teaching elementary general music and middle school chorus in North Carolina public schools and as instructor of music education at Florida State University (1999–2000).

In 2003–2004, Robinson was visiting professor and director of music education at Virginia Commonwealth University in Richmond, where she developed and implemented a master of music education degree. Her professional and research interests include effective pre-service teacher preparation, teacher training, curriculum development, music and literacy, and using music to reach and educate at-risk students. Robinson is currently serving as an advisor for the Tennessee Music Education Association. She is division head and assistant professor of music at the University of Memphis. She has presented workshops, clinics, and research on the state, regional, and national levels and has published in various professional journals.

Sharon Robinson

EDUCATION, SPORTS. Sharon Robinson is the daughter of Major League Baseball legend Jackie Robinson. She received a bachelor's degree from Howard University in 1973 and a master's degree from Columbia University in 1976. She went on to receive a post-master's certificate in teaching from the School of Nursing at the University of Pennsylvania. She earned a doctor of humane letters, honoris causa, from Medaille College.

Robinson served for 20 years as a nurse and educator. She has taught at Yale, Columbia, Howard and Georgetown. She directed the Rev. Jesse L. Jackson's PUSH for Excellence program from 1985 to 1990 and was a fund-raiser for the United Negro College Fund and A Better Chance. She authored *Jackie's Nine: Jackie Robinson's Values to Live By,* and anthology that explores the nine values that helped her father achieve his goals. Other books include the romance novel *Still the Storm,* the memoir *Stealing Home,* and her most recent, *Promises to Keep: How Jackie Robinson Changed America,* a photographic children's biography about her father, the first African American to play major league baseball.

Robinson joined Major League Baseball as vice president of educational programming. She also serves on the Board of Directors of the Jackie Robinson Foundation and the Roberto Clemente Sports City Complex in Carolina, Puerto Rico.

Sharon B. Robinson

STATE GOVERNMENT. Sharon B. Robinson is a native of Baton Rouge, Louisiana. She received a bachelor's degree in accounting from Southern University in 1988 and earned her master's degree in business administration from Louisiana State University in 2001. She is a member of the Louisiana Society of Certified Public Accountants and is a licensed certified public accountant.

Robinson was an auditor for the Louisiana Legislative Auditor's Office for 16 years. Near the end of her time there, she was promoted to assistant legislative auditor and worked closely with local governmental entities and associations to assist them in complying with various aspects of state law. On March 15, 2005, Governor Kathleen B. Blanco appointed Robinson as the second state inspector general. She is the first African American to hold this position. In this capacity, she leads a staff of 12 auditors. The office's mission is to help prevent waste, mismanagement, abuse, fraud, and corruption in the executive branch of state government without regard to partisan allegiances, status or influence.

Sharon P. Robinson

EDUCATION. Sharon P. Robinson received her bachelor's degree, master's degree and doctorate in education administration and supervision from the University of Kentucky. She has also received an honorary doctorate from the University of Louisville. Robinson has held a variety of leadership positions at the National Education Association (NEA), including director of the National Center for Innovation, nea's research and development arm, and she recently served as interim deputy director of the National PTA's Programs and Legislation Office. She was president of the Educational Testing Service's Educational Policy Leadership Institute. She is a lifelong civil rights activist. Robinson was named president and chief executive officer of the American Association of Colleges for Teacher Education.

Joan Robinson-Berry

ENGINEERING. Joan Robinson-Berry is one of nine children brought up in the midst of gang violence in eastern Los Angeles County in California. She received a bachelor of science degree in mechanical and manufacturing engineering from California Polytechnic in Pomona, California. She earned a master of science degree in engineering from West Coast University and a master of business administration from the University of California in Riverside.

Robinson-Berry joined the Boeing Company in 1986 after working in design and manufacturing engineering for General Dynamics and co-founding and operating a small engineering company in the inner city of Los Angeles. At Boeing, she progressed through various technical and program management assignments. At the Boeing Company, she is the corporate director of external technical affairs and director of integrated defense systems supplier diversity. She is the first African American to win an Amelia Earhart Award, the first African American woman to set on a Boeing engineering process council, and the first African American woman to become a program manager in multi-billion dollar commercial airplane program.

Rene D. Rochester

MINISTRY. Rene D. Rochester received a bachelor of science degree from the University of Texas at Austin. She also earned both her master of science degree and Ph.D. in education from the University of Texas at Austin. She was an adjunct professor at North Park University and the Reformed Bible College. She has served as a consultant, guest lecturer, workshop facilitator, program developer and evaluation specialist for organizations such as Compassion International, Youth Specialties, Urban Outreach, Urban Impact and the Texas Department of Health's Center on Cultural Competency. In 1997, Rochester presented "Meeting the Needs of At Risk Adolescents in the State of Texas" to Governor George Bush's senior staff. Rochester is the president and chief executive officer of Urban S.E.T. (Strengthening, Educating, Training) Inc., and senior director of community ministries for Youth for Christ/USA.

Stephen W. Rochon

MILITARY. Rear Admiral Stephen W. Rochon is a native of New Orleans, Louisiana. He enlisted in the United States Coast Guard in 1970 and was commissioned as an ensign in 1975 from the Officer Candidate School at Yorktown. He received a bachelor of science degree in business administration from Xavier University. He is a graduate of the Naval War College. In 2007, he was the highest ranking black officer serving in the U.S. Coast Guard. He is the guard's director of personnel management. He was selected by the Bush Administration to serve as the eighth chief usher of the White House, in charge of overseeing what's officially known as the Executive Residence at the White House. The chief usher supervises the staff that handles the official and ceremonial activities of the president. He is the first African American to hold the post.

Maya Rockeymoore

BUSINESS. Maya Rockeymoore received a bachelor of arts degree in political science and mass communications from Prairie View A&M University. She earned a master of arts degree and a Ph.D. in political science and public policy from Purdue University. Rockeymoore was a member of the professional staff on the U.S. House of Representatives Committee of Ways and Means; was chief of staff and senior policy advisor to U.S. Congressman Charles Rangel in the late 1990s; and was the senior resident scholar for health and income security at the National Urban League's policy think tank. She served as the vice president for research and programs at the Congressional Black Caucus Foundation, where she successfully led the implementation of the organization's five year strategic plan. Rockeymoore is the founder, president and chief executive officer of Global Policy Solutions, a public affairs and organizational development consulting firm based in Washington, D.C. She also serves as a professional lecturer at American University.

Britt A. Rodgers

ENGINEERING. Britt A. Rodgers received a bachelor's degree in electrical engineering from the University of Delaware. She previously worked on a U.S. Postal Service program and a space-based sensor system program. Rodgers serves as the C4ISRT Networked Systems, Navy Systems Integration and Test integrated product team leader in Baltimore, Maryland, with responsibility for ensuring that military systems are designed, integrated and tested per government requirements. A major responsibility is managing the day to day system integration and sell-off activities and schedules to ensure on time delivery of the product to the government. In addition, she supports system level factory ac-

ceptance testing and site acceptance testing for all C4ISRT Networked Systems programs.

John W. Rogers, Jr.

BUSINESS. John W. Rogers is a native of Chicago, Illinois. In 1980 he received a bachelor of arts degree in economics from Princeton University, where he was the captain of the varsity basketball team. Rogers founded Ariel Capital Management in 1983 on the idea that wealth can be created by investing great companies at bargain prices, whose true value would be realized over time. He has transformed Ariel into a widely recognized mutual fund company and money management firm with more than $15.5 billion in assets under management. He was chairman, chief executive officer, chief investment officer and lead portfolio manager for Ariel Fund and Ariel Appreciation Fund.

Tawanda R. Rooney

FEDERAL GOVERNMENT. Tawanda R. Rooney received a bachelor of science degree in business administration from Virginia State University in Petersburg and earned a master of business administration degree from the University of Maryland, University College. She completed Squadron Officer School at Maxwell Air Force Base in Alabama; the women's leadership program, Office of Personnel Management, Management Development Center, Aurora, Colorado; and the senior executive service air and space seminar, Maxwell Air Force Base in Alabama.

Rooney began her federal career in 1984 through the Air Force summer-hire program at the Pentagon. From September 1988 to December 1993, she was budget and program analyst, Management Support Office, Directorate of Space Programs, assistant secretary of the Air Force for acquisition, in Washington, D.C. Five years later she transitioned to the Defense Evaluation Support Activity, where her positions included project manager, contracting officer and directorate budget representative. In 1997, Rooney became a deputy program manager at the Intelligence Systems Support Office in Arlington, Virginia. In November 1999, she was assigned as a staff officer to the deputy assistant secretary of defense for program analysis and evaluation in Washington, D.C.

In January 2001, she became deputy director for Information Engineering and Assessment Laboratory, Intelligence Systems Support Office, Fort Washington, Maryland. From November 2006 to February 2007, she was the director for Information Engineering and Assessment Laboratory. In February 2007, Rooney became the director for Intelligence Systems Support Office, which supports the initiatives and activities of the Office of the Under Secretary of Defense for Intelligence.

George E. Ross

EDUCATION. George E. Ross received a bachelor's degree and a master's degree in business administration from Michigan State University. He earned a Ph.D. in higher education from the University of Alabama. He completed his postdoctoral studies at Harvard University. He is also a certified public accountant. Ross has than 30 years in finance and management experience in the corporate and non-profit sectors, as well as in higher education. He has held positions at Clark Atlanta University in Atlanta, Georgia, the University of Tennessee at Chattanooga, and Tuskegee University in Tuskegee, Alabama. He served as the vice president for finance and administrative services at Central Michigan University. He was the 17th president of Alcorn State University.

Kevin G. Ross

JUDICIAL. Kevin G. Ross received both his bachelor of arts degree and his juris doctor with high distinction and other honors from the University of Iowa. He began his career serving as a police officer for five years in Iowa City. He served a judicial clerkship in the United States Court of Appeals, Eighth Circuit, for the Honorable Donald P. Lay in St. Paul. This followed a judicial clerkship in the U.S. District Court, District of Minnesota, for the Honorable Paul A. Magnuson, chief judge. In 1997, he joined a law firm and worked in private law practice in the areas of constitutional law, employment consultation and litigation, and general litigation. Ross was appointed to the Minnesota Court of Appeals on February 23, 2006, by Governor Tim Pawlenty.

James M. Rosser

EDUCATION. James M. Rosser is a native of East St. Louis, Illinois. He earned academic degrees in health ed-

ucation administration and microbiology from Southern Illinois University at Carbondale (bachelor of arts in 1962; master of arts in 1963; and a Ph.D. in 1969). He was a researcher at the Eli Lilly and Company Research Laboratories in Indianapolis from 1963 to 1966; he held several academic and administrative posts at Southern Illinois University at Carbondale from 1967 to 1970; from 1970 to 1979, he was associate vice chancellor for academic affairs at the University of Kansas in Lawrence and was a tenured faculty member in pharmacology and toxicology and higher education, while also serving as a member of the editorial board of the University Press of Kansas. Rosser has served since 1979 as president of California State University in Los Angeles, where he also holds academic appointment as professor of health care management. He has held senior administrative positions in two major universities and one statewide university system.

Vince Rozier

JUDICIAL. Vince Rozier is a native of Tar Heel, North Carolina, and a graduated as valedictorian of Tar Heel High School in 1994. He received a bachelor of arts degree in political science from the University of North Carolina at Chapel Hill and earned his juris doctor degree from North Carolina Central University School of Law. Rozier began his career as a Wake County assistant district attorney. On February 9, 2006, North Carolina Governor Michael Easley appointed him to a seat on the Wake County District Court vacated by the resignation of Judge Alice Stubbs.

Fanon Rucker

JUDICIAL. Fanon Rucker received a bachelor's degree from Hampton University in Virginia and earned his juris doctor from the University of Cincinnati. He was admitted to the Ohio bar in 1996. Rucker began his career as an assistant city prosecutor for the City of Cincinnati from 1996 to 2000, prosecuting misdemeanor cases and representing the city in civil and administrative cases. He worked in private law practice before receiving an appointment from Governor Ted Strickland to fill a vacancy on the Hamilton County Municipal Court.

Robert D. Rucker

JUDICIAL. Robert D. Rucker is a native of Canton, Georgia, and grew up in Gary, Indiana. He received a bachelor of arts degree from Indiana University in 1974 and earned his juris doctor degree from the University of Virginia Law School. Rucker has worked in private law practice, as attorney for the City of Gary, Indiana, and as a deputy prosecuting attorney for Lake County. In 1991, he was appointed to the Indiana Court of Appeals by Governor Evan Bayh. Rucker was appointed to the Indiana Supreme Court in 1999 by Governor Frank O'Bannon.

Cathy Runnels

EDUCATION. Cathy Runnels is a native of Dallas, Texas. She received a bachelor's degree from Chapman College in Orange, California, and a master's degree from Syracuse University in Syracuse, New York. Runnels has served with the Montgomery County Public Schools, the University of the District of Columbia, and the Harlem Hospital Speech and Hearing Center. She is presently a faculty associate at Johns Hopkins University and a national consultant for Pearson/AGS publishing and the Bureau of Educational Leadership. Runnels is president of Accent on Speech, a practice specializing in the language learning needs of school-aged children, public speaking, accent modification, and delivery skills of broadcasters. She conducts training workshops for governments, corporations, and non-profit organizations in the Washington, D.C., metroplex.

Bobby L. Rush

FEDERAL GOVERNMENT. Bobby L. Rush is a native of Albany, Georgia, and a graduate of Marshall High School in Marshall, Illinois. He received a bachelor of arts degree from Roosevelt University in Chicago, Illinois, in 1974. He earned a master of arts degree from the University of Chicago in 1994 and a master of arts degree from McCormick Theological Seminary in Chicago.

Rush served in the United States Army from 1963 to 1968. He

was an insurance agent in Chicago. He was an alderman elected to the Chicago City Council, 1983 to 1993, and in 1990 he was deputy chairman of the Illinois Democratic Party. He was an unsuccessful candidate for mayor of Chicago in 1999 and served as a minister in Chicago. Rush was elected as a Democratic to the 103rd and the seven succeeding Congresses (January 3, 1993, to present).

Dorothy Sumners Rush

EDUCATION. Dorothy Sumners Rush received a bachelor of science degree in mathematics and science from the College of New Jersey and a master of education in educational administration from Temple University. Rush has served as an educator for 19 years in elementary, middle and high schools teaching mathematics, science and reading. While a teacher and administrator, she wrote curricula, developed standards and conducted staff development for fellow educators. She then was vice principal of Ada H.H. Middle School for 11 years and was principal for eight years. She has been a member of the Philadelphia Board of Education since 2002, and currently serves as the board's vice president.

Tiffany C. Rush-Wilson

MEDICINE. Tiffany C. Rush-Wilson received a master of arts degree from John Carroll University in 1996 and earned her doctor of philosophy from the University of Akron in 2003. Rush-Wilson is a licensed professional clinical counselor with supervision credential with the State of Ohio Counselor, Social Worker and Marriage and Family Board. Her career includes serving as a social service worker with the Cuyahoga Department of Children and Family; as a community respite worker with the Berea Children's Home; as a clinical supervisor for the Baldwin Wallace College Counseling Center; as an adjunct professor at the John Carroll University Graduate School counseling program; and as coordinator of skill development at Walden University Graduate School, psychology program, Minneapolis, Minnesota.

Dr. Rush-Wilson has worked in private practice during the past eight years with clients diagnosed with eating disorders and a variety of other concerns such as women's issues and identity development. She is co-owner of the Chagrin Counseling Associates and Eating Recovery Clinic in Pepper Pike, Ohio.

Michael Russell

BUSINESS, ENGINEERING. Michael Russell is a native of Atlanta, Georgia. He received a bachelor of science degree in civil engineering from the University of Virginia and earned his master's in business administration from Georgia State University. He worked for 19 years in the construction and real estate development industry. He has been involved in the construction industry since he was a youngster and early in his career worked with renowned developer and architect John Portman, who provided him with invaluable experience in all aspects of the development business, including engineering, field supervision, project management and business development.

He spent most of his career with H.J. Russell and Company, serving in a variety of executive positions, most recently as executive vice president. He was promoted to chief executive officer of H.J. Russell and Company in October 2003, succeeding his father, Herman Russell, who founded the company in 1952 and led it for 50 years. Russell is chief executive officer of Concessions International, another Russell company and one of the leading food service management companies in the country.

Shantel L. Samuel

ENGINEERING. Shantel L. Samuel received a bachelor's degree in computer engineering from North Carolina State University and is pursuing her master's degree in systems engineering at the Johns Hopkins University. She is an electronics engineer at Northrop Grumman Electronic Systems and provides development and support for several antenna and radar technologies. She joined the company as a rotational engineer in the Professional Development Program.

David Sanders

BUSINESS. David Sanders graduated with honors from Princeton University with a bachelor's degree in psychology; he earned a Ph.D. in clinical psychology from the University of Minnesota. Sanders has served as senior human services director at the Hennepin County Children, Family and Adult Services Department, managing a social service department of 1,450 staff, responsible for all state and federally mandated social services to children, families and adults. Sanders was director of all operations for the Los Angeles County Department of Children and Family Services, the largest county system in the country, with about a 6,000 staff serving about 22,000 children in care. He currently is executive vice president of Systems Improvement for Casey Family Programs and leads the organization's efforts to partner with and support state, local and tribal child welfare jurisdictions in improving outcomes for children and youth that they serve.

Hank Sanders

STATE GOVERNMENT. Hank Sanders is a native of Selma, Alabama, the second of 13 children and a graduate of Douglasville High School. He received a bachelor's degree from Talladega College and a juris doctor from Harvard Law School. Sanders served in Huntsville, Alabama, with Madison County Legal Aid Society and in private law practice. In 1983, he was elected to the Alabama State Senate, becoming the first African American state senator from the Alabama Black Belt.

Luther L. Santiful

FEDERAL GOVERNMENT. Luther L. Santiful is a native of Waverly, Virginia. After completing his apprenticeship, he received a certificate in industrial management from the University of Virginia and later a bachelor of general studies from George Washington University. Santiful was deputy for equal employment opportunity (EEO) policy and director of the U.S. Army Equal Employment Opportunity Agency following his tour as director of EEO for the U.S. Army in Europe, headquartered in Heidelberg, Germany. Prior to that, he served as EEO officer for U.S. Army V Corps, headquartered in Frankfurt, Germany. Before his assignment with the U.S. Army, he held several positions in EEO, public affairs and production departments with the U.S. Naval Air Rework Facility in Norfolk, Virginia.

In January 2005, Santiful became director of equal employment opportunity and civil rights for the Department of the Army. As a member of the senior executive service, he is responsible for policy, guidance, direction, and oversight of all plans and programs affecting equal employment opportunity for Army civilian personnel. In addition to directing the EEO staff, he has oversight of accessibility issues that affect the Army workplace and public use of Army facilities.

David Satcher

MEDICINE, PUBLIC HEALTH. David Satcher was born in Anniston, Alabama. He graduated from Morehouse College in Atlanta, Georgia, in 1963. He received his medical doctor degree and Ph.D. from Case Western Reserve University and completed his residency training at Memorial Hospital, University of Rochester, University of California Los Angeles, and King-Drew in Los Angeles. From 1977 to 1979, he served as the interim dean of the Charles R. Drew Postgraduate Medical School, during which time he negotiated the agreement with UCLA School of Medicine and the board of regents that led to a medical education program at King-Drew. He also directed the King-Drew Sickle Cell Research Center for six years.

Dr. Satcher was professor and chairman of the Department of Community Medicine and Family Practice at Morehouse School of Medicine from 1979 to 1982. He is a former faculty member of the ucla School of Medicine and Public Health and the King-Drew Medical Center in Los Angeles, where he developed and chaired the King-Drew Department of Family Medicine. In 1993, President Bill Clinton appointed him director of the Centers for Disease Control and Prevention and administrator of the Agency for Toxic Substances and Disease Registry, where he served until 1998.

President Clinton selected him to serve as

the surgeon general for the United States; on February 13, 1998, Dr. Satcher was sworn in as the 16th surgeon general. He was also named assistant secretary for health. He became only the second person in history to hold simultaneously the positions of surgeon general and assistant secretary for health. In these roles, he is the secretary's senior advisor on public health matters and director of the Office of Public Health and Science. The surgeon general holds the military rank of admiral. Dr. Satcher was named director of the new National Center for Primary Care at the Morehouse School of Medicine in Atlanta, Georgia, in September 2002. From March to September 2002, he was a senior visiting fellow with the Kaiser Family Foundation, where he spent time reflecting and writing about his experiences in government and speaking. He also was president of Morehouse School of Medicine.

Robert Lee "Bobby" Satcher, Jr.

ASTRONAUT. Robert Lee (Bobby) Satcher, Jr., is native of Hampton, Virginia, and attended Denmark-Olar High School in Denmark, South Carolina. He received a bachelor of science degree chemical engineering from the Massachusetts Institute of Technology in 1986 and a Ph.D. in chemical engineering from mit in 1993. He earned his medical doctor degree from Harvard University Medical School in 1994. Dr. Satcher joined NASA in 2004 as an astronaut candidate while serving as a researcher at Northwestern University in Illinois. He was an orthopedic surgeon at Northwestern Memorial Hospital in Chicago. In his medical practice, Dr. Satcher treats patients who suffer from cancer in their arms and legs. At NASA he is a mission specialist.

Patricia P. Satterfield

JUDICIAL. Patricia P. Satterfield earned her juris doctor degree from St. John's University School of Law in 1977. She was a teacher living in Queens, New York, prior to attending law school. Satterfield serves as a justice on the New York Supreme Court of Queens County (Civil Division).

Eugene G. Savage

LAW ENFORCEMENT. Eugene G. Savage earned a master's degree in public administration from Florida Atlantic University in Fort Lauderdale, Florida, in 1990. He was a doctoral student in the School of Public Administration at Florida Atlantic University and at Lynn University in Boca Raton, Florida. He is a graduate of the 72nd administrative officers' course, Southern Police Institute at the University of Louisville, and a graduate of the John F. Kennedy School of Government at Harvard University.

His career in law enforcement began on October 5, 1970, as a patrol officer with the West Palm Beach, Florida, Police Department, after completing a tour in the U.S. Army that included meritorious service in the Vietnam War. He served in all the operational and administrative theaters of the police department, working up through the ranks to become its first African American captain. Additionally, he established its first community-oriented policing program and served as its first African American assistant chief. On February 24, 1997, Savage was name chief of police for the Fort Pierce, Florida, Police Department, becoming the first African American to head the department in its 96-year history.

Frank Savage

BUSINESS. Frank Savage received a bachelor of arts degree from Howard University in 1962 and a master of arts degree from the John Hopkins University Nitze School of Advanced International Studies in 1968. He has also received an honorary doctorate of humanities from Howard University. Savage has a distinguished 33-year career in international banking, corporate finance, and global investment management. He spent the early part of his career with the International Division of Citicorp in the Middle East and Africa. After a brief period as a principal in an international leasing company, taw International Leasing, he spent several years as an investment officer with Equitable Life, lending directly to U.S. and foreign companies. He rose to management chairman of Equitable Capital Management Corporation, a subsidiary of Equitable Life, and built the firm's global investment management business. He was chairman of Alliance Capital Management International, a division of Alliance Capital Management Corporation. Savage is now chief executive officer of Savage Holding LLC, a global financial services company.

Gale Sayers

SPORTS, BUSINESS. Gale Sayers is a native of Wichita, Kansas. He received a bachelor's degree in physical education from Kansas University and a master's degree in education administration from Southern Illinois University. Sayers was the fourth draft pick in the National Football League's first round in 1965. He was chosen by the Chicago Bears and went on to be named Rookie of the Year for that first season. During his career, Sayers had nearly 9,500 combined net yards and almost 5,000 yards rushing, and scored 336 points. He also is the NFL's lifetime kickoff return leader. He was named the Pro Bowl's Player of the Game in 1967, 1968

and 1970, and was named to the 75th Anniversary All Time NFL Team. He was also named to the Chicago Sports Hall of Fame in 1980, the Black Sports Hall of Fame in 1975 and the NFL All-time Millennium Team. In 1977, he was the youngest player ever inducted into the NFL Hall of Fame.

After his professional football career, Sayers returned to Kansas University to complete his degree and served as assistant athletic director. He then accepted the assignment as assistant director of the Williams Education Fund for three years. From 1976 to 1981, he was athletic director at Southern Illinois University. Following a successful career at Southern Illinois, he moved back to Chicago and launched a sports marketing and public relations firm, Sayers and Sayers Enterprises. In 1984, Sayers and his wife started a computer reseller firm. Today, the Sayers Group is a national technology solutions provider with locations across the United States and revenues of more than $300 million.

Andre H. Sayles

MILITARY. Andre H. Sayles is a 1973 graduate of the United States Military Academy. He holds a master's and Ph.D. in electrical engineering from the Georgia Institute of Technology. He also received a master of science degree in general management from Salve Regina University and a master of arts degree in national security and strategic studies from the U.S. Naval War College. He is a graduate of the U.S. Naval College of Command and Staff and the U.S. Army War College.

Sayles has 30 years of military service and developed the diversity process model based on observations during his time at West Point and in the Army. He served as a U.S. Military Academy admissions outreach officer, and in 1997 founded the student chapter of the National Society of Black Engineers at West Point. He is a professor and head of the Department of Electrical Engineering and Computer Science at the U.S. Military Academy at West Point.

Charles H. Scales

FEDERAL GOVERNMENT. Charles H. Scales received a bachelor's degree in general business from Alabama A&M University in Huntsville, Alabama, and then joined the Marshall Center as a communications specialist. Scales began his career with NASA as a cooperative education student while attending college. In 1976, he became a program analyst in Marshall's communications division. He was appointed chief of the program control office in the Marshall Facilities Office in 1986. Two years later, he was appointed chief of the resources management branch in the Information Systems Office. In 1994, Scales was named director of the plans and analysis office in the Institutional and Program Support Directorate, and he became director of the Business Management Office in 1995.

He was appointed deputy director of Marshall's Equal Opportunity Office in 1996 and was director from 1997 to 2004. He was selected to serve as deputy director in the Officer of Center Operations at the agency's Marshall Space Flight Center in Huntsville, Alabama. He was the associate administrator for the Office of Institutions and Management. Scales assumed the position of NASA's associate deputy administrator on April 16, 2007.

Errol R. Schwartz

MILITARY. Errol R. Schwartz received a bachelor of science degree in electrical engineering from the University of the District of Columbia in 1980 and a master of science degree in business management from Central Michigan University in 1984. He also received a master of science in national security strategy from the National Defense University in 2000.

Schwartz enlisted in the District of Columbia Army National Guard in 1976. He was commissioned in June 1979 and appointed a platoon leader in the 104th Maintenance Company. He served in numerous leadership positions as a staff officer and as a commander. Some of his previous assignments include battalion commander, 372nd Military Police Battalion, deputy director of information management, director of logistics, commander, 74th Troop Command, and deputy commanding general of the District of Columbia National Guard. He assumed duties as the adjutant general, Joint Force Headquarters, and commander of the District of Columbia Army National Guard on June 27, 2003.

David Scott

FEDERAL GOVERNMENT. David Scott is a native of Aynor, South Carolina. He received a bachelor of arts degree from Florida A&M, Tallahassee, Florida, in 1967 and earned a master of business administration from the Wharton School of Finance at the University of Pennsylvania in Philadelphia. He was a business owner, elected a member of the Georgia State House of Representatives in 1974, and elected to the Georgia State Senate (1982–2002). Scott was elected a Democrat to the 108th and to the two succeeding Congresses (January 3, 2003, to present).

Mark Anthony Scott

JUDICIAL. Mark Anthony Scott received an associate in science degree in business administration and a bachelor of arts degree in speech communication from California State University in 1980. He earned a juris doctor degree from Howard University School of Law in Washington, D.C. He spent three and a half years in the United States Air Force, receiving an honorable discharge. He served in private law practice with a primary legal concentration focused on criminal defense work throughout the United States. He has served on the faculty of Gerry Spence's Trial Lawyers College in Jackson Hole, Wyoming. He was elected as a Superior Court judge for the 4th Judicial District position in DeKalb County, Georgia. Judge Scott presides over civil, domestic relations, and criminal felony matters as a Superior Court judge in the Stone Mountain Judicial Circuit.

Raytheon K. Scott

MILITARY. Raytheon K. Scott received a bachelor of arts degree in social work from Alabama State University in Montgomery, Alabama, and a master of arts degree in human resource management and personnel administration from Webster University in Colorado Springs, Colorado. His military education includes Squadron Officers School at Maxwell Air Force Base in Alabama, Air Command and Staff College, and the Air War College.

Colonel Scott received his commission through the Air Force Reserve Officer Training Corps (ROTC) program as a distinguished graduate. He was a Titan intercontinental ballistic missile crew member, then transitioned to missile maintenance in 1986. He has served in all levels of missile maintenance and was a squadron commander for the 30th Transportation Squadron at Vandenberg Air Force Base, California. He served as the director of the U.S. Air Force logistics group commanders course, U.S. Air Force maintenance group commanders course and U.S. Air Force wing commanders seminar at Maxwell Air Force Base. From 2004 to June 2006, he was chief of logistics, MILSATCOM (Military Satellite Communications), Space and Missile Systems Center at Peterson Air Force Base in Colorado. In June 2006, he was assigned as commander of the 91st Maintenance Group at Minot Air Force Base in North Dakota.

June E. Seay

MILITARY. June E. Seay is a native of Worcester, Massachusetts. She received a bachelor of science degree in liberal arts from Excelsior College. She is a graduate of all the non-commissioned officer courses; the first sergeants course; the direct support unit standard supply system course; standard supply operators course; contracting officers representative course; the standard army intermediate level supply ABX system course; and the United States Army Sergeants Major Academy (Class 52) at Fort Bliss, Texas.

Seay entered the U.S. Army on February 22, 1983. She has held a wide variety of key military staff and command assignments, including as a squad leader, material management supervisor, platoon sergeant, property book manager, integrated logistics support manager, theater sustainment maintenance manager, first sergeant, S-4 sergeant major, and troop support battalion command sergeant major.

Seay participated in numerous combat operations, humanitarian missions, Operation Desert Storm/ Shield, Team Spirit in Korea, Hurricane Andrew in Homestead, Florida, and Operation Rugged Seahorse in Costa Rica. She directly supported Operation Joint Endeavor in Kaposar, Hungary; Operation Support Hope, Rwanda; and Operation Iraqi Freedom. She currently serves as Mannheim Garrison command sergeant major.

Valencia Seay

STATE GOVERNMENT. Valencia Seay attended DeKalb College, Clayton College and State University, and is a graduate of the Flemming Fellows Leadership Institute. Seay served 22 years in the banking industry before retiring. She is now president and CEO of Seay and Associates. She was elected a state representative to the Georgia House of Representatives in 2001. In 2002, she was elected a Georgia state senator for District 34. She currently is secretary of the State Institutions and Property Committee and member of the Public Safety and Homeland Security, Transportation, and Appropriations committees.

Willa Seldom

BUSINESS. Willa Seldom received a bachelor of arts degree in economics from Bryn Mawr College and a master of business administration from Harvard Graduate School of Business Administration. She earned her juris doctor degree from Yale Law School. Seldom spent seven years as an executive at AirTouch Communications, a multi-billion-dollar wireless company. She identified and completed numerous strategic investments, acquisitions and joint ventures, including the $6 billion acquisition of USWest's wireless business and the purchase of a controlling stake in Telecel in Portugal. She was one of two executives charged with the starting up AirTouch's Mobile Satellite Services Group.

Seldom is executive director of the Tides Center, an infrastructure support organization and fiscal sponsor providing financial, human resources and administrative services to 250 projects with combined budgets of $50 million.

Fred Seraphin

JUDICIAL. Fred Seraphin immigrated from Haiti to the United States in 1967, arriving in New York to join the rest of his family. His mother, Madeline, arrived first, having fled Haiti during the Duvalier years after his father, Franck, a parliamentary opponent of President Jean-Claude Duvalier, was murdered by the regime. He was the last of seven siblings to come to the United States. He worked for more than seven years for the Miami-Dade Public Defender's Office, handling criminal cases, and also has served in private law practice. He was appointed by Florida Governor Jeb Bush as a judge for Miami-Dade's Criminal Division, Eleventh Judicial Circuit of Florida.

Pamela Sharpe

PUBLIC SAFETY. Pamela Sharpe is the author of *The History of the New York State Police 1917 to 1987*, the first complete history of the agency. She was appointed to the New York State Police as one of the first nine women hired and the first African American female. She currently serves as the lieutenant in charge of member hiring in the Office of Human Resources. She is assigned to Division Headquarters in Albany, New York. She manages all state police hiring for sworn positions.

Alfred (Al) Charles Sharpton, Jr.

MINISTRY. Alfred Charles Sharpton, Jr. (Al Sharpton) is a native of Brooklyn, New York, graduated from Samuel J. Tilden High School in Brooklyn, and attended Brooklyn College, dropping out after two years in 1975. Sharpton preached his first sermon at the age of four and toured with gospel singer Mahalia Jackson. He was licensed and ordained a Pentecostal minister at age nine by Bishop F.D. Washington. In 1969, Sharpton was appointed by Jesse Jackson as youth director of Operation Breadbasket. In 1971, he founded the National Youth Movement to raise resources for impoverished youth. He became a tour manager for James Brown in 1971.

In 1994, he was re-baptized as a member of Bethany Baptist Church by Reverend William Jones and became a Baptist minister. He ran unsuccessfully for president of the United States in 2004. The Rev. Sharpton, known as a fiery orator, was the nation's leading black activist during the late 1990s and in the 2000s. He has led many protests; in September 2007 he led over 20,000 demonstrators in Jena, Louisiana, to protest what was perceived as differences in how black and white suspects are treated. He appeared before a Congressional Committee in October 2007 to testify about the Jena 6 and the lack of federal involvement. On November 16, 2007, he led a march on the U.S. Justice Department in Washington, D.C., protesting the department's lack of response on hate crime issues.

Booker T. Shaw

JUDICIAL. Booker T. Shaw is a native of St. Louis, Missouri. He received a bachelor of arts degree from Southern Illinois University in Carbondale in 1973 and earned his juris doctor degree from Catholic University of America in 1976. He has served as assistant circuit attorney; with the U.S. Department of Justice; at the Federal Trade Commission; Columbus Community Legal Services in Washington, D.C.; from 1983 to 1995 as an associate circuit judge in the Missouri 22nd Judicial District; and from 1995 to 2002, as a circuit judge in the Missouri 22nd Judicial District. Judge Shaw was appointed in 2002 to the Court of Appeals for the State of Missouri and retained in the November 2004 general election for a 12-year term expiring December 31, 2016. He began serving in July 2006 as chief judge of the Missouri Court of Appeals, Eastern District.

Frances Lynne Shell

MILITARY. Frances Lynne Shell is a native of Meridian, Mississippi, but calls Chattanooga, Tennessee, home. She received a bachelor of science in criminal justice from the University of Maryland, University College, in College Park, Maryland. In 1983, she graduated from the U.S. Air Force Special Investigations Academy at Bolling Air Force Base in Washington, D.C.

Shell enlisted in the U.S. Air Force in October 1975. She was assigned to Misawa Air Force Base in Japan as a security police officer. She completed tours at Hellenikon Air Force Base in Greece and Nellis Air Force Base in Nevada, as a security police investigator on both tours. Her leadership assignments include serving as superintendent at a large detachment; special agent in charge; region superintendent; headquarters staff officer; and as the chief of majcom (Major Command) enlisted assignments. On April 28, 2002, she became command chief master sergeant for the Air Force Office of Special Investigations, Andrews Air Force Base, Maryland. She is the advisor to the commander on utilization, management, training and quality of life issues impacting the command's 1650 enlisted special agents and support personnel.

Martha Lynn Sherrod

JUDICIAL. Martha Lynn Sherrod received a bachelor of arts degree from Fisk University in Nashville, Tennessee, and earned her juris doctor from the University of Houston and the University of Alabama School of Law. She has worked in private law practice and as an assistant district attorney from 1993 to 1997. In 1997, she was appointed by the mayor and city council as a judge on the Municipal Court of Huntsville, Alabama. She served as the presiding judge of the Municipal Court of Huntsville in 1998. In 1999, she was elected judge to the Alabama 23rd Judicial Circuit in the Madison County District. She is the first African American to win an at-large election in Madison County. Judge Sherrod has developed and presides over the Madison County Drug Court.

George L. Shine

MILITARY. George L. Shine joined the United States Marine Corps in July 1983 and attended boot camp at Marine Corps Recruit Depot Parris Island, South Carolina. He reported to Camp Lejeune, North Carolina, where he attended Infantry Training School and completed Drill Instructor School.

Shine has served for twenty-five years in the Marine Corps, as an infantry fire team leader, squad leader, drill instructor and battalion drill master. In November 1989, he reported to 3rd Battalion, 7th Marine Brigade, to serve as an infantry platoon sergeant. While there, he was deployed to the Persian Gulf in support of Desert Storm and Desert Shield. In June 1995, he reported to the 22nd Marine Expeditionary Unit to serve as operations chief. He was deployed to Landing Forces Sixth Fleet 1-96 as the joint operations center operation chief in support of Operations Assured Response and Quick Response.

In September 1996, he reported to Echo Company, 2nd Battalion, 2nd Marines, where he was the company gunnery sergeant. In February 1998, he reported to Golf Company, 2nd Battalion, 8th Marines, as the company first sergeant. In February 2003, he was transferred to the 1st Recruit Training Battalion at Parris Island as the battalion sergeant major. In February of

2005, he was transferred to the Support Battalion at Parris Island, where he served until being transferred to Marine Aviation Logistics Squadron 29 in April 2006. In November 2006 Sergeant Major Shine was transferred from Marine Aviation Logistics 29 to Marine Aircraft Group 29 as the group sergeant major.

Aaron Shirley

MEDICINE. Aaron Shirley received a bachelor's degree from Tougaloo College in Tougaloo, Mississippi, and earned his doctor of medicine from Meharry Medical School in Nashville, Tennessee. He completed his pediatrics residency at the University of Mississippi in 1965 and was the first African American to accomplish this feat.

Dr. Shirley helped establish the Jackson Hinds Comprehensive Health Center, which became the largest community health center in the state in 1970. He also established a comprehensive school-based clinic to provide health and counseling services to help reduce teen pregnancy, drug abuse, teen violence, sexually transmitted diseases, and mental health issues. The clinic became a national model for school-based clinics. Dr. Shirley serves as chairman of the board for the Jackson Medical Mall Foundation and is director of community health services with the University of Mississippi Medical Center.

Kenneth T. Shivers

MILITARY. Kenneth T. Shivers is a graduate of the Navy's Basic Electricity and Electronics and AE "A" School in Millington, Tennessee, and the Air Force Senior Noncommissioned Officer Academy, Class 03-E. Shivers enlisted in the U.S. Navy through the delayed entry program in October 1984. He has held numerous key leadership positions, including with the Air Test and Evaluation Squadron One stationed at Naval Air Station Patuxent River, Maryland, and with the Commander Fleet Air Western Pacific, in Atsugi, Japan. He currently is the command master chief, Airborne Early Warning Squadron 115 at Naval Air Facility, Atsugi, Japan, deploying with Carrier Air Wing Five aboard the USS *Kitty Hawk*.

Darin D. Simmons

MILITARY. Darin D. Simmons enlisted in the Marine Corps in June 1978 and attended recruit training at Marine Corps Recruit Depot Parris Island, South Carolina. Upon graduation from the 3rd Recruit Training Battalion, he attended Infantry Training School at Camp Pendleton, California. He has also completed Drill Instructor School at Parris Island and Recruiters School in San Diego, California.

His key leadership assignments include serving as a canvassing recruiter, sub-station noncommissioned officer in charge, program coordinator and military entrance processing station noncommissioned officer in charge at the 8th Marine Corps Detachment in San Antonio, Texas. He was assigned to the Staff Noncommissioned Officer Academy as a faculty advisor and instructor for the career course at Marine Corps Combat Development Command at Quantico, Virginia. He was a company first sergeant at Officer Candidate School. In March 2001 he was transferred to 4th Marine Corps Detachment Recruiting Station Frederick, Maryland, where he was the recruiting station sergeant major. In April 2004, he was transferred to the School of Infantry (East) as the battalion sergeant major, Headquarters and Support Battalion. In September 2006, he was transferred to Combat Logistics Regiment 27.

Russell Simmons

MUSIC. Russell Simmons is a native of Queens, New York. He attended City College of New York but left his studies to begin promoting local rap music acts, including Kurtis Blow and Run-DMC (whom he would later sign to his record label), and producing records. In 1984, he and Rick Rubin founded Def Jam Records, signing the Beastie Boys, LL Cool J, Public Enemy and other acts.

Def Jam became just one piece in Simmons' corporation, Rush Communications, which included a management company, a clothing company called Phat Farm, a movie production house, television shows such as Def Comedy Jam, a magazine, and an advertising agency. Simmons sold his stake in the record company for

$100 million to Universal Music Group in 1999. The Rush Communications is the sneaker company Run Athletics, which produces the Legacy and Arthur Ashe shoes.

Since May 2005 he has been a contributing blogger at *The Huffington Post*. Simmons is the fourth richest hip hop entertainer, behind Jay-Z, 50 Cent, and Diddy.

Wallington Sims, Jr.

MILITARY. Wallington Sims, Jr., attended college at Central Methodist College in Fayetteville, Missouri, and Central Texas University School, from which he was awarded an associate degree in general studies. He enlisted in the United States Marine Corps on April 4, 1983, and attended boot camp at Marine Corps Recruit Depot San Diego, California. Sims' key leadership assignments include serving as a drill sergeant and senior drill sergeant at Marine Corps Recruit Depot San Diego, California. In July 1992 he was transferred to the 1st Marine Expeditionary Battalion at Kaneohe Bay, Hawaii, and was platoon sergeant for 2nd Platoon. In July 1994, he transferred to the 1st Marine Aircraft Wing, Marine Wing Support Squadron in Iwakuni, Japan, and was the embarkation chief.

In July 1995, he received orders to Okinawa, Japan, to serve with the 3rd Force Service Support Group, G-3 LMCC. He was the embarkation chief and strategic mobility chief. During his tour his oversight of the embarkation of personnel and equipment to over 30 demanding exercises in the Republic of Korea, Japan, Australia, and the Kingdom of Thailand was superior in all respects. Returning to the United States, he assumed duties as the enlisted field sponsor for installations and logistics, Logistic, Plans and Capabilities Section, Headquarters Marine Corps in Washington, D.C. In May 2002, he was promoted to first sergeant and was assigned to Marine Aviation Detachment in Patuxent River, Maryland. In March 2006, he assumed his duties as the Marine Wing Support Squadron 373 sergeant major.

Leander Singletary

MILITARY. Leander Singletary is a native of Fort Lauderdale, Florida. He received an associate degree in applied science in management from El Paso Community College and an associate in arts in technology from Pierce Community College. He earned a bachelor of applied science in resources management from Troy State University and a master of business administration in leadership studies from Baker College Center for Graduate Studies. His military education includes all noncommissioned officers courses, first sergeant course, drill sergeant course, the army maintenance management course, nuclear biological chemical defense course, equal opportunity leadership course and the master fitness course. He is a graduate of the U.S. Army Sergeants Major Academy class 55.

He entered the U.S. Army in January 1985 as a light wheeled vehicle mechanic. He attended basic training, advanced individual training and the light wheeled (recovery specialist course) at Fort Dix, New Jersey. He was then assigned to the 78th Engineer Battalion in Ettlingen, Germany. He auditioned and was accepted as a tuba player with the 62nd Army Band and soon attended the United States Army Element School of Music in March 1989. He distinguished himself with high academic achievement by obtaining the C1 additional skill identifier. He then served in the now 56th Army Band as a drum major, squad leader, platoon sergeant and operations noncommissioned officer in charge. He has been assigned to the 282nd Army Band; the 21D Band; and 1CAV Band; and the 3rd Infantry Division Band as the first sergeant, deployed with the unit to Operation Enduring Freedom and Operation Iraqi Freedom. He was band sergeant major of the 323rd Army Band (Medical Command Band) at Fort Sam Houston, Texas. His present duty is with the U.S. Army Band in Japan (296th Army Band) as the band sergeant major.

LaToya E. Sizer

MILITARY. LaToya Sizer is a native of Springfield, Illinois. She received a master's degree in human resources management and is pursuing a doctorate in business administration. Her military education includes all the noncommissioned officer courses, the equal opportunity representatives course, mountaineering and rappelling course, first sergeants course with honors, and the United States Army Sergeants Major Academy (Class 55).

Sizer entered the U.S. Army in November 1987. She attended basic training at Fort Dix, New Jersey, and the basic journalist course at Fort Benjamin Harrison, Indiana. She was deployed to Haiti in support of Operation Uphold Democracy as a media relations noncommissioned officer. In 1995, she moved to Fort Meade, Maryland, to teach at the Defense Information School. In 1998, she was assigned to Fort Huachuca, Arizona, as the U.S. Army Intelligence Center and Fort Huachuca public affairs noncommissioned officer in charge. During this assignment she was platoon sergeant and later first sergeant of a company of more than 300 soldiers.

Sizer was first sergeant of the Defense Information School and sergeant major of the 1st Corps and Fort Lewis Public Affairs Office. In 2005, she made history when she was selected to serve as the first woman, first African American and first print journalist to hold the highest enlisted position at the American Forces Network Europe in its 63-year history. In August 2006, she became the network's first command sergeant major and one of five command sergeants major in the history of Army public affairs.

Richard Sizer

MILITARY. Richard Sizer received an associate degree in supervisory leadership from Hawaii Pacific University and is currently working toward his bachelor of science degree in information technology from the University of Phoenix. His military education includes all the non-commissioned officer courses, the battle staff non-commissioned officer course, combat life savers course, the air assault course; and the basic and advance instructors course.

Sizer entered the U.S. Army in 1982 as a tactical communication equipment repairman. His numerous leadership assignments include serving as the first sergeant with A Company, 102nd Military Intelligence Battalion, Korea; as the 2nd Military Intelligence Battalion rear detachment command sergeant major; and as the command sergeant major of the 105th Military Intelligence Battalion.

Gwendolyn D. Skillen

BUSINESS. Gwendolyn D. Skillen received a bachelor of science degree from the University of California at Berkeley and earned a master of business administration from Stanford University. She was director of internal audits for the Northwestern Health Unit Division of Kaiser Foundation Health Plan, Inc. She served as a vice president and controller and vice president of internal audits for Bass Hotels and Resorts. She currently is a senior vice president and general auditor for CareFirst BlueCross BlueShield in Maryland, responsible for directing internal audit services, quality control activities, and special investigations for its essential operations. Skillen was also elected to serve as the president and chief executive officer of the National Association of Black Accountants, Inc., Board of Directors.

Sylvester Small

EDUCATION. Sylvester Small is a native of Akron, Ohio, and graduate of Hower High School. He received a bachelor's degree, a master's degree and his Ph.D. from the University of Akron. Small began his career in education as a substitute teacher in the Akron Public Schools. He later worked as a teacher, assistant principal, and principal. He also served in many capacities as an administrator before becoming superintendent. Small became the first African American superintendent of Akron Public Schools in May 2001.

Thomas C. Smalls

LAW ENFORCEMENT. Thomas C. Smalls is a native of Hampton County, South Carolina, where he attended public schools and is a 1972 graduate of Wade Hampton High School. He is a 1984 graduate of the South Carolina Criminal Justice Academy. Smalls has served as a minister in the Church of Our Lord Jesus Christ of the Apostolic Faith Inc. and now serves as interim pastor of Greater Refuge Church in Varnville, South Carolina. His career in law enforcement began in 1983 when he joined the Hampton County Sheriff's Department. From 1984 to 1994, he was chief deputy. In 1991, he was named "Officer of the Year." From 1995 to 1998, he was Lieutenant of Operations. During 2000 and 2001, he was chief of investigations. He served as school resource officer for the Varnville Police Department from 2002 to 2006. In 2006, he was elected sheriff of Hampton County.

Allison Smith

MILITARY. Allison Smith is a native of Portsmouth, Virginia. She received a bachelor of arts degree from the University of Maryland and a master's in public administration from Troy State University. She attended U.S. Army basic training at Fort Dix, New Jersey. She graduated from the U.S. Army

Drill Sergeants School at Fort Jackson, South Carolina; all the noncommissioned officer courses; equal opportunity representative course; instructor training course; and the United States Army Sergeants Major Academy (Class 55).

Smith has served at Headquarters V Corps, where she was the secretary of the general staff noncommissioned officer in charge. She was a drill sergeant with D-Company, 4/13th Infantry Regiment at Fort Jackson, South Carolina, and the professional development noncommissioned officer for the Army's administrative specialist at the Human Resources Command. In 2001, she was assigned to Korea as the first sergeant of the 1st Replacement Company, then in 2002 she was first sergeant of B Company, 2/13th Infantry Regiment. Smith was selected to serve as the command sergeant major of 1st Battalion, 1st Infantry, at West Point, New York.

Calvin E. Smith, Jr.

MILITARY. Calvin E. Smith, Jr., is a native of Calvert County, Maryland. He entered the Marine Corps on August 8, 1985. Upon completion of recruit training, he attended Marine Aviation Machinist Mate School in Millington, Tennessee, in January 1986. He also attended Drill Instructor School. Smith began his military career as a marine aviation machinist mate assigned to Marine Light Attack Helicopter Squadron 367 at Camp Pendleton, California. His numerous leadership assignments include serving as a drill instructor and senior drill instructor at the Drill Instructor School at Marine Corps Recruit Depot in San Diego, California.

In September 1996, he received orders to work as an AH-1W plane captain as the noncommissioned officer in charge for the Flight Line Division at Marine Light Attack Helicopter Squadron and Marine Aircraft Group at Camp Pendleton, where he was promoted to staff sergeant in November 1996. One year later, he was reassigned to Marine Light Attack Helicopter Squadron 369, Marine Aircraft Group 39, at Camp Pendleton as flight line detachment commander for the 31st Marine Expeditionary Unit. He was gunnery sergeant, drill instructor and senior drill instructor with the 1st Recruit Training Battalion. From September 2000 to September 2002, he was first sergeant for Alpha Company. He was assigned as the first sergeant for Company A, 3rd Assault Amphibian Battalion, with the 1st Marine Division at Camp Del Mar. He was the first sergeant for Alpha, Echo and Headquarters Companies with the 1st Marine Division. He was promoted to sergeant major in November 2005 and assigned to Headquarters and Headquarters Squadron at Marine Corps Air Station, Marine Corps Base, Camp Pendleton.

Carol I. Smith

MEDIA. Carol I. Smith received a bachelor's degree from Yale University, Occidental College, and a master of science degree in public administration from Temple University. Smith established the Telecommunications Technology Task Force in 1994 to increase awareness of the importance of technology in shaping Philadelphia's 21st century economy. She has been the executive director of the Mayor's Commission on Technology since 1996. She is also president and chief executive officer of DigitalSistas.Net, and online network for African American women in technology.

Smith is the Philadelphia coordinator for Black Family Technology Awareness Week, a national program sponsored by Career Communications, Inc., and IBM. She has served as president of the Greater Philadelphia Chapter of the National Forum for Black Public Administrators. She was inducted into the Temple University League for Entrepreneurial Women Hall of Fame, which recognizes leadership, entrepreneurship and excellence in the community.

George Bundy Smith

JUDICIAL. George Bundy Smith is a native of New Orleans, Louisiana, and graduated from Phillips Academy. He received a bachelor of arts degree from Yale University in 1959 and a LL.B. degree from Yale Law School in 1962. He earned a master of arts degree in political science in 1967 and a Ph.D. in government from New York University in 1974.

Smith's judicial career began in May 1975 when he was named to an interim term on the Civil Court of New York City. He was elected to a 10-year term on that bench the following November. He was elected to a 14-year term on the State Supreme Court in 1979, and worked in New York County until his promotion to the Appellate Division, First Department. He was an associate justice of the State Supreme Court, Appellate Division, First Department, from January 1987 to September 1992, when Governor Mario M. Cuomo appointed him to the Court of Appeals. He was confirmed by the State Senate on September 24, 1992. He is the senior associate judge for the New York State Court of Appeals. Smith's twin sister, Inez Smith Reid, is a judge on the District of Columbia Court of Appeals.

Lizalyn Smith

ENGINEERING. Lizalyn Smith earned a master's degree in engineering from North Carolina Agricultural and Technical State University in 2004.

After receiving her master's degree she joined NASA's Glenn staff, where she has a role in developing a simulated upper stage for NASA's new Ares I rocket, which will eventually carry astronauts to the moon. Smith is president of the Northeast Ohio Chapter of the National Society of Black Engineers. She networks with society members, facilitates meetings, establishes community programs and fosters relationships with corporations and other technical organizations. Smith is a facilitator in the Footprints for Girls program, which provides role models for at-risk students.

Lovie Smith

SPORTS. Lovie Smith is a native Big Sandy, Texas, where he led the Big Sandy Wildcats to three consecutive state championships in high school and was all-state three years as an end and linebacker.

He received his bachelor's degree from the University of Tulsa. While at the University of Tulsa he was a linebacker and safety and was a two-time All-American.

Smith began coaching at his hometown high school in 1980. He coached the Cascia Hall Preparatory School football team in 1981. By 1983, he began coaching linebackers on the college level, at the University of Tulsa from 1983 to 1986, and then at the University of Wisconsin at Madison in 1987. He coached at Arizona State University from 1988 to 1991, the University of Kentucky in 1992, the University of Tennessee from 1993 to 1994, and the Ohio State University in 1995.

Smith began his pro football coaching career as a linebacker coach for the Tampa Bay Buccaneers. Under the guidance of Tony Dungy, Smith helped develop the Tampa 2 defense. After four years he was hired as the defensive coordinator of the St. Louis Rams, helping the Rams win the 2001 NFC Championship and advance to Super Bowl XXXVI (36). The Rams lost the Super Bowl to the New England Patriots.

The Chicago Bears hired Smith as head coach in 2004. The team finished the 2006 season with a 13–3 record, earning the NFC's top playoff seed. The Bears finished the season with the NFC's second-ranked scoring offense and fifth-ranked overall defense, winning the NFC Championship and representing the NFC in the Super Bowl. Smith led the Chicago Bears into the 2006 Super Bowl against Tony Dungy of the Indianapolis Colts. Lovie Smith and Tony Dungy became the first two African Americans to coach a team in the Super Bowl. The Colts won that contest.

Orlando "Tubby" Smith

SPORTS. Orlando "Tubby" Smith is a native of Scotland, Maryland. He is the sixth of 17 children born to sharecroppers Guffrie and Parthenia Smith. He is a graduate of Great Mills High School in Great Mills, Maryland, and received a bachelor of science degree in health and physical education from High Point College (now High Point University).

Smith was the basketball coach at his high school alma mater; assistant coach at Virginia Commonwealth University from 1979 to 1986; assistant coach at the University of South Carolina; assistant coach at the University of Kentucky; and from 1991 to 1995, head coach at the University of Tulsa. On March 29, 1995, he accepted the head coaching job at the University of Georgia, becoming the school's first African American in the post. He was named the 20th head coach of the University of Kentucky on May 12, 1997. Coach Smith led Kentucky to one national championship in 1998, a perfect 16–0 regular season conference record in 2003, five sec (Southeastern) regular season championships (1998, 1999, 2001, 2003, and 2005) and five sec tournament titles (1998, 1999, 2001, 2003, and 2004), with six Sweet Sixteen finishes and four Elite Eight finishes in his nine seasons.

Smith was selected to help coach the 2000 U.S. Olympic men's basketball team in Sydney, where the American team captured the gold medal. In 2007, Smith was named the head coach for the University of Minnesota basketball team.

Robin A. Smith

ENGINEERING. Robin A. Smith received a bachelor of science degree in electrical engineering from Howard University, a master's in business administration from the University of the District of Columbia, and a master's certificate in information technology management from George Washington University. Smith served as a project manager with Bell Atlantic in Virginia and joined Verizon in 2000. She is senior consulting engineer at Verizon Communications. She is responsible for planning, initiating and overseeing the development and life-cycle management of business plans and systems ensuring that user, cost, quality and specific objectives are met.

Ron Smith

ENGINEERING. Ron Smith received a bachelor's degree in electrical engineering from California Polytechnic State University, San Luis Obispo, with post-baccalaureate studies at California State University at Long Beach. Smith is vice president of Six Sigma for Northrop Grumman's Space Technology sector. He is responsible for the strategy and development of a tailored approach to implementing business transformation through process improvement. He is also acting vice president of Directed Energy Systems, which includes directed energy technology development, business development and program execution elements. All of the sector's laser programs and initiatives report to director Energy Systems, including Airborne Laser, the Joint-High-Power Solid-State Laser Program and other laser technology efforts, active protection systems efforts, and company affiliates Cutting Edge Optronics and Synoptic.

Rosa A. Smith

EDUCATION. Rosa A. Smith received a bachelor's degree and master's degree from Indiana State University. She earned a Ph.D. from the University of Minnesota and an honorary doctorate from Ohio Dominican University. Smith has served as a teacher, high school principal, an assistant superintendent in Minneapolis and Saint Paul and South Bend, Indiana. She served as superintendent in Columbus, Ohio. From June 2001 to May 2007 she was president and CEO of the Schott Foundation for Public Education. Smith is currently the New Leaders for New Schools' regional education manager.

Ella Louise Smith-Simmons

MINISTRY, EDUCATION. Ella Louise Smith-Simmons received a master's degree from Andrews University and earned her Ph.D. from the University of Louisville. She has been an educator throughout her career, in departments of education, as chair at Kentucky State University, as associate dean at the University of Louisville, and as professor at Oakwood College and La Sierra University. She had administrative experience as academic vice president of Oakwood College and academic vice president for La Sierra. Smith-Simmons was selected as vice president of the world Seventh-day Adventist Church, the first woman in that post.

Jimme Lee Solomon

SPORTS. Jimme Lee Solomon received a bachelor of arts from Dartmouth College and earned a juris doctor degree from Harvard University. Solomon joined Major League Baseball in 1991 as director of minor league operations. He was promoted to executive director of minor league operations and then to senior vice president of baseball operations for five years, overseeing Major League, Minor League, and international baseball operations, the Major League Scouting Bureau, the Arizona Fall League and numerous special projects, including launching the Major League Baseball Youth Academy at Compton College in Compton, California. He is executive vice president for baseball operations, responsible for such additional areas as on-field discipline, security, and facility management.

Otha L. Solomon

MILITARY, MEDICAL. Otha L. Solomon is a native of Kinston, North Carolina. He received a bachelor of science degree in biology from Winston-Salem State University in Winston-Salem, North Carolina. He earned a doctor of dental surgery from the University of North Carolina at Chapel Hill and completed an advanced clinical dentistry residency at Eglin Air Force Base in Florida. He also completed a dental service fellowship, Headquarters U.S. Air Force Office of the Surgeon General; medical executive skills training course

(Uniformed Services School of Health Care Science); Military Health System Executive Skills Capstone Symposium; Air Command and Staff College; and Air War College.

Solomon was commissioned a second lieutenant in December 1981 and entered active duty in January 1982 with the rank of captain. His key leadership assignments include serving as commander of the 6th Dental Squadron at MacDill Air Force Base, in Florida; commander of the 89th Dental Squadron, Andrews Air Force Base in Maryland; commander of the 380th Expeditionary Medical Group, Al Dhafra Air Base, United Arab Emirates; and in 2005, as chief of dental operations at Headquarters Air Force Medical Center at Wright Patterson Air Force Base in Ohio. He is the commander of the 71st Medical Group, Vance Air Force Base, in Oklahoma.

Jeri K. Somers

JUDICIAL. Jeri K. Somers was born at McConnell Air Force Base in Wichita, Kansas. She received a bachelor of arts degree from George Mason University in 1983 and a juris doctor degree from American University Washington College of Law in 1986.

Somers served on active duty in the U.S. Air Force from 1986 to 1991; she has held various reserve positions in Air Force Reserves and D.C. Air National Guard. She was a trial attorney, Department of Justice, Civil Division, Commercial Litigation Branch,1991 to 1994; assistant United States attorney, United States Attorney's Office, Eastern District of Virginia, 1994 to 2001; and in private law practice, 2001 to 2003. Somers was appointed to the Department of Transportation Board of Contract Appeals in April 2004. She became a member of the Civilian Board of Contract Appeals on January 6, 2007.

She has served as a military judge with the United State Air Force Reserves since 2004; as an adjunct professor, Embry-Riddle Aeronautical University (Graduate Program), 1988 to 1990; and as an adjunct professor at the University of Maryland, University College, from 1994 to 2001.

Michelle Spence-Jones

LOCAL GOVERNMENT. Michelle Spence-Jones is a native of Miami, Florida, and a graduate of North Miami High School. She attended Tallahassee Community College. She was on the staff of Miami Mayor Manny Diaz. Her accomplishments include being instrumental in obtaining $5 million to revitalize the Carver Theater in the Model City area. She also spearheaded efforts to secure $3 million for the redevelopment of a former grocery store site on Martin Luther King Boulevard. In November 2005 Spence-Jones made history by becoming the first African American female to be elected to the City of Miami Commission in forty years.

Charles Thomas Spurlock

JUDICIAL. Charles Thomas Spurlock is a native of Chicago, Illinois, where he attended public schools. He received a bachelor's degree from Boston University and earned his juris doctor degree from Boston University School of Law. Spurlock served in the District Attorney's Office in Middlesex County, Massachusetts, and the United States Attorney's Office in Washington, D.C. He worked in private law practice as a defense attorney. He serves as a Massachusetts Superior Court judge in Boston.

Earl Stafford

BUSINESS. Earl Stafford received a bachelor's degree from the University of Massachusetts and earned a Master's in Business Administration from Southern Illinois University. He entered the United States Air Force, serving for twenty distinguished years.

After retiring from the Air Force, in 1988 he founded UNITECH, a telecommunications company that has integrated services for engineering, business support systems and simulation and training services for the military.

Mr. Stafford serves as the chairman and CEO of his company, which has more than 350 employees. UNITECH is one of the mid–Atlantic region's fastest growing companies. Headquartered in Centreville, Virginia, within Northern Virginia's Dulles corridor and only minutes from Washington, D.C., UNITECH has operating locations nationwide with the major branch offices in Washington, D.C.; Orlando, Florida; Des Moines, Iowa; and Albuquerque, New Mexico. The company earned approximately $78 million in revenue in 2008.

On December 4, 2008, Mr. Stafford announced that he would provide more than 100 wounded veterans, battered women and terminally ill patients an all expense paid trip to Washington, D.C., for Barack Obama's inauguration. He purchased a $1 million inaugural package at a D.C. hotel, which included 200 rooms, $200,000 in food and beverage, and $600,000 in inaugural balls. The project was funded by his family's Stafford Foundation.

Terry D. Stanford

MILITARY. Terry D. Stanford enlisted in the Marine Corps on July 13, 1981, and attended recruit training at Marine Corps Recruit Depot Parris Island, South Carolina. Stanford has served for over 27 years in the U.S. Marine Corps with many leadership positions, including at Guantanamo Bay, Cuba, as the noncommissioned officer in charge of the fuels facility. In October 1985 he was transferred to Marine Corps Recruit Depot Parris Island as an assistant drill instructor and the section noncommissioned officer in charge for recruits awaiting disposition. He was an advisor at the Noncommissioned Officers Academy. In September 1990, he participated in Operations Desert Shield and Desert Storm as platoon sergeant for the Fuels Detachment 10. After this deployment he served was platoon sergeant, section chief, refueling point coordinator maintenance management chief, section leader, and first sergeant. In June 2003, he was transferred to the School of Infantry (East), Infantry 2nd Combat Engineer Battalion, 2nd Marine Division, where he remained until his transfer as the squadron sergeant major, Marine Light/Attack Helicopter Squadron 29, Marine Corps Forces Command in Jacksonville, North Carolina.

June Werdlow Stansbury

LAW ENFORCEMENT. June Werdlow Stansbury received a bachelor of science degree in criminal justice from Wayne State University in 1980 and a master of arts degree in counseling from Central Michigan University in 1982. She earned a Ph.D. in criminal justice and criminology from the University of Maryland in August 1997. In April 1983 Stansbury became a special agent with the U.S. Department of Justice, Drug Enforcement Administration (DEA). She conducted numerous narcotic investigations including extensive successful undercover assignments in Detroit, Michigan, and Baltimore, Maryland. In 2002, Stansbury was promoted to associate special agent in charge at the Houston Division Office. Through two assignments she has been responsible for management of all the enforcement and intelligence programs in Houston, Texas, and all of the sub offices throughout the division. In January 2005, Stansbury was named the New England Field Division's special agent in charge by DEA Administrator Karen Tandy.

Bonnie Stanton

LAW ENFORCEMENT. Bonnie Stanton is a native of San Francisco Bay Area, where she attended Elcerrito High School in 1968. Her career began at a local radio station. At age 26, she started the California State Police Academy; after graduation she was assigned as a California Highway Patrol officer. In 1982, Stanton was offered a special assignment in the Background Investigations and Recruitment Unit in the Golden Gate Division. Next, she did undercover assignments with the Auto Theft Unit in her agency. She was the first female in her department to receive an award for stolen vehicle recoveries and she received the Commissioner's Citation for outstanding achievement in the area of vehicle theft. In 1991, she was assigned as acting sergeant in the Patrol Division in the Oakland area.

In 1992, she was promoted to sergeant. She was assigned as the statewide coordinator to the Applicant Investigations Unit in Sacramento. In 1993, she returned to the Patrol Division. In 1997 Stanton became the first African American female to reach the rank of lieutenant. Her assignment was as field operations officer in San Francisco. In July 2000, Stanton became a captain and the first African American female to reach this pinnacle as well. As captain, she was transferred to the Golden Gate Communications center as commander. On August 30, 2002, Stanton made history again when she was promoted to the rank of assistant chief of the California Highway Patrol. She is the only African American female to have reached this rank in California Highway Patrol history.

Michael Steele

STATE GOVERNMENT. Michael Steele was born at Andrews Air Force Base in Prince George's County. He graduated from Archbishop Carroll High School and received a bachelor's degree in international relations from Johns Hopkins University in 1981. He earned his law degree from Georgetown University Law Center in 1991, and also attended the Augustinian Friars Seminary at Villanova University in Villanova, Pennsylvania.

He has taught high school history and economics an worked in private law practice. He rose through the ranks in Prince George's County to become the first African American county Republican Party chairman in 2000. He was the first-ever African American to be elected chairman of a state Republican Party. He co-chaired the African American Steering Committee for the Bush-Cheney campaign and served as a national spokesman delivering President George W. Bush's message to communities across the country. In January 2003, Steele made history when he became the first African American elected to a statewide office and the first-ever Republican lieutenant governor in Maryland.

In February 2009 he was elected the first black chairman of the Republican Party.

Gwendolyn Stephenson

EDUCATION. Gwendolyn Stephenson received a bachelor's degree in education from Harris Teachers College and holds a Management Certificate from Harvard University. She earned a master's degree in counselor education and a doctorate in education with a minor in research methodology from St. Louis University. Stephenson was chancellor of St. Louis Community College, with an enrollment of over 120,000 credit and non-credit students and an annual budget of $108 million. She has served as the president of Hillsborough Community College in Tampa, Florida, since August 1997. As the chief academic and executive officer of Hillsborough Community College Stephenson oversees an institution with campuses also in Dale Mabry, Plant City, and Ybor City with more than 42,000 credit and non-credit students annually. Hillsborough Community College employs more than 2,278 people full and part time.

Matthaw Stevenson

JUDICIAL. Matthaw Stevenson received a bachelor of arts degree in criminology in 1975 and earned his juris doctor from Florida State University College of Law in 1978. She served as assistant public defender in the Fifteenth Judicial Circuit from 1978 to 1979 and as a law clerk for the Honorable Joseph W. Hatchett on both the Florida Supreme Court and the United States Court of Appeals for the Fifth (now the Eleventh) Circuit, from 1979 to 1980. From 1981 to 1985, he was a commissioned officer, with the Judge Advocate General's (JAG) Corps in the United States Navy; from 1985 to 1987, he served as a Chapter 120 administrative hearing officer, Florida Division of Administrative Hearing. He worked in private law practice from 1987 to 1990. From 1990 to 1994, he was circuit judge for the Fifteenth Judicial Circuit; and from July 1, 2005, to June 30, 2007, he served was chief judge, Fourth Court of Appeals, Florida.

Cleveland Steward, Jr.

EDUCATION. Cleveland Steward, Jr., is a native of Greensburg, Pennsylvania, and a graduate of Greensburg-Salem High School. He received a bachelor's degree in education from Cal University in 1973 and a master's degree in education administration from Duquesne University. He earned his Ph.D. in education administration and his principal certification from Indiana University of Pennsylvania. He was the primary elementary principal at Wilkins Primary Elementary School. He served as a middle school principal in the Gateway School District from 1990 to 1991. Since then he has been assistant superintendent for Gateway's District of Elementary Education. Steward was named superintendent of the Gateway School District, which serves the communities of Monroeville and Pitcairn, Pennsylvania, 15 miles east of Pittsburgh.

David Steward

BUSINESS. David Steward is a native of Chicago, Illinois, and grew up in Clinton, Missouri. He attended Lincoln School then integrated Franklin School in 1957 and graduated from Clinton High School in 1969. Steward is chairman, chief executive officer and founder of World Wide Technology in 1990. Founded with a staff of four people and 4,000 square feet of office space, World Wide Technology has grown to employ over 900 people in one million plus square feet of facilities with over $3 billion in sales. It specializes in supplying technological and supply chain solutions to customers, suppliers and partners.

Alfred J. Stewart

MILITARY. Alfred J. Stewart received a bachelor of science degree in management and business administration from the United States Air Force Academy in Colorado Springs, Colorado. He earned a master of arts degree in national security and strategic studies from the College of Naval Command and Staff, Naval War College, Newport, Rhode Island. He was a national security management fellow at the Maxwell School of Citizenship and Public Affairs, Syracuse University, New York.

Stewart was commissioned in 1981 as a graduate of the U.S. Air Force Academy. He served in a variety of assignments, including Combat Crew Training School instructor, training program manager and as an operations officer. He commanded an air refueling squadron, an operations group, and a flying training wing. His staff assignments include tours on the Air Staff, with U.S. Transportation Command's Joint Deployment Training Center, and Headquarters U.S. Air Forces in Europe. In 1983, Stewart flew air refueling missions in support of Operation Urgent Fury, the rescue of United States students from Grenada. In 1985, during the Iran-Iraq War, he deployed to Southwest Asia to fly air refueling missions over the Persian Gulf in support of Operation Elf One. Most recently, he served as director of the Combined Joint Task Force, Horn of Africa, Air Component Coordination Element. Prior to his current assignment, the general was vice commander, Air Command Europe, at Ramstein Air Base in Germany. He is the commander of the 21st Expeditionary Mobility Task Force at McGuire Air Force Base in New Jersey.

Gina Marcia Stewart

MINISTRY. Gina Marcia Stewart is a graduate of Memphis Catholic High School. She earned a bachelor of business administration in marketing from the University of Memphis in 1982 and a master of education in administration and supervision from Trevecca Nazarene College in Nashville, Tennessee, in 1989. She also earned a master of divinity cum laude from Memphis Theological Seminary in May 1996. She attended the Harvard Divinity School Summer Leadership Institute for Church Based Community and Economic Development in 2000 and earned a doctor of ministry degree from the Interdenominational Theological Center in Atlanta, Georgia.

Stewart has served as an admissions representative for Control Data Institute from 1986 to 1989 and as director of admissions at Memphis Institute of Technology. She was director of admissions at Shelby State Community College for six years. She was elected to serve as pastor of Christ Missionary Baptist Church in Memphis, Tennessee. She is the first African American female elected to serve a Baptist congregation in Shelby County.

James Edward Stewart, Sr.

JUDICIAL. James Edward Stewart, Sr., is a native of Louisiana and a graduate of C.E. Byrd High School in Shreveport, Louisiana, in 1973. He received a bachelor of arts degree from the University of New Orleans, Louisiana, in 1977 and a juris doctor degree from Loyola University School of Law, New Orleans, Louisiana, in 1980. He was assistant city attorney in the Shreveport City Attorney's Office

from 1980 to 1982; assistant district attorney for Caddo Parish District Attorney's Office from 1982 to 1989; and first assistant district attorney at the Caddo Parish District Attorney's Office from 1989 to 1990. He was elected judge to the First Judicial District Court in 1991. In 1994, Stewart was elected a judge on the Second Circuit Court of Appeals in Louisiana.

Vincent R. Stewart

MILITARY. Vincent R. Stewart received his bachelor's degree from Western Illinois University in Macomb, Illinois, and a master's degree in national security and strategic studies from the United States Naval War College in Newport, Rhode Island, in 1984. He also earned a master's degree in national resource strategy from the Industrial College of the Armed Forces, National Defense University, Washington, D.C., in 2002. His military education includes: basic school at Quantico, Virginia; armor officer basic course at Fort Knox, Kentucky, in 1982; basic communications officer's course at Quantico in 1985; cryptologic division officer's course in Washington, D.C., 1986; Amphibious Warfare School at Quantico; Naval Command and Staff at the Naval War College, Newport, Rhode Island; the School of Advanced Warfighting at Quantico; and the Industrial College of the Armed Forces at the National Defense University in Washington, D.C.

He has been a tank platoon leader; executive officer; company commander; project officer, Light Armored Vehicle, Anti-Tank, Twenty-Nine Palms in California; intelligence officer and chief, Command, Control, Communications and Intelligence; deputy director, intelligence policy, Office of the Assistant Secretary of Defense; deputy intelligence chief, Marine Forces Central Command in 2002; and from 2003 to 2005, director of strategy, contingency planning and assessment, Office of the Under Secretary of Defense for Intelligence. He served as the commanding officer of the II Marine Expeditionary Force Headquarters Battalion.

Charles Stith

MINISTRY, FEDERAL GOVERNMENT. Charles Stith is a native of St. Louis, Missouri, and a graduate of Charles Sumner High School in 1966. He received a bachelor's degree from Baker University in Baldwin, Kansas, in 1973. He earned a master of divinity degree from the Interdenominational Theological Center in Atlanta, Georgia, in 1975 and a master's degree in theology from Harvard University Divinity School in Cambridge, Massachusetts, in 1977. He has also received an honorary doctorate from his alma mater, Baker University.

Stith was appointed senior minister of Union United Methodist Church in Boston at the age of 30, the youngest person ever appointed senior minister at the church. In 1985, while still pastoring at Union United, he founded the Organization for the New Equality (one), a not-for-profit organization with the goal of generating economic opportunity for women and people of color. In 1998, he was appointed by President Bill Clinton as ambassador to Tanzania. On September 17, 1998, Ambassador Stith received his letters of credence as ambassador extraordinary and plenipotentiary of the United States of America to the United Republic of Tanzania. He is the founder and director of the African Presidential Archives and Research Center at Boston University.

Eugene A. Stockton

MILITARY. Eugene A. Stockton received an associate degree in applied science from John Tyler Community College and an associate degree in liberal arts from St. Leo University. He earned a bachelor of arts from St. Leo University and received a baccalaureate certificate from Northwestern University Traffic Institute. He also earned a master of science from Virginia Commonwealth University and a master of strategic studies from the Army War College.

Stockton began his military career in 1968 as a recruit at the U.S. Marine Corps Recruit Depot Parris Island, South Carolina. In 1969 he was assigned to the 1st Marine Division in the Republic of Vietnam. He was discharged from the Marines in 1975 with the rank of staff sergeant. In July 1980 he joined the Virginia Army National Guard and served as a platoon leader with the 116th Infantry Brigade.

General Stockton has held numerous leadership positions, including as detachment commander at Headquarters, State Area Command, with the Virginia Army National Guard; as inspector general, Headquarters, State Area Command; inspector general, 29th Infantry Division; commander, 4th Battalion, 183rd Regiment (Regional Training Institute); and commander, 183rd Regiment. On November 5, 2005, he became assistant adjutant general for Army, Joint Force Headquarters, at Fort Pickett, Virginia Army National Guard.

Tammy Cox Stokes

JUDICIAL. Tammy Cox Stokes is a native of Savannah, Georgia, and graduate of Beach High School. She received a bachelor's degree and a juris doctor degree from the University of Georgia in 1987. She began her legal

career with the federal Board of Veterans Appeals in Washington, D.C. She then moved to the Atlanta area, where she spent a year with the DeKalb County Juvenile Court before joining the DeKalb County Solicitor's Office. She later joined the Fulton County District Attorney's Office. She left the post to become a litigator with State Farm Insurance Company. She then entered private law practice, first in Atlanta and later in Savannah. She was appointed as the first female and first African American to hold the position of Recorder's Court Judge in Chatham County, Savannah, Georgia.

Gale Stallworth Stone

FEDERAL GOVERNMENT. Gale Stallworth Stone is a native of Evergreen, Alabama. She received a bachelor's degree cum laude from Huntingdon College in Montgomery, Alabama, in 1987 and a master of science degree in information systems from Johns Hopkins University in Baltimore, Maryland. She is a certified public accountant.

Stone began her federal career as a cooperative education student in the Birmingham, Alabama, field office of the Department of Health and Human Services Office of the Inspector General. In 1996, Vice President Al Gore honored Stone with the Hammer Award for her significant contribution to the successful completion of the 1996 audit of Social Security Administration's financial statements. She was director of the Systems and the Financial Audit Division for 3 years for the Social Security Administration Office of the Inspector General. In 2000, she was promoted to deputy assistant inspector general for audit in the same office.

George A. Strait, Jr.

MEDIA. George A. Strait, Jr., is a native of Boston, Mass. He received a bachelor's degree in biology at Boston University in 1967. While he was completing the coursework for a master's degree in biochemical genetics at Atlanta University, he began to explore the world of broadcast journalism with a job as an anchor at a local TV station. Following stints at a Philadelphia station and at CBS News, he joined ABC News where he covered Jimmy Carter, Walter Mondale and George H.W. Bush. In 1983, Roone Arledge, then president of ABC News, chose Strait to be the first medical and health reporter in network television news. He held the position of chief medical correspondent until he left ABC in 1999. He co-anchored, wrote and produced *Black in White America*, a critically acclaimed documentary on race, and produced a documentary on the syphilis experiments on African American men in Tuskegee, Alabama.

In 1975, he helped found the National Association of Black Journalists. Strait has served as senior advisor for policy at the public relations firm IssueSphere in Washington, D.C. He has also been devoting himself full-time to MedComm, a healthcare and communications consulting firm he formed in 1996. In 2000, during the height of the dot-com boom, Strait shifted gears and moved to California to embark on a new venture with the Dr. Spock Company, where he was senior vice president of content and media until September 2001. He is vice chancellor for public affairs at the University of California at Berkeley.

Howard T. Strassner, Jr.

MEDICINE. Howard T. Strassner, Jr., received a bachelor's degree from the University of Chicago and his medical doctor degree from the University of Chicago Pritzker School of Medicine. His postdoctoral clinical training includes a four-year residency in obstetrics and gynecology at Columbia-Presbyterian Medical Center, the Sloan Hospital for Women in New York, and a two-year fellowship in maternal-fetal medicine at the Women's Hospital, the University of Southern California Los Angeles County Medical Center. He is board certified in obstetrics and gynecology and in maternal-fetal medicine.

Dr. Strassner serves as the John M. Simpson Professor and chairman of the Department of Obstetrics and Gynecology. He is also director of the Section of Maternal-Fetal Medicine and co-director of the Rush Perinatal Center and the Rush Regional Perinatal Network. Dr. Strassner has received two gubernatorial appointments to statewide bodies: the Infant Mortality Reduction Advisory Board and the Governor's Task Force on AIDS in Healthcare.

John Street

LOCAL GOVERNMENT. John Street was born in rural poverty in Norristown, Pennsylvania, and graduated from Conshohocken High School. He received a bachelor's degree from Oakwood College in Huntsville, Alabama, and earned his juris doctor from Temple University Law School. His professional career began as an English teacher at an elementary school and, later, at the Philadelphia Opportunities Industrialization Center. He served as a law clerk with Common Pleas Court Judge Mathew W. Bullock, Jr., and with the U.S. Department of Justice. He worked in private law practice prior to entering into public service.

Street was elected to the Philadelphia City Council in 1979 and assumed office in 1980. For nearly 20 years, he represented the city's Fifth Council District. He was chosen unanimously by members of the council to serve as president in 1992 and 1996. He retired from Philadelphia City Council on December 17, 1998, to run for mayor of Philadelphia. On November 2, 1999, he was elected to serve as the city's first mayor of the new millennium.

Thomas E. Stringer, Sr.

JUDICIAL. Thomas E. Stringer, Sr., received a bachelor of arts degree in mathematics from New York University (Washington Square College) in 1967 and earned his juris doctor degree from Stetson University College of Law in 1974. He was an assistant state attorney from 1974 to 1976. He served in private law practice until his appointment to the Hillsborough County Court in Florida as a judge. He was a member of the executive committee of the Conference of County Court Judges and served as administrative judge of the County Court. In 1987, he was appointed to the Thirteenth Judicial Circuit Court by Florida Governor Bob Martinez. He was the administrative judge for the Family Law Division until January 1994. In February 1999, Florida Governor Jeb Bush appointed Judge Stringer to the Florida Second District Court of Appeals.

Todd H. Stroger, Jr.

LOCAL GOVERNMENT. Todd H. Stroger, Jr., is a graduate of St. Ignatius College Prep and of Xavier University in New Orleans, Louisiana, where he earned a bachelor of arts degree in history. He was an investment banker at SBK-Brooks Investment Corporation. His career in public service began as an employee for the office of the chief judge of Cook County, where he served as jury supervisor to the assistant for the Chicago Park District. In 1992, he was elected state representative for the 31st Legislative District. On September 5, 2001, he was appointed by Mayor Richard Daley to fill the office of the late Alderman Lorraine Dixon and in February 2003 was elected to that office. On December 4, 2006, Stroger was sworn in as the 33rd president of the Cook County Board of Commissioners.

Emmet G. Sullivan

JUDICIAL. Emmet G. Sullivan is a native of Washington, D.C., and a graduate of McKinley High School in D.C. He received a bachelor of arts degree in political science from Howard University in 1968 and the juris doctor degree from the Howard University School of Law in 1971. He was the recipient of a Reginald Heber Smith fellowship and was assigned to the Neighborhood Legal Services Program in Washington, D.C.

Sullivan was a law clerk to Superior Court Judge James a Washington, Jr., a former professor and acting dean of Howard University School of Law. In 1973, he entered private law practice. On October 3, 1984, President Ronald Reagan appointed him a judge in the Superior Court of the District of Columbia. As an associate judge of the Superior Court, Sullivan was one of only seven judges in the twenty-four year history of that court to have served full-time in every division. He was the deputy presiding judge and president judge of the Probate and Tax Divisions, as well as chairperson of the Rules Committee for those divisions. On November 25, 1991, Judge Sullivan was appointed by President George

H.W. Bush to serve as an associate judge of the District of Columbia Court of Appeals. In addition to his full-time case management responsibilities, Judge Sullivan was chairperson for the Nineteenth Annual Judicial Conference of the District of Columbia in June 1994. On September 28, 1994, he was appointed by Chief Judge Wagner to chair the Task Force on Families and Violence for the District of Columbia Courts.

On June 16, 1994, Sullivan was appointed by President Bill Clinton to serve as U.S. District Court judge for the District of Columbia. Upon his appointment, Judge Sullivan became the first person in the District of Columbia to have been appointed by three United States presidents to three judicial positions.

Horacena Tate

STATE GOVERNMENT. Horacena Tate was born in Griffin, Georgia, and raised in Atlanta, Georgia. She attended Atlanta City Schools and graduated from Frederick Douglass High School in 1973. She received a bachelor of science degree in education from the University of Georgia in 1977. She earned a master's degree in education administration from Atlanta University in 1988 and her education doctorate from Clark-Atlanta University in 1992. Tate began her career in the Georgia Department of Labor in 1977. She spent several years as an employee of United Airlines and Apollo Travel Service. She currently is president of Tate, Marsh and Associates, Inc., software training, management training and technical writing firm. Tate was first elected to the Georgia State Senate from the 38th District in 2003. Senator Tate, a Democrat, represents part of Fulton County, Georgia.

Marcia Tate

EDUCATION. Marcia Tate received a bachelor's degree in psychology and elementary education from Spelman College and a master of arts degree in remedial reading from the University of Michigan. She has also earned an educational specialist degree from Georgia State University and a Ph.D. in educational leadership from Clark Atlanta University. Tate has served for over 30 years in a career of education with the DeKalb County School System, Decatur, Georgia. She has been a classroom teacher, reading specialist, language arts coordinator, and staff development director. In 2001, Tate received the Distinguished Staff Developer Award for the State of Georgia and her department was chosen to receive the 2002 Exemplary Program Award for the state.

Wilbert A. Tatum

MEDIA. Wilbert A. Tatum received a bachelor's degree from Lincoln University and a master's degree in urban studies at Occidental College in Los Angeles, California. He received an honorary doctor of letters degree from Lincoln University in 1958. Tatum also attended Yale University as a National Urban fellow. He purchased the *Amsterdam News* with his partners in 1971. In 1972, also with partners, he purchased radio stations WLIB and WBLS in New York City. These stations became the flagships of the Inner City Broadcasting Corporation with stations in California, Michigan, Texas, Indiana and New York, as well as corporate stock ownership of the famed Apollo Theatre in Harlem.

Bernard Taylor, Jr.

EDUCATION. Bernard Taylor, Jr. received a bachelor of arts degree, a master of public administration degree and a Ph.D. in education degree from the University of Pittsburgh. Taylor has served as a teacher, and as a principal in the Pittsburgh Public Schools. He was superintendent of Schools in the Kansas City, Missouri School District. Taylor was appointed as superintendent of Grand Rapids Public Schools, Michigan's third largest district, effective July 1, 2006.

Carole Y. Taylor

JUDICIAL. Carole Y. Taylor received a bachelor of arts from the University of North Carolina in 1971 and earned her juris doctor from the University of North Carolina Law School in 1974. From 1974 to 1976 she was a staff attorney for Legal Aid Society of Durham County, North Carolina. She has served as a staff attorney for New Hanover Legal Services; as an associate university attorney at the University of Florida from 1977 to 1979; as an assistant public defender from 1979 to 1982; and from 1982 to 1983, as an assistant United States attorney. She worked in private law practice until 1991, then was a County Court judge for Florida's 17th

Judicial Circuit from 1991 to 1995. Since 1998, Judge Taylor has served on the Florida's Fourth District Court of Appeals. She was inducted into the Broward County Women's Hall of Fame in 1999.

Ephren W. Taylor

BUSINESS. Ephren W. Taylor at age 23 was appointed chief executive officer of City Capital Corporation, a publicly-owned company. Taylor became America's youngest African American CEO of a publicly-owned company and one of the youngest CEOs of any race in the United States.

At age 12, Taylor began his first company, designing 3-D computer games. He grew his second company, a job search portal for teens and college students called GoFerrelGo, to a street value of $3.2 million, fourth among all teen businesses nationwide (*YoungBiz* magazine). He was recognized as Kansas Young Entrepreneur of the Year in 2002 by the Kansas Department of Commerce for his exceptional investment strategies, originally developed to assist churches with their investment and funding needs. He later expanded the concepts to include other non-profit endowments, especially those of entertainment of entertainment and sports figures.

Taylor's diverse business portfolio is quickly transforming him into a household name. He appears weekly on *Fox News* and has been featured on network shows such as ABC's *20/20* and CNBC's *Business Nation*. He has had regular appearances in print and radio media, including PBS, *Black Enterprise*, and the *Miami Herald*. In 2007, at City Capital Corporation, Taylor started the subsidiary Goshen Energy Resources, becoming a national leader in producing alternative energy specializing in biofuels. His commitment to green energy is part of his concept of empowering local communities with both profitable and socially conscious investing and development. Through his actions he is leading a new wave of ceos focusing on corporate social responsibility.

Leah Landrum Taylor

EDUCATION, STATE GOVERNMENT. Leah Landrum Taylor is a native of Phoenix, Arizona. She attended Xavier College Preparatory and Arizona State University, where she received bachelor's and master's degrees in political science. She is a graduate of the John F. Kennedy School of Government at Harvard University. Taylor is a founder and vice-president of the Landrum Foundation, a non-profit organization designed to provide financial support and preparation for students throughout their post-secondary education. During her spare time she is an adjunct faculty member for Maricopa Community College. She was elected an Arizona State Senator for District 16.

Valerie Taylor

ENGINEERING. Valerie Taylor received a bachelor of arts and master of science in electrical engineering from Purdue University. She earned a Ph.D. in electrical engineering and computer sciences from the University of California at Berkeley. Taylor works with Sigma Xi, the scientific research society. Her research areas include performance of parallel scientific applications, computer architecture, and visual supercomputing environments. Specifically, she's interested in development of techniques for systematically analyzing and improving application performance in the context of parallel and distributed scientific applications, visual supercomputing environments and distributed systems.

Willie C. Tennant, Sr.

MILITARY. Willie C. Tennant, Sr., is a native of Pleasantville, New Jersey. He received an associate in science degree in general studies from Central Texas College and a bachelor of science degree in business management from Liberty University. He is a graduate of the Airborne School, the Air Assault School, the first sergeant course, the U.S. Army Sergeants Major Academy; and the U.S. Army Command Sergeants Major Course.

Tennant entered the United States Army in September 1978. He has served at every leadership position, including squad leader, section sergeant, platoon sergeant, operations sergeant, first sergeant, sergeant major, and command sergeant major. He was deployed as the command sergeant major of Task Force Special Operations Task Force 20 in support of Operation Iraqi Freedom. He returned to Germany and assumed the duties as command sergeant major of Special Troops Battalion, 3rd Corps Support Command, Wiesbaden Airfield in Germany. He has been command sergeant major of the 7th Corps Support Group, Bamberg, Germany, since October 2004. He selected to serve as the command sergeant major of the 3rd Corps Support Command.

Don I. Tharpe

BUSINESS. Don I. Tharpe is a native of Kentucky. He received a bachelor's degree and master's degree from Murray State University in Kentucky. He earned his doctorate in education administration from Virginia Polytechnic and State University in Blacksburg, Virginia. Tharpe's career in association management spans more than 25 years. He was employed at the Missouri State Department of Education as its director of trade and vocational education. He moved to the Washington, D.C., metropolitan area and has served as executive vice president and chief operation officer of the Council on Foundations and was responsible for the management of its internal operations. He has also served as the executive director of the Association of School Business Officials International, a position he held for 12 years. Tharpe was named president and CEO of the Congressional Black Caucus Foundation in May 2005.

Ronald R. Thaxton

MILITARY. Ronald R. Thaxton received a bachelor of science degree in education from the University of Maryland, Eastern Shore, and a master of science in national security strategy from the National Defense University. His military education includes the infantry officer's basic and advance courses, Army Combined Arms Services and Staff School, Army Command and General Staff College, and the National War College. Thaxton enlisted in the Army as an infantryman in 1979 and became an officer upon completion of Officer Candidate School in 1981, when he was commissioned an Infantry Second Lieutenant. He has held numerous staff and command assignments in the United States and overseas: U.S. Special Operations Command at MacDill Air Force Base in Florida; U.S. Army Civil Affairs and Psychological Operations Command (Airborne) at Fort Bragg, North Carolina; the Federal Republic of Germany; the Republic of Panama; Bosnia and Herzegovina; and in Afghanistan. He is currently deputy chief of staff for information operation, U.S. Army South, Fort Sam Houston, Texas

Cecil Thomas

LOCAL GOVERNMENT. Cecil Thomas is a native of Birmingham, Alabama. He attended St. Anthony Catholic School in the Queensgate area of Cincinnati and graduated from Withrow High School in Cincinnati. Thomas joined the Cincinnati Police Cadet Program, which officered a free college education. Upon graduation from college, he joined the ranks of the Cincinnati Police Department. He spent twenty-seven years with the Cincinnati Police Department and worked in every district, including all 52 neighborhoods. He also worked in numerous special assignments, such as undercover narcotics, robbery task force, investigative unit and homicide task force.

Thomas retired in 2000 to assume the executive directorship of the embattled Cincinnati Human Relations Commission. Under his leadership, the commission became recognized nationally as one of the premier human relations organizations in the country. He serves as a member of the Cincinnati City Council.

Deborah Scott Thomas

BUSINESS, MILITARY. Deborah Scott Thomas received a bachelor's degree in accounting and management from Alabama State University and a master's degree in public administration and management from Webster College. After 31 years of honorable military duty with the United States Air Force Reserve, she retired as a colonel. She now serves as the president and chief executive officer of Data Solutions and Technology Incorporated. Her professional and business experience spans more than 30 years of human resource management, training and development in senior management positions.

Emmitt Thomas

SPORTS. Emmitt Thomas is a native of Angleton, Texas. He was quarterback and receiver at Bishop College in Dallas, Texas. He was converted to defensive back as an undrafted rookie free agent with the Kansas City Chiefs. Thomas was a standout defensive back for 13 years with the Chiefs (1966–78). He played in 181 National Football League games, including in Super Bowls I and IV, and was selected to play in five Pro Bowls. He finished his career with 58 interceptions, including one in Super Bowl IV against Minnesota, the ninth-most in NFL history. He led the league in interceptions twice in a single season. He is a member of the Chiefs Hall of Fame and his name is etched on the walls at Arrowhead Stadium.

Thomas' coaching career began at Central Missouri State University, where he coached the secondary from 1979 to 80, and his NFL coaching career started with the then St. Louis Cardinals in 1981. He next served with the Washington Redskins for nine seasons from 1986 to 1994 as a wide receivers coach and then as a defensive backs coach. His time with the Redskins was marked with five trips to the playoffs, two NFC championships and victories in Super Bowls XXII (22) and XXVI (26). He served as a defensive coordinator for the Philadelphia Eagles from 1995 to 1998 before taking a similar post with the Green Bay Packers in 1999.Thomas was the defensive coordinator for the Minnesota Vikings from 2000 to 2001. In his first season in Minnesota, he helped the Vikings win the NFC Central crown and advance to the NFC championship game. He joined the Atlanta Falcons in 2002 and help improved Atlanta's pass defense from 30th to 16th in 2002. Also in 2002, he guided the Falcons to finish tied for third in the NFL with 24 interceptions and a top 10 ranking among NFL teams for total interceptions with 86. After serving with the Atlanta Falcons for five years as a defense coach, he was named head coach in December 2007 when the head coach quit with three games left in the season. Thomas is the first African American to serve as the Atlanta Falcons' head coach.

Everett H. Thomas

MILITARY. Everett H. Thomas received a bachelor of science degree in environmental health from Mississippi Valley State University in Itta Bena, Mississippi, and a master of science degree in industrial safety from Central Missouri State University in Warrensburg, Missouri. He has also earned master of arts degree in national security and strategic studies from the Naval War College in Newport, Rhode Island. His military education includes the Squadron Officer School at Maxwell Air Force Base in Alabama and the Air Command and Staff College at Maxwell.

Thomas was commissioned through the ROTC program in 1980 and entered the U.S. Air Force as a second lieutenant in September 1980. His numerous staff and command assignments include most recently serving as executive officer to the Air Force vice chief of staff; as assistant deputy director for politico-military affairs, Africa, and international negotiations on the Joint Staff. In this position he represented the chairman of the Joint Chiefs of Staff on the Moscow Treaty delegation. Thomas was vice commander of the 45th Space Wing at Patrick Air Force Base in Florida; from July 2004 to April 2006, he was the commander of the 341st Space Wing at Malmstrom Air Force Base, Montana; and in April 2006, he was selected as the vice commander of the U.S. Air Force Warfare Center at Nellis Air Force Base in Nevada. He was promoted to brigadier general on December 2, 2006.

Herman Y. Thomas

JUDICIAL. Herman Y. Thomas received a bachelor's degree in political science from the College of Arts and Sciences at the University of South Alabama in 1983 and earned his juris doctor degree from Florida State University in 1985. He was an adjunct faculty member in the Political Science and Criminal Justice Department from 1991 to 1997. He is an Alabama State Court judge.

Isiah Lord Thomas III

SPORTS. Isiah Lord Thomas III is a native of Chicago, Illinois. He led his high school basketball team to the state title game in 1978 and the next year was a member of the United States team at the Pan-American games; the team won a gold medal. In the fall of 1979, he enrolled at Indiana University and led the team to the 1981 ncaa championship as a sophomore. He passed up his final two years of collegiate eligibility and entered the 1981 National Basketball Association draft. The Detroit Pistons picked him second overall in the draft. He earned a bachelor's degree in criminal justice from Indiana University in 1987.

Thomas was named to the 1980 U.S. Olympic team,

but never played because the United States boycotted the Moscow Games. He turned pro and began a now-legendary 13-year career with the Detroit Pistons. He was an integral part of the Pistons' first-ever NBA title in 1989 as they swept the Los Angeles Lakers. The Piston's second NBA title came the following year against the Portland Trail Blazers. Thomas was named MVP of the NBA finals, averaging 27.6 points and 7.0 assists. He was named to the All-Star team every year of his career except 1994 and named MVP in 1984 and 1986. During the 1993-94 season, he was plagued by injuries. He retired with 18,822 points (19.2 per game), 9,061 assists (9.3 per game) and 1,861 steals in 979 games.

Thomas was named one of the "50 Greatest Players in NBA History." In October 1999, he purchased a majority ownership in the Continental Basketball League, eliminating individual team owners and proposing to make a "farm team" system for the NBA. On October 13, 2000, Thomas was inducted into the Basketball Hall of Fame in Springfield, Massachusetts. He was named president of the New York Knicks on December 22, 2003, and in June 2006 he took over as head coach.

Keith Allen Thomas

MILITARY. Keith Allen Thomas is a native of Montgomery, Alabama. He holds a bachelor of science degree. He enlisted in the United States Navy in January of 1983. After completing initial nuclear propulsion training he was transferred to his first ship, the USS *Theodore Roosevelt* (CVN 71). He was One Plant leading chief petty officer on the USS *Mississippi* (CGN 40). In April 1993, he was transferred to Naval Nuclear Power Training Command in Orlando, Florida, as a staff instructor. He taught enlisted reactor principles and was an enlisted section advisor during his tour. In September 1996, he was assigned to the USS *George Washington* (CVN 73). During this five-year tour he was reactor electrical leading chief petty officer, department career counselor, and department senior enlisted advisor.

He qualified as propulsion plant watch officer and was advanced to senior chief petty officer. In July 2001, he was assigned to Commander Naval Air Force Pacific on the Nuclear Propulsion Mobile Training Team in San Diego, California. He was the fleet nuclear electrical assistant and nuclear career counselor. He was advanced to master chief petty officer during this tour. In October 2003, he was selected to serve as command master chief, Naval Nuclear Power Training Command, in Charleston, South Carolina.

Lydia W. Thomas

SCIENCE. Lydia W. Thomas received a bachelor of science degree in zoology from Howard University in 1965. She earned a master of science in microbiology from American University in 1971 and a Ph.D. in cytology from Howard University in 1973. Thomas was with Mitretek Systems as president and chief executive officer. She was responsible for strategic planning and leadership of Mitretek's Center for environment, resources and space. She now serves as a member of the board of trustees and president and chief executive officer of Mitretek Systems. She is on the advisory board of the Research and Technology Campus of George Washington University.

Patty Ball Thomas

EDUCATION. Patty Ball Thomas is a native of Jacksonville, Florida. She received a bachelor of science degree in elementary education from Florida A&M University in 1967 and a master of science degree in reading and language education from Florida State University. She earned her Ph.D. in educational leadership from Florida A&M University in 2001.

Thomas was a teacher in the Duval County Public Schools in Jacksonville, Florida; on the staff of the Department of Health and Rehabilitative Services in Tallahassee, Florida; a teacher in the Leon County Public Schools; and administrator for the Office of Early Intervention and School Readiness with the Department of Education. She is an assistant professor in the College of Education at Florida A&M University and has been a licensed Unity teacher at Unity

Eastside since 1997. Prior to 1997, she served Unity of Tallahassee as youth education director for 14 years. Thomas is president of Phi Delta Kappa (Florida A&M University Chapter).

Preston G. Thomas

JUDICIAL. Preston G. Thomas received his juris doctor degree from Wayne State University Law School in 1982. He was a legislative auditor for the Pontiac City Council and a deputy city attorney for the City of Pontiac. He was elected a judge to the Michigan 50th District Court in the City of Pontiac in November of 1998. He was appointed chief judge in 2007. He was president of the Oakland County District Judges Association. He has also taken his courtroom to area high schools where actual court proceedings are conducted, to engage and educate students about the justice system.

Priscilla D. Thomas

LOCAL GOVERNMENT. Priscilla D. Thomas is a native of Savannah, Georgia, and graduated from Tompkins High School. She received a bachelor of science degree in elementary education from Savannah State College and a master's degree in education and administration and supervision from Bradley University. She earned a Ph.D. in psychology and educational administration from the University of North America.

Thomas has taught and retired as a principal of Haven Elementary School after 30 years in education. She was elected to the Chatham County, Georgia, Commission in 1990. Her fellow commissioners elected her vice chairman of the board, becoming the first female and first African American in that post.

Regina Thomas

STATE GOVERNMENT. Regina Thomas is a native of Savannah, Georgia, and a graduate of A.E. Beach High School. She attended the Community College of Baltimore in Maryland. Thomas was first elected to the Georgia State Senate from District 2 in a special election on January 11, 2000. She also served in the Georgia House of Representatives from 1995 to 1998, where her efforts were focused on education, children's issues and welfare reform. She served as assistant majority whip in the House in 1997–1998.

Stephen Thomas

MILITARY. Stephen Thomas is a native of Centerville, Illinois. He enlisted in the United States Marine Corps in May 1987 and attended recruit training at Marine Corps Recruit Depot Parris Island, South Carolina. In October 1987, he completed Communications School in 29 Palms, California, and later Drill Instructor School in Marine Corps Recruit Depot San Diego, California. He served in July 1989 with the 1st Reconnaissance Company, 1st Marine Expeditionary Force, at Camp Pendleton. There he was a radio operator, assistant team leader, team leader and platoon sergeant.

He deployed to Southwest Asia with 1st Force from 1990 to 1991 in support of Operation Desert Shield and Desert Storm, to the Western Pacific with the 11th Marine Expeditionary Unit in 1992 in support of Operation Provide Comfort, and numerous other operations and exercises. In January 1994, he was ordered to Drill Instructor School and assigned subsequent duty as a drill instructor in Hotel Company, 2nd Recruit Training Regiment, in San Diego, California. In April 2000 he assumed duties of assistant marine officer instructor for the Navy Reserve Officer Training Corps unit at North Carolina State University from 2000 to 2003. In April 2006, he was ordered to Marine Corps Security Force Company in Bahrain to serve as the company first sergeant until June 2007. He was then Third Battalion sergeant major for 2nd Marine Division at Camp Lejeune, North Carolina.

Anita Favors Thompson

LOCAL GOVERNMENT. Anita Favors Thompson is a native of Kansas. She received a bachelor of arts degree from Park College in Parkville, Missouri, and was honored as a presidential scholar. She earned a master's de-

gree from Central Michigan University in Mount Pleasant, Michigan.

Her top management positions have included executive director of the Area Agency on Aging in Kansas City; assistant to the finance commissioner in Kansas City, Kansas; assistant city administrator, Kansas City, Kansas; commissioner of adult services for the Kansas State Department of Social and Rehabilitation Services; senior assistant city manager, City of Tallahassee; and city manager for Tallahassee since April 1997. She is responsible for administration of all city services, encompassing 2896 employees, an operating budget of $465.5 million and a five year capital improvement plan of $701.6 million.

Don Thompson

BUSINESS. Don Thompson received a bachelor's degree in electrical engineering from Purdue University in 1984. His professional career at McDonald's includes serving as senior vice president, restaurant support officer of the Midwest Division; president of the Midwest Division; executive vice president and innovation orchestration leader for McDonald's Restaurant Solutions Group; executive vice president and chief operations officer; and his current position of president of McDonald's USA. In this role, he is responsible for the entire McDonald's system in the United States, which includes 13,700 restaurants.

Errington C. Thompson

MEDICINE. Errington C. Thompson received an education from Emory University and a medical degree from Southwestern Medical School in Dallas, Texas. He completed his surgical training at Louisiana State University in Shreveport, Louisiana. Dr. Thompson was a trauma surgeon and associate director of trauma and surgical critical care at Mission Hospital in Asheville, North Carolina. He previously served as clinical assistant professor and director of trauma at Louisiana State University Medical Center in Shreveport. As a member of the Society of Black Academic Surgeons, he is on the executive committee.

George N. Thompson

MILITARY, MUSIC. George N. Thompson grew up in Philadelphia, Pennsylvania, where he began his early musical training on piano. He is a graduate of the Westminster School in Simsbury, Connecticut. He studied at Phillips Exeter Academy in Exeter, New Hampshire. He earned degrees from Amherst College in Amherst, Massachusetts, and the University of Pennsylvania's Wharton School of Finance and Commerce. His military schools include basic training at Great Lakes; the School of Music intermediate course; Officer Indoctrination School at Naval Air Station in Pensacola; and advance training in the Navy's enlisted bandleader course at the School of Music.

Thompson enlisted in the Navy in 1977. He first served with the Navy Band in Orlando, Florida, where he performed on piano with the contemporary music ensemble. In January 1980 he transferred to Navy Band Newport in Rhode Island, where he was assigned as a keyboard player and vocalist with the Northeastern Navy Showband. He served with the United States Sixth Fleet Band, homeported in Naples, in Italy, where he was leader of the jazz-rock unit The Diplomats. He was selected to serve as an enlisted bandleader with the Navy Band in Seattle, where he was promoted to chief petty officer and was later selected for commissioning as a limited duty officer bandmaster. On November 1, 1990, he became the first African American to be commissioned a bandmaster in the history of the United States Navy. He was officer in charge of the Ceremonial Unit and head of the Operations and Administration Departments. In June 1994, he was director of the Seventh Fleet Band on board the USS *Blue Ridge*, homeported in Yokosuka, Japan. He was director of the Navy Band Southeast in 1997. He was assigned to the Navy School of Music as executive officer and took command in July 2002. From April 2005 to April 2007, he was head of the Navy Music Program at Naval Support Activity Mid-South in Millington, Tennessee. In April 2007, he was selected to serve as commanding officer of the United States Navy Band.

John W. Thompson

BUSINESS. John W. Thompson received a bachelor's degree in business administration from Florida A&M University and a master's degree in management science from Massachusetts Institute of Technology's Sloan School of Management. He joined Symantec after 28 years at IBM Corporation, where he was general manager of Personal Software Products, responsible for Personal systems and other products. He served most recently as general manager of IBM Americas; he was responsible for sales and support of IBM's technology products and services in the United States, Canada and Latin America. He led the transformation of the company from a consumer software publisher to the global leader in information security solutions for individuals and enterprises. He has led global operations in more than 35 countries. Thompson has been chairman of the board and chief executive officer of Symantec Corp., Cupertino, California, a provider of software and Internet security technology, since April 1999. Symantec has defined a new category of information security software for consumers under Thompson's leadership, and has made a number of strategic acquisitions to enhance its ability to serve the rapidly changing security and management needs of large global enterprises. He was president of Symantec Corp from April 1999 to January 2002.

In September 2002, President George W. Bush appointed Thompson to the National Infrastructure Advisory Committee. He has served as the chair of the Silicon Valley Blue Ribbon Task Force on Aviation Security and Technology to identify and evaluate technology-driven solutions to improve the security and efficiency of national and local aviation. He has been a director of United Parcel Service, Inc., since 2000 and is a Director of Symantec and Seagate Software (Cayman) Holdings Corporation.

Larry Thompson

BUSINESS, FEDERAL GOVERNMENT. Larry Thompson received a bachelor of arts degree in sociology from Culver-Stockton College and a master of arts in sociology from Michigan State University. He earned his juris doctor degree from the University of Michigan. He worked in private law practice in Atlanta, Georgia, from 1977 to 1982. From 1982 to 1986, he was the United States Attorney for the Northern District of Georgia. In 1986, he returned to private law practice in Atlanta. In July 1995, Thompson was appointed independent counsel for the Department of Housing and Urban Development Investigation by a special panel of United States Supreme Court. In April 2000, Mr. Thompson was selected to chair the Judicial Review Commission on Foreign Asset Control. In 2002, Attorney General John Ashcroft named Thompson to lead the National Security Coordination Council.

He served as a deputy U.S. attorney general under President George W. Bush until August 2003. In 2004, he was selected as a visiting professor of law at the University of Georgia Law School. In October 2004, he assumed the position of senior vice president of government affairs, general counsel, and secretary for PepsiCo. He is responsible for PepsiCo's worldwide legal function, as well as its government affairs organization and the company's charitable foundation. He is a visiting professor at the University of Georgia Law School and a senior fellow at the Brookings Institution.

Neville Thompson

ENGINEERING. Neville Thompson received a bachelor of science degree in electrical engineering in 1989 and a master of science degree in electrical engineering in 1996 from Tuskegee University. He has worked for over 23 years in research and development for the Department of the Navy and the Air Force. He is a senior engineer in the office of the deputy assistant secretary of Air Force Science, Technology and Engineering. He is the Air Force's conventional munitions program element monitor. He provides guidance, management, and oversight of a $100 million research and development munitions portfolio. His responsibilities include planning, programming, and budgeting, as well as representing munitions programs to senior Air Force leaders, the Office of the Secretary of Defense, and the U.S. Congress.

William C. Thompson, Jr.

LOCAL GOVERNMENT. William C. Thompson, Jr., is a native of Brooklyn, New York. The son of a judge and a public school teacher, he attended New York City public schools. He received a bachelor's degree from Tufts University and was awarded an honorary doctorate in humane letters from Mercy College. Thompson worked for a Brooklyn congressman, and he was the borough's youngest-ever deputy borough president.

He was appointed to the New York City Board of Education in 1994. Two years later, he began the first of five consecutive terms as president of the board. He led a reform agenda that resulted in improved student achievement and greater public accountability. Thompson was a senior vice president for public finance at an investment banking firm in the early 1990s. He became New York City's 42nd comptroller on January 1, 2002. He was re-elected in November 2005 and began his second term on January 1, 2006.

Patricia Timmons-Goodson

JUDICIAL. Patricia Timmons-Goodson is a native of Southport, North Carolina. She received a bachelor of arts degree in speech from the University North Carolina at Chapel Hill and earned her juris doctor from the UNC Chapel Hill School of Law in 1979.

She has served as a prosecutor and legal aid lawyer. In 1984, at the age of 29, she was appointed a District Court judge in North Carolina. She was elected in 1986 and subsequently was re-elected twice without opposition. In 1997 she was appointed as judge of the N.C. Court of Appeals and in 1998 was elected to a full term. Her election marked the first occasion that an African American woman was elected to an appellate court in North Carolina. She is a justice on the North Carolina Supreme Court, the first African American female to serve in this position.

Henry N. Tisdale

EDUCATION. Henry N. Tisdale is a native of Kingstree, South Carolina. He received a bachelor of science degree in mathematics magna cum laude from Claflin University in 1965 and a master of education degree in mathematics from Temple University in 1967. He earned a master of arts degree in mathematics from Dartmouth College in 1975 and a doctor of philosophy degree in mathematics from Dartmouth College in 1978. He received an honorary doctorate degree from South Carolina State University in 2004.

Tisdale has taught mathematics in the Philadelphia school system; served as an instructor for the Summer Engineering Institute; and was a professor of mathematics and assistant director of institutional research and planning at Delaware State University in Dover. In 1985 he was selected by the American Council on Education Center for Leadership Development in Washington, D.C. In 1986, Tisdale was appointed assistant academic dean for administration, planning and information management at Delaware State University. From 1987 to 1994 he was the senior vice president and chief academic officer there. In 1994, he was named the eighth president of Claflin University.

Charles H. Toliver IV

JUDICIAL. Charles H. Toliver IV received a bachelor of arts from Hampton Institute in Hampton, Virginia, in 1972 and earned his juris doctor from the University of Virginia School of Law in 1975. From 1975 to 1978 he was an assistant city solicitor for the City of Wilmington and from 1978 until 1990 he served in private law practice. On February 9, 1990, he became a judge of the Superior Court of Delaware.

Mike Tomlin

SPORTS. Mike Tomlin is a native of Hampton, Virginia, and attended Denbigh High School in Newport News, Virginia. He was a three-year starter at wide receiver for the College of William and Mary and finished his career with 101 receptions for 2,046 yards and a school record 20 touchdown catches.

His career began in 1995 as the wide receiver coach at Virginia Military Institute. He spent the 1996 season as a graduate assistant at the University of Memphis, where he worked with the defensive backs and special teams. Following a brief stint on the Uni-

versity of Tennessee at Martin's coaching staff, he was hired by Arkansas State University in 1997 to coach its defensive backs. After two seasons at the University of Cincinnati, he was hired by the Tampa Bay Buccaneers as defensive backs coach. In January 2003, following the 2002 season, the Buccaneers won Super Bowl XXXVII (37). In 2002 and 2005, the Buccaneers led the National Football League in total defense (fewest yards allowed per game). On January 10, 2006, Tomlin was selected by Vikings head coach Brad Childress to be his defensive coordinator. At 33 years old, he became the youngest defensive coordinator in the NFL. Following the 2006 season, he interviewed for head coaching positions with the Miami Dolphins and Pittsburgh Steelers. On Sunday January 22, 2007, the Pittsburgh Steelers announced Tomlin as the new head coach. At age 35, he was the second youngest head coach in any of the four major North American professional sports, including the NFL, National Hockey League, Major League Baseball and the National Basketball Association (NBA).

In 2008, he coached the Steelers to the AFC Championship on February 1, 2009. He was the winning coach of Super Bowl XLIII. Michael Tomlin, at age 36, became the youngest head coach in history to win a Super Bowl.

Edward Toussaint, Jr.

JUDICIAL. Edward Toussaint, Jr. received his juris doctor degree from DePaul University Law School. From 1975 to 1981 he was claim counsel for American Family Insurance. From 1981 to 1987 he served as a Workers' Compensation judge and from 1987 to 1992 he was a Workers' Compensation Court of Appeals judge. In 1992, he was appointed a Hennepin County District Court judge. In 1995, Judge Toussaint was appointed chief judge of the Minnesota Court of Appeals and was reappointed in 1998, 2001, and 2004. He is an adjunct professor at William Mitchell College of Law. Toussaint was elected president of the Council of Chief Judges in November 1998 and since 1996 has served on the executive committee of the Council of Chief Judges.

Randolph F. Treece

JUDICIAL. Randolph F. Treece earned his juris doctor from Albany Law School in 1976. He has served as an adjunct law professor at Albany Law School; as an assistant public defender for Rensselaer County; in private law practice; as first deputy of the Capital Defender Office; and as general counsel for the Office of the Comptroller of the State of New York. Treece was appointed in 2001 as a U.S. Magistrate judge for the Northern District of New York. He serves on the boards of trustees of Albany Law School and Siena College and on the board of directors of the New York Bar Foundation.

Alphonso Trimble

MILITARY. Alphonso Trimble entered the United States Marine Corps in December 1982 as an aviation supply clerk. In June 1986, he was awarded a Navy ROTC scholarship to Morehouse College, graduating in May 1990 with a bachelor of science degree in physics. He was commissioned a second lieutenant. He also graduated from the Marine Corps Command and Staff College, the Marine Corps' advanced logistics officers' course, and the U.S. Army's advanced joint logistics course. He then completed the basic school in Quantico, Virginia, and the aviation supply officers course in Athens, Georgia.

He reported to Marine Corps Headquarters in July 1998 for duty as an analyst in the Program and Resources Department, where he monitored the flying hour, future aviation logistics support and unmanned aerial vehicle programs. Later, he served as the Marine liaison to the chief of naval operations, Programs and Budget Division. In December 2000, Colonel Timble was selected to serve as aide-de-camp to commandants of the Marine Corps.

Frank O. Tuck

FEDERAL GOVERNMENT. Frank O. Tuck entered the Air Force in 1970 after completing his bachelor of science degree in mechanical engineering at Tuskegee Institute in Alabama. While in the Air Force, he earned a master's degree in business administration from the University of Rochester, and then was assigned to Wright-Patterson Air Force Base as a systems acquisition officer.

After leaving the Air Force, he entered federal civil service. Tuck has managed and directed a variety of Air Force acquisitions programs, including engine support equipment projects, numerous common and standard avionics programs, electronic warfare systems and major aircraft programs. He also has served as director of technology and industrial support at the Sacramento Air Logistics Center. Tuck was the director of the Air Combat System Program Office, Aeronautical Systems Center, Air Force Materiel Command, Wright-Patterson Air Force Base, in Ohio. As director, his responsibilities included planning, acquisition and sustainment activities related to Air Combat Command.

His education includes: the program management course, Defense Systems Management College, Fort Belvoir, Virginia; program for senior officials in national security, John F. Kennedy School of Government, Harvard University, Cambridge, Massachusetts; Federal Executive Institute, Charlottesville, Virginia; program management level III certification; senior managers in government, John F. Kennedy School of Government, Harvard University; national security leadership course, Johns Hopkins University, Baltimore, Maryland.

Joyce E. Tucker

BUSINESS. Joyce E. Tucker is a native of Illinois. She received a juris doctor degree from the John Marshall Law School and is a member of the Illinois bar. She was president of Tucker Spearman and Associates. In 2001, she was appointed to the White House Initiative Advisory Board for Historically Black Colleges and Universities. She currently serves on the board of directors for the National Conference for Community and Justice, Chicago and Northern Illinois Region. Tucker is the vice president for global diversity and employee rights for Boeing Company. She is a nationally recognized expert with more than thirty years of experience in equal employment opportunity (EEO) and affirmative action in both the public and private sectors.

Jeffrey E. Turner

LAW ENFORCEMENT. Jeffrey E. Turner moved to Clayton County, Georgia, with his family in 1978. He attended and graduated from Morrow High School in 1982 and earned a bachelor of science degree in criminal justice from West Georgia University in 1986. He is a graduate of the FBI National Academy, Session 217. Turner joined the Clayton County Police Department in 1987, at which time he was one of only four African American officers on the force.

During his 20 year tenure he has worked as a uniformed patrolman, conducted criminal investigations as a detective, supervised officers on the street as a sergeant and lieutenant, and was assigned as the administrative captain to the former chief of police. Turner was assistant chief of police, then was appointed as the tenth chief of the Clayton County Police Department on March 20, 2007.

Patricia L. Turner

MEDICINE. Patricia L. Turner received her medical degree at Bowman Gray School of Medicine, Wake Forest University, in Winston-Salem, North Carolina, and completed her surgical residency at Howard University Hospital. Dr. Turner is a general surgeon and assistant professor of surgery at the University of Maryland Medical Center. She is associate program director for the General Surgery Residency Program there. She is also chair of the Surgical Caucus of the American Medical Association Young Physicians Section.

William Turner

EDUCATION. William Turner received his bachelor's degree in sociology from the University of Kentucky in 1968. He earned a master's degree in sociology in 1971 and a doctorate in sociology and anthropology from Notre Dame University in 1974. He worked at the University of Kentucky from 1979 through 1983. He has taught, performed research, and held administrative posts at several other colleges and universities, including Fisk University, Howard University, and Winston-Salem State University. He was distinguished visiting professor of black and Appalachian studies at Berea College from 1988 to 1989 and visiting research professor at Brandeis University from

1990 to 1991. From 1979 to 1991, Turner was a research associate to Alex Haley, author of *Roots.* For the 1983-1984 academic year, he served as dean of the College of Arts and Sciences at Kentucky State University; from January 2003 to April 2004, he was interim president. Turner is vice president for university engagement and associate provost for multicultural and academic affairs at the University of Kentucky.

Gloria J. Twilley

MILITARY, HEALTH. Gloria J. Twilley received an associate degree in nursing from Meridian Junior College, Meridian, Mississippi, and a bachelor of science in nursing from William Carey College in Hattiesburg, Mississippi. She earned a master of arts in management from Webster University in St. Louis, Missouri. Her military education includes Squadron Officer School; the Air Command and Staff College and the Air War College.

Twilley entered the Air Force in 1982 following a direct commission into the United States Nurse Corps. She has served in a variety of leadership positions in the medical service career field, including staff nurse, charge nurse, flight nurse, flight nurse instructor, flight commander, deputy squadron commander, squadron commander, and deputy chief, medical operations and policy.

From June 2003 to June 2004 she served in the Office of the Surgeon General at Bolling Air Force Base in Washington, D.C. From June 2004 to July 2005, she was assigned to the Office of the Command Surgeon, Air Mobility Command, Scott Air Force Base in Illinois. She currently is the commander, 509th Medical Group, 509th Bomb Wing, at Whiteman Air Force Base, Missouri. The 509th Medical Group maintains readiness for deployment in support of Air Force missions and provides medical care for 11,600 active and retired military members and their families.

Stephen M. Twitty

MILITARY. Stephen M. Twitty is a native of Spartanburg, South Carolina. He is a 1985 distinguished military graduate from South Carolina State University. He earned a master's degree in public administration from Central Michigan University and a master's degree in National Military Strategy from the National War College. His staff and command positions include serving as a Joint Chiefs of Staff intern in the Directorate for Strategic Plans and Policy in the Pentagon; from 1994 through 1995, speechwriter for the army deputy chief of staff for operations and plans; G-3 operations officer with V Corps in Heidelberg, Germany; battalion executive officer for the 1st Battalion, 26th Infantry Regiment in April 1997 in Schweinfurt, Germany; and bridge operations officer (S3) for the 2nd Brigade, 1st Infantry Division.

From June 1999 to June 2001, he was in Mons, Belgium, at the Supreme Headquarters Allied Powers Europe as the aide-de-camp to the supreme allied commander Europe and commander in chief, United States European Command. From June 2001 to June 2003, he served in the 3rd Infantry Division as the Battalion Commander, 3rd Battalion, 15th Infantry Regiment, including during Operation Iraqi Freedom, and in June 2003 he was assigned as the division operations officer for the 3rd Infantry Division at Fort Stewart Georgia. He currently is the commander of the 4th Brigade Combat Team, 1st Cavalry Division.

Raymond Tymas-Jones

EDUCATION, MUSIC. Raymond Tymas-Jones received a bachelor of music degree from Howard University and a master of music degree in conducting and voice from Washington University (St. Louis). He earned a Ph.D. in performance practice in voice from Washington University in St. Louis. From 1990 to 1993 he was the associate dean of the faculty of Humanities and Fine Arts at Buffalo State College. He was director of the School of Music at the University of Northern Iowa, 1993 to 1998. From 1998 to 2005, he was the dean of the College of Fine Arts at Ohio University. In September 2005, he was appointed associate vice president for the arts and dean of the College of Fine Arts at the University of Utah. He oversees the academic departments of art and art history, ballet, modern dance, theater, the school of music, the division of film studies and an interdisciplinary arts technology program. He is also responsible for on-campus arts organizations, including Pioneer Theater Company, the Utah Museum of Fine Arts and Kingsbury Hall.

Neil deGrasse Tyson

SCIENCE. Neil deGrasse Tyson is a native of the Bronx, New York, and a graduate of the Bronx High School of Science. He received a bachelor of arts in physics from Harvard University in 1980, where he also rowed on the crew team, joined the wrestling team, and was the team captain and editor-in-chief of the school's *Physical Science Journal.* He earned a master's degree from the University of Texas at Austin in 1983 and a Ph.D. in astrophysics from Columbia University in New York in 1991.

Tyson was an astrophysicist and research scientist at Princeton University, a columnist for *Stardate* magazine, and from 1996, he was the first occupant of the Frederick P. Rose directorship of the Hayden Planetarium in New York City (the youngest director in the long history of the planetarium). His association with Princeton continues; he is a visiting research scientist in astrophysics and also teaches. In 2001, President George W. Bush appointed Tyson to serve on the Commission on the Future of the United States Aerospace Industry and in 2004 to serve on the President's Commission on Implementation of United States Space Exploration Policy, "Moon, Mars and Beyond." In 2004, he hosted the four-part *Origins* miniseries on pbs's *Nova* and co-authored it with Donald Goldsmith. He was awarded the NASA Distinguished Public Service Medal, the highest civilian honor bestowed by the U.S. space agency.

Gene Upshaw

SPORTS. Gene Upshaw is a native of Robstown, Texas. He received a bachelor of science degree from Texas A&I University in 1968. He has also done postgraduate studies at Golden Gate University and Lincoln University. Upshaw was a National Football League player for 16 years for the Oakland Raiders and in Los Angeles. He received four All-Pro, five All-Conference, six Pro Bowl selections and eventually was named to the NFL Hall of Fame. He is the only one in history to play in a Super Bowl in three different decades, 1960, 1970 and 1980. After his retirement, he was chosen by his peers as executive director of the NFL Players Association. He was enshrined in the Bay Area Sports Hall of Fame in 1996.

Pat Upshaw-Monteith

PUBLIC SERVICE. Pat Upshaw-Monteith received a bachelor's degree from Albany State University and a master's degree from Bowling Green State University. She is executive director of Leadership Atlanta, an organization dedicated to the growth and development of Atlanta by imparting to new generations of leaders the legacy of core values that have traditionally been central to Atlanta' s success. She chaired the Board for the Community Leadership Association with over 800 leadership directors and volunteers in attendance from around the world. Upshaw-Monteith has the distinct honor of being one of the first blacks hired in management by a major symphony orchestra. She spent 13 years with the Atlanta Symphony Orchestra as assistant general manager. In that capacity she was producer of the orchestra's successful pops series at Chastain Park and directed the symphony's education program.

Hannah Valantine

MEDICINE. Hannah Valantine was born in the West African country of Gambia and moved with her family to England at age 13. Her education includes bachelor of medicine and bachelor of surgery, medical doctor and Ph.D. degrees from St. George's Hospital Medical School in London, England (1978). She completed an internship at St. Georges' and Kingston Hospital, England, (1979); a residency at St. George's Hospital Medical School in London, England (1981); a residency at Brompton Hospital in England (1982); and fellowships at Hammersmith Hospital in London in 1984. She graduated from Stanford University Medical Center, Stanford, California, in 1986. She holds a board certification in internal medicine from the Royal College of Physicians in the United Kingdom.

Dr. Valantine is a professor of cardiology at Stanford University School of Medicine. Her specialties are cardiology (heart) and lung transplantation and heart transplant cardiovascular risk assessment. She has been selected to serve as senior associate dean for diversity and leadership at the Stanford School of Medicine. As with the other senior associate deans at the medical school, Dr. Valantine's job is a half-time position that will allow her to continue her research, teaching and clinical activities.

Peggy Valentine

EDUCATION, NURSING. Peggy Valentine received her bachelor of science degree and master of arts degree from Howard University. She earned a doctor of education degree from Virginia Tech in Blacksburg, Virginia, in 1987 and was awarded a certificate for "Promising Doctoral Research in Education" for the state. Valentine joined Howard University in 1980 as a lecturer in psychiatry. She has served in various clinical and academic capacities, including department chairman for six years, and currently holds academic rank of professor in the physician assistant department. Her clinical experiences have been as registered nurse, nursing coordinator, and physicians' assistant. She was elected fellow in the Association of Schools of Allied Health Professions in 2003.

Valentine has directed the Targeted Provider Education Demonstration Grant, funded by the Ford Foundation, the National AIDS Minority Information and Education Program, funded by the Centers for Disease Control and Prevention (CDC), and many others. She was principal investigator of the Malawi Project University Technical Assistance Program, funded by the cdc's Global AIDS Program. She served as associate dean for the division of allied health sciences in the College of Pharmacy, Nursing and Allied Health Sciences, overseeing seven academic programs. She was appointed the second dean of the School of Health Science at Winston-Salem State University effective January 2, 2006.

Ricky T. Valentine

MILITARY. Ricky T. Valentine received a bachelor of science in accounting from North Carolina Agricultural and Technical State University in Greensboro. He earned a master's in business administration from Auburn University in Montgomery, Alabama, and a master of science in national resource strategy from the Industrial College of the Armed Forces at Fort McNair, Washington, D.C. His military education includes Squadron Officer School at Maxwell Air Force Base in Alabama; Professional Military Comptroller School at Maxwell; Air Command and Staff College at Maxwell; Joint and Combined Staff Officer School, Armed Forces Staff College, at Norfolk, Virginia; and Air War College.

Valentine was commissioned into the United States Air Force in May of 1982 after graduating from North Carolina A&T. He served in U.S. Special Operations Command and as squadron commander with the 51st Fighter Wing in Korea. He has an acquisition professional development program level III certification in program management and in financial management. He is a fully qualified joint specialty officer and previously served as executive officer to the Air Force director of budget, assistant secretary of the Air Force for financial management, in Washington, D.C. In July 2004, he was assigned as director of financial management, Electronic Systems Center, Hanscom Air Force Base in Massachusetts.

Jefferson Varner III

MILITARY. Jefferson Varner III is a native of Clanton, Alabama. He received an associate degree from Gadsden State Community College and a bachelor of science degree from Excelsior College. He earned a graduate certificate in emergency and disaster management. His military education includes courses for noncommissioned officers, supervisor development, manager development, military operations on urban terrain, physical security, instructor training, master fitness trainer, and U.S. Army first sergeants course. He also completed Drill Sergeant School and the U.S. Army Sergeants Major Academy.

Varner has been squad leader, 44th Chemical 2nd Armored Division at Fort Hood; squad leader, 4th Chemical Company, 2nd Infantry Division in Korea; drill sergeant with D Company, 82nd Chemical Battalion; master fitness trainer, Fitness Training Company at Fort McClellan, Alabama; instructor at Headquarters and Headquarters Company, 84th Chemical Battalion; first sergeant at Headquarters and Headquarters Detachment, Engineer Brigade, First Cavalry Division; first sergeant for the 7th Chemical Company, 83rd Chemical Battalion at Fort Polk; division chemical staff sergeant major for the 3rd Infantry Division at Fort Stewart; and command sergeant major at 23rd Chemical Battalion at Fort Lewis, Washington. He is the command sergeant major and commandant for the Joint Readiness Training Center and Fort Polk Noncommissioned Officer Academy in Louisiana.

Michael Vass

BUSINESS. Michael Vass is a native of the Bronx, New York. He is a graduate of Evander Childs High School and attended Rutgers University. While at the university he joined the U.S. Marine Corps Reserve. He studied philosophy, English, and chemistry at Rutgers.

After leaving Rutgers, Vass went to Russia, where he was a director for an international import-export company. He lived in Moscow and Tblisi, where he experienced an attempted coup and a civil war. Upon returning to the United States he went to Los Angeles to join a start-up theatrical production company and experienced the Los Angeles riots as well as the Northridge earthquake. He returned to New York to pursue a career in securities markets, where he enjoyed a nearly decade long career as a successful securities account executive (stockbroker). In addition to the work in investor relations, he has explored the growing field of weblogs. He has created management and improvement of nearly a dozen weblogs and websites. The culmination of this experience has been the creation of Black Entertainment USA in December 2005 and MV Consulting, Inc., in August 2006.

Arlinda Vaughn

BUSINESS. Arlinda Vaughn received a bachelor's degree in German with a minor in bio-medical physics from Washington University in St. Louis, Missouri, and a master's degree in international business from Webster University in Webster Groves, Missouri. Vaughn has held marketing and sales positions with Ployrack GmbH and Global Risk Consultants' Latin American service region. In addition to English, she is fluent in German and Spanish. Volk Optical has appointed Vaughn as regional manager for Africa, Asia, the Caribbean, Latin America, the Middle East, and Oceania.

Gayle Vaughn-Wiles

EDUCATION. Gayle Vaughn-Wiles is the superintendent of the Department of Defense Dependents Schools, Okinawa. She oversees twelve schools serving over 8300 students from kindergarten to high school. She is the first African American in this position. Her schools serve families from all branches of the United States military, Department of Defense civilians, and other authorized personnel. The schools offer a comprehensive curriculum comparable to any mid-sized school district in the U.S.

Luis Raul Visot

MILITARY. Luis Raul Visot received a bachelor of arts degree in Spanish from Marquette University and a master of education degree in higher education administration from the University of Georgia. He has earned a master of strategic studies degree from the United States Army War College. His military schools include the quartermaster officer basic course, the transportation officer advanced course, and the U.S. Army Command and General Staff College. Visot has held numerous staff and command assignments, most recently as commander, 6th Transportation Battalion, 7th Transportation Group, Fort Eustis, Virginia; commander, 32nd Transportation Group (Composite), Tampa, Florida; commander, 32nd Transportation Group (Composite), U.S. Army, Kuwait; and currently as the deputy commander (TPU), 1st Support Command (Theater) (Multi-Component) at Fort Bragg, North Carolina. He was promoted to brigadier general on May 7, 2006. Visot is the executive director, Joint Military Science Leadership Center, University of South Florida, in Tampa.

Leon Vorters, Jr.

MILITARY. Leon Vorters, Jr., enlisted in the United States Navy through the delayed entry program in December 1982. He completed basic training at the Recruit Training Command San Diego in August 1983, and then attended Dental Technician "A" School, Naval School of Dental Assisting and Technology, San Diego. He is a graduate of Hospital Corpsman Surgical Technology "C" School and the inaugural class of Medical Department Administrative Technician "C" School, both at Naval School of Health Sciences San Diego. He is a graduate of the Navy Senior Enlisted Academy.

Vorters has served as leading chief petty officer and battalion S3/S4 with the First Force Service Support Group, First Dental Battalion and as the dental de-

partment leading chief aboard the USS *Frank Cable* (AS 40), Agana, Guam. In August 2003 he reported aboard Naval Dental Center at Great Lakes. After the integration of Naval Hospital and Naval Dental Center at Great Lakes he was the dental directorate senior enlisted leader and was selected for advancement to master chief hospital corpsman. Vorters is the command master chief, Hospital Corpsman Aviation.

Dale Wainwright

JUDICIAL. Dale Wainwright received a bachelor's degree summa cum laude from Howard University and earned his juris doctor degree from the University of Chicago Law School. He studied at the London School of Economics. He worked in private law practice and was appointed judge to the Texas 334th Civil District Court in Harris County in 1999 by then Governor George W. Bush. He later served as the presiding judge of the 334th Civil District Court. In 2001, Texas Governor Rick Perry appointed Wainwright to a temporary commission as justice on the Supreme Court. On November 5, 2002, he was elected to the Supreme Court of Texas.

LeRoy H. Walden, Jr.

BUSINESS. LeRoy H. Walden, Jr., is a native of Highland Park, Michigan. He received his formal education at Washtenaw Community College and Eastern Michigan University in Graphic Design and Creative Studies. In 1996, he completed an advanced training course in computer operations offered by New Horizon Computer Learning Center. Walden became an instructor of html and graphic design at Lawrence Technological University for 30 Detroit Public School students with exceptional grade point averages. He instructed his students in graphic and website design, basic ethics, time management, career guidance and counseling. He was the student dean and operating manager and owner of all media advertising for Youth Links USA. He currently is president of 1111 Records.

Allen Walker

MILITARY. Allen Walker is a native of Homerville, Georgia. He enlisted in the United States Navy and reported to Navy Recruit Training in Orlando, Florida, in September 1980. Following graduation he reported to his first ship, the USS *Caloosahatchee*.

Walker was a repair leading petty officer aboard the USS *Wainwright* in 1984. Beginning in 1989, he completed three consecutive sea tours, serving onboard to the USS *Orion* as leading petty officer, USS *Ray* for a short theater air defense assignment, USS *Hue City*, as a leading chief petty officer for R Division, and USS *Shenandoah*. In 1995 he reported to Great Lakes Training Center as a recruit division commander. He reported to CVW5, embarked in the USS *Kitty Hawk* in 2000, as a command master chief and in 2002 he transferred to Naval Support Activity La Maddalena as command master chief. He is command master chief onboard the USS *Laboon* (DDG-58).

Cynthia Walker

JUDICIAL. Cynthia Walker received her juris doctor degree from Valparaiso University Law School. She has held a variety of civil, criminal, and administrative positions, having previously served as court administrator for the 50th District Court, as city attorney for Pontiac, and as an instructor for the American Institute of Paralegal Studies. She also worked as a staff attorney for the United Auto Workers Legal Services and Legal Services of Eastern Michigan. Walker was appointed judge to the Michigan 50th District Court in the City of Pontiac by Governor Jennifer Granholm in September 2003 and was elected in November 2004. She is the first woman to serve as a judge in the 50th District of Michigan.

E. Thurman Walker

MINISTRY. E. Thurman Walker received his bachelor of arts degree in accounting from Colorado College, a master of divinity from

the ITC/Morehouse School of Religion, and a doctor of ministry degree from United Teleological Seminary in Dayton, Ohio. Walker was named pastor of Antioch Church in San Antonio, Texas, in March 1993. Under his leadership, Antioch has grown to some 3,000 members and tripled its budget. Walker is only the third pastor in the 69 year history of Antioch Church.

Janice Walker

EDUCATION. Janice Walker grew up in a small town in Florida. She received a bachelor of arts degree from Tuskegee Institute (now Tuskegee University) in Alabama, graduating in 1971. She earned a master of arts degree from the University of Michigan in 1972 and her Ph.D. from the University of Michigan, in Ann Arbor, in 1982.

Walker has served as an associate professor and chair of the Mathematics and Computer Science Department at Xavier University in Cincinnati, Ohio. She is now the dean of the College of Arts and Sciences at Xavier University, where she oversees 14 academic departments and 30 programs. She is the first female dean of a college at Xavier University.

Kara Walker

ARTIST. Kara Walker was born in Stockton, California, and moved to Atlanta, Georgia, at age 13. She received a bachelor of fine arts degree from the Atlanta College of Art in 1991 and a master fine arts from the Rhode Island School of Design in 1994. She has become one of the leading black artists in the United States, best known for exploring the raw intersection of race, gender, and sexuality through her iconic, silhouetted figures. She unleashes the traditionally proper Victorian medium of the silhouette directly onto the walls of the gallery, creating a theatrical space in which her unruly cut-paper characters fornicate and inflict violence on one another. In 2000, her work *Darkytown Rebellion* (2000), she uses overhead projectors to throw colored light onto the ceiling, walls, and floor of the exhibition space. Walker's work has been exhibited at the Museum of Modern Art, the San Francisco Museum of Modern Art, the Solomon R. Guggenheim Museum, and the Whitney Museum of American Art. She is a 1997 recipient of the John D. and Catherine T. MacArthur Foundation Achievement Award and was the United States representative to the 2002 Sao Paolo Bienal in Brazil. She is on the faculty of the master of fine arts program at Columbia University.

John E. Wallace, Jr.

JUDICIAL. John E. Wallace, Jr., is a native of Pitman, New Jersey. He received a bachelor of arts degree from the University of Delaware in 1964 and earned his juris doctor from Harvard University Law School in 1967. He was in the United States Army from 1968 to 1970, attaining the rank of captain. His legal career includes serving in private law practice, as the Municipal Court Judge for Washington Township in Gloucester County, and as a New Jersey Superior Court Judge in 1984. Wallace was promoted to the Appellate Division in 1992.

Wallace was nominated by Governor James E. McGreevey on April 12, 2003, to serve on the New Jersey Supreme Court. He was confirmed by the New Jersey Senate on May 19, 2003, and was sworn in the next day.

Christopher A. Walls

MILITARY. Christopher A. Walls entered the United States Army from Indianapolis, Indiana, in 1983. He attended basic training at Fort Leonard Wood, Missouri, and advanced individual training for Military Occupational Specialty 91B at Fort Sam Houston, Texas. His military education includes all levels of the noncommissioned officer education system courses, Drill Sergeant School, first sergeant course, and the United States Army Sergeants Major Academy at Fort Bliss, Texas.

Command Sergeant Major Walls' leadership assignments include drill sergeant, C Company, 232 Medical Battalion at Fort Sam Houston, Texas; platoon sergeant for C Company, 296th Forward Support Battalion, 2nd Infantry Division, Fort Lewis, Washington; and first

sergeant for the following companies: C Company, 15th Forward Support Battalion at Fort Hood, Texas; 377th (Air Artillery), Camp Humphreys in Korea; Medical Element, Soto Cano Air Base Honduras; and C Company, 25th Forward Support Battalion, 25th Infantry Division (Light) at Fort Lewis, Washington. He was sergeant major, distributed mission operations centers, 25th Infantry Division (Light). Walls is now the command sergeant major for the 226th Medical Battalion, Logistics (Rear) Detachment.

Kimberly Walton

FEDERAL GOVERNMENT. Kimberly Walton holds a law degree from the Catholic University of America's Columbus School of Law and is a member of the District of Columbia Bar. She studied psychology at the University of Tennessee and organizational psychology at Columbia. Walton was director of Civil Rights for the United States Department of Commerce. Before that, she was an attorney with the U.S. Equal Employment Opportunity Commission. She was the deputy chief administrative officer for the U.S. Patent and Trademark Office. Additionally, she was a key member of the chief financial officer/chief administrative officer's immediate policy planning group and participated in formulation oversight to, and coordinating the activities of, the Human Resources, Administrative Services, Security and Civil Rights offices. She currently serves as the special counselor to the administrator of the Transportation Security Administration.

Reggie Walton

JUDICIAL. Reggie Walton is a native of North Charleroi, Pennsylvania. He received a bachelor of arts degree from West Virginia State College in 1971 and earned his juris doctor degree from American University Washington College of Law in 1974. He was a staff attorney; assistant U.S. attorney and executive assistant U.S. attorney for the U.S. Attorney's Office in the District of Columbia from 1976 to 1981.

He was appointed to the Washington, D.C., Superior Court in 1981 by Ronald Reagan. In 1989, he was appointed by George H.W. Bush as the deputy drug czar under Bill Bennett. He was reappointed to the District of Columbia Superior Court by the senior President George Bush in 1991. On September 4, 2001, President George W. Bush appointed him to serve as a United States judge on the U.S. District Court for the District of Columbia. He was confirmed by the Senate on September 21, 2001, and received his commission on September 24, 2001.

Tanya Walton-Pratt

JUDICIAL. Tanya Walton-Pratt is a graduate of Cathedral High School. She received a bachelor of arts degree from Spelman College in 1981 and earned her juris doctor from Howard University in 1984.

Judge Walton-Pratt worked in private law practice in Indianapolis, Indiana. She has served as a public defender in Marion County Superior Court, Criminal Division Room 2, for five years. She was a master commissioner for Criminal Division 1 from 1993 to 1996. In January 1997 she was elected judge to the Marion Superior Court, Criminal 1. From 2007 to 2008, she was the associate presiding judge of Marion Superior Court, Indiana. She is the supervising judge of the Juvenile Detention Center in Marion County. On May 21, 2001, Governor Frank O'Bannon appointed Walton-Pratt the chairperson of the Indiana Martin Luther King, Jr., Holiday Commission. On September 12, 2003, Governor Joseph E. Kernan appointed her to the State Sentencing Policy Study Committee.

Jeffrey Ward

PUBLIC SAFETY. Jeffrey Ward attended Indiana University. He joined the Gary, Indiana, fire service in 1969 as a private and firefighter and was promoted to the positions of engineer, lieutenant, captain, battalion chief, and division chief. In October of 2006, he was appointed fire chief by the Honorable Mayor Rudolph Clay. Ward is the first Gary Fire Chief to have experience as a certified paramedic (25 years) and as an industrial firefighter (U.S. Steel, five years).

William Edward Ward

MILITARY. William Edward Ward is a native of Baltimore, Maryland. He received a bachelor of arts degree in political science from Morgan State University and a master of arts degree in political science from Pennsylvania State University. His military education includes the infantry officer basic and advanced courses, the U.S. Army Command and General Staff College, and the U.S. Army War College.

He began his military career with Company A, 3rd Battalion, 325th Infantry, 82nd Airborne Division, at Fort Bragg, North Carolina. He has served in Washington, D.C.; at Fort Wainwright, Alaska; in Hawaii; in Korea; at the American Embassy in Egypt; as U.S security coordinator for Israel-Palestinian Authority in Tel Aviv; and in Germany. He was an instructor of social sciences, later assistant professor, at the United States Military Academy at West Point, New York, from 1978 to 1982.

He was promoted to major on January 1, 1983, lieutenant colonel on February 1, 1989, colonel on June 1, 1992, brigadier general on April 1, 1996, and major general on February 1, 1999. In 2007, he was nominated by President George W. Bush to command the new Africa Command and became its first commanding general on October 1, 2007.

Carole Ward-Allen

LOCAL GOVERNMENT. Carole Ward-Allen received a bachelor of arts degree and a master of fine arts degree from San Jose State University in San Jose, California. She earned a doctorate in education from Nova Southeastern University, Florida, in 2000. She has also studied politics and art of West Africa at Forah Bay College, Sierra Leone, University of Ile-Ife, Nigeria; the University of Kumasi, Ghana; and University of Nairobi, Kenya.

Ward-Allen was first elected to the Bay Area Regional Transit (bart) board on November 3, 1998, to represent the 4th District, which includes Alameda and portions of Oakland. She was sworn into office on December 8, 1998. In December 2005, BART became the first major transit agency in American history to be led by two African American women after the nine-member board unan imously elected Ward-Allen president and Lynette Sweet vice president, BART's most powerful posts.

Dartanian Warr

MILITARY. Dartanian Warr earned a bachelor's degree in behavioral sciences (human factors) from the United States Air Force Academy in Colorado and a master's degree in applied behavioral sciences from Wright State University in Ohio. His master's degree in business administration management (with honors) is from Golden Gate University in California. He also has a master's degree in national resource strategy from the Industrial College of the Armed Forces in Washington, D.C. His military education includes Squadron Officer School at Maxwell Air Force Base in Alabama; advance program management, Defense Systems Management College in Virginia; Air Command and Staff College in Alabama; Center for Creative Learning, executive leadership program; and national security management course, Syracuse, New York.

Warr was commissioned into the U.S. Air Force in 1980 upon graduating from the U.S. Military Academy. His most recent assignments include serving as chief, senior officer matters, at Headquarters Air Force Materiel Command at Wright-Patterson Air Force Base in Ohio; from August 1999 to March 2002, as system program director, Human Systems Program Office, Brooks Air Force Base in Texas; and from April 2002 to February 2004, as inspector general at Headquarters Air Force Materiel Command at Wright-Patterson. He is commander, Battle Management Systems Wing, Electronic Systems Center, at Hanscom Air Force Base in Massachusetts.

Thomas Warren

LAW ENFORCEMENT. Thomas Warren is a native of Omaha, Nebraska. He graduated from Omaha Technical High School in 1979 and received a bachelor's degree in criminal justice from Morningside College in Omaha in 1983. He earned a master's degree from the University of Nebraska Omaha in 1989.

Warren joined the Omaha Police Department in 1983 and served in a variety of assignments, including patrol division, internal affairs, information services and the investigation bureau. He was promoted to captain in 1999 and became Northeast Precinct commander in 2002. After scoring highest on tests, interviews and other criteria among nine candidates for the job, on December 3, 2003, Warren was sworn in as Omaha's chief of police. He is the first African American ever selected to serve in that post.

Denzel Washington

ENTERTAINMENT, FILM. Denzel Washington is a native of Mount Vernon, New York. He is a graduate of Oakland Academy, a prep school for boys in the upstate New York town of New Windsor. He received a bachelor's degree in drama and journalism from Fordham University. He attended the American Conservatory Theatre in San Francisco for a year.

Washington landed his first professional acting assignment in the NBC made for television movie *Wilma* in 1977. In 1979 he was featured in the CBS television-film *Flesh and Blood* and made his film debut in the 1981 film *Carbon Copy.* He landed the role of Malcolm X in 1981 in the New Federal Theater's production of *When the Chickens Come Home to Roost.* He starred in the popular television hospital drama *St. Elsewhere* from 1982 to 1988. He played leading man in *The Pelican Brief*; *Crimson Tide*; *Much Ado About Nothing*; *The Preacher's Wife*; *Virtuosity* in 1995; and *The Hurricane* in 1999. In 2000, he appeared in the Disney film *Remember the Titans*; in 2001, the cop thriller *Training Day*; in 2002, *John Q.*; then he directed his first film, *Antwone Fisher,* in which he also co-starred. Between 2003 and 2004, Washington appeared in a series of thrillers, *Out of Time, Man on Fire,* and *The Manchurian Candidate.* In 2005, he appeared as Brutus in Shakespeare's *Julius Caesar* on Broadway. In 2006 he starred in *Inside Man,* a Spike Lee film; *Déjà Vu,* released in November 2006; and in 2007, *American Gangster.* He directed and starred in *The Great Debaters.*

Washington won an Academy Award in the category of Best Actor (for *Training Day*), becoming only the second African American performer to win an Academy Award in that category. Sidney Poitier was the first.

Kelvin Washington

LAW ENFORCEMENT. Kelvin Washington is a native of Hemingway, South Carolina, and a graduate of Hemingway High School. He attended South Carolina State University and received a bachelor of science degree in criminal justice from American Intercontinental University. He is currently enrolled at Troy University for his master's degree in criminal justice. He also graduated from the South Carolina Criminal Justice Academy, the FBI sponsored Carolina Command College, and the National Sheriff's Institute.

Washington began his law enforcement career with the City of Florence (South Carolina) Police Department in 1990. He was a patrolman, narcotics agent, and an investigator. In 1993, Washington joined the Williamsburg County Sheriff's Office as the chief investigator and was later promoted to chief deputy. In January 1999, he was elected sheriff of Williamsburg County, making South Carolina history. Sheriff Washington is the youngest African American to be elected sheriff in the state. He was re-elected in 2000 and 2004.

Willie Anthony Waters

MUSIC. Willie Anthony Waters was appointed conductor general and artistic director of the Connecticut Opera in Hartford in July 1999. He has been a guest conductor for operas all over the U.S. and the Cologne Opera (Germany), Manitoba Opera (Winnipeg, Canada), L'Opera de Montreal, Vancouver Opera and the opera companies of Cape Town, Pretoria, and Durban, South Africa. Among his orchestral engagements are performances with the Florida Philharmonic, Detroit Symphony, Hartford Symphony, Bavarian Radio Orchestra (Munich), Essen Philharmonic (Germany), Brucknerhaus Orchester (Linz, Austria), and Indianapolis Symphony. Maestro Waters is also artistic advisor and conductor of the Houston Ebony Opera Guild, where he has conducted *Otello, Tosca, Suor, Angelica and Highway One, USA* (William Grant Still), *The Barber of Seville,* and *La Boheme,* set during the Harlem renaissance of the 1920s.

During the 2001-2002 season, Waters was a guest with the Hartford Symphony on three occasions: Handel's *Messiah* featuring the Hartford Chorale, a subscription concert featuring music of Wagner and Tchaikovsky, and the third annual Martin Luther King Celebration. He also conducted the African American Gala with the chorus of the Houston Ebony Music Society. In September 2002, Waters conducted a gala concert with Denyce Graves in celebration of the 20th anniversary of Opera Colorado in Denver. In November, Maestro Waters made his New York City Opera debut conducting *Rigoletto.* His schedule during the 2003-

2004 season included *Rigoletto* for Houston Ebony Opera, his return to New York City Opera for Carlisle Floyd's *Of Mice and Men*, and *Salome* for the Kentucky Opera. For Connecticut Opera, he conducted *Lucia Di Lammermoor*.

Melvin L. Watt

FEDERAL GOVERNMENT. Melvin L. Watt is a native of Steele Creek, North Carolina, and a graduate of York Road High School in Charlotte, North Carolina, in 1963. He received a bachelor of science degree from University of North Carolina at Chapel Hill in 1967 and earned his juris doctor degree from Yale University School of Law in New Haven, Connecticut. Watt worked in private law practice and was elected in 1985 as a North Carolina state senator. He was elected as a Democrat to the 103rd and to the seven succeeding Congresses (January 3, 1993, to present).

Sidney D. Weatherspoon

MILITARY. Sidney D. Weatherspoon is a native of Panama City, Florida. He is a graduate of all courses in the noncommissioned officer education system. His military education includes the first sergeant course and the U.S. Sergeants Major Academy (Class 50). He enlisted in the U.S. Army in 1978 as an operations intelligence assistant. He has served in enlisted leadership positions from squad leader to command sergeant major. His assignments include first sergeant of 2nd Battalion, 7th Air Defense Artillery (Patriot) during Operation Desert Shield and Desert Storm, Fort Bliss, Texas; first sergeant, 5th Battalion, 2nd Air Defense Artillery Avenger, Bamberg, Germany; operations sergeant major, 2nd Battalion, 1st Sir Defense Artillery (Patriot), at Fort Bliss, Texas; 35th Air Defense Artillery Brigade operations sergeant major; command sergeant major, Task Force Iron Fist during Operation Enduring Freedom and Operation Iraqi Freedom; and command sergeant major of 2nd Battalion, 1st Air Defense Artillery (Patriot) at Gwangju Air Base, Republic of Korea.

Frank C. Weaver

ENGINEERING. Frank C. Weaver received a bachelor of science degree in electrical engineering from Howard University and earned a masters of business administration from the University of North Carolina. He also has received honorary doctorates in science from Saint Augustine's College and humane letters from Shaw Divinity School. Weaver has over 25 years of experience in government and private industry, and has marketed over $1 billion in communication satellite and launch vehicles to NASA and the Department of Defense. He serves as director for telecommunications policy, Office of Government Relations, at the Boeing Company in Washington, D.C.

Carl P. Webb

BUSINESS. Carl P. Webb is a graduate of the Art Institute of Atlanta and attended North Carolina Central University. He is a 25-year veteran of the advertising and marketing communications industry, now serving as president and chief operating officer of Webb Patterson Communication, a Durham, North Carolina, based advertising, marketing communications and public relations agency. Webb Patterson Communications has relationships with such clients as McDonald's, First Citizens Bank, University of North Carolina Hospitals, North Carolina GlaxoSmithKline Foundation, GlaxoSmith Kline, Mechanics and Farmers Bank, Allergan Inc., Duke University and the State of North Carolina.

Sandra Webb-Brooker

MILITARY, HEALTH. Sandra Webb-Brooker is a native of Chicago, Illinois. She holds a Ph.D. and entered the United States Army in February 1985. Just prior to entering the military she served as a nursing instructor for Chicago State University. After serving

more than 20 years as an Army Reserve nurse, she took over as commander of the 801st Combat Support Hospital at Fort Sheridan in Illinois. She is the first nurse in that post, spending a year in Kuwait and Iraq from 2003 to 2004. As commander, she is responsible for the battalion-size unit of about 500 personnel, including medics, nurses, anesthesiologists, and surgeons. She also runs the licensed practical nurse program for the Chicago Public Schools.

Yvonne Welbon

FILM. Yvonne Welbon is a native of Chicago who attended Vassar College in Poughkeepsie, New York. She spent six years in Taipei, Taiwan, where she taught English, learned Mandarin Chinese, and founded and published a premier arts magazine for five years. She returned to the United States and enrolled in the School of the Art Institute of Chicago and obtained a master of fine arts with a concentration in film and video in 1994. She earned a Ph.D. in radio, television and film from Northwestern University.

Welbon is a film director, producer, writer, and editor. Her work as a filmmaker is experimental and often autobiographical, exploring identity through memory, history, culture, race, and sexuality. Her films illustrate people's need to recognize their heritage, history and places in society as individuals. One of her more recent projects, *Sisters in Cinema* (2003), is a documentary outlining the history of African American women directors.

Teresa M. Wesley

MEDICINE. Teresa Wesley received a bachelor's degree and earned her doctor of medicine degree from the University of Kansas. Dr. Wesley is an internal medicine physician and national medical expert. She has appeared in print, radio, and television, including *The Montel Williams Show*, BET's Rap It Up forums, *Lancet* medical journal, and is a contributor to the book *100 Words of Wisdom for Women*. The vision and mission of DrTeresaWesley.com is to create a host of resources. This includes medical information via a continuum of web based information, conferences, teleseminars, articles, and health education materials.

Mildred West

EDUCATION. Mildred West was reared in Tulsa, Oklahoma. She received a bachelor of science degree from Northeast Oklahoma and a master of education degree from the University of Nevada in Las Vegas. She earned her mid-management certification at Texas Christian University in Fort Worth and her Ph.D. in educational administration from the University of Texas in Austin.

Her many positions in public education have included assistant superintendent, high school principal, and teacher of business and technology courses. Her supervisory experience includes overseeing the design and alignment of curriculum, professional development, instruction, assessment, and analysis of accountability measures. She was also employed by the Jerry Savelle Ministries International. Her work as director of a correspondence school provided direction for the International Bible School offices in Asia, Australia, Canada, South Africa, Tanzania, the United Kingdom and the United States.

West has served as a clinical professor at Trinity University in San Antonio, Texas, and has been a national and international conference presenter. She was named superintendent of Kendleton Independent School District. She is the first superintendent to be selected through the use of a national headhunter search firm. Her appointment was the result of a 7–0 vote by the Kendleton Independent School Board of Trustees.

Corliss Hill White

LOCAL GOVERNMENT. Corliss Hill White is a native of Atlanta, Georgia. She graduated from Southwest High School in 1977 and received a bachelor of science degree in journalism from the University of Georgia in 1980.

White began her career with the U. S. Postal Service in 1983 as a clerk. Over the years, she moved up the ranks through various promotions and assignments, including communications specialist, retail analyst, community relations coordinator and Olympics liaison. White has also been a speech writer for the Atlanta District Office of the U. S. Postal Service and served as the official

spokesperson for the media. In preparation for the 1996 Summer Olympic Games in Atlanta, she was part of a select group to prepare the U. S. Postal Service for the Games. $20 million was appropriated to renovate and build new post offices that could accommodate and serve the thousands of visitors to Atlanta during the Olympic Games. The long term benefits from this effort including establishing a post office at the Hartsfield-Jackson Atlanta Airport and increasing revenue by placing post offices in more visible and better positions.

In 2001, she was sworn into her first postmaster position in Zebulon, Georgia. In 2003, she was sworn in as postmaster in Tyrone, Georgia, and was appointed postmaster in Fairburn, Georgia in 2006. White holds three historical accomplishments in the postmaster positions. She became the first African-American female postmaster in Fayette County; the first African-American Postmaster in Tyrone, Georgia; and the first female African-American postmaster in Fairburn, Georgia.

Woodrow Whitlow, Jr.

SCIENCE. Woodrow Whitlow, Jr. received a bachelor of science degree, a master of science degree and a doctor of philosophy degree in aeronautics and astronautics from the Massachusetts Institute of Technology. He has written nearly 40 technical papers, most in the areas of unsteady transonic flow and aeroelasticity. Whitlow began his professional career in 1979 as a research scientist at the NASA Langley Research Center in Hampton, Virginia. He assumed various positions of increasing responsibility before moving to the Glenn Research Center in 1998. In 1994, he was director of the Critical Technologies Division, Office of Aeronautics, at NASA Headquarters. He served as director of research and technology at the Glenn Research Center. From September 2003 through December 2005, he was the deputy director of the NASA John F. Kennedy Space Center.

Whitlow has been the director of the National Aeronautics and Space Administration (NASA) John H. Glenn Research Center at Lewis Field in Cleveland, Ohio since December 25, 2005.

Robert Whyms

ENGINEERING. Robert Whyms received a bachelor's degree in electrical engineering from the University of Florida and a master's degree in electrical engineering from Johns Hopkins University. Whyms is an advisory engineer with responsibility for the design of advanced digital-processor architectures to support key military sensors programs, such as the F-22 radar processor and the Longbow Block III program radar electronics unit, at Northrop Grumman Electronic Systems in Baltimore, Maryland.

Whyms has supported the company's Discover "E" (Engineer) Program, visiting inner city schools to speak about engineering careers and has co-mentored Baltimore high-school students as part of the Worthwhile to Help High School Youth (Worthy) program.

Susan D. Wigenton

JUDICIAL. Susan D. Wigenton received a bachelor of arts degree in political science from Norfolk State University in 1984 and earned her juris doctor degree from the College of William and Mary in 1987. She was a judicial clerk for Judge Lawrence M. Lawson, the assignment judge for Monmouth County in New Jersey, from 1987 to 1988. Following her clerkship she was the public defender for the city of Asbury Park. She next worked in private law practice in Middletown, New Jersey, from 1988 to 2000. In 2000, she was appointed a U.S. magistrate judge, United States District Court for the District of New Jersey.

In January 2006, Judge Wigenton was nominated by President George W. Bush to serve as a U.S. District Judge for the District of New Jersey. She was confirmed by the Senate on May 26, 2006, to the lifetime position. She received her commission and was officially appointed by President Bush on June 12, 2006.

Kate Wiley

FEDERAL GOVERNMENT. Kate Wiley is a native of Michigan. She received an associate degree in communications from Ohio Dominican College and a bachelor of arts degree magna cum laude from Ohio Dominican College in 1977. Wiley joined the U.S. Postal Service in 1977 as a letter sorting machine clerk in the Columbus, Ohio, processing plant. Her management assignments include serving as a tour superintendent in Columbus and senior manager for the seven processing centers in the Kentuckiana District. She helped design the processing and distribution center near the airport in Columbus, but left before the $160 million

facility was constructed. In 2000, became plant manager in Stamford, Connecticut, then manager of the Southern Connecticut Processing and Distribution Center and Columbus district manager. She is the first Columbus employee appointed to a local executive position since 1986. On October 1, 2006, she was the first black female to serve as the Central Florida District manager. In October 2007, she became the first woman to serve as the Atlanta District manager.

Gina P. Wilkerson

MEDICAL. Gina P. Wilkerson received a bachelor of science degree in animal and poultry sciences and biology from Tuskegee University in 1980 and earned her doctor of veterinary medicine degree from Tuskegee University in 1985. Dr. Wilkerson has served as a veterinarian in private practice and for the U.S. Department of Agriculture before entering private industry. She was named director of veterinary medicine at AstraZeneca Pharmaceuticals, where she oversees all animal projects at the company's Wilmington (Delaware) Research and Development facility.

Adrian D. Williams

MILITARY. Adrian D. Williams is a native of Hamtramck, Michigan, and graduated in 1973 from Mackenzie High School in Detroit, Michigan. He attended Wayne State Community College in Detroit and Eastern Michigan University in Ypsilanti for two years. Williams attempted to enlist in the U.S. Navy in August 1976, but was turned away due to having a metal plate in his leg. He had surgery to have the plate removed, then enlisted in the Navy by way of the delayed entry program in April 1977. After completing Recruit Training Command and Operations Specialist "A" school, both in Great Lakes, Illinois, he was promoted to master chief petty officer in April 1993. He was selected for the Command Master Chief program in December 1996. He has attended the Navy's Senior Enlisted and Air Force's Senior Noncommissioned Officers Academy. His first command master chief assignment was onboard the USS *Lake Erie* (CG-70), home ported at Pearl Harbor, Hawaii. He was command master chief for Naval Security Group Activity at Fort Gordon, Georgia, and Strike Fighter Squadron 15 (VFA-15) at Oceana Master Jet Base, Virginia Beach, Virginia. Command Master Chief Williams reported to Naval Recruiting District Michigan for his fourth command master chief tour in April 2007.

Felicia Toney Williams

JUDICIAL. Felicia Toney Williams is a graduate of McCall Senior High School with honors in Tallulah, Louisiana, in 1974 and received a bachelor of arts degree magna cum laude from Southern University in Baton Rough, in Louisiana in 1977. She earned her juris doctor degree cum laude from Southern University School of Law in Baton Rouge, Louisiana, in 1980 and completed the Appellate Judge's Program at New York University School of Law in 1994.

Williams was an attorney with the U.S. Department of Justice in 1980; an attorney with Central Louisiana Legal Services from 1980 to 1981; an assistant district attorney for Madison Parish District Attorney's Office in Tallulah, Louisiana, and has worked in private law practice. She was elected in 1991 to serve as judge, Division B, Sixth Judicial District Court, Tallulah, Louisiana.

Judge Williams was elected as appellate judge, Second Circuit Court of Appeals, in Shreveport, Louisiana, in 1993. She served on the Louisiana Supreme Court, New Orleans, as associate justice pro tem from September 1, 1994, through December 28, 1994. She is the first African American female to serve on the Louisiana Supreme Court.

James Herbert Williams

EDUCATION. James Herbert Williams received a master of social work degree from Smith College and a master of public administration degree from the University of Colorado. He earned his Ph.D. from the University of Washington in Seattle. From 1995 to 2006, he was a faculty member and administrator at the George Warren Brown School of Social Work at Washington University in St. Louis, Missouri. Most recently, he served as E. Desmond Lee pro-

fessor of racial and ethnic diversity and associate dean at George Warren Brown School of Social Work at Washington University, as well as assistant to the chancellor for urban community initiative at Washington University. He was foundation professor of youth and diversity at the School of Social Work in the College of Public Programs at Arizona State University. Williams was named dean of the University of Denver Graduate School of Social Work.

Janet Williams

MUSIC. Janet Williams received a bachelor of music education as well as a bachelor of voice degree from Michigan State University. She earned a master of music degree in vocal performance from Indiana University. Williams is a soprano who has delighted audiences and critics internationally. She was a vocal coach for both the African American Choral Ensemble and the Indiana University Soul Revue from 1984 to 1987. She also was a vocal instructor at the School of Music during this time. She has won critical acclaim for performances in leading roles at the Metropolitan Opera, Berlin Staatsoper, Paris Opera, Theatre des Elysees, Opera de Lyon, Nice Opera, Geneva Opera, Frankfurt Opera, Cologne Opera, Leipzig Opera, Theatre Royal de la Monnaie, San Francisco Opera, Washington Opera, Dallas Opera and Michigan Opera Theatre; festivals in Spoleto, Innsbruck, Halle and New York; as well as in concerts throughout Europe, North America, Canada, Israel and Japan with numerous acclaimed conductors. Williams' operatic and concert repertoire spans genres of musical styles from Baroque to contemporary. Williams also leads a variety of performance enhancement seminars throughout Europe and the United States. She maintains a voice studio in Berlin, Germany. She received the Indiana University African American Arts Institute's Herman C. Hudson Alumni Award.

Karen Hastie Williams

FEDERAL GOVERNMENT. Karen Hastie Williams received a bachelor's degree from Bates College and earned her juris doctor from the Catholic University School of Law. She was a law clerk for Supreme Court Justice Thurgood Marshall and Judge Spottswood W. Robinson III of the United States Court of Appeals for the District of Columbia Circuit. She also served as chief counsel to the U.S. Senate Committee on the Budget, and as administrator of the Office of Federal Procurement Policy in the Office of Management and Budget. From October 2000 to September 2003, she served with distinction as a public life member of the Internal Revenue Oversight Board, appointed by the president of the United States.

Lisa Williams

EDUCATION. Lisa Williams is the first African American female to graduate from the Ohio State University's Marketing and Logistics Department, and she also holds a Ph.D. She is the second woman in her discipline to become a full professor at Penn State University and a two time endowed chair holder. She was the first female to hold a multimillion dollar endowed chair in her field. She has dedicated her life to educating and developing excellence in future and current leaders. Major corporations and President Bill Clinton's Commission on Critical Infrastructure Protection have sought her advice. Her research has practical and global implications and as such she has spoken to audiences in the United States, Belgium, Austria, Canada, London and Australia. Williams is president and chief executive officer of Williams Research, Inc., and author of the book *Leading Beyond Excellence*.

Marcellette G. Williams

EDUCATION. Marcellette G. Williams received a bachelor of arts degree with highest honors in comparative literature and a master of arts in English and comparative literature from Michigan State University. She also earned a Ph.D. in English from Michigan State University. She has served as a professor of English and comparative literature, and for almost a decade she taught and consulted throughout Asia and in Europe through Michigan State University's Graduate Studies in Education Overseas program. She was associate director of the English Language Center at Michigan State University; acting chair in the Department of English; project coordinator and as assistant to the provost for internal institutional advancement in the Office of the Provost; and executive assistant to the president and corporate secretary of the board of trustees. She served seven and a half years as deputy chancellor at the University of Massachusetts at Amherst.

On February 7, 2001, the Board of Trustees of the

University of Massachusetts ratified the appointment of Williams as chancellor effective July 1, 2001.

Michael L. Williams

STATE GOVERNMENT. Michael L. Williams is a native of Midland, Texas. He received a bachelor's degree in political science from the University of Southern California College. He earned a master of arts in public administration and his juris doctor degree from the University of Southern California. He is a former assistant district to attorney in his hometown of Midland, Texas. From 1984 to 1988, he was a federal prosecutor. From January 1988 to June 1989, was special assistant to Attorney General Richard Thornburgh in the U.S. Department of Justice. He served as deputy assistant secretary for law enforcement at the U.S. Department of the Treasury from August 1989 to June 1990. In 1990, President George H.W. Bush appointed him to be assistant secretary of education for civil rights at the U.S. Department of Education. Texas Governor George W. Bush appointed him in 1998 to the Texas Railroad Commission to fill the vacancy created by the election of Carole Keeton Strayhorn, as Texas comptroller. He was the first African American in Texas history to serve in a nonjudicial statewide office. He was re-elected chairman of the Texas Railroad Commission in 2002 to a full six-year term.

Montel Williams

MEDIA. Montel Williams is a native of Baltimore, Maryland. In 1975, he became the first black Marine selected to the Naval Academy Prep School. He received a bachelor of science degree in engineering and a minor in international security affairs from the United States Naval Academy, Annapolis, Maryland, in 1980. Williams began his professional career in the U.S. Marine Corps in 1974, when he enlisted after graduating high school, and after six months was selected to attend the U.S. Naval Academy. He served on the USS *Sampson* during the United States' invasion of Grenada. He retired after 22 years of military service as a lieutenant commander in the Navy Reserves.

In 1991 Williams began hosting his own television show, *The Montel Williams Show*, syndicated by CBS Paramount Television. In 1996, he received a Daytime Emmy Award for Outstanding Talk Show Host. As an actor he has also starred in the action adventure film *The Peacekeeper*; had a role in *Matt Waters*, a one-hour drama series that aired on CBS; appeared in the CBS series *Touched by an Angel*; appeared twice on *JAG*; and was in TNT's *The New Adventures of Robin Hood*.

Moses Williams

MARTIAL ARTS. Moses Williams graduated from Southwest Texas State University in 1983 with an associate degree in criminal justice. He has worked as a University of Texas police officer and as a chief of security. Master Williams has studied under some of the world's greatest grand masters, including Rick Reed, John S. Wong, Daniel Baker and high priest Rick Anderson. He has achieved two world titles, one in black belt soft style kung fu and the other in continuous fighting. He has been ranked third in the world by the National Black Belt League, Super Heavyweight Division. In 1997, 1998, and 1999 he won three Texas Golden Greek Awards in the Executive Black Belt Division 35 years or older in both fighting and form. He owns and operates the Fire Dragon Martial Arts Institute, which he established in 1994. He was inducted into the Universal Martial Art Hall of Fame as Grand Master of the Year — Kung Fu in 2002, as Head Founder — Spiritual Kung Fu, his own system, in 2003, and in 2005 for the Diamond Life Achievement Award, capturing two more world titles in Chinese kung-fu forms and weapons.

Williams is a 10th degree black sash in spiritual kung fu and siu lum pai gung fu, and an 8th degree black belt in zen-u-zen kung fu and kajukenbo karate. Williams also has a 5th degree black belt in American kempo karate. He has 37 years' experience in the martial arts. He specializes in youth development, discipline and educational programs. He has worked in the Austin Community for more than 28 years. He trained law enforcement officers and judges as well as the children of the community. He has students throughout the United States spreading his art, spiritual kung-fu.

Nathaniel Williams

LAW ENFORCEMENT. Nathaniel Williams is a native of East Feliciana Parish, Louisiana. He is a graduate of the Louisiana State University Basic Training Academy; Drug Enforcement Agency (dea) training; police internal affair training; police supervisory training and many other law enforcement courses. Williams joined

the St. Helena Parish in May 1990 as a patrolman, working his way through the ranks to chief of operations (later called chief deputy), overseeing the day to day operation of the department. He was appointed interim sheriff in February 2007 and was elected sheriff of St. Helena Parish on October 20, 2007, for the unexpired term and regular term of sheriff.

Ronnie M. Williams

LAW ENFORCEMENT. Ronnie M. Williams began his law enforcement career in 1973 with the Los Angeles County Sheriff's Department, when he attended the department's Training Academy. After graduating as a deputy sheriff in 1974, he served at the Hall of Justice Jail, Los Angeles County, University of Southern California Medical Center Jail Ward, Lenox Station, Operation Safe Streets Bureau, and Men's Central Jail. In 1985, he was promoted to sergeant and held assignments at Crescenta Valley Station, Homicide Bureau, and the Internal Affairs Bureau. In 1990, he was promoted to lieutenant and took on assignments at the Mira Loma Detention Facility, Men's Central Jail, the Los Angeles County Safety Police Department, Lennox Station. As captain beginning in 1999, he held assignments at the Altadena Station and Narcotics Bureau. In 2003, he was promoted to commander and assigned to the Detective Division. Williams was promoted to chief on April 7, 2004.

Tatia L. Williams

LAW, MEDIA. Tatia L. Williams is a native of Washington, D.C. She received a bachelor of arts degree from the University of Virginia and earned a juris doctor from Harvard Law School. Williams began her career in private law practice. She has served as the vice president of legal affairs for Oxygen Media. She previously served as a political appointee in the Clinton Administration, first as a special counsel to the president, and then as a senior advisor in the Department of Commerce. Williams currently is director of sales planning and strategy at mtv Networks in New York City, where she provides legal, cable and regulatory advice to the Affiliate Sales and Marketing Group to help meet its distribution goals.

Theodore J. Williams

FEDERAL GOVERNMENT. Theodore J. Williams received a bachelor of science degree in business administration from Northwestern State University of Louisiana, Natchitoches. He earned a master of business administration in management and accounting at Rensselaer Polytechnic Institute, Troy, New York, and a master of science in management and accounting from Rensselaer Polytechnic Institute. Other education includes professional military comptroller course; program management course, Fort Belvoir, Virginia; and Senior Managers in Government Program, John F. Kennedy School of Government, Harvard University, Cambridge, Massachusetts.

Williams served in the Air Force for more than 26 years, retiring in rank of colonel in 1999. While on active duty, he worked for the Air Force Audit Agency (AFAA) for more than 11 years as an acquisition auditor, audit manager, branch chief, acting office chief, program manager and executive officer to the Air Forces auditor general.

He was assigned to the Defense Finance and Accounting Service Headquarters as the assistant deputy director for customer service and the first director of program control in the services accounting systems program office. His assignments in the Senior Executive Service have included as assistant auditor general for field activities, AFAA, Arlington, Virginia, and as assistant auditor general for acquisition and logistics audits, AFAA, Wright-Patterson Air Force Base in Ohio. Williams was selected to serve as deputy auditor general for financial and support audits for the AFAA in Washington, D.C.

Virgil S.L. Williams

MILITARY. Virgil S.L. Williams received a bachelor's degree in liberal arts from the University of Toledo, a master of arts in management from Webster University, and a master's degree in strategic studies from the United States Army War College. His military schooling includes the armor officer basic course; the quartermaster officer advance course; the Combined Arms Ser-

vice Staff School; the Command and General Staff College; and the U.S. Army War College.

Williams has served in a variety of command and staff assignments, most recently as the director of logistics, Multi-National Force — Iraq, from August 2004 to June 2005. Other key assignments include chief, Logistics Plans and Exercises Division, United States Pacific Command, Camp Smith, Hawaii; commander, 101st Forward Support Battalion, 1st Infantry Division, Fort Riley, Kansas; senior logistics advisor to the Saudi Arabian National Guard Director of Logistics, Riyadh, Saudi Arabia; support operation officer for the 3rd Brigade Combat Team, 2nd Infantry Division, and chief of supply and services, 1st Corps at Fort Lewis in Washington.

Andrea D. Willis

HEALTH. Andrea D. Willis is a native of Alabama. She received a bachelor of science degree from the University of Alabama at Birmingham and her medical doctor degree from Georgetown University. She earned a master of public health from Johns Hopkins University and was a fellow of the American Academy of Pediatrics. Dr. Willis has served in private group practice, as deputy commissioner of health for a state, and started the State Children's Health Insurance Program in Alabama. She is the founder of DiagnosisDestiny, LLC. She speaks to a wide variety of audiences including medical students, health workers and providers, church groups, community organizations, and women's conferences.

Vannia Willis

ENGINEERING. Vannia Willis received a bachelor's degree in electrical engineering from Temple University and a master's degree in business administration from Averett University. She joined Northrop Grumman Newport News as lead engineer for the multi-million dollar Engineer Change proposal. She is a senior engineer in the company's Washington, D.C., engineering office and has responsibilities ranging from combat systems to exterior communications for both new aircraft carriers and the aircraft carrier overhaul. Willis has worked on the CVN 78 as the exterior communication systems and topside.

Blenda J. Wilson

EDUCATION. Blenda J. Wilson grew up in a small New Jersey town in the 1950s. She received a bachelor's degree in English and secondary education from Cedar Crest College. She earned a master's degree in education from Seton Hall and a Ph.D. in higher education from Boston College. She was awarded an honorary doctor of humane letters from Eckerd College in 2004.

Wilson was the director of the Middlesex County Economic Opportunity Corporation. She began her career in higher education administration at Rutgers University in New Jersey in 1969. From 1972 to 1982, she was senior associate dean at the Harvard University Graduate School of Education. After she left Harvard in 1988, she became chancellor of the University of Michigan. From 1992 to 1999, she was president of California State University, Northridge, California, and led the university's recovery from the Northridge earthquake in January of 1994. Wilson was named the first president and chief executive officer of the Nellie Mae Foundation, one of the largest foundations in New England, and the largest focused exclusively on education.

Chandra Wilson

ENTERTAINMENT. Chandra Wilson is a native of Houston, Texas. She was a student at Houston's High School for the Performing and Visual Arts. She received a bachelor of fine arts degree in drama from New York University's Tisch School of Arts. Her career in the entertainment industry began at age five. She worked with Theater Under the Stars and appeared in more than ten musical productions. In college, she was trained at the Lee Strasberg Theater Institute. Her first major television appearance was in the short-lived sitcom *Bob Patterson*, written by actor Jason Alexander. Since then she has

worked in several TV shows such as *The Sopranos, Law and Order: Special Victims Unit, Third Watch, Sex and the City*, and *The Cosby Show*. She also had recurring roles on *One Life to Live* and *Queens Supreme*. She is now part of the TV show *Grey's Anatomy* as Dr. Miranda Bailey. The role earned Wilson a Screen Actors Guild Award for Outstanding Female Actor in a Drama Series in 2007. She was also nominated for the Supporting Actress in a Drama Series award at the 2007 Emmys for this role.

Charlotte L. Wilson

MILITARY. Charlotte L. Wilson received a bachelor of science in education from the University of Georgia in Athens, Georgia, and a master of science in human resource management from Chapman University in Orange County, California. She has also earned a master's degree in strategic studies from the Air War College at Maxwell Air Force Base in Alabama. Her military schools include Squadron Officer School, Air Command and Staff College, and Air War College.

Colonel Wilson was commissioned in 1984 through the Air Force Reserve Officer Training Corps program at the University of Georgia. She has served in multiple crew and squadron staff positions including deputy crew commander, crew commander, chief of training, chief of deployment plans and chief of space support. She was on the initial cadre at the 14th Air Force on the operations staff. Following her operations command tour, she became the special advisor for space and missile defense issues at the Arms Control Bureau, Department of State in Washington, D.C. She was previously chief of staff and the Chief Director's Action Group for the National Security Space Office, Office of the Undersecretary of the Air Force, in Washington, D.C. Colonel Wilson is the vice commander of the 460th Space Wing at Buckley Air Force Base in Colorado.

M. Roy Wilson

EDUCATION. M. Roy Wilson received his medical degree from Harvard University Medical School in 1980 and his master of science in epidemiology from the University of California at Los Angeles School of Public Health in 1990. He performed both his ophthalmology residency and glaucoma fellowship at the Massachusetts Eye and Ear Infirmary at Harvard University and an internship in internal medicine at the Harlem Hospital Center in New York City. He also completed a fellowship in glaucoma at the Massachusetts Eye and Ear Infirmary.

Dr. Wilson was a professor of ophthalmology at UCLA's Jules Stein Eye Institute and at Charles R. Drew University of Medicine and Science. In 1998, he was appointed dean of the Creighton University School of Medicine in 1998, and served as both dean and vice president for health sciences from 1999 to 2003. In 2003 he was appointed president of Texas Tech University Health Sciences Center and inducted into the Institutes of Medicine, National Academy of Sciences. Dr. Wilson was selected to serve as chancellor of the University of Colorado at Denver and Health Sciences Center on July 1, 2006.

Valarie D. Wilson

LOCAL GOVERNMENT. Valarie D. Wilson received a bachelor of arts degree in communications from Clark College and earned her master's degree in public administration from Troy State University. From 1991 to 1996 she was director of the Office of Aging for the Human Services Department of Fulton County, in Atlanta, Georgia. She was named director of the Fulton County Human Services Department in 1999. Wilson was named executive director of the BeltLine Partnership by Atlanta Mayor Shirley Franklin, who established the agency in 2005 to foster advocacy and coordinate private sector engagement in the city's visionary 25-year BeltLine initiative.

Henry T. Wingate

JUDICIAL. Henry T. Wingate received a bachelor of arts degree in philosophy from Grinnell in 1969 and earned a juris doctor degree from Yale University Law School in 1972. He has also received an honorary degree from Grinnell in 1986. Wingate served from 1973 to 1976 as a lieutenant in the United States Navy's Judge Advocate General's (JAG) Corps. During that time he was the only African American lawyer in the entire U.S. Navy.

He has taught at Golden Gate University, Mississippi College School of Law, Mississippi Judicial College, and the University of Houston Law Center. After serving with the United States Attorney and District Attorney's Office in Mississippi, he was appointed to the federal bench in 1985 by President Ronald Reagan. Judge Wingate became the first African American appointed to the U.S. District Court for the Southern District of Mississippi.

Roland A. Winston

MILITARY. Roland A. Winston enlisted in the U.S. Marine Corps in June 1984 and began Recruit Training at Parris Island, South Carolina, in July 1984. He completed Drill Sergeant Instructor School; the technician's theory course and ground radar technician's course; Noncommissioned Officer Leadership School; and the Senior Noncommissioned Officer Academy. Winston has held every enlisted supervisory position, including assistant team leader, drill instructor, senior drill instructor, radar maintenance chief, platoon sergeant, first sergeant, and sergeant major.

In January 2003, the 2nd Marine Expeditionary Brigade was activated, and he assumed the duties as the senior enlisted advisor for the Brigade Headquarters Group and deployed in support of Operations Enduring Freedom and Iraqi Freedom. In June 2003, the brigade was ordered to the coast of Liberia in support of Joint Task Force 58. In August 2003, he was reassigned to the 2nd Radio Battalion for duty as company first sergeant for Headquarters and Service Company. He was the acting sergeant major for the Battalion Remain Behind Element from August 2004 to June 2005. He was promoted to sergeant major in November 2005. In April 2006, he was ordered to Marine Air Control Squadron One, 3rd Marine Aircraft Wing, to serve as the squadron sergeant major.

Brenda Wood

MEDIA. Brenda Wood received a bachelor of arts degree in speech communication and mass media summa cum laude from Loma Linda University in Southern California. She began her broadcasting career in 1977 in Huntsville, Alabama, at WAAY-TV. In 1978 she was a general assignment reporter at WSM-TV in Nashville, Tennessee. One year later, Wood was back at WAAY-TV, this time as an anchor. She then spent eight years as an anchor for WMC-TV in Memphis, Tennessee. In 1988, joined the news team at WAGA-TV in Atlanta. She has received numerous honors, including 15 Emmy awards from the National Academy of Television Arts and Sciences.

Bobby B. Woods

MILITARY. Bobby B. Woods enlisted in the United States Marine Corps in 1977. He completed boot camp at Parris Island, South Carolina, and attended Infantry Training School at Camp Pendleton, California. He has also completed the Aircraft Firefighting and Rescue Field at Naval Air Station Millington, Tennessee; Drill Instructor School at San Diego, California; senior noncommissioned officer advance course; and the first commandant of the Marine Corps' first sergeants course in Quantico, Virginia.

His leadership positions include section leader, training chief, drill instructor, first sergeant and sergeant major. His served two deployments with the 31st Marine Expeditionary Unit in the Kuwait from December 1998 to April 1999. He was company first sergeant for Weapons Company, Golf Company, and Headquarters and Service Company. In June 1999, he was transferred to Headquarters and Support Battalion, Marine Corps Base, Camp Pendleton, serving as the company first sergeant for Support Company until his promotion to sergeant major in March 2000. Woods was transferred to Assault Amphibian School Battalion (Del Mar), Camp Pendleton, and served as the school sergeant major and area sergeant major until December 2002. He was sergeant major, Recruiting Station Chicago, from December 2002 to January 2005, then sergeant major of the 12th Marine Corps District beginning January 20, 2005. He is the sergeant major of the Marine Corps Recruit Depot San Diego and Western Recruiting Region.

Jonathan Woodson

MILITARY. Jonathan Woodson received a bachelor of science degree in biomedical sciences from City College of New York and a medical doctor degree from New York University. He earned a master of strategic studies degree from the United States Army War College. His military education includes the Army medical department officer basic and advanced courses; the U.S. Army Command and General Staff College; and the U.S. Army War College.

His medical assignments to include serving as a surgeon with 351st General Hospital at Hanscom Air Force Base, Massachusetts; chief of surgery, 399th Combat Support Hospital in Taunton, Massachusetts; commander of the 399th Combat Support Hospital; chief of surgical services, Task Force Medical Falcon IV, 30th

Medical Brigade (Forward), Camp Bondsteel, Kosovo; deputy commander, Clinical Services, 865th Combat Support Hospital (Forward) Kuwait; commander, 804th Medical Brigade at Ayer, Massachusetts; and commander, 330th Medical Brigade, Fort Sheridan, Illinois. He was promoted to brigadier general on October 1, 2006.

Dr. Woodson's civilian occupation includes serving as vascular surgeon, Boston University Medical Center; associate professor of surgery at Boston University School of Medicine; and as associate chief medical officer for Boston Medical Center in Massachusetts.

Kym Loren Worthy

JUDICIAL. Kym Loren Worthy received a bachelor's degree in economics and political science from the University of Michigan and earned her juris doctor from the University of Notre Dame. She began her legal career in the Wayne County Prosecutor's Office in 1984, where she became the office's first African American special assignment prosecutor. She was elected judge of the Recorder's Court for the City of Detroit in 1994. She became a judge for the Wayne County Circuit Court in October 1997 when that court merged with the Recorder's Court. After nine years on the bench she retired in 2003 to become a candidate for the office of Wayne County prosecutor. On January 6, 2004, in Detroit, Michigan, Worthy was sworn in as the first African American and the first woman to be Wayne County prosecutor. The 63-member bench of the Wayne County Circuit Court appointed Worthy to the position. In November 2004, she ran unopposed for re-election.

Anthone R. Wright

MILITARY. Anthone R. Wright received his commission in May 1988 following graduation from the United States Naval Academy with a bachelor of science degree in economics. He earned a master of science degree in financial management from the Naval Postgraduate School, Monterey, California, in 1998. He attended the aviation supply officer's course in Athens, Georgia, and completed the Professional Military Comptroller School at Maxwell Air Force Base in Alabama in 1999.

Wright served with Marine Aviation Logistics Squadron 31, Marine Corps Air Station Beaufort, South Carolina, where he was assistant repairable management division officer. With the Command Element, 22nd Marine Expeditionary Unit at Camp Lejeune, North Carolina, he served as the headquarters commandant. During this 13-month tour, he participated in Operation Sharp Edge, the noncombatant evacuation and defense of the U.S. Embassy in Monrovia, Liberia. In May 1991, he reported for duty with Marine Corps Recruiting Station Buffalo, New York, as the recruiting operations officer. He was promoted to captain and assigned as the executive officer, serving in that capacity until June 1994.

He was the assistant aviation supply officer and assistant operations officer with the Marine Aviation Logistics Squadron 14, Marine Aircraft Group 14, Marine Corps Air Station Cherry Point, North Carolina. He was assigned as the aviation supply officer for Marine Aviation Logistics Squadron 36 with the 1st Marine Aircraft Wing, Marine Corps Air Station Futenma, Japan. Returning to the United States in June 2003, he was assigned to the office of the chief of naval operations, Air Warfare Division, where he was the assistant head for aviation material support. He was promoted to lieutenant colonel in June 2004. Wright was transferred to Marine Aviation Logistics Squadron 29, Marine Corps Air Station New River, North Carolina, in July 2005.

Dawn Wright

SCIENCE. Dawn Wright received a bachelor of science degree in geology from Wheaton College in Illinois and a master of science in oceanography from Texas A&M University. She also earned a Ph.D. in physical geography and marine geology in 1994. After graduation, she spent three years traveling the world aboard a 470-foot ship as a marine technician for the International Ocean Drilling Program, helping to collect sediment and rock samples from the sea floor.

Wright's research interests include geographic information science, benthic terrain and habitat characterization, tectonics of mid-ocean ridges, and the processing and interpretation of high-resolution bathymetry and underwater videography and photography. She as competed oceanographic fieldwork in some of the most geologically active regions of the planet, including the East Pacific Rise, the Mid-Atlantic Ridge, the Juan de Fuca Ridge, the Tonga Trench, and volcanoes under the Japan Sea and the Indian Ocean. She has dived three times in the deep submergence vehicle *Alvin* and twice in the *Pisces V*. Wright is a professor in the Department of Geosciences at Oregon State University in Corvallis, Oregon.

Eve Wright

SPORTS. Eve Wright received a bachelor of arts degree in economics from DePauw University. She earned her juris doctor for Indiana University School of Law and participated in the consortium program at Howard University School of Law. She has worked in private law practice. She currently serves as the senior director of legal affairs of the Ladies Professional Golf Association (LPGA), a non-profit corporation promoting women's golf through its tour and teaching and club professional memberships. As the senior director of legal affairs, she is involved in several facets of the organization, including tournament contracts, sponsorship, licensing and retail merchandising initiatives, all legal matters related to lpga.com, trademark management and foreign trademark prosecution, and television broadcast initiatives. She also provides legal advice regarding advertising campaigns, sweepstakes and other LPGA promotions.

LaNette N. Wright

MILITARY. LaNette N. Wright is a native of Boca Raton, Florida. She enlisted in the United States Marine Corps on March 6, 1989, and completed recruit training at Marine Corps Recruit Depot Parris Island, South Carolina. Upon completion of recruit training, she reported to Marine Corps Communications Electronics School, Marine Corps Air Ground Combat Center, Twenty-nine Palms, California, and attended the telecommunication center operators course. After graduating, she transferred to Communication Company, Headquarters Battalion, 3rd Marine Division, in Okinawa, Japan, and served as a communication center operator. In 1996, she transferred to Marine Security Guard School in Quantico, Virginia.

Her most recent assignments include serving as assistant Marine Security Guard commander, American Embassy in Bridgetown, Barbados; assistant Marine Security Guard Detachment commander, American Embassy, Hong Kong, China; Marine Security Guard detachment commander, American Embassy, Canberra, Australia; and assistant Marine Security Guard Detachment commander, American Embassy in Tokyo, Japan.

Wright was assigned as career course faculty instructor and advisor, Staff Non-Commissioned Officer's Academy, Marine Corps Base, Okinawa, Japan, in April 2002. In May 2004, she was promoted to first sergeant and assigned as the company first sergeant for Tenant Activities Company, Headquarters and Service Battalion, Marine Corps Base Quantico, Virginia. She transferred to 3rd Marine Logistics Group, Combat Logistics Regiment 35, 3rd Maintenance Battalion, as first sergeant in May 2007. She is currently the sergeant major of the Marine Medium Helicopter Squadron 265.

Otis D. Wright II

JUDICIAL. Otis D. Wright II is a native of Tuskegee, Alabama. He received a bachelor of science degree from California State University in Los Angeles in 1976 and earned his juris doctor degree from Southwestern University Law School in 1980. He served in the United States Marine Corps, where he obtained the rank of sergeant. He served 11 years as a deputy sheriff in Los Angeles. He began his legal career as a deputy attorney general in the Criminal Appeals Section of the California Department of Justice. During his three years in the office, he handled more than 200 appeals before the state's Court of Appeals and the Supreme Court. He next served in private law practice for more than 20 years.

In November 2005, Governor Arnold Schwarzenegger appointed Judge Wright to the Superior Court, where he was assigned to the Substance Abuse Court. He was nominated to the federal bench by President George W. Bush on January 9, 2007, and was confirmed by the United States Senate on March 15, 2007, for a seat on the U.S. District Court, Central District of California.

Robert C. Wright

JUDICIAL. Robert C. Wright was born and raised in the city of Chester, Pennsylvania, and was a 1962 graduate of Chester High School. He received a bachelor's degree from George Washington University and earned his juris doctor degree from Villanova University Law School. He completed the general jurisdiction course at the National Judicial College at the University of Nevada in Reno. Wright served ten years in the Penn-

sylvania House of Representatives. He was elected in 1991 to the Delaware County, Pennsylvania, Court of Common Pleas for a full ten-year term commencing in January of 1992. He began a second ten year term in January 2002 following his retention election.

Robert F. Wright, Jr.

MILITARY. Robert F. Wright, Jr., received a bachelor of science degree from the United States Air Force Academy in Colorado and a master of science degree in systems management from the University of Southern California. His military education includes Squadron Officer School at Maxwell Air Force Base in Alabama; Air Command and Staff College at Maxwell Air Force Base; Armed Forces Staff College at Norfolk Naval Station in Virginia; John Malone fellowship in Arabic and Islamic studies, Department of Defense Executive Leadership Development Program at the Pentagon in Washington, D.C.; and National Defense fellowship at Clark Atlanta University, Atlanta, Georgia.

He was commander of the 4404th, then 363rd, Communications Squadron at Prince Sultan Air Base in Saudi Arabia. In September 1999, he was assigned as chief, information assurance operations branch, Headquarters, Air Force Communications and Information Center at the Pentagon in Washington, D.C. In July 2001, he was assigned as the commander of the Communications Support Squadron at Headquarters Air Space Command, Peterson Air Force Base, Colorado. He served on the air staff at the office of the Secretary of the Air Force (Space Systems) at the United States Command Headquarters. He is the vice commander of the 14th Air Force (space force) at Vandenberg Air Force Base in California. The 14th Air Force provides ready forces and command and control capabilities with 28 weapon systems and 12,000 personnel in 155 units at 44 locations worldwide. In July 2003, Wright was assigned as commander of the 55th Communications Group, Offutt Air Force Base, Nebraska. In July 2007, he was selected to serve as the commander of Space Innovation and Development Center, Schriever Air Force Base in Colorado. The center is the centerpiece of Air Force space command's efforts to fully integrate space into the daily operational Air Force.

Ron D. Wright

EDUCATION. Ron D. Wright received an associate degree from Northeastern Christian Junior College and a bachelor's degree in applied psychology from Pepperdine University. He earned a master's degree in counseling psychology from Antioch University and a Ph.D. in public policy and management from Cornell University. Wright has over 30 years of experience in community college administration in Pennsylvania, Maryland, Delaware, and Ohio. In Ohio, he has served on the Governor's Workforce Policy Board and Commission for Student Success. Wright has been president of Cincinnati State Technical and Community College in Cincinnati, Ohio, since August 1997.

Val Wurster

LAW ENFORCEMENT. Val Wurster received a bachelor of science degree from Metropolitan State University and is a graduate of the Senior Management Institute for Police. She began her law enforcement career with the Minneapolis Police Department in April 1981. She has served in every rank from patrolman to deputy chief. Her assignments include serving as the commander of Domestic Assault Unit, where she developed the department's vulnerable adult protocols. She was commander of the Internal Affairs Unit, 3rd Precinct Sector Two, as a lieutenant. She most recently served as inspector of the 2nd Precinct. She is currently deputy chief of the Minneapolis Police Department.

Albert Russell Wynn

FEDERAL GOVERNMENT. Albert Russell Wynn is a native of Philadelphia, Pennsylvania, and a graduated from DuVal High School in Lanham, Maryland, in 1969. He received a bachelor of science degree from the University of Pittsburgh, Pennsylvania, and attended Howard University Graduate School of Political Science in Washington, D.C. He earned his juris doctor from Georgetown University School of Law in Washington, D.C., in 1977.

Wynn was director of the Prince George's County, Maryland, Consumer Protection Commission from 1977 to 1982; he was elected to the Maryland State

House of Delegates in 1982 and was elected to the Maryland State Senate in 1986. He was elected as a Democrat to the 103rd and to the seven succeeding Congresses (January 3, 1993, to present).

Phail Wynn

EDUCATION. Phail Wynn received a bachelor of science degree from the University of Oklahoma and a master of business administration from the Kenan-Flagler School of Business at the University of North Carolina at Chapel Hill. He earned a master's degree in educational psychology and a Ph.D. from North Carolina State University.

He served with the 82nd Airborne Division and the U.S. Army Special Forces and as chairman of the Greater Durham (N.C.) Chamber of Commerce. He sits on the corporate board of directors of SunTrust Bank and on the board of directors of University of North Carolina Health Care System; he is a member of the board of directors of the Triangle Community Foundation and founding member of the Greater Triangle Regional Council. Wynn was appointed president of Durham Technical Institute, now Durham Technical Community College, in 1980. He is the first African American community college president in North Carolina.

Clarease Rankin Yates

JUDICIAL. Clarease Rankin Yates was working as an attorney in Washington, D.C., when she was appointed to serve as a United States immigration judge in Houston, Texas. She is the first African American female to serve in that judicial position in Texas.

Lloyd Yates

BUSINESS. Lloyd Yates received a bachelor of science degree in mechanical engineering from the University of Pittsburgh and a master's degree in business administration from St. Joseph's University in Philadelphia. He attended the advanced management program at the University of Pennsylvania Wharton School and the executive management program at the Harvard Business School.

Yates has more than 25 years of experience in the energy business, including fossil generation, energy delivery, and nuclear generation. He worked for PECO Energy for 16 years in several line operations and management positions. He came to Progress Energy, predecessor to Carolina Power and Light, in 1998, and served for five years in the role of vice president for fossil generation. He was vice president of transmission and senior vice president of energy delivery for Progress Energy Carolinas. On July 1, 2007, he was promoted to his current position as president and chief executive officer for Progress Energy Carolinas, an electric utility serving 1.4 million customers in a 30,000-square-mile service area in North Carolina and South Carolina. He oversees the four operational and customer service regions and the distribution, transmission and system planning functions.

Clarence Young

MEDICINE. Clarence Young earned a medical degree from Harvard Medical School and completed training in internal medicine at Columbia-Presbyterian Medical Center and in infectious diseases at the Massachusetts General Hospital and the Hospital of the University of Pennsylvania. He is board certified in internal medicine and infectious diseases. He is a fellow of the Infectious Diseases Society of America.

Dr. Young has held faculty positions at the University of Pennsylvania and the University of Florida in Gainesville, Florida. He has served as an infectious disease physician for over fourteen years of pharmaceutical industry experience. He held several positions at GlaxoSmithKline directing clinical programs in genital herpes, viral hepatitis and community and hospital-acquired infections. In his most recent role, he was vice-president and clinical head for anti-infective in the Infectious Diseases Medicines Development Center at GlaxoSmithKline, responsible for developing and implementing clinical strategy for anti-infectives and providing medical affairs support for anti-infective products in the United States. He is the chief medical officer for Protez Pharmaceuticals.

Robert P. Young, Jr.

JUDICIAL. Robert P. Young, Jr., received a bachelor's degree with honors from Harvard College in 1974 and earned his juris doctor degree from Harvard Law School in 1977. He began his career in private law practice in 1978. In 1992, he was selected to serve as vice president, corporate secretary, and general counsel of AAA Michigan. In 1995, he was appointed a judge on the Michigan Court of Appeals and was elected to the Court of Appeals in 1996. In 1999, he was appointed to serve as a member of the Michigan Supreme Court. He was elected in 2002 to a term that will expire January 1, 2011.

Tamiko M. Youngblood

ENGINEERING. Tamiko M. Youngblood received a bachelor of science degree in mining engineering, a master of science in engineering management, and a Ph.D. in engineering management, all from the University of Missouri Rolla. She is the first African American woman to receive a Ph.D. in engineering from the University of Missouri Rolla. She has also received a graduate certificate in business intelligence and data warehousing from Loyola University at Chicago's Graduate School of Business.

Youngblood has served as an information technology specialist for IBM Global Services, a visiting scholar for Lockheed Martin Technologies, and as member of the technical staff at nasa's Jet Propulsion Laboratory. She is an adjunct faculty member at National Louis University, where she teaches graduate and undergraduate management courses. She is the founder and CEO of Youngblood Enterprises, a consulting firm that specializes in project management, information technology and business management practices.

Valerie Youngblood

MEDICINE. Valerie Youngblood received a bachelor's degree in nursing from Purdue University and earned her medical doctor degree from Michigan State University. Dr. Youngblood completed an internal medicine residency and spent 12 years blending internal and emergency medicine with meditation, yoga, and fine arts to focus on holistic medicine. Dr. Youngblood founded Continuum Center in 2003 as a holistic-aesthetic medical practice focused on traditional medicine intermixed with evidence-based complementary, functional 21st century medicine and anti-aging services.

John Milton Younge

JUDICIAL. John Milton Younge is a native of Philadelphia, Pennsylvania, where he attended public schools and graduated from Central High School in 1973. He received a bachelor of business administration from Boston University in 1977 and earned his juris doctor degree from Howard University School of Law in 1981. He worked in private law practice, then from 1985 to 1995, he was an attorney with the Redevelopment Authority of the City of Philadelphia. He served as deputy executive director and general counsel. Younge was elected to a ten year term on the Pennsylvania Superior Court of Common Pleas in Philadelphia in 1995 and retained in 2005.

Dhyana Ziegler

MEDIA. Dhyana Ziegler has a Ph.D. in academic administration, a master of arts in radio and television, and an undergraduate degree in the areas of journalism and music. She also attended Harvard University's Management and Leadership in Education Institute as part of her post-doctoral work and was awarded a Fulbright-Hays scholarship for a special seminar to China in 2004.

Ziegler is the host and co-producer of *The Delta see Connection*, a one-hour radio program highlighting the contribution of African American scientists in math, science, technology and engineering. She is the assistant vice president of instructional technology and academic affairs at Florida A&M University. She was the acting vice president for research and director of university planning and analysis for the 2002-2003 academic year. Ziegler has worked for several mass media entities in New York City, such as WCBS-TV and WNEW-TV, as a reporter and producer.

Al Zollar

ENGINEERING. Al Zollar received a master of arts degree in applied mathematics from the University of California at San Diego and is a graduate of the John F. Kennedy School for Government at Harvard University. He joined IBM in 1977 as a systems engineer trainee in San Francisco, California. He currently serves as general manager of Lotus Development Corp., an IBM company offering messaging, collaboration and knowledge management. He is a member of IBM's Worldwide Management Council, the senior-most management team.

Appendix A: Occupational Listing

Activism

Angela Yvonne Davis

Artist

Synthia Saint James
Aaron McGruder
Kara Walker

Arts

Clarence A. Hedge

Astronaut

Robert Lee "Bobby" Satcher, Jr.

Author

Walter L. Hawkins
Aaron McGruder

Business

Ivye L. Allen
Deborah L. Alleyne
Shelly "Butch" Anthony
Arlene Holt Baker
Dawn Rivers Baker
James A. Bell
Rosalind Brewer
Shirley Bridges
Percy Dean Butler
Roy L. Clay, Sr.
Tanya Clemons
Delores Crowell
H. James Dallas
Erroll B. Davis, Jr.
Terri Dean
Willie A. Deese
Anne Doris
Thomas W. Dortch
Donna Elam
Cedric Ferrell
Eugene Flood, Jr.
Stephenie Frazier
Brenda Gaines
Willie E. Gary
Denise J. Gatling
Mirian Graddick-Weir
William J. Harvey
Larry Hawkins
Samara P. Heaggans
Wyllstyne D. Hill
Melvin Andre Hooks
Rosalind Hunt
Cheryl Boone Isaacs
Yvonne R. Jackson
Renaldo M. Jensen
Arthur E. Johnson
Emanuel Jones
Jethro Joseph
C. Ray Kennedy
Nathelyne A. Kennedy
Aylwin B. Lewis
Jonathan D. Mariner
Joshua Martin
Barry Mayo
Gloria S. McCall
Teri Plummer McClure
Larry Miller
Ernest Stanley O'Neal
Rodney O'Neal
Clarence Otis, Jr.
Vallerie Parrish-Porter
Russell Perry
Stephen A. Perry
Myrtle Potter
Deborah Pryor
Maya Rockeymoore
John W. Rogers, Jr.
Michael Russell
David Sanders
Frank Savage
Gale Sayers
Willa Seldom
Gwendolyn D. Skillen
Earl Stafford
David Steward
Ephren W. Taylor
Don I. Tharpe
Deborah Scott Thomas
Don Thompson
John W. Thompson
Larry Thompson
Joyce E. Tucker
Michael Vass
Arlinda Vaughn
LeRoy H. Walden, Jr.
Carl P. Webb
Lloyd Yates

Culinary Arts

Wayne Johnson

Education

Robert "Bobby" Adams
Ilesanmi Adesida
Winser Alexander
Anita L. Allen
Danielle Allen
Ivye L. Allen
Linda L. Ammons
Claudia S. Averette
Delbert W. Baker
Jacqueline Bardwell
Michael A. Battle
Stanley F. Battle
Ray L. Belton
Daniel O. Bernstine
Rosie Phillips Bingham
Wilson G. Bradshaw
Nelvia Brady
Carolyn B. Brooks
Peggy Brooks-Bertram
Anita Brown
Walter G. Bumphus
Warrick L. Carter
Gwen Chandler
Karen Chandler
Constance R. Clark
Arlene W. Clinkscale
Thomas Cole
Allen J. Coles
Lisa A. Cooper
Elaine Johnson Copeland
Mildred C. Crump
Angela Yvonne Davis
Erroll B. Davis, Jr.
Myrtle Dorsey
Charlene M. Dukes
Cheryl E. Easley
Teresa Dawn Edwards
Evelynn Ellis
Charles H. Epps, Jr.
Elson S. Floyd
Everette J. Freeman
George T. French, Jr.
Maria Goodloe-Johnson
Bernadette Gray-Little
Bobbie Green
Lloyd "Vic" Hackley
Willie Hagan
John M. Hairston
Delon Hampton
Robert L. Hampton
Zelema Harris
Muriel Hawkins
Gerry House
Lillie Howard
Freeman A. Hrabowski, III
Rosalind Hunt
Stanley Jackson
Adrienne C. James
Charlene Drew Jarvis

Carolyn Jefferson-Jenkins
Esther J. Jenkins
Robert R. Jennings
Carol R. Johnson
Jim Johnson
Melvin N. Johnson
Otis Johnson
Deneese L. Jones
Paul Killpatrick
Walter M. Kimbrough
Bernard Kincald
Linda Lacey
Wright Lassiter
LaDawn Law
Howard N. Lee
Audre Levy
DeLores Mack
Carolyn R. Mahoney
Helen T. McAlpine
Gloria S. McCall
Anita D. McDonald
Saundra Yancy McGuire
Irving Pressley McPhail
Sidney A. McPhee
Lester P. Monts
Eddie N. Moore, Jr.
Yolonda T. Moses
Cynthia Nance
Eucharia E. Nnadi
Cheryl L. Nunez
Beverly J. O'Bryant
Toney C. Parks
Karyn Pettigrew
Edna J. Ragins
Wilhelmina Reuben-Cooke
Wayne Joseph Riley
Neriah Roberts
Jon Robertson
Nicole R. Robinson
Sharon Robinson
Sharon P. Robinson
George E. Ross
James M. Rosser
Cathy Runnels
Dorothy Sumners Rush
Sylvester Small
Rosa A. Smith
Ella Louise Smith-Simmons
Gwendolyn Stephenson
Cleveland Steward, Jr.
Marcia Tate
Bernard Taylor, Jr.
Leah Landrum Taylor
Patty Ball Thomas
Henry N. Tisdale
William Turner
Raymond Tymas-Jones
Peggy Valentine
Gayle Vaughn-Wiles
Janice Walker
Mildred West
James Herbert Williams
Lisa Williams
Marcellette G. Williams
Blenda J. Wilson
M. Roy Wilson
Ron D. Wright
Phail Wynn

Engineering

Lilia A. Abron
Winser Alexander
Arthur B. Anderson
Treena Livingston Arinzeh
Robert Auten
Lisa Barker
Gwendolyn Elizabeth Boyd
Shirley Bridges
Tulanda D. Brown
Roy A. Burrell
Stephen Clarke
Norma Clayton
Linda Clement-Holmes
Mark E. Dean
Walter L. Dixon
Gregory C. Dudley
Kerron R. Duncan
Teresa Dawn Edwards
Paul Engola
Greg Frazier
Cedric George
Kevin Greenaugh
Dorothea Grimes-Frederick
Delon Hampton
Tameika N. Hollis
Rhonda Holt
Ted E. Imes
Yvonne T. Jackson
Michael K. Johnson
Sandra K. Johnson
LeVerne W. Kelley
Nathelyne A. Kennedy
Tracy Mack
Sharon Meadows
Timothy Mark Pinkston
Joan Robinson-Berry
Britt A. Rodgers
Michael Russell
Shantel L. Samuel
Lizalyn Smith
Robin A. Smith
Ron Smith
Valerie Taylor
Neville Thompson
Frank C. Weaver
Robert Whyms
Vannia Willis
Tamiko M. Youngblood
Al Zollar

Entertainment

Sean Combs
Jermaine Dupri
Kedar Massenburg
Andrea Nelson Meigs
Tyler Perry
Antonio "L.A." Reid
Denzel Washington
Chandra Wilson

Film

Julie Dash
Jeff Friday
Cheryl Boone Isaacs
Denzel Washington
Yvonne Welbon

Government—Federal

Joyce Anne Barr
Sanford Dixon Bishop, Jr.
Eric M. Bost
Terry Bowie
William Lacy Clay, Jr.
Emanuel Cleaver, II
James Enos Clyburn
Marsha Coleman-Adebayo
Elijah Eugene Cummings
Gilda R. Daniels
Artur Davis
Danny K. Davis
Clark Kent Ervin
Alcee Lamar Hastings
Alphonso Jackson
Jesse L. Jackson, Jr.
Yvonne T. Jackson
Hank Johnson
William E. Kennard
Ronald N. Langston
John R. Lewis
Craig Manson
James D. McGee
Kendrick B. Meek
Thomas Hill Moore
Charles W. Nesby
Barack Obama
Felton Page
Mamie Parker
Donald Milford Payne
Buddie J. Penn
Colin Luther Powell
Charles A. Ray
Laura Richardson
Tawanda R. Rooney
Bobby L. Rush
Luther L. Santiful
Charles H. Scales
David Scott
Charles Stith
Gale Stallworth Stone
Larry Thompson
Frank O. Tuck
Kimberly Walton
Melvin L. Watt
Kate Wiley
Karen Hastie Williams
Theodore J. Williams
Albert Russell Wynn

Government—Local

Charles P. Austin, Sr.
Andre Birotte, Jr.
Stephanie T. Bolden
Cherry Houston Brown
Farrell J. Chiles
Roy L. Clay, Sr.
Y. Laketa Cole
Wanda Collier-Wilson
RoseMary Covington
Mildred C. Crump
Ronald V. Dellums
C. Jack Ellis
Adrian M. Fenty
Betty Hager Francis
Andrew D. Gillum
Carla D. Hayden
Willie W. Herenton
Curtis T. Hill, Jr.
Melvin "Kip" Holden
Stanley Jackson
Vera Jean-White
Patricia Coats Jessamy
Otis Johnson
Samuel L. Jones
Diane Jordan
Bernard Kincald
Samuel Lloyd
Alfred Davis Lott
Mark Mallory
John Marks
Janet T. May
Regina M. McDuffie
Rhine McLin
Sheila McNeil
Frank E. Melton

Malinda Miles
Juanita D. Miller
Bruce T. Moore
Allegra Webb Murphy
C. Ray Nagin
Harris Odell
Barbara Buckles Paxton
Lewis Reed
Fredrick D. Richardson, Jr.
Michelle Spence-Jones
John Street
Todd H. Stroger, Jr.
Cecil Thomas
Priscilla D. Thomas
Anita Favors Thompson
William C. Thompson, Jr.
Carole Ward-Allen
Corliss Hill White
Valarie D. Wilson

Government — State

Thurbert E. Baker
J. Kenneth Blackwell
Charles E. Box
Cloves Campbell, Jr.
Wilmer Amina Carter
Charles T. Epps, Jr.
Grindley Johnson
Emanuel Jones
Valeria A. Lemmie
Gerald Malloy
Frank E. Melton
Bettye Henderson Neely
Linda V. Parker
David Alexander Paterson
Deval Patrick
Sharon B. Robinson
Hank Sanders
Valencia Seay
Michael Steele
Horacena Tate
Leah Landrum Taylor
Regina Thomas
Michael L. Williams

Health

Curry Avery
Gloria Addo Ayensu
Verdelle Bellamy
Cherry Houston Brown
H. Westley Clark
Ozena Floyd
Beverly J. O'Bryant
Gloria J. Twilley
Sandra Webb-Brooker
Andrea D. Willis

Interior Design

Cecil Hayes

Judicial

Sheila Abdus-Salaam
Gregory A. Adams
Cheryl L. Allen
Linda Randle Anderson
Reuben V. Anderson
Marvin S. Arrington, Sr.
Nannette A. Baker
Vicki Ballou-Watts
Randolph Baxter
Karen Baynes
Robert Mack Bell
Karen Bennett-Haron
Irene Berger
Adolpho A. Birch, Jr.
Clyde Bishop
Fred Bonner
Frederick L. Brown
Joe Brown
Linda E. Brown
Vanessa Lynne Bryant
Michael B. Calvin
U.W. Clemon
Tom Colbert
John Creuzot
Denise L. Cross
Roosevelt Currie
Angelita Blackshear Dalton
Carr L. Darden
Lynda Van Davis
Michael J. Davis
Robert N. Davis
Clinton E. Deveaux
Laura G. Douglas
Michael Douglas
George W. Draper, III
Jules D. Edwards, III
John H. England, Jr.
Aubrey Ford, Jr.
Henry E. Frye
Darrin P. Gayles
Wendell M. Graham
James E. Graves, Jr.
Clifford Scott Green
Henry W. Green, Jr.
James E. Green
Tomie Zean Turner Green
Walter M. Green
Clayton Greene, Jr.
Wendell Griffen
Sophia Hall
Charlotte Hardnett
Lisa White Hardwick
Lubbie Harper, Jr.
Sara J. Harper
Leroy Rountree Hassell, Sr.
Alcee Lamar Hastings
Grant W. Hawkins
Judith Warren Hawkins
Thelton Henderson
Paul B. Higginbotham
Judith M. Hightower
Eric Himpton Holder, Jr.
George W. Holifield
Marcella A. Holland
Jan Bromell Holmes
Denise Page Hood
Roderick L. Ireland
Janet E. Jackson
Leon N. Jamison
Michael T. Jamison
Mabel M. Jasper
Wallace B. Jefferson
Martin J. Jenkins
Faith Johnson
Justin Morris Johnson
Mamie Bush Johnson
Sterling Johnson, Jr.
William Johnson
C. Darnell Jones, II
Nathaniel R. Jones
Richard A. Jones
Theodore T. Jones, Jr.
Pandora Jones-Glover
Claudia J. Jordan
Damon Jerome Keith
Leslie D. King
Tammy Bass-Jones LeSure
Casandra Lewis
David B. Lewis
Yvonne Lewis
Sam Lindsay
Benjamin H. Logan, II
Herman Marable, Jr.
Nikki Marr
Mable Martin-Scott
W. Dwayne Maynard
William E. McAnulty
Alice O. McCollum
Frances E. McGee
Yolanda Y. McGowan
Vanzetta Penn McPherson
Tyrone E. Medley
Harold Melton
Brian S. Miller
William D. Missouri
Leonard Murray
Clifton B. Newman
Flemming L. Norcott, Jr.
Eugene Oliver, Jr.
Alan C. Page
Jeff Payton
Andrea C. Peeples
James E.C. Perry
Matthew James Perry, Jr.
Tanya Walton Pratt
Orlando A. Prescott
Johnnie B. Rawlinson
Inez Smith Reid
Tynia D. Richard
Kevin G. Ross
Vince Rozier
Fanon Rucker
Robert D. Rucker
Patricia P. Satterfield
Mark Anthony Scott
Fred Seraphin
Booker T. Shaw
Martha Lynn Sherrod
George Bundy Smith
Jeri K. Somers
Charles Thomas Spurlock
Matthaw Stevenson
James Edward Stewart, Sr.
Tammy Cox Stokes
Thomas E. Stringer, Sr.
Emmet G. Sullivan
Carole Y. Taylor
Herman Y. Thomas
Preston G. Thomas
Patricia Timmons-Goodson
Charles H. Toliver, IV
Edward Toussaint, Jr.
Randolph F. Treece
Dale Wainwright
Cynthia Walker
John E. Wallace, Jr.
Reggie Walton
Tanya Walton-Pratt
Susan D. Wigenton
Felicia Toney Williams
Henry T. Wingate
Kym Loren Worthy
Otis D. Wright, II
Robert C. Wright
Clarease Rankin Yates
Robert P. Young, Jr.
John Milton Younge

Law

John Marks
Joshua Martin
Tatia L. Williams

Law Enforcement

Frank J. Anderson
Charles P. Austin, Sr.
Ed Banks
Jacquelyn Harris Barrett
John R. Batisle
Anthony W. Batts
A.D. Baylor
Gwendolyn V. Boyd
Thomas E. Brown
Joseph C. Carter
Lora Cole
Silvester Dawson
Cassandra Deck-Brown
Ira Edwards, Jr.
Cathy Ellison
Christopher B. Epps
Warren Evans
Preston L. Felton
Gwen Keyes Fleming
Myron Eugene Freeman
Ida L. Gillis
LeRoy Green, Jr.
Stanley Griffin
Marlin N. Gusman
Beverly J. Harvard
Walter L. Hawkins
George W. Hayman
Victor Hill
Sylvester M. Johnson
Tim K'Nuckles
Kevin E. Masters
Walter McNeil
David T. Moore
Charles Alexander Moose
Richard J. Pennington
Cheryl Price
Monica Ray
Warren J. Riley
James B. Rivers
Eugene G. Savage
Thomas C. Smalls
June Werdlow Stansbury
Bonnie Stanton
Jeffrey E. Turner
Thomas Warren
Kelvin Washington
Nathaniel Williams
Ronnie M. Williams
Val Wurster

Martial Arts

Sifu Larry Miller
Moses Williams

Media

Karyn Greer
Melvin "Kip" Holden
Carol Jenkins
Tom Joyner, Sr.
William E. Kennard
Donna Lowry
Barry Mayo
Bernadette A. Morris
Monica Pearson
Carol I. Smith
George A. Strait, Jr.
Wilbert A. Tatum
Montel Williams
Tatia L. Williams
Brenda Wood
Dhyana Ziegler

Medicine

Roosevelt Allen
Richard S. Baker
Jacqueline Bardwell
Eliot F. Battle, Jr.
Regina Marcia Benjamin
James K. Bennett
Marilyn Benoit
Lisa D. Benton
Karyn L. Butler
Veronica Butler
Benjamin S. Carson, Sr.
Mark S. Clanton
Beverly Coleman-Miller
Edward E. Cornwell, III
Simone Cummings
Kenneth Davis, Jr.
Cheryl Dorsey
Lisa Eghuonu-Davis
Tellis B. Ellis, III
Charles H. Epps, Jr.
Jenelle E. Foote
Carol D. Harris
Gloria Harris
Sharon M. Henry
Cheryl Howard-Young
Mildred F. Jefferson
Risa J. Lavizzo-Mourey
Sharon Malone
Calvin W. McLarin
Lori Moore
Linda Rae Murray
Evelyn M. Nelson
Jeanne Nizigiye
Ewaul B. Persaud, Jr.
Carla M. Pugh
Sarah Reeder
Tiffany C. Rush-Wilson
David Satcher
Aaron Shirley
Otha L. Solomon
Howard T. Strassner, Jr.
Errington C. Thompson
Patricia L. Turner
Hannah Valantine
Teresa M. Wesley
Gina P. Wilkerson
Clarence Young
Valerie Youngblood

Military

Renita D. Alexander
David J. Allen
Ronald Allen
Roosevelt Allen
Benjamin Anderson
Marcia Mahan Anderson
Jerry L. Bailey
John H. Bailey
Ronald L. Bailey
Anthony E. Baker, Sr.
Valerie Barnes
Donald L. Battle
Frank E. Batts
Sheila R. Baxter
Edward L. Bolton, Jr.
Charles L. Booker
Voresa E. Booker
Timothy K. Bridges
Anthony Brinkley
Charles Q. Brown, Jr.
Kevin M. Brown
Manson K. Brown
Mark Brown
Rodney Bryan
Pamela Carmouche
Joseph C. Carter
Richard M. Clark
Vincent E. Clark
Alfred Collins, Sr.
Elroy Combs, Jr.
Barbara A. Cooper
Willie W. Cooper, II
Kirk D. Crawley
Timothy A. Crisp
Jesse R. Cross
Derrick D. Crowley
Bobby Dandridge
Merryl David
Don D. Davis
Brian S. Dawson
Garry C. Dean
Robert A. Dews
Masicia Sonya Lee Diggs
Carol A.M. Dockery
Larry Donaldson
Donald G. Drummer
Robert Edmunds
Anthony L. Edwards
Norman L. Elliott
Gloria D. Farrow
Gerald W. Felder
Mark W. Flemon
Jeffrey Fletcher
Ozena Floyd
Joey A. Fondren
Leana A. Fox
Kenneth Funderburg
Ronald Gaines
Cedric George
Barbara Gilchrist
Larry D. Gilpin
Samuel A. Greaves
Edgar L. Green
Samuel Green
Carolyn Hamilton-Evans
Cecil D. Haney
Leroy Harris
Michael T. Harrison, Sr.
Mark A. Harvey
Emile H. Hawkins
Anthony M. Henderson
Wayne Hester
Enrique X. Hines
Sanford Eugene Holman
Charles Wayne Hooper
Christina Hopper
Vera Hughes
James P. Humphrey
Shirley Ann Hunt
Kym Ingram
George E. James
Anthony D. Johnson
Edward L. Johnson
Frederick J. Johnson
Jack Johnson, Jr.
Robert Johnson
Robert S. Johnson
Elijah Jones, Jr.
Michael F. Jones
Voresa Jones
Linus Jordan, Jr.
Beverly Leedom
Grover C. Lewis
Juan C. Lewis
Delice Liggon
Yolanda J. Lomax
Darlene A. Lovell

Sammie L. Lymon
Alphonso C. Mack, Jr.
Donald J. Massey
Joseph F. Mayfield
Joseph S. McClain
Garry McClure
William S. McCoy
Darren W. McDew
Bernard C. McPherson
Cherry A. McPherson
Lloyd Miles
Lawrence Miller
Jimmy L. Mincey
Edward W. Mitchell
Keith Moncrief
Timothy A. Mullins
William L. Nelson
Bruce W. Nichols
Samuel Thomas Nichols, Jr.
Angela M. Odom
Elizabeth A. Okoreeh-Baah
Charles H. Oldham
Joseph C. Persaud
Michael E. Phelps
Audre F. Piggee
Phillip S. Rhoda
Jeffrey L. Richardson
Adam M. Robinson, Jr.
Stephen W. Rochon
Andre H. Sayles
Errol R. Schwartz
Raytheon K. Scott
June E. Seay
Frances Lynne Shell
George L. Shine
Kenneth T. Shivers
Darin D. Simmons
Wallington Sims, Jr.
Leander Singletary
LaToya E. Sizer
Richard Sizer
Allison Smith
Calvin E. Smith, Jr.
Otha L. Solomon
Terry D. Stanford
Alfred J. Stewart
Vincent R. Stewart
Eugene A. Stockton
Willie C. Tennant, Sr.
Ronald R. Thaxton
Deborah Scott Thomas
Everett H. Thomas
Keith Allen Thomas
Stephen Thomas
George N. Thompson
Alphonso Trimble
Gloria J. Twilley
Stephen M. Twitty
Ricky T. Valentine
Jefferson Varner III
Luis Raul Visot
Leon Vorters, Jr.
Allen Walker
Christopher A. Walls
William Edward Ward
Dartanian Warr
Sidney D. Weatherspoon
Sandra Webb-Brooker
Adrian D. Williams
Virgil S.L. Williams
Charlotte L. Wilson
Roland A. Winston
Bobby B. Woods
Jonathan Woodson
Anthone R. Wright
LaNette N. Wright
Robert F. Wright, Jr.

Ministry

Maxine Allen
Michael A. Battle
Dale Bronner
Anita Brown
Claudette A. Copeland
Gerald W. Felder
Yvette Flunder
Leah Gaskin-Fitchue
Terrance D. Grant-Malone
Wilton D. Gregory
Emile H. Hawkins
Jesse Louis Jackson, Sr.
Mamie Bush Johnson
Norman S. Johnson
Eddie L. Long
Brenda Salter McNeil
Charlene Monk
Otis Moss, Jr.
C. Anthony Muse
Beverly Wilkes Null
Janet Bell Odom
Toney C. Parks
Rene D. Rochester
Alfred (Al) Charles Sharpton, Jr.
Ella Louise Smith-Simmons
Gina Marcia Stewart
Charles Stith
E. Thurman Walker

Music

James Abbington
Anton Armstrong
Angela Small Blalock
Karen Chandler
Leslie B. Dunner
William Eddins
Steven Ford
James "Jimmy Jam" Harris, III
Curtis James Jackson, III
Lester P. Monts
Michael Morgan
Jon Robertson
Russell Simmons
George N. Thompson
Raymond Tymas-Jones
Willie Anthony Waters
Janet Williams

Nursing

Cheryl E. Easley
Della McGraw Goodwin
Beverly Malone
Peggy Valentine

Public Health

John O. Agwunobi
Beverly Coleman-Miller
Michelle Gourdine
Shiriki K. Kumanyika
David Satcher

Public Policy

Angela Glover Blackwell
Tina Patterson

Public Safety

Lloyd Ayers
Douglas L. Barry
Niles Ford
Charles N. Hood
Darryl Jones
Warren E. McDaniels
Charles Parent
Debra Pryor
Pamela Sharpe
Jeffrey Ward

Public Service

Cory A. Booker
Marian L. Heard
Wanda E. Irving
Jaicy John
Pat Upshaw-Monteith

Publishing

Cloves Campbell, Jr.
Earl G. Graves, Jr.

Science

Claudia Alexander
Carolyn B. Brooks
Sonya Summerour Clemmons
Tene Hamilton Franklin
Edith Amos Hambie
Erich D. Jarvis
Shirley Malcom
Patricia A. Newby
Marcia L. Page
Samuel R. Reid, Jr.
Lydia W. Thomas
Neil deGrasse Tyson
Woodrow Whitlow, Jr.
Dawn Wright

Sports

Willie Adams
Barry Lamar Bonds
Jim Brown
Michael "Mike" Carey
Romeo Crennel
Tony Dungy
Herm Edwards
Tanya Forrest Hall
Hue Jackson
Paula Jackson
Earvin Effay (Magic) Johnson, Jr.
Marvin Lewis
Carl Martin
Willie Larry Randolph
Jerry Reese
Sharon Robinson
Gale Sayers
Lovie Smith
Orlando "Tubby" Smith
Jimme Lee Solomon
Emmitt Thomas
Isiah Lord Thomas, III
Mike Tomlin
Gene Upshaw
Eve Wright

Television

Amanda Davis
Mark Hayes

Theater

Tyler Perry

Appendix B: Geographical Listing

Alabama

Baylor, A.D.
Benjamin, Regina Marcia
Boyd, Gwendolyn Elizabeth
Brinkley, Anthony
Clemon, U.W.
Davis, Artur
Davis, Don D.
Ellis, Evelynn
England, John H., Jr.
Ford, Aubrey, Jr.
Franklin, Tene Hamilton
French, George T., Jr.
Johnson, Frederick J.
Jones, Samuel L.
Kincald, Bernard
May, Janet T.
McAlpine, Helen T.
McPherson, Vanzetta Penn
Nichols, Samuel Thomas, Jr.
O'Neal, Ernest Stanley
Price, Cheryl L.
Richardson, Fredrick D., Jr.
Sanders, Hank
Scales, Charles H.
Sherrod, Martha Lynn
Stone, Gale Stallworth
Thomas, Deborah Scott
Thomas, Herman Y.
Thompson, Neville
Varner, Jefferson, III
Willis, Andrea D.

Alaska

Easley, Cheryl E.

Arizona

Campbell, Cloves, Jr.
Doris, Anne
Hill, Wyllstyne D.
Taylor, Leah Landrum

Arkansas

Allen, Maxine
Griffen, Wendell
Jamison, Leon N.
Kimbrough, Walter M.
K'Nuckles, Tim
Miller, Brian S.
Moore, Bruce T.
Nance, Cynthia
Parker, Mamie
Piggee, Audre F.

California

Adams, Robert "Bobby"
Alexander, Claudia
Allen, David J.
Auten, Robert
Baker, Arlene Holt
Baker, Delbert W.
Baker, Richard S.
Barker, Lisa
Barry, Douglas L.
Batts, Anthony W.
Bell, James A.
Benton, Lisa D.
Birotte, Andre, Jr.
Blackwell, Angela Glover
Bonds, Barry Lamar
Booker, Charles L.
Brown, Jim
Carey, Michael "Mike"
Carter, Wilmer Amina
Chiles, Farrell J.
Clark, H. Westley
Clark, Richard M.
Clay, Roy L., Sr.
Davis, Angela Yvonne
Davis, Danny K.
Dean, Mark E.
Dellums, Ronald V.
Ellis, C. Jack
Ferrell, Cedric
Flemon, Mark W.
Floyd, Ozena
Flunder, Yvette
Fondren, Joey A.
Greaves, Samuel A.
Hagan, Willie
Harvey, Mark A.
Henderson, Thelton
Hooks, Melvin Andre
Howard, Lillie
Hughes, Vera
Isaacs, Cheryl Boone
Jackson, Yvonne R.
James, George E.
James, Synthia Saint
Jenkins, Martin J.
Johnson, Earvin Effay (Magic), Jr.
Johnson, Michael K.
Johnson, Norman S.
Jones, Michael F.
Kelley, LeVerne W.
Law, LaDawn
Levy, Audre
Lewis, Juan C.
Lovell, Darlene A.
Manson, Craig
McDew, Darren W.
Meadows, Sharon
Meigs, Andrea Nelson
Nesby, Charles W.
Pinkston, Timothy Mark
Pryor, Deborah
Pryor, Debra
Richardson, Laura
Robinson, Sharon
Robinson-Berry, Joan
Rosser, James M.
Sanders, David
Savage, Frank
Smith, Ron
Smith-Simmons, Ella Louise
Solomon, Jimmie Lee
Stanton, Bonnie
Strait, George A., Jr.
Strassner, Howard T., Jr.
Taylor, Valerie
Thompson, John W.
Upshaw, Gene
Valantine, Hannah
Walker, Kara
Ward-Allen, Carole
Williams, Ronnie M.
Wright, Otis D., II
Zollar, Al

Canada

Eddins, William

Colorado

Engola, Paul
Jefferson-Jenkins, Carolyn
Jordan, Claudia J.
Williams, James Herbert
Wilson, Charlotte L.
Wilson, M. Roy
Wright, Robert F., Jr.

Connecticut

Avery, Curry
Bryant, Vanessa Lynne
Harper, Lubbie, Jr.
Norcott, Flemming L., Jr.
Seldom, Willa

Delaware

Bishop, Clyde
Martin, Joshua
Tisdale, Henry N.
Toliver, Charles H., IV
Wilkerson, Gina P.

Florida

Anderson, Arthur B.
Bailey, Ronald L.
Boyd, Gwendolyn V.
Dawson, Silvester
Gary, Willie E.
Gayles, Darrin P.
Gillum, Andrew D.
Graham, Wendell M.
Green, Walter M.
Harris, Leroy
Hastings, Alcee Lamar
Hawkins, Judith Warren
Holt, Rhonda
Johnson, William
Jones, Voresa
Joyner, Phyllis M.
Marks, John
Massey, Donald J.
McClure, Teri Plummer
McNeil, Walter
Meek, Kendrick B.
Moore, Thomas Hill
Morris, Bernadette A.
Murphy, Allegra Webb
Perry, James E.C.
Prescott, Orlando A.
Richardson, Jeffrey L.
Roberts, Neriah
Robertson, Jon
Savage, Eugene G.
Seraphin, Fred
Spence-Jones, Michelle
Stephenson, Gwendolyn
Stevenson, Matthaw
Stringer, Thomas, Sr.
Taylor, Carole Y.
Thomas, Patty Ball
Weatherspoon, Sidney D.
Wiley, Kate F.
Wright, LaNette N.
Young, Clarence

Georgia

Abbington, James
Adams, Gregory A.
Anthony, Shelly "Butch"
Arrington, Marvin S., Sr.
Baker, Thurbert E.
Barrett, Jacquelyn Harris
Battle, Michael A.
Baynes, Karen
Bellamy, Verdelle
Bennett, James K.
Bishop, Sanford Dixon, Jr.
Brewer, Rosalind
Bridges, Shirley
Bronner, Dale
Brown, Thomas E.
Butler, Percy Dean
Clarke, Stephen
Clemmons, Sonya Summerour
Cloud, Rosemary R.
Cole, Thomas
Collins, Alfred, Sr.
Crowell, Delores
Dash, Julie
Davis, Amanda
Dockery, Carol A.M.
Dortch, Thomas W.
Drummer, Donald G.
Dupri, Jermaine
Edwards, Ira, Jr.
Eghuonu-Davis, Lisa
Fleming, Gwen Keys
Foote, Jenelle E.
Frazier, Stephenie
Freeman, Everette J.
Freeman, Myron Eugene
Gilpin, Larry D.
Green, Samuel
Greer, Karyn
Gregory, Wilton D.
Hall, Tanya Forrest
Hambie, Edith Amos
Harris, Gloria
Harris, James "Jimmy Jam," III
Harvard, Beverly J.
Hawkins, Walter L.
Hayes, Cecil
Hayes, Mark
Hill, Victor
Jackson, Hue
Jackson, Paula
Johnson, Arthur E.
Johnson, Edward L.
Johnson, Hank
Johnson, Otis
Johnson, Robert S.
Jones, Emanuel
Lewis, John R.
Long, Eddie L.
Lott, Alfred Davis
Lowry, Donna
Marr, Nikki
McDuffie, Regina M.
McLarin, Calvin W.
Melton, Harold
Miles, Lloyd
Mincey, Jimmy L.
Moss, Otis, Jr.
Odell, Harris
Paxton, Barbara
Pearson, Monica
Pennington, Richard J.
Perry, Tyler
Persaud, Ewaul B., Jr.
Rivers, James B.
Russell, Michael
Satcher, David
Sayles, Andre H.
Scott, David
Scott, Mark Anthony
Seay, Valencia
Stokes, Tamy Cox
Tate, Horacena
Tate, Marcia L.
Thomas, Priscilla D.
Thomas, Regina
Thompson, Larry
Turner, Jeffrey E.
Twitty, Stephen M.
Upshaw-Monteith, Pat
Walker, Allen
Walker, E. Thurman
White, Corliss Hill
Wiley, Kate F.
Wilson, Valarie D.
Wood, Brenda

Germany

Fletcher, Jeffrey
Lomax, Yolanda J.

Hawaii

Moncrief, Keith
Moose, Charles Alexander
Rhoda, Phillip S.

Honduras

Mullins, Timothy A.

Illinois

Adesida, Ilesanmi
Allen, Danielle
Bardwell, Jacqueline
Box, Charles E.
Carter, Warrick L.
Davis, Erroll B., Jr.
Elliott, Norman L.
Felder, Gerald W.
Gaines, Brenda
Gaines, Ronald
Gillis, Ida L.
Graves, Earl G., Jr.
Hall, Sophia
Hampton, Delon
Harris, Zelema
Ingram, Kym
Jackson, Jesse L., Jr.
Jackson, Jesse Louis
Jenkins, Esther J.
Jones, Elijah, Jr.
Lewis, Casandra
McClure, Garry
McGee, James D.
McGruder, Aaron
McNeil, Brenda Salter
Murray, Leonard
Murray, Linda Rae
Pettigrew, Karyn
Potter, Myrtle
Pugh, Carla M.
Rogers, John W., Jr.
Rush, Bobby
Satcher, Robert Lee "Bobby," Jr.
Sayers, Gale
Sizer, LaToya E.
Steward, David
Stewart, Vincent R.
Stroger, Todd H., Jr.
Tucker, Joyce E.
Vorters, Leon, Jr.
Webb-Brooker, Sandra
Welbon, Yvonne
Youngblood, Tamiko M.

Indiana

Anderson, Frank J.
Brown, Linda E.
Darden, Carr L.
Dungy, Tony
Edwards, Anthony L.
Hawkins, Grant W.
Hill, Curtis T., Jr.
Mack, Tracy
Martin-Scott, Mable
Penn, Buddie J.
Pratt, Tanya Walton

Ray, Monica
Rucker, Robert D.
Thompson, Don
Walton-Pratt, Tanya
Ward, Jeffrey
Williams, Janet

Iowa

Butler, Veronica

Iraq

Farrow, Gloria D.
Liggon, Delice

Japan

Donaldson, Larry
Leedom, Beverly
Lewis, Grover C.
Shivers, T.
Singletary, Leander

Kansas

Diggs, Masicia Sonya Lee
Green, Henry W., Jr.
Green, LeRoy, Jr.
Masters, Kevin E.
Parrish-Porter, Vallerie
Taylor, Ephren W.
Thompson, Anita Favos

Kentucky

Mayfield, Joseph F.
McAnulty, William E.
McCall, Gloria S.
Robinson, Adam M., Jr.
Thape, Don I.
Turner, William

Korea

Sizer, Richard

Louisiana

Anderson, Benjamin
Burrell, Roy A.
Combs, Elroy, Jr.
Creuzot, John
Davis, Lynda Van
Dorsey, Myrtle
Edwards, Jules D., III
Griffin, Stanley
Gusman, Marlin N.
Holden, Melvin "Kip"
Jordan, Linus, Jr.
McDaniels, Warren E.
McGuire, Saundra Yancy
Nagin, C. Ray
Parent, Charles
Riley, Warren J.
Robinson, Sharon B.
Rochon, Stephen W.
Stewart, James Edward, Sr.
Thompson, Errington, C.
Williams, Felicia Toney
Williams, Nathaniel
Belton, Ray L.

Maryland

Arinzeh, Treena Livingston
Ayensu, Gloria Addo
Bailey, Jerry L.
Baker, Anthony E., Sr.
Ballou-Watts, Vicki
Bell, Robert Mack
Brooks, Carolyn B.
Chandler, Gwen
Cummings, Elijah Eugene
Dorsey, Cheryl
Dukes, Charlene M.
Duncan, Kerron R.
Dunner, Leslie B.
Francis, Betty Hager
Frazier, Greg
Gourdine, Michelle
Greenaugh, Kevin
Greene, Clayton, Jr.
Hayden, Carla D.
Henry, Sharon M.
Holland, Marcella A.
Hollis, Tameika N.
Hrabowski, Freeman A., III
Imes, Ted E.
Jessamy, Patricia Coats
Lloyd, Samuel
Miles, Malinda
Miller, Juanita D.
Missouri, William D.
Monk, Charlene
Muse, C. Anthony
O'Bryant, Beverly J.
Reid, Samuel R., Jr.
Rodgers, Britt A.
Rooney, Tawanda R.
Shell, Frances Lynne
Simmons, Darin D.
Sims, Wallington, Jr.
Skillen, Gwendolyn D.
Smith, Calvin E., Jr.
Somers, Jeri K.
Steele, Michael
Turner, Patricia L.
Ward, William Edward
Whyms, Robert
Williams, Montel

Massachusetts

Brown, Frederick L.
Carter, Joseph C.
Coleman-Adebayo, Marsha
Edwards, Teresa Dawn
Heard, Marian L.
Ireland, Roderick L.
Irving, Wanda E.
Jefferson, Mildred F.
Johnson, Carol R.
Langston, Ronald N.
Patrick, Deval
Seay, June E.
Spurlock, Charles Thomas
Stansbury, June Werdlow
Tuck, Frank O.
Williams, Marcellette G.
Woodson, Jonathan

Michigan

Adams, Willie
Carson, Benjamin S., Sr.
Evans, Warren
Goodwin, Della McGraw
Hood, Denise Page
Jensen, Renaldo M.
Joseph, Jethro
Keith, Damon Jerome
Marable, Herman, Jr.
Monts, Lester P.
Moore, Lori
O'Neal, Rodney
Parker, Linda V.
Ross, George E.
Taylor, Bernard, Jr.
Thomas, Preston G.
Walden, LeRoy H., Jr.
Walker, Cynthia
Wiley, Kate F.
Williams, Adrain D.
Worthy, Kym Loren
Young, Robert P., Jr.
Youngblood, Valerie

Minnesota

Brady, Nelvia
Davis, Michael J.
Page, Alan C.
Ross, Kevin G.
Smith, Orlando "Tubby"
Toussaint, Edward W., Jr.
Wurster, Val

Mississippi

Allen, Ivye L.
Allen, Ronald
Anderson, Reuben V.
Cole, Lora
Collier-Wilson, Wanda
Crowley, Derrick D.
Ellis, Tellis B., III
Epps, Christopher B.
Graves, James E., Jr.
Green, Tomie Zean Turner
Harris, Carol D.
King, Leslie D.
Lymon, Sammie L.
Mack, DeLores
Melton, Frank E.
Neely, Bettye Henderson
Nizigiye, Jeanne
Null, Beverly Wilkes
Odom, Angela M.
Otis, Clarence, Jr.
Shirley, Aaron
Wingate, Henry T.

Missouri

Baker, Nannette A.
Calvin, Michael B.
Clay, William Lacy, Jr.
Cleaver, Emanuel, II
Draper, George W., III
Floyd, Elson S.
Hardwick, Lisa White
Jamison, Michael T.
Johnson, Anthony D.
Mahoney, Carolyn R.
Reed, Lewis
Shaw, Booker T.
Stith, Charles
Wesley, Teresa M.

Nebraska

Ford, Niles, Jr.
Funderburg, Kenneth
Warren, Thomas

Nevada

Bennett-Haron, Karen
Coles, Allen J.
Douglas, Michael
Nnadi, Eucharia E.
Thomas, Everett H.

New Jersey

Clayton, Norma
Crump, Mildred C.
Deese, Willie A.
Deveaux, Clinton E.
Edwards, Herm
Epps, Charles T., Jr.
Gaskin-Fitchue, Leah
Hayman, George W.
Heaggans, Samara P.
Mariner, Jonathan D.
Nelson, Evelyn M.
Payne, Donald Milford
Stewart, Alfred J.
Tennant, Willie C., Sr.
Wallace, John E., Jr.
Wigenton, Susan D.
Wilson, Blenda J.

New Mexico

Green, Bobbie
Hopper, Christina
Lacey, Linda

New York

Abdus-Salaam, Sheila
Brooks-Bertram, Peggy
Brown, Anita
Clark, Constance R.
Clemons, Tanya
Clinkscale, Arlene W.
Combs, Sean
David, Merryl
Douglas, Laura G.
Elam, Donna
Felton, Preston L.
Friday, Jeff
Graddick-Weir, Mirian
Harrison, Michael T., Sr.
Hines, Enrique X.
Holder, Eric Himpton, Jr.
Holman, Sanford Eugene
Hunt, Rosalind
Jackson, Curtis James, III
Jenkins, Carol
John, Jaicy
Johnson, Sterling, Jr.
Jones, Theodore T., Jr.
Lewis, Yvonne
Malcom, Shirley
Malone, Beverly
Massenburg, Kedar
Mayo, Barry
McPhail, Irving Pressley
Moore, David T.
Oliver, Eugene, Jr.
Page, Felton
Paterson, David Alexander
Persaud, Joseph C.
Powell, Colin Luther
Richard, Tynia D.
Satterfield, Patricia P.
Sharpe, Pamela
Simmons, Russell
Smith, Allison
Tatum, Wilbert A.
Thomas, Isiah Lord, III
Thompson, William C., Jr.
Treece, Randolph F.
Tyson, Neil deGrasse
Vass, Michael
Washington, Denzel
Waters, Willie Anthony
Williams, Tatia L.
Ziegler, Dhyana

North Carolina

Alexander, Winser
Banks, Ed
Battle, Donald L.
Battle, Stanley F.
Bolden, Stephanie T.
Bost, Eric M.
Cooper, Willie W., II
Dawson, Brian S.
Deck-Brown, Cassandra
Flood, Eugene, Jr.
Frye, Henry E.
Gatlin, Denise J.
Gray-Little, Bernadette
Grimes-Frederick, Dorothea
Hackley, Lloyd "Vic"
House, Gerry
Humphrey, James P.
Jarvis, Erich D.
Jennings, Robert R.
Johnson, Jim
Kennedy, C. Ray
Lee, Howard N.
Mack, Alphonso C., Jr.
McPherson, Cherry A.
Okoreeh-Baah, Elizabeth A.
Ragins, Edna J.
Rawlinson, Johnnie B.
Rozier, Vince
Samuel, Shantel L.
Shine, George L.
Smith, Lizalyn
Stanford, Terry D.
Thomas, Stephen
Timmons-Goodson, Patricia
Trimble, Alphonso C.
Valentine, Peggy
Watt, Melvin L.
Webb, Carl P.
Wright, Anthone R.
Wynn, Phail

North Dakota

Allen, Rosevelt
Scott, Raytheon K.

Ohio

Ammons, Linda L.
Anderson, Linda Randle
Baxter, Randolph
Bridges, Timothy K.
Brown, Tulanda D.
Butler, Karyn L.
Clement-Holmes, Linda
Cole, Y. Laketa
Cross, Denise L.
Davis, Kenneth, Jr.
Green, James E.
Hairston, John M.
Harper, Sara J.
Jackson, Janet E.
James, Adrienne C.
Jasper, Mabel M.
Jons, Nathaniel R.
Maynard, W. Dwayne
McCollum, Alice O.
McGee, Frances E.
McLin, Rhine
Nelson, William L.
Nunez, Cheryl L.
Payton, Jeff
Peeples, Andrea C.
Perry, Stephen A.
Reid, Antonio "L.A."
Rucker, Fanon
Rush-Wilson, Tiffany C.
Small, Sylvester
Smith, Rosa A.
Thomas, Cecil
Vaughn, Arlinda
Walker, Janice
Whitlow, Woodrow, Jr.
Wright, Ron D.

Oklahoma

Colbert, Tom
Crisp, Timothy A.
Dews, Robert A.
Hawkins, Emile H.
Hedge, Clarence A.
LeSure, Tammy Bass-Jones
Lewis, David B.
Perry, Russell
Solomon, Otha L.

Oregon

Dean, Garry C.
Wright, Dawn
Killpatrick, Paula

Pennsylvania

Allen, Anita L.
Allen, Cheryl L.
Alleyne, Deborah L.
Averette, Claudia S.
Ayers, Lloyd
Baker, Dawn Rivers
Bradshaw, Wilson G.
Cooper, Barbara A.
Dean, Terri
Ford, Steven
Fox, Leana A.
Green, Clifford Scott
Hamilton-Evans, Carolyn
Jean-White, Vera
Johnson, Justin Morris
Johnson, Sylvester M.
Jones, C. Darnell, II
Jones, Darryl
Kumanyika, Shiriki K.
Lavizzo-Mourey, Risa J.
Lewis, Marvin
Martin, Carl
McDonald, Anita D.
Miller, Larry
Newby, Patricia A.
Nichols, Bruce W.
Reeder, Sarah
Rush, Dorothy
Smith, Carol I.
Steward, Cleveland, Jr.
Street, John
Williams, Lisa
Wright, Robert C.
Wynn, Albert Russell
Younge, John Milton

South Carolina

Austin, Charles P., Sr.
Blalock, Angela Small
Brown, Cherry Houston
Clyburn, James Enos
Copeland, Elaine Johnson
Goodloe-Johnson, Maria

Holmes, Jan Bromell
Hunt, Shirley Ann
Jones-Glover, Pandora
Malloy, Gerald
McCoy, William S.
Miller, Lawrence
Newman, Clifton B.
Parks, Toney C.
Perry, Matthew James, Jr.
Randolph, Willie Larry
Smalls, Thomas C.
Thomas, Keith Allen
Washington, Kelvin
Winston, Roland A.
Woods, Bobby B.
Yates, Lloyd

South Dakota

Alexander, Renita D.

Tennessee

Bingham, Rosie Phillips
Birch, Adolpho A., Jr.
Booker, Voresa E.
Chandler, Karen
Clark, Vincent E.
Dalton, Agelita Blackshear
Hampton, Robert L.
Herenton, Willie W.
Johnson, Melvin N.
Jordan, Diane
McPhee, Sidney A.
Reese, Jerry
Riley, Wayne Joseph
Robinson, Nicole R.
Stewart, Gina Marcia
Thompson, George N.

Texas

Armstrong, Anton
Bailey, John H.
Bumphus, Walter G.
Carmouche, Pamela
Copeland, Claudette A.
Crawley, Kirk D.
Dallas, H. James
Ellison, Cathy
Ervin, Clark Kent
Gilchrist, Barbara
Grant-Malone, Terrance D.
Hawkins, Larry
Hester, Wayne
Hood, Charles N.
Howard, Michelle J.
Howard-Young, Cheryl
Jefferson, Wallace B.
Johnson, Faith
Johnson, Mamie Bush
Johnson, Sandra K.
Kennedy, Nathelyne A.
Lassiter, Wright
Lewis, Aylwin B.
Lindsay, Samuel L.
McNeil, Sheila
Miller, Sifu Larry
Mitchell, Edward W.
Odom, Janet Bell
Oldham, Charles H.
Page, Marcia L.
Patterson, Tina
Ray, Charles A.
Rochester, Rene D.
Smith, Lovie
Thaxton, Ronald R.
Thomas, Emmitt
Wainwright, Dale
Warr, Dartanian
West, Mildred
Williams, Michael L.
Williams, Moses
Wilson, Chandra
Yates, Clarease Rankin

United Kingdom

Dandridge, Bobby

Utah

Medley, Tyrone E.
Tymas-Jones, Raymond

Virginia

Batts, Frank E.
Bolton, Edward L., Jr.
Brown, Kevin M.
Crennel, Romeo
Cross, Jesse R.
Dixon, Walter L.
Dudley, Gregory C.
Edmunds, Robert
Green, Edgar L.
Harvey, William J.
Hassell, Leroy Rountree, Sr.
Johnson, Grindley
Jones, Deneese L.
Lemmie, Valeria A.
McClain, Joseph S.
McPherson, Bernard C.
Moore, Eddie N., Jr.
Phelps, Michael E.
Santiful, Luther L.
Smith, Robin A.
Stafford, Earl
Stockton, Eugene A.
Tomlin, Mike

Washington

Barr, Joyce Anne
Batisle, John R.
Baxter, Sheila R.
Bonner, Fred
Bryant, Rodney
Currie, Roosevelt
Davis, Robert N.
Hightower, Judith M.
Holifield, George W.
Jarvis, Charlene Drew
Johnson, Wayne
Jones, Richard A.
Logan, Benjamin H., II
Walls, Christopher A.
Williams, Virgil S.L.

Washington, D.C.

Abron, Lilia A.
Agwunobi, John O.
Barnes, Valerie
Battle, Eliot F., Jr.
Benoit, Marilyn
Bernstine, Daniel O.
Blackwell, J. Kenneth
Booker, Cory A.
Bowie, Terry
Brown, Charles Q., Jr.
Brown, Joe
Brown, Manson K.
Brown, Mark
Clanton, Mark S.
Coleman-Miller, Beverly
Cooper, Lisa A.
Cornwell, Edward E., III
Covington, RoseMary R.
Cummings, Simone
Daniels, Gilda R.
Epps, Charles H., Jr.
Fenty, Adrian M.
George, Cedric
Haney, Cecil D.
Hardnett, Charlotte
Henderson, Anthony M.
Hooper, Charles Wayne
Jackson, Alphonso
Jackson, Stanley
Jackson, Yvonne T.
Jarvis, Charlene Drew
Johnson, Jack, Jr.
Johnson, Robert
Kennard, William E.
Malone, Sharon
Morgan, Michael
Moses, Yolonda T.
Obama, Barack
Reid, Inez Smith
Reuben-Cooke, Wilhelmina
Robinson, Sharon P.
Rockeymoore, Maya
Runnels, Cathy
Schwartz, Errol R.
Sharpton, Alfred (Al) Charles, Jr.
Smith, George Bundy
Sullivan, Emmet
Thomas, Lydia W.
Twilley, Gloria J.
Valentine, Ricky T.
Vaughn-Wiles, Gayle
Walton, Kimberly
Walton, Reggie
Weaver, Frank C.
Williams, Karen Hastie
Williams, Theodore J.
Willis, Vannia
Wright, Eve

West Virginia

Berger, Irene

Wisconsin

Anderson, Marcia Mahan
Hawkins, Muriel
Higginbotham, Paul B.
McGowan, Yolanda Y.